Applications in Basic Marketing

Clippings from the Popular Business Press

2005-2006 Edition

William D. Perreault, Jr.
University of North Carolina

and

E. Jerome McCarthy
Michigan State University

McGraw-Hill
Irwin

Boston   Burr Ridge, IL   Dubuque, IA   Madison, WI   New York   San Francisco   St. Louis
Bangkok   Bogotá   Caracas   Kuala Lumpur   Lisbon   London   Madrid   Mexico City
Milan   Montreal   New Delhi   Santiago   Seoul   Singapore   Sydney   Taipei   Toronto

The McGraw·Hill Companies

 **McGraw-Hill
Irwin**

APPLICATIONS IN BASIC MARKETING:
CLIPPINGS FROM THE POPULAR BUSINESS PRESS 2005-2006 EDITION

Published by McGraw-Hill/Irwin, a business unit of The McGraw-Hill Companies, Inc., 1221 Avenue of the Americas, New York, NY, 10020. Copyright © 2005 by The McGraw-Hill Companies, Inc. All rights reserved. No part of this publication may be reproduced or distributed in any form or by any means, or stored in a database or retrieval system, without the prior written consent of The McGraw-Hill Companies, Inc., including, but not limited to, in any network or other electronic storage or transmission, or broadcast for distance learning.

Some ancillaries, including electronic and print components, may not be available to customers outside the United States.

This book is printed on acid-free paper.

1 2 3 4 5 6 7 8 9 0 QPD/QPD 0 9 8 7 6 5

ISBN   0-07-286471-0
ISSN   1099-5579

Editorial director: *John E. Biernat*
Publisher: *Andy Winston*
Coordinating editor: *Lin Davis*
Managing developmental editor: *Nancy Barbour*
Executive marketing manager: *Dan Silverburg*
Senior project manager: *Christine A. Vaughan*
Manager, New book production: *Heather D. Burbridge*
Director of design: *Keith J. McPherson*
Senior digital content specialist: *Brian Nacik*
Compositor: *Electronic Publishing Services, Inc., TN*
Printer: *Quebecor World Dubuque, Inc.*

www.mhhe.com

Preface

This is the sixteenth annual edition of *Applications in Basic Marketing*. We developed this set of marketing "clippings" from popular business publications to accompany our texts—*Basic Marketing* and *Essentials of Marketing*. All of these clippings report interesting case studies and current issues that relate to topics covered in our texts and in the first marketing course. We will continue to publish a new edition of this book *every year*. That means that we can include the most current and interesting clippings. Each new copy of our texts will come shrinkwrapped with a free copy of the newest (annual) edition of this book. However, it can also be ordered from the publisher separately for use in other courses or with other texts.

Our objective is for this book to provide a flexible and helpful set of teaching and learning materials. We have included clippings (articles) on a wide variety of topics. The clippings deal with consumer products and business products, goods and services, new developments in marketing as well as traditional issues, and large well-known companies as well as new, small ones. They cover important issues related to marketing strategy planning for both domestic and global markets. The readings can be used for independent study, as a basis for class assignments, or as a focus of in-class discussions. Some instructors might want to assign all of the clippings, but we have provided an ample selection so that it is easy to focus on a subset which is especially relevant to specific learning/teaching objectives. A separate set of teaching notes discusses points related to each article. We have put special emphasis on selecting short, highly readable articles—ones which can be read and understood in 10 or 15 minutes—so that they can be used in combination with other readings and assignments for the course. For example, they might be used in combination with assignments from *Basic Marketing,* exercises from the *Learning Aid for Use with Basic Marketing,* or *The Marketing Game!* micro-computer strategy simulation.

All of the articles are reproduced here in basically the same style and format as they originally appeared. This gives the reader a better sense of the popular business publications from which they are drawn, and stimulates an interest in ongoing learning beyond the time frame for a specific course.

We have added this component to our complete set of **P**rofessional **L**earning **U**nits **S**ystems (our **P.L.U.S.**) to provide even more alternatives for effective teaching and learning in the first marketing course. It has been an interesting job to research and select the readings for this new book, and we hope that our readers find it of value in developing a better understanding of the opportunities and challenges of marketing in our contemporary society.

William D. Perreault, Jr. and E. Jerome McCarthy

Acknowledgments

We would like to thank all of the publications that have granted us permission to reprint the articles in this book. Similarly, we value and appreciate the work and skill of the many writers who prepared the original materials.

Lin Davis played an important role in this project. She helped us research thousands of different publications to sort down to the final set, and she also contributed many fine ideas on how best to organize the selections that appear here.

The ideas for this book evolved from and built on previous editions of *Readings and Cases in Basic Marketing*. John F. Grashof and Andrew A. Brogowicz were coauthors of that book. We gratefully recognize the expertise and creativity that they shared over the years on that project. Their fine ideas carry forward here and have had a profound effect on our thinking in selecting articles that will meet the needs of marketing instructors and students alike.

We would also like to thank the many marketing professors and students whose input have helped shape the concept of this book. Their ideas—shared in personal conversations, in focus group interviews, and in responses to marketing research surveys—helped us to clearly define the needs that this book should meet.

Finally, we would like to thank the people at McGraw-Hill/Irwin, our publisher, who have helped turn this idea into a reality. We are grateful for their commitment to making these materials widely available.

W.D.P. and E.J.M.

Contents

Getting Information for Marketing Decisions

Product

Place

Promotion

Price

Marketing Strategies: Planning, Implementation, and Control

Ethical Marketing in a Consumer-Oriented World: Appraisal and Challenges

Marketing's Value to Consumers, Firms, and Society

Probing Shoppers' Psyche

In Designing New Products, Companies Try to Determine Consumers' 'Unmet Needs'

DEBORAH BALL, SARAH ELLISON AND JANET ADAMY. *WALL STREET JOURNAL.*

THREE YEARS AGO, **Procter & Gamble** Co. set out to build a better air freshener.

P&G researchers learned some useful things when they asked people in focus groups to describe their "desired scent experience." Many people, after about half an hour, seem to adjust to a scent and can't smell it anymore. Most air-freshener scents don't spread evenly across a room. People complained that many scents smell artificial.

P&G took it all in and came back with a solution: a scent "player," that looks like a CD player and plays one of five alternating scents every 30 minutes. The gadget, named Febreze Scentstories and priced at $34.99, has a tiny fan inside that circulates the scent throughout the room. With it, P&G sells five different discs, each $5.99 and holding a variety of scents with trademarked names such as "Relaxing in the Hammock" and "Wandering Barefoot on the Shore."

"Nobody could have articulated Scentstories," says Steve McGowan, a product-development manager for Febreze, "but if you really watch the consumer, they'll tell you what they wish."

Ingenuity has taken an extreme turn in the high-stakes world of product development. Desperate to increase sales and market share, companies are digging deeper into shoppers' homes and habits to discover "unmet needs" and then design new products to meet them. Last year, marketers launched a dizzying 34,000 new foods, drinks and beauty products—representing more unmet needs than most people ever guessed they had.

The strategy is turning out to be expensive, with the costs of marketing and promoting a new product often topping $50 million. In September, a sharp rise in marketing spending led **Colgate-Palmolive** Co. and **Unilever** to slash their 2004 earnings forecasts—but also to resolve to continue spending heavily

on marketing to help spur sales. In July, **Kraft Foods** Inc. reported a sharp decline in its quarterly earnings and lowered its full-year forecast amid increased marketing spending.

Even Procter & Gamble, which has led the charge into new products, is feeling the weight of additional costs. Yesterday P&G reported that its operating margins were being squeezed by increased spending on marketing.

Marketers of everything from pet food to soft drinks feel pressure to innovate, for a variety of reasons. Powerful retailers such as **Wal-Mart Stores** Inc. are quicker than ever to pull a lagging product off their shelves, sometimes substituting their own private-label version. Stores also are apt to cut prices of branded items unless shoppers find something new or exciting in them. Marketers must work harder than ever to stand out in superstores that in many cases stock as many as 100,000 different items.

General Mills Inc. rolled out 92 new products this past summer—including Betty Crocker pourable cake-frosting and square-bottomed Old El Paso taco shells—for an increase of more than 30% from the 70 new products launched the previous summer. "Limited-edition" products match shoppers' short attention spans: **PepsiCo** Inc. launched a grape-flavored Mountain Dew, called Mountain Dew Pitch Black, last month just for Halloween and plans to follow with a spicy version of Pepsi for Christmas.

When P&G last month launched a version of Tide laundry detergent with Downy fabric softener, the company said it had "identified an unmet need among a subset of women who want clean and soft laundry, but for various reasons are either unwilling to add liquid fabric softener or are inconsistently adding it because they simply forget."

New products face tough odds. The average American family turns to the same 150 items for as much as 85% of its household needs, says Jack Trout, president of marketing firm Trout & Partners Ltd. Only about 2% of new brands and brand extensions hit $100 million in first-year sales, considered the threshold for success, according to Information Resources Inc.

Sales of C2, **Coca-Cola Co.**'s reduced-calorie, reduced-carbohydrate cola and the company's biggest product introduction since Diet Coke, already have started to fall, just months after the product's introduction. About 25% of so-called line extensions produce no incremental sales, says Valerie Skala Walker, an analyst at Information Resources.

"Consumers are more elusive and harder to reach," says Jim Stengel, head of marketing for

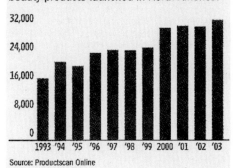

Freshening Up

New food, tobacco, beverage, health and beauty products launched in North America:

```
32,000

24,000

16,000

8,000

0
    1993 '94 '95 '96 '97 '98 '99 2000 '01 '02 '03
```

Source: Productscan Online

P&G. "We are trying to bring true category-building innovations . . . not just another flavor of ice cream." Such an effort requires what salesmen call a "missionary sale," in which the seller first must teach customers what their unmet need is before offering to fill it.

There is no need too small for new products to address. Among the new products P&G has successfully sent out to market are Swiffer Sweep+Vac, the latest iteration in its successful Swiffer line of dust mops and disposable cloths. P&G introduced the Sweep+Vac, a small, battery-operated vacuum-cleaner with a Swiffer mop head attached, during the summer, after focus-group participants said they get on their hands and knees to wipe up the small pile of dirt left on the floor after mopping with a dry Swiffer cloth. "We knew that was a compensating behavior that consumers wouldn't want to do," says Joe Miramonte, a product-development manager for the Swiffer line.

P&G appears to have hit the jackpot with an unmet need it discovered among those consumers who wash their own cars. They told P&G that half of the time they devoted to washing the car was actually spent drying the car, so that water spots won't form. For these consumers, P&G designed Mr. Clean AutoDry Carwash, a sponge along with a nozzle and a liquid-soap cartridge that attaches to a garden hose. A filter in the nozzle removes the minerals in water that cause the spots.

Retailers liked the kit's $24.99 price tag. And the price of refills—$6.99—beats the pennies that consumers might spend on soap to give their car an old-fashioned wash. The AutoDry product is on track to generate more than $100 million in first-year sales, P&G says.

Imitators nip at the heels of successful new products. **Pfizer** Inc. blazed a new trail in packaged products in 2001 with Listerine PocketPaks. The thin, edible, plastic-like mouthwash strips quickly caught on with

(Cont.)

teens and raked in $175 million in first-year sales. Today, supermarket checkout aisles are brimming with all kinds of strips, from Novartis's Theraflu Thin Strips, to Momentus Solutions' Healthy Moments Arthur watermelon-flavored vitamin strips for kids—and even Hartz mint-flavored breath strips for dogs. In the first nine months of this year, 128 different strip products were launched, up fivefold from 2002, according to Productscan Online.

Such innovations rarely stay hot for long, though, Last week, **Wm Wrigley Jr.** Co. said it would close the Phoenix plant where its strips are made because of waning U.S. demand.

"You might be able to hold on to an innovation for six months now, maybe 12 if you're really strong," says Bart Becht, chief executive of Reckitt Benckiser PLC, the maker of Woolite and Lysol. The company says it derived about 40% of its 2003 revenue of $6.81 billion from products introduced within the past three years. Among its recent innovations is Finish Glass Protector, a dishwasher detergent that protects glassware from mineral corrosion.

"We aren't big believers in coming out with just the lemon variant," Mr. Becht says. "We tend to work more towards breakthrough innovations."

Minding the Store

Analyzing Customers, Best Buy Decides Not All Are Welcome

Retailer Aims to Outsmart Dogged Bargain-Hunters, And Coddle Big Spenders

Looking for 'Barrys' and 'Jills'

GARY MCWILLIAMS. *WALL STREET JOURNAL.*

Brad Anderson, chief executive officer of Best Buy Co., is embracing a heretical notion for a retailer. He wants to separate the "angels" among his 1.5 million daily customers from the "devils."

Best Buy's angels are customers who boost profits at the consumer-electronics giant by snapping up high-definition televisions, portable electronics, and newly released DVDs without waiting for markdowns or rebates.

The devils are its worst customers. They buy products, apply for rebates, return the purchases, then buy them back at returned-merchandise discounts. They load up on "loss leaders," severely discounted merchandise designed to boost store traffic, then flip the goods at a profit on eBay. They slap down rock-bottom price quotes from Web sites and demand that Best Buy make good on its lowest-price pledge. "They can wreak enormous economic havoc," says Mr. Anderson.

Best Buy estimates that as many as 100 million of its 500 million customer visits each year are undesirable. And the 54-year-old chief executive wants to be rid of these customers.

Mr. Anderson's new approach upends what has long been standard practice for mass merchants. Most chains use their marketing budgets chiefly to maximize customer traffic, in the belief that more visitors will lift revenue and profit. Shunning customers—unprofitable or not—is rare and risky.

Mr. Anderson says the new tack is based on a business-school theory that advocates rating customers according to profitability, then dumping the up to 20% that are unprofitable. The financial-services industry has used a variation of that approach for years, lavishing attention on its best customers and penalizing its unprofitable customers with fees for using ATMs or tellers or for obtaining bank records.

Best Buy seems an unlikely candidate for a radical makeover. With $24.5 billion in sales last year, the Richfield, Minn., company is the nation's top seller of consumer electronics. Its big, airy stores and wide inventory have helped it increase market share, even as rivals such as Circuit City Stores Inc. and Sears, Roebuck & Co., have struggled. In the 2004 fiscal year that ended in February, Best Buy reported net income of $570 million, up from $99 million during the year-earlier period marred by an unsuccessful acquisition, but still below the $705 million it earned in fiscal 2002.

But Mr. Anderson spies a hurricane on the horizon. Wal-Mart Stores Inc., the world's largest retailer, and Dell Inc., the largest personal-computer maker, have moved rapidly into high-definition televisions and portable electronics, two of Best Buy's most profitable areas. Today, they rank respectively as the nation's second- and fourth-largest consumer-electronics sellers.

Mr. Anderson worries that his two rivals "are larger than us, have a lower [overhead], and are more profitable." In five years, he fears, Best Buy could wind up like Toys 'R' Us Inc., trapped in what consultants call the "unprofitable middle," unable to match Wal-Mart's sheer buying power, while low-cost online sellers like Dell pick off its most affluent customers. Toys 'R' Us recently announced it was considering exiting the toy business.

This year, Best Buy has rolled out its new angel-devil strategy in about 100 of its 670 stores. It is examining sales records and demographic data and sleuthing through computer databases to identify good and bad customers. To lure the high-spenders, it is stocking more merchandise and providing more appealing service. To deter the undesirables, it is cutting back on promotions and sales tactics that tend to draw them, and culling them from marketing lists.

As he prepares to roll out the unconventional strategy throughout the chain, Mr. Anderson faces significant risks. The pilot stores have proven more costly to operate. Because different pilot stores target different types of customers, they threaten to scramble the chain's historic economies of scale. The trickiest challenge may be to deter bad customers without turning off good ones.

"Culturally I want to be very careful," says Mr. Anderson. "The most dangerous image I can think of is a retailer that wants to fire customers."

Mr. Anderson's campaign against devil customers pits Best Buy against an underground of bargain-hungry shoppers intent on wringing every nickel of savings out of big retailers. At dozens of Web sites like FatWallet.com, SlickDeals.net and TechBargains.com, they trade electronic coupons and tips from former clerks and insiders, hoping to gain extra advantages against the stores.

At SlickDeals.net, whose subscribers boast about techniques for gaining hefty discounts, a visitor recently bragged about his practice of shopping at Best Buy only when he thinks he can buy at below the retailer's cost. He claimed to purchase only steeply discounted loss leaders, except when forcing Best Buy to match rock-bottom prices advertised elsewhere. "I started only shopping there if I can [price match] to where they take a loss," he wrote, claiming he was motivated by an unspecified bad experience with the chain. In an e-mail exchange, he declined to identify himself or discuss his tactics, lest his targets be forewarned.

Mr. Anderson's makeover plan began taking shape two years ago when the company retained as a consultant Larry Selden, a professor at Columbia University's Graduate School of Business. Mr. Selden has produced research tying a company's stock-market value to its ability to identify and cater to profitable customers better than its rivals do. At many companies, Mr. Selden argues, losses produced by devil customers wipe out profits generated by angels.

Best Buy's troubled acquisitions of MusicLand Stores Corp. and two other retailers had caused its share price and price-to-earnings ratio to tumble. Mr. Selden recalls advising

Holding Steady

Best Buy still ranks first in terms of consumer-electronics revenue, but emerging rivals are climbing fast.

Estimated 1997 consumer-electronics sales

Best Buy	$7.6 billion
Circuit City	$6.8
CompUSA	$5.1
RadioShack	$3.2
Sears Roebuck	$3.2

Estimated 2003 consumer-electronics sales

Best Buy	$19.5 billion
Wal-Mart	$15.7
Circuit City	$9.8
Dell	$6.3
Target Stores	$5.0

Source: Retail Forward

Mr. Anderson: "The best time to fix something is when you're still making great money but your [price-to-earnings ratio] is going down."

Mr. Selden had never applied his angel-devil theories to a retailer as large as Best Buy, whose executives were skeptical that 20% of customers could be unprofitable. In mid-2002, Mr. Selden outlined his theories during several weekend meetings in Mr. Anderson's Trump Tower apartment. Mr. Anderson was intrigued by Mr. Selden's insistence that a company should view itself as a portfolio of customers, not product lines.

Mr. Anderson put his chief operating officer in charge of a task force to analyze the purchasing histories of several groups of customers, with an eye toward identifying bad customers who purchase loss-leading merchandise and return purchases. The group discovered it could distinguish the angels from the devils, and that 20% of Best Buy's customers accounted for the bulk of profits.

In October 2002, Mr. Anderson instructed the president of Best Buy's U.S. stores, Michael P. Keskey, to develop a plan to realign stores to target distinct groups of customers rather than to push a uniform mix of merchandise. Already deep into a cost-cutting program involving hundreds of employees, Mr. Keskey balked, thinking his boss had fallen for a business-school fad. He recalls telling Mr. Anderson, "You've lost touch with what's happening in your business."

Mr. Anderson was furious, and Mr. Keskey says he wondered whether it was time to leave the company. But after meeting with the chief operating officer and with Mr. Selden, Mr. Keskey realized there was no turning back, he says.

Best Buy concluded that its most desirable customers fell into five distinct groups: upper-income men, suburban mothers, small-business owners, young family men, and technology enthusiasts. Mr. Anderson decided that each store should analyze the demographics of its local market, then focus on two of these groups and stock merchandise accordingly.

Best Buy began working on ways to deter the customers who drove profits down. It couldn't bar them from its stores. But this summer it began taking steps to put a stop to their most damaging practices. It began enforcing a restocking fee of 15% of the purchase price on returned merchandise. To discourage customers who return items with the intention of repurchasing them at an "open-box" discount, it is experimenting with reselling them over the Internet, so the goods don't reappear in the store where they were originally purchased.

"In some cases, we can solve the problem by tightening up procedures so people can't take advantage of the system," explains Mr. Anderson.

In July, Best Buy cut ties to FatWallet. com, an online "affiliate" that had collected referral fees for delivering customers to Best Buy's Web site. At FatWallet.com, shoppers swap details of loss-leading merchandise and rebate strategies. Last October, the site posted Best Buy's secret list of planned Thanksgiving weekend loss leaders, incurring the retailer's ire.

Timothy C. Storm, president of Roscoe, Ill.-based FatWallet, said the information may have leaked from someone who had an early look at advertisements scheduled to run the day after Thanksgiving.

In a letter to Mr. Storm, Best Buy explained it was cutting the online link between FatWallet and BestBuy.com because the referrals were unprofitable. The letter said it was terminating all sites that "consistently and historically have put us in a negative business position."

Mr. Storm defends FatWallet.com's posters as savvy shoppers. "Consumers don't set the prices. The merchants have complete control over what their prices and policies are," he says.

Shunning customers can be a delicate business. Two years ago, retailer Filene's Basement was vilified on television and in newspaper columns for asking two Massachusetts customers not to shop at its stores because of what it said were frequent returns and complaints. Earlier this year, Mr. Anderson apologized in writing to students at a Washington, D.C., school after employees at one store barred a group of black students while admitting a group of white students.

Mr. Anderson says the incident in Washington was inappropriate and not a part of any customer culling. He maintains that Best Buy will first try to turn its bad customers into profitable ones by inducing them to buy warranties or more profitable services. "In most cases, customers wouldn't recognize the options we've tried so far," he says.

Store clerks receive hours of training in identifying desirable customers according to their shopping preferences and behavior. High-income men, referred to internally as Barrys, tend to be enthusiasts of action movies and cameras. Suburban moms, called Jills, are busy but usually willing to talk about helping their families. Male technology enthusiasts, nicknamed Buzzes, are early adopters, interested in buying and showing off the latest gadgets.

Staffers use quick interviews to pigeonhole shoppers. A customer who says his family has a regular "movie night," for example, is pegged a prime candidate for home-theater equipment. Shoppers with large families are steered toward larger appliances and time-saving products.

The company hopes to lure the Barrys and Jills by helping them save time with services like a "personal shopper" to help them hunt for unusual items, alert them to sales on preferred items, and coordinate service calls.

Best Buy's decade-old Westminster, Calif., store is one of 100 now using the new approach. It targets upper-income men with an array of pricey home-theater systems, and small-business owners with network servers, which connect office PCs, and technical help unavailable to other customers.

On Tuesdays, when new movie releases hit the shelves, blue-shirted sales clerks prowl the DVD aisles looking for promising candidates. The goal is to steer them into a back room that showcases $12,000 high-definition home-theater systems. Unlike the television sections at most Best Buy stores, the room has easy chairs, a leather couch, and a basket of popcorn to mimic the media rooms popular with home-theater fans.

At stores popular with young Buzzes, Best Buy is setting up videogame areas with leather chairs and game players hooked to mammoth, plasma-screen televisions. The games are conveniently stacked outside the playing area, the glitzy new TVs a short stroll away.

Mr. Anderson says early results indicate that the pilot stores "are clobbering" the conventional stores. Through the quarter ended Aug. 28, sales gains posted by pilot stores were double those of traditional stores. In October, the company began converting another 70 stores.

Best Buy intends to customize the remainder of its stores over the next three years. As it does, it will lose the economies and efficiencies of look-alike stores. With each variation, it could become more difficult to keep the right items in stock, a critical issue in a business where a shortage of a hot-selling big-screen TV can wreak havoc on sales and customer goodwill.

Overhead costs at the pilot stores have run one to two percentage points higher than traditional stores. Sales specialists cost more, as do periodic design changes. Mr. Anderson says the average cost per store should fall as stores share winning ideas for targeting customers.

THE SMARTEST COMPANY OF THE YEAR AND THE WINNER IS . . . TOYOTA

Hot cars. Hot brands. Hot technology. Here's how Japan's largest automaker keeps firing on all cylinders.

By: Andrew Tilin

WHAT YOU CAN LEARN FROM TOYOTA

Nothing says smart like great results, and during the past year *Business 2.0's* smartest company certainly delivered. After leapfrogging Ford to become the No. 2 automaker worldwide, Toyota saw profits soar to a record $11.1 billion. Behind the numbers were intelligent moves in every corner of the operation, from product design and marketing to manufacturing and leadership. On the following pages, we spotlight some of the winning practices that put Toyota at the top of our list. Take a look—you might find an idea or two to make your own business smarter.

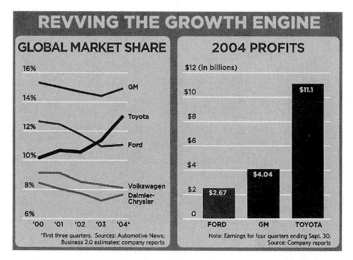

MARKETING

1. KNOW THE LIMITS OF YOUR BRAND.

It was a strange place to hype a new car: Last June, just outside iMi Jimi, a hipster clothing shop in Denver, stood four new coupes from Toyota, a brand better known for Camrys than cool. The hope was that young fashionistas would take time away from trying on Vans sneakers to go for a spin.

That's just what they did, by the hundreds, at iMi Jimi and other trendy clothing and record stores, cafes, and pubs nationwide. The attraction wasn't mega-rebates or zero-percent financing. It was the tC coupe, a stylish hatchback from Toyota's new youth-focused marque, Scion. Thanks to clever positioning, smart marketing, and a trio of edgy-looking, sub $20,000 vehicles, Scion sold some 100,000 cars last year—about as many as Gen Y-targeted competitors Honda Element and Mini Cooper combined.

Toyota launched Scion because it recognized the limitations of its existing brands. The average Toyota driver is 50, and buyers of the company's big Lexus sedans are even older. But Scion is attracting an entirely new cadre of customers with a median age of only 35, extending Toyota's reach to the 63 million-strong "echo boomer" generation. "You have to be who you are," says marketing consultant John Winsor, author of *Beyond the Brand.* "If you're going to switch directions, you'd better start fresh."

That includes creating a completely new approach to selling cars. Because its target market is notoriously skeptical of advertising, Scion relies more on experiential marketing. Thus the informal test-drives at youth-centric hangouts as well as sponsorships of events like hip-hop concerts and graffiti art shows. Even Scion's showrooms look different: Tucked within larger Toyota dealerships, they're outfitted with flat-screen TVs and industrial-chic brushed metal. As a result, the new line

DIFFERENT MARQUES FOR DIFFERENT FOLKS

SCION
MEDIAN BUYER AGE:
35

TOYOTA
MEDIAN BUYER AGE:
50

LEXUS
MEDIAN BUYER AGE:
55

isn't cannibalizing its parent: 85 percent of Scion owners have never purchased a Toyota. Of course, the company hopes that Scion drivers will become Toyota customers for life. "It's a good toe in the water," says Brian Bolain, Scion's national sales promotions manager. "Toyota gets a lot of experience with a group of consumers that's going to be around for a long time."

CULTURE

2. MAKING GREAT PRODUCTS MEANS GOING THE EXTRA MILE (OR 53,000).

An old Toyota proverb goes something like this: To make a better product, get off your rear end and experience the marketplace. Charged with revamping the Sienna minivan for 2004, Toyota chief engineer Yuji Yokoya did just that. To improve on the previous Sienna—small and underpowered—Yokoya embarked on a 53,000-mile North American minivan road trip that included five cross-continent treks, visits to every Mexican state and Canadian province, and loops around Puerto Rico, Hawaii, and the Virgin Islands. "When we asked Mr. Yokoya about his vision, he got very prophetic," recalls Mark Amstock, a Toyota marketing manager. "He said, 'The road will tell us.'"

Driving to the beat of the Pet Shop Boys' "Go West," Yokoya had many epiphanies. In Santa Fe, N.M., narrow downtown streets convinced him that the new Sienna should have a tighter turning radius. On the gravel of the Alaska Highway, he understood the need for

all-wheel-drive. After squinting in the Mississippi sun along the Gulf Coast, he ordered roll-up sunshades for the second- and third-row side windows. There were small triumphs as well: On Utah's Bonneville Salt Flats, he tried to make the minivan fishtail. He was happy to report that "it's difficult to put the Sienna into a spin."

Soon after its debut, the 2004 Sienna became the car critics' darling. Through the first 11 months of last year, Sienna sales were up 60 percent over the same stretch in 2003, moving it into second place in the U.S. minivan race behind the perennial top seller, the Dodge Caravan. While Yokoya's trek took product testing to new extremes, it's also emblematic of Toyota's unswerving focus on the nitty-gritty of the user experience. "Occasionally he'd stop to take a breather or shoot a picture of something pretty," Amstock says. "But mostly it was to fix a flat or because he was lost."

INNOVATION

3. STUDY THEIR MISTAKES— AND YOUR OWN.

The first hybrid car sold in the United States, the wedge-shaped Honda Insight, certainly stood out. But weird looks plus a teeny cabin that could barely contain two early adopters added up to a tough sell. Between 1999 and 2004, Honda moved fewer than 13,000 of the vehicles. Figuring that consumers wanted something more conventional, Honda did somewhat better in the 2003 model year with a Civic hybrid that's indistinguishable from its gas-only twin. But it took Toyota's 2004 Prius, a car that walks the line between Honda's futuristic and familiar extremes, to make six-month waiting lists for hybrids a reality.

Mining niches pioneered by others is a Toyota specialty. In 1989, Toyota introduced its high-end Lexus line, which within three years outsold BMW and Mercedes-Benz to become the No. 1 luxury import. The company's family-oriented Camry sedan out-Taurused the Taurus in quality and function and is still a perennial chart topper. With hybrids, Toyota stumbled out of the gate: The first Prius, a four-door introduced in the United States in 2000, suffered from a lack of cargo space, poor acceleration, and plain-Jane looks.

(Cont.)

But the slow and steady path to success is signature Toyota. For the 2004 Prius, Toyota set out to deliver the power and roominess of a family sedan in a design that screams eco-friendly. To make the $20,000 car perform better, Toyota engineers packed 50 percent more power into the electric motor and modified the engine so it could switch power sources 50 times faster. Meanwhile, the Prius's sloped, aerodynamic contours ensure that drivers look PC while they're getting high MPG. Soaring gas prices make the design seem all the more brilliant. "Honda's hybrid appeals on a rational basis," says Jim Hossack, a vice president at AutoPacific, an automotive market research firm in Tustin, Calif., "while the Prius says, 'Look at me!'"

As a result, the Prius outsells the Civic hybrid two to one and has ignited a mania for hybrids. Toyota's new Lexus RX 400h, scheduled to start shipping in April, already has more than 10,000 confirmed orders. Back in 2001, people laughed at Toyota president Fujio Cho when he predicted that Toyota would sell 300,000 hybrids by 2005. Turns out he wasn't far off: The company expects to sell 228,000 worldwide by the end of the year.

GLOBAL MANUFACTURING

4. TO EXPORT QUALITY, FIRST EXPORT COMPANY VALUES.

Don't be fooled by the leather furniture, rich brown walls, and giant chrome Lexus symbol perched proudly on gleaming hardwood floors. This isn't a swanky Lexus showroom; it's the lobby of the automaker's new plant in Cambridge, Ontario. But the similarity is absolutely intentional. "It reminds our workers of what customers expect from Lexus," says Ray Tanguay, president of Toyota Motor Manufacturing Canada.

Toyota has long manufactured cars outside Japan. But to do so for Lexus, the company had to export the brand's culture of perfection—a level of expectation that

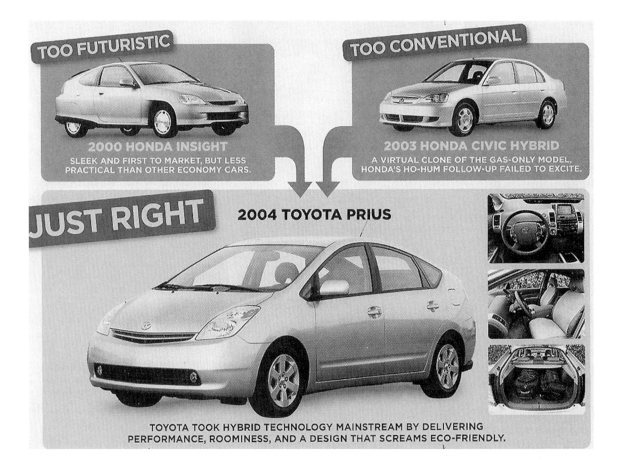

TOO FUTURISTIC

2000 HONDA INSIGHT
SLEEK AND FIRST TO MARKET, BUT LESS PRACTICAL THAN OTHER ECONOMY CARS.

TOO CONVENTIONAL

2003 HONDA CIVIC HYBRID
A VIRTUAL CLONE OF THE GAS-ONLY MODEL, HONDA'S HO-HUM FOLLOW-UP FAILED TO EXCITE.

JUST RIGHT

2004 TOYOTA PRIUS

TOYOTA TOOK HYBRID TECHNOLOGY MAINSTREAM BY DELIVERING PERFORMANCE, ROOMINESS, AND A DESIGN THAT SCREAMS ECO-FRIENDLY.

(Cont.)

surpasses even that of the exacting mother brand. On a Toyota, for instance, a 1-millimeter gap between hood and grille is acceptable; on a Lexus, the separation can't be thicker than an eyelash. Cambridge workers receive special training in Lexus manufacturing processes, and if no one on the floor responds to computer-detected manufacturing flaws within 15 minutes, upper management is paged by BlackBerry. "'Can I prevent it, can I predict it, can I see it?' That's the mentality we're always reinforcing to the staff," Tanguay says.

Before launching the new plant, Tanguay, a 13-year veteran of Toyota Manufacturing, toured every Lexus factory in Japan, looking for ways to improve on what he saw. The upscale entrance is one of his innovations, as are the quality-control systems that *triple*-check every stage of the Lexus-making process. Tanguay also extended the drive for improvement to suppliers, inspiring a Michigan-based maker of wood steering wheels to turn to a piano manufacturer for better lacquering techniques.

The impeccable execution of Cambridge's very first Lexus product—a 2004 RX 330 sport utility vehicle—should be the envy of any company competing in the global marketplace. That's because replicating manufacturing success across borders is easier said than done: When Nissan opened its Canton, Miss., plant in 2003, it experienced manufacturing glitches galore. Still, Tanguay believes that a better measure of his $470 million facility is how well it stacks up against other Lexus plants. An April 2004 J.D. Power & Associates quality survey showed that the differences are indeed minimal. "The only way to distinguish a Japanese RX 330 from a Canadian one?" Tanguay says. "The sticker."

LEADERSHIP

5. ACT, IMPROVE, REPEAT

Since Fujio Cho became its president in 1999, Toyota has been riding an unprecedented wave of prosperity. Sales are up 39 percent, and profits a whopping 141 percent to more than $11 billion. After joining the company in 1960 at age 23, Cho transplanted Toyota's famed manufacturing process to American factories in the 1980s. Known for spotting opportunities the Prius hybrid and the youth-oriented Scion brand debuted under his watch, Cho says smart companies are always striving to do better.

What makes Toyota so smart? I'm not sure the term "smart" really suits Toyota. Rather than dealing with problems neatly in our heads, we execute. If our solutions don't work, we try something else. I like to think

of Toyota as a company that's not afraid to get its hands dirty. If you want to call that smart, OK.

Let's use your definition then. How does Toyota stay smart year after year? Toyota grew out of Sakichi Toyoda's invention of automated looms, and the spirit of the inventor is alive and well. It's a focus on results, where action is key. I learned when I was young that you had to get out into the field—you're always surprised by what you find. And I learned not to give up. If I failed at some project, my bosses never talked about blame. Rather, they sent me back to the drawing board. Good managers never say, "Do what you're told," because that tells subordinates that it's OK not to use their heads.

Companies worldwide are studying the Toyota Production System. Can they become as smart as Toyota? Some people think that if they just implement our techniques, they can be as successful as we are. But those that try often fail. That's because no mere process can turn a poor performer into a star. Rather, you have to address employees' fundamental way of thinking. At Toyota we start with two questions: "Where are we wasting resources like time, people, or material?" and "How can we be less wasteful?" Take conveyor belts. Some manufacturers use them to move a product from worker to worker on an assembly line. But belts can actually waste time because workers have to take the product off the belt at each manufacturing step. It's faster to keep the component stationary and have workers approach it as necessary. The Toyota we know today is the result of challenging ourselves to get rid of waste for more than 40 years.

How does Toyota maintain quality as it expands globally? This is a big problem, and something we have to conquer. We have strict standards, but sometimes those standards are not met. So we need a culture that is not afraid to halt production. When I worked in America, people were afraid to stop the line at first because they didn't want to upset their managers. But within a year, they became really skilled at knowing when to do it. Last year we opened our global support centers, where plant managers from around the world go for training. Our 40 or so factories worldwide compete on quality, and some from overseas are starting to give those in Japan a run for their money.

What other companies do you think are smart? You can learn a lot about brand image from Shiseido, the cosmetics company. Canon is a model for global expansion. And I have long admired GM: When it moved into Europe in the 1950s and '60s, its subsidiaries there became truly European. For students of success, every company can be a teacher.

9

Advertising

To get their messages across, more and more nonprofit organizations are going commercial.

BY NAT IVES

With an ad in Parade magazine on Sunday, the American Heart Association will begin its first-ever paid advertising campaign, a $36 million, three-year effort to raise awareness of heart disease and stroke. The group hopes that writing checks will help deliver its message more effectively compared with donated advertising, which often translates into "far from prime time."

With the decision to go commercial, the heart association becomes the latest prominent nonprofit group to buy both media time and creative services. The American Cancer Society made the same decision four years ago and now spends $10 million to $12 million a year on ads.

Research suggests that charitable groups overall have increased their ad outlays recently. Spending by charities increased to $576.5 million in 2003, from $497.7 million in 2002, a gain of 15.8 percent, according to Nielsen Monitor-Plus. By comparison, overall ad spending climbed to $99.7 billion last year from $94.9 billion in 2002, up 5.1 percent.

Nonprofits and advocacy groups face many of the same challenges that confront corporate advertisers, marketing experts said, citing the deluge of come-ons directed at ever-more-splintered audiences.

"It's been common for charities to get donated advertising in the past," said Stephen M. Adler, chief executive at JAMI Charity Brands in New York, which helps match nonprofit groups with corporate benefactors. "But what's happening now is charities are having a harder time reaching their target audience."

Jerry Della Femina, chairman at Della Femina Rothschild Jeary & Partners in New York, said counting on donated time and space had become a bigger gamble than before. "Public service announcements basically are unfortunately the beggars of the advertising industry," he said. "The networks put them on at 3:30 in the morning, somewhere between guys selling you knives and guys selling you dumpling makers."

Specialists in issues and advocacy advertising at the Seattle office of DDB Worldwide, part of the **Omnicom** Group, say that they, too, have seen changing demands from their nonprofit clients.

"Increasingly, nonprofits are getting more sophisticated," said Candy Cox, managing part-

ner. "They want to play in the very best media in order to communicate their messages."

At the Advertising Council in New York, which facilitates public service campaigns that use donated services and media, executives acknowledged the limits of donated time but said that many groups had few other options.

"From time to time, some organizations decide to make an investment in paid campaigns to complement their public service campaigns," said Peggy Conlon, president and chief executive at the Ad Council. "It's a perfectly good strategy, but year after year, the donated-media, public-service-advertising model really is the best for nonprofits."

The heart association's decision to open its purse stemmed from research revealing a decline in brand awareness, said Claire Bassett, a board member at the association in Dallas. "Everywhere from California to the Northeast to Omaha, Neb., by and large everyone said we have to raise the awareness," Ms. Bassett said.

So the group conducted a review for its first agency of record, selecting Campbell-Ewald in Warren, Mich., to create a paid campaign that would include print and broadcast elements directed at both English and Spanish speakers. It bought time on network shows like "60 Minutes" and "Everybody Loves Raymond," programs that would be nearly out of the question for public service announcements surviving on donated time.

The association also bought time on cable networks including A&E, Discovery Health and Lifetime. In addition to Parade, print ads will appear in publications including Essence, Ladies' Home Journal, Oprah and Reader's Digest.

Planning the media buy was in some ways more clear-cut than striking the right tone with the content, which is intended to remind consumers that heart disease affects not only men but also women and children, said Jeff Scott, president for integrated account services at Campbell-Ewald, part of the **Interpublic Group** of Companies.

"We took a look at depicting a world in which the American Heart Association didn't exist," Mr. Scott said, describing images of an emergency room filled with poorly trained staff and little or no equipment. "That was potentially alienating," he said.

Instead, the campaign emphasizes real families that have faced heart disease. One

ad reads, "Heart disease affects three kinds of people. Children. Women. Men." A somber couple is shown in front of an small empty chair. "John Godleski died of heart disease," the ad continues. "He was just 2 years old."

All elements of the campaign encourage consumers to visit the association's Web site or call a special number to take a "Learn and Live Health Quiz." The level of participation in the quiz will help measure the effort's effectiveness, Mr. Scott said.

The heart association did not retain a big-name corporate sponsor to defray costs because it wanted to control the message as completely as possible at this point, but executives did not rule out future corporate involvement.

Outsiders pointed to partnerships between nonprofits and companies as a major source of financing in the future.

For nonprofits with possibly controversial messages to spread, paying for advertising is often the only way to gain wide distribution. That was the case with a new campaign against job discrimination from the Gill Foundation, a group that advocates lesbian, gay, bisexual and transgender rights.

"With free media, the best way to get on the air is to make a spot that won't offend anybody," said Eric Gutierrez, associate creative director at DDB Seattle, which created the campaign. "When you're making a spot about something like gay rights, you're probably going to offend somebody."

Like the heart association work, the Gill Foundation commercials portrays real people, in this case gay Americans who had not previously disclosed their sexual orientation at work, but publicly reveal their orientation in the spots.

One print ad reads, "For gays and lesbians, America is 14 states that recognize our right to live free from job discrimination, and 36 states that don't."

It is still possible for public service campaigns to receive exposure in desirable times and venues. An Ad Council study of its campaigns from 1999 through 2002 found that only 30 percent of its public service announcements appeared during the overnight hours.

Then there was a spot appearing during the Super Bowl pregame show this year that raised awareness of H.I.V. But that spot, also created by DDB Seattle, had a little help: the clients behind it were the Henry J. Kaiser Family Foundation and **Viacom**, owner of CBS, which broadcast the game.

Microsoft Hopes People See SPOTs When Glancing At Watches

New Data-Enabled Timepieces

. . . .

Two companies start selling wristwatches that will bring news, other info—for fee.

. . . .

By Patrick Seitz
Investor's Business Daily

Microsoft Corp. thinks your wristwatch should do more than tell the time. It also should give you the news, weather, traffic, sports and stock prices, plus send you instant messages and Outlook calendar reminders.

The debut last month of watches using Microsoft's smart personal objects technology, or SPOT, and its service for bringing content to those objects, called MSN Direct, marks the company's first foray into what it calls "glanceable" displays.

Using new MSN Direct-powered watches from Fossil Inc. and Suunto, people can glance at data that's important to them during meetings, business lunches and other places where a cell phone, pager or handheld computer would be obtrusive or rude.

"We're very excited about the watch and its potential," said Doug Kramp, Fossil's senior vice president of consumer technology. "Technology is really merging with fashion for the first time. On the wrist you basically have oceanfront property in terms of accessibility, convenience and discreetness."

The MSN Direct watches from Fossil and Suunto let users customize the data they receive wirelessly. The watches cost from $179 to $300. The MSN Direct service is available in the 100 largest U.S. cities and costs $9.95 a month, or $59 a year. That cost is likely to be the biggest challenge to adoption of the technology, says Matt Rosoff, an analyst with independent research firm Directions on Microsoft.

"Most consumers won't be willing to pay $10 a month for the kind of information that's available on MSN Direct," Rosoff said. "It seems a little pricey for what you get."

He says Microsoft is still mulling price. If sales are low, the Redmond, Wash., company could cut prices, he says.

Microsoft also needs to show that the service will be updated with new features and channels of information, Rosoff says. Among the channels yet to roll out are traffic, sports, movie show times and restaurant recommendations.

With the annual payment plan, MSN Direct comes to less than $5 a month. "That's a couple of lattes," Fossil's Kramp said. Plus, the service will only get better, he says.

The notion of paying a fee for data delivered to your watch is new to most people and will take time to sink in, says Bill Mitchell, corporate vice president of Microsoft's mobile platforms unit.

Another challenge is to get people used to the idea of having to recharge their watches like cell phones every few days, Mitchell says. Consumers also have to take the time to personalize their watches online from their PCs, he says.

Coverage area is another potential drawback. The service is delivered over FM subcarrier bandwidth in the top 100 metropolitan markets, but coverage in the suburbs can be spotty. In Chicago, for example, coverage misses large portions of the prosperous north and west suburbs.

The MSN Direct watches are bigger than most watches, but compare in size to many designer watches. The size is comparable to watches Fossil makes under license for the Diesel, Armani and DKNY brands, Kramp says.

"Big is in fashion now, so this is pretty consistent with a lot of the watches we're selling," he said.

Suunto opted to make its first MSN watches thicker and heavier than Fossil's SPOT watches by adding a bigger battery. Suunto claims to get double Fossil's battery life from its rechargeable lithium ion battery, about five or six days, says Suunto President Dan Colliander.

Suunto sees a good fit with the SPOT watches and its sports instruments. Suunto

SPOT On

Two companies last month came out with the first watches that use Microsoft's SPOT technology, which lets the watches receive such data as stock quotes, news and weather forecasts

Suunto N3 smart wristwatch with MSN Direct service

A Dick Tracy brand Fossil Wrist Net watch with MSN Direct service

sells watches with such features as integrated satellite navigation, heart rate monitors, altimeters and barometers. It targets divers, bikers, hikers, climbers, golfers and other active lifestyles with its products.

"We expect this will significantly increase our user base in the U.S. and allow people a nice way to understand what Suunto is about," Colliander said. "This brings us different types of users, perhaps more of the sports enthusiasts who sit on their couch and watch sports rather than the ones who are actively participating."

Besides news and other services, the SPOT watches display accurate time. The MSN Direct service references an atomic clock as its standard and broadcasts this time to SPOT watches over the local FM radio waves.

The MSN Direct business will be "minuscule" to Microsoft for the foreseeable future, Rosoff says. But he says it's important for several reasons.

First, the devices are another attempt by Microsoft to extend the reach of its software beyond personal computers. With the SPOT watches, Microsoft has shown that its software can run in small-memory, low-power devices and offer competition to Sun Microsystems Inc.'s Java software. Microsoft wants to use its SPOT technology and MSN Direct service in a host of devices, such as key chains, traveling alarm clocks and refrigerator magnets.

Also, the FM subcarrier network that Microsoft has built out—it had to put some equipment at FM towers—with local radio stations could conceivably be put to other uses, Rosoff says. Delivering traffic and other information to in-dash car receivers is one possibility, he says.

Microsoft sees the MSN Direct watches as being like TV sets and will continue to improve the programming they can receive, Mitchell says. He expects refinements in location-based data such as weather and traffic in the months ahead.

Microsoft has lots of bandwidth to broadcast data to its subscribers. A typical radio station can deliver about 125 megabytes of such content a day, he says.

Sales Team

P&G's Gillette Edge: The Playbook It Honed at Wal-Mart

Consumer-Products Giant Helps Huge Retailer Make Specialty Items Mainstream

Coffee Beans for Beginners

SARAH ELLISON, ANN ZIMMERMAN AND CHARLES FORELLE. *WALL STREET JOURNAL.*

Procter & Gamble Co. Chief Executive A.G. Lafley has a strategy in mind for Gillette Co., and he learned it from navigating one of the business world's most intertwined relationships—P&G and Wal-Mart Stores Inc. His approach: Take mundane products and make them so glamorous and distinctive that the world's largest retailer won't be able to resist them.

Mr. Lafley realized soon after becoming CEO nearly five years ago that Wal-Mart's strategy is not only to supply products at the lowest cost but to get people to turn to Wal-Mart for things they normally find elsewhere, at specialty stores, restaurants or even the doctor's office.

So P&G is upgrading its Olay face creams and marketing them as better than department-store brands and just as good as a botox shot from a plastic surgeon. Tooth-whitening used to be an expensive process that was available only at the dentist's office. P&G's Crest Whitestrips gave it a $25 price tag and made it possible for the masses. P&G, maker of the Actonel osteoporosis drug, helps women get bone-density tests in stores instead of a doctor's office. All of this is available at Wal-Mart. And now that P&G is buying Gillette for $52.4 billion based on Friday's close, P&G is likely to push even more such programs using Gillette brands.

For P&G and Wal-Mart, "it's a lot like a marriage," says Lou Pritchett, who, as P&G vice president of sales, met with Wal-Mart founder Sam Walton to establish the companies' relationship in 1987. "Sometimes you want to slice each other's throats, and there are other times when it's a love-in."

Fully 17%, or $8.7 billion, of P&G's $51.4 billion in sales come from Wal-Mart's

5,100 stores world-wide. The companies link their computer systems and share sales data and marketing plans. One of P&G's largest offices outside its Cincinnati headquarters is in Fayetteville, Ark., down the road from Wal-Mart headquarters. The two companies cozy up to each other, only at times to pull back and compete fiercely.

Being the best-selling brand is always a goal for consumer-products companies. But it has become a matter of survival as Wal-Mart has become a bigger player in the world of retail. Wal-Mart is brutally focused on stocking only a few brands on its shelves. Moving products quickly through its stores is crucial to the company's profitability, so Wal-Mart swiftly abandons products that aren't selling well.

Before becoming CEO, Mr. Lafley ran P&G's beauty business, which trained him in the power of selling an upscale image. He aims to push brands that were once mid-tier into the premium echelons. "Here's our real strategy—secret sauce. We want to make the . . . middle to the top of the market as big as it can possibly be through innovation and new ideas," said Mr. Lafley, in an interview as he was laying out his strategy in the summer of 2003.

The drive by P&G, Gillette and Wal-Mart to offer increasingly elaborate products at reasonable prices is helping reshape consumer taste across America. Items like cappuccino makers and spa treatments that were once the domain of specialty stores in cities on the coasts are now common throughout the country. Wal-Mart argues that it forces suppliers to become more efficient and passes gains to consumers in the form of lower prices and a broader selection.

P&G's acquisition was not driven by a

desire to have greater leverage with Wal-Mart, Mr. Lafley said in an interview Friday. Asked if the balance of power has shifted to suppliers, he likes to reply, "The power has shifted to the consumer." P&G says it offers the same programs to all its suppliers and doesn't give any special treatment to Wal-Mart.

Instead, Mr. Lafley spoke of the potential of expanding into products like women's shaving, a market Gillette leads with its Venus brand but one that isn't nearly as developed compared with its men's lines.

Mr. Lafley, who had already established himself as P&G's most acquisitive CEO, buying up beauty companies like Clairol and Wella, wasn't looking for a deal. After expanding a restructuring that had begun under his predecessor, Mr. Lafley was finally shaking the nagging concern on Wall Street that P&G relied on one kind of restructuring program or another to achieve earnings growth. In recent months, he has told investors P&G was focused on internal growth, not deal-making.

So when Gillette CEO James Kilts initially approached Mr. Lafley last fall, the talks didn't go far. Then earlier this month, Mr. Lafley, attracted by Gillette's brands, went back to Mr. Kilts and they quickly hammered out a deal. The acquisition of Gillette would be far larger than any previous acquisition in P&G's 168 years. Its next largest was Wella for $7 billion.

For both P&G and Gillette, Wal-Mart is the largest single seller of their products. It accounts for 13% of Gillette's $9.25 billion in annual sales. P&G's sales at Wal-Mart traditionally have grown faster than its total company growth rate, which was 19% in its last fiscal year, ended June 30. Wal-Mart has even lately worried about suppliers becoming too reliant on it, noting that any time companies rely too much on each other, they inherit all the risks of the other.

Close partnerships between stores and manufacturers are becoming more common now, with such retailers as Costco Wholesale Corp., Target Corp. and Carrefour SA of France moving to that model. P&G and Wal-Mart pioneered the idea and created the template for others. So many manufacturers have offices near Wal-Mart that they dub the town "Vendorville." P&G and Wal-Mart representatives declined to discuss their relationship, citing a policy not to discuss supplier-retailer relationships.

About 300 people work in P&G's Arkansas office, overseeing sales of its brands to Wal-Mart and devising cross-marketing and other tie-ins. After a few years on the account, P&G tends to send managers on to the next assignment because they can often start to identify as much with Wal-Mart's needs as with P&G's, says Tom Muccio, who headed P&G's Wal-Mart team until retiring last year.

Well-Groomed

Percentage of Procter & Gamble's and Gillette's sales that are to Wal-Mart.

Procter & Gamble

Gillette (2004 figure N/A)

Threshold below which companies don't have to disclose sales

1998 '99 '00 '01 '02 '03 '04*

*P&G acquired Wella, a German maker of hair-care products that does little business with Wal-Mart.

Sources: the companies

(Cont.)

"The people were paid by P&G and sat in P&G's office, but it was like they were working for Wal-Mart and P&G equally," Mr. Muccio says. "The payroll just happened to come from P&G."

When Wal-Mart discovered a downside to P&G's and Gillette's pricier products like Crest Whitestrips and Mach3 razors—these products were the most popular to steal—it turned to the suppliers for an answer. One Saturday in January 2001, Tom Coughlin, a Wal-Mart vice-chairman, summoned executives from both companies to Bentonville, asking them to fix the problem, Mr. Muccio recalls.

So, P&G altered its packaging to make its products harder to steal. It changed its Olay package from a box to a clear plastic container with a flat piece of cardboard, known as a "clamshell" because it is so difficult to open. It made the Crest Whitestrips package larger and added an extra layer of plastic. It assumed the extra cost. Gillette also adopted clamshell packaging for its razor packs. For the blade refills, it created a clear-front, plastic dispenser system fitted with drawers that let customers take just one package at a time.

Until Messrs. Walton and Pritchett canoed down Arkansas' Spring River for two days in the summer of 1987, there was barely a relationship between the two companies. "We shipped them products and they sent us a check back," says Mr. Pritchett. "It was we sell. You buy. Good-bye." Years before, Wal-Mart had named P&G its supplier of the year, and P&G hadn't bother to show up to pick up the award.

But advances in technology made Mr. Pritchett believe the two could work together to sell P&G products more efficiently. Mr. Pritchett proposed that P&G share some of its consumer research with Wal-Mart in exchange for a better picture of how P&G's products were selling. Mr. Walton agreed, as long as Mr. Pritchett could sell the idea to his "Yankee bosses." Mr. Pritchett realized then how little the two companies knew about each other. "Cincinnati is in the Midwest," he recalls thinking. (Mr. Walton died in 1992. Mr. Pritchett, who retired from P&G in 1989, now advises companies on the importance of partnerships.)

Early on, P&G employees, who relocated to Fayetteville to be close to Wal-Mart, called their adopted home Fayette-nam, and often griped about Wal-Mart's demands. Still, P&G and Wal-Mart came up with specific goals. In their first collaboration, Wal-Mart complained that Pampers diapers sat for too long in its warehouses, costing it money. Wal-Mart buyers were shipping diapers from the factory every two weeks. After gaining access to Wal-Mart's sales data, P&G assigned one manager to monitor the data and order just enough Pampers to meet sales but not too much so that the diapers sat in the warehouse.

By the mid-nineties, as P&G was starting to struggle to maintain its sales and earnings momentum, Wal-Mart's business was taking off with the rapid expansion of its supercenters. Wal-Mart was quick to take advantage of a P&G miscalculation. P&G had let the trademark on its White Cloud toilet paper lapse in 1994, in order to concentrate on its pricier Charmin brand. A private entrepreneur snapped up the trademark and sold it to Wal-Mart. Wal-Mart started displaying White Cloud with open rolls so shoppers could touch and compare. White Cloud sales quickly increased, hurting P&G's Charmin.

P&G executives felt betrayed, executives involved in the business at the time say. All the consumer market research P&G had shared with Wal-Mart on how to sell toilet paper was being used against it. "The beauty about White Cloud for Wal-Mart was that we had built that Mercedes image and they brought it in at Chevy prices," Mr. Muccio says.

When Mr. Lafley hastily became CEO in June 2000, P&G was reeling from months of turmoil under his predecessor, Durk Jager. Mr. Jager realized P&G needed to innovate more quickly to keep its products relevant, but he went about it by trying to invent new ones like at-home dry cleaning kits and fruit-and-vegetable washes and neglected some of P&G's core brands like Tide and Pampers. Mr. Lafley reversed that. He said he wanted innovation in the company's top 10 brands.

Mr. Lafley, who has a B.A. in history from Hamilton College and briefly pursued a master's degree in medieval and Renaissance history at the University of Virginia, latched onto Wal-Mart's effort to fill an ever-greater role in its shoppers' lives. P&G's consumer research helped develop specific programs for Wal-Mart that bundle P&G's products into a theme, like "Speaking of Women's Health," a nonprofit program that hosts several thousand women each year at a meeting in Cincinnati and hosts dozens of smaller events, to discuss topics like breast cancer and osteoporosis in Wal-Marts across the country. Another, "Babies First," is an initiative that supports children's immunizations, safety seats and a healthy diet. It is sponsored by Pampers, Wal-Mart and the American Academy of Pediatrics.

While P&G doesn't necessarily promote its products at such events, company marketers calculate that such events lend both P&G and Wal-Mart a halo, presenting P&G as an authority on parenting and health and Wal-Mart as a place to get an education on such topics. P&G thinks its sales of diapers increase as a result, giving its brand the clout to expand into new products like foaming wash mittens and disposable bibs.

In 2001, Mr. Muccio says P&G developed a brand of coffee, called Veneto, just for Wal-Mart. Seattle's Best Coffee, a midsize brand then owned by AFC Enterprises, had approached Wal-Mart about selling its coffee beans for about $2 more than P&G's canned Folgers and about $2 less than P&G's higher-end Millstone brand. P&G's Mr. Muccio quickly suggested another option to Wal-Mart: P&G would develop a new mid-tier coffee specifically for Wal-Mart.

P&G came up with Veneto, a whole-bean coffee not as strong as Millstone or the similarly priced Starbucks. P&G and Wal-Mart employees on the project joked that Veneto was the Fisher-Price version of whole bean coffee, as in "my first whole bean." The product was specifically designed to appeal to consumers who had a taste for Folgers or its main competitor, Kraft Foods Inc.'s Maxwell House, but who wanted to participate in the Starbucks phenomenon. P&G's team helped Wal-Mart run consumer taste tests comparing Veneto with Seattle's Best, which is now owned by Starbucks Corp. Today, Wal-Mart stocks Seattle's Best at some stores and Veneto at others, but the P&G brand helped keep the competition from dominating that middle tier, according to Wal-Mart.

Coffee isn't even a priority product for P&G, and, with Veneto, P&G designed a product to get consumers to trade up from its own Folger's. The product, though, showed what has become one of P&G's greatest strengths under Mr. Lafley—making consumers pay a premium for products that are only marginally different from the staples they've purchased for years.

Similarly, Gillette introduces major new product shifts in its razors every five to 10 years, and with them substantial price increases. Its trade-up strategy has a second part: As it introduces new razors, Gillette slowly pulls up the price of its "tail" brands, the older generations. Eventually, the company figures, a Mach3 user will notice that the new Mach3Turbo isn't that much more and will jump to the costlier product.

P&G is planning to leave Gillette's razor and battery businesses and its Braun line of small appliances intact, but meld the rest of the company's deodorant and other products into P&G's structure, according to a person familiar with the negotiations between the two firms. Mr. Kilts sees male skincare as an area where the companies could possibly team up to develop new products. P&G's knowledge of skincare, with its Olay anti-aging creams for women, combined with Gillette's reach with male consumers, makes it a natural, Mr. Kilts said in an interview. "That's something that exists as a sort of East Coast West Coast phenomenon now," says Mr. Kilts, "but we see it moving into the middle of the country and really taking off."

Chinese Youth League Turns to a New Path: Madison Avenue

Ogilvy & Mather Joins Group To Promote Capitalism

A Picture of Mickey Mouse

GEOFFREY A. FOWLER. WALL STREET JOURNAL.

BEIJING—As a university student, Li Wenbin is required to attend training sessions run by the Communist Youth League of China. He learns how to advance the cause of the Communist Party and to help the elderly. And, in one recent exercise, he learned how to sell Chinese mothers on a new flavor of Tang.

Across China, programs organized by the 70 million-member league are coaching young people in today's paramount ideology: capitalism. Some pitch fertilizer on roadshows to farmers, while others teach tots to draw pictures of Mickey Mouse.

They are working with Red Force, an unlikely marketing joint venture between the Communist Youth League and New York advertising firm Ogilvy & Mather. In exchange for helping clients including petroleum and chemical giant Sinochem Corp. and Hong Kong Disneyland make pitches to Chinese shoppers, Ogilvy has groomed more than 3,500 youth-league members in doing promotions and running a business.

Founded in 1922 as a training ground for the Communist Party, the youth league is still intimately tied to the affairs of the often-opaque Communist Party. China's President Hu Jintao was the youth league's first secretary—its highest rank—in 1984.

Now the league hopes Red Force will aid it in a new kind of revolution: finding jobs for the first generation to grow up under China's economic reforms. For all its economic promise and racing growth, China is pumping out more college graduates than it can employ—about 2.8 million new ones in 2004, a third more than in the previous year.

Gathering at Beijing's Great Hall of the People in July 2003 for their 15th National Congress, league officials admitted they were losing appeal. "We used to stress our role as an educator of youth. But now we should listen to the young people's needs

on an equal basis," said Ma Chunlei, deputy secretary of the league's Shanghai branch, according to official reports.

The league's transformation opened the door for its unusual partnership with Ogilvy, which is part of the sprawling British marketing company WPP Group PLC. On a hunch at the end of 2002, Estela Kuo, the managing director of Ogilvy's field marketing unit, gave officials at the social services center of the league her "elevator pitch" for a joint venture.

"We need young people, and I know the mission of the CYL is to help young people get better lives," she remembers saying. To her surprise, the league called her back at 8 the next morning. "They said, 'This is a great idea, but we'll have to do it very carefully,'" recalls Ms. Kuo.

The league's new efforts remain a sensitive topic since it doesn't want to be seen as a profit-driven institution. It rarely speaks to the foreign press and didn't respond to repeated written questions about Red Force. But in state-controlled local press reports, the League's Central Committee has identified Red Force as a top model program.

It targets young people like Mr. Li, who found the league's sober communist morality lessons of little help in the face of a jobs crisis. "The biggest influence of the youth league to me is [teaching me] to love the country and love the Party," says Mr. Li.

A 22-year-old from a lower-middle-class family in Guzhen county, he says his parents, whose lives were largely directed by the state, promised him "full freedom to design my own life." But lately, choosing his dream career—be it as an army officer or a tycoon—has given way to finding a job of any sort at all.

"Job-hunting is getting tougher nowadays," says the e-commerce student at Mingxing College, who will graduate in the spring. "I can feel the stress on campus."

One year in, Red Force's training sessions are so popular it has had to turn students away. At a Beijing session last month, Ogilvy staff taught the entire two-day seminar, beginning with a lecture on communication and personality style, as well as an overview of mantras of Ogilvy corporate culture: "Deliver your brand to the last mile," repeated Ogilvy executive Jeffrey Wu.

Students listened to four hours of case studies on how to promote everything from fruit to phones, all the while scribbling notes on the vocabulary of marketing. There was "P.O.P." (point-of-purchase display), "on-site events," and even "promotion girls"—the attractive women hired to sit at bars with products to "become friends with the customers."

There was to be a test on all of this: an assignment, given on the last day, to create a promotional event proposal for an imaginary youth brand. Those who e-mailed in a report would be considered for future employment by Red Force.

As an enticement, Ms. Kuo closed the session by offering a few jobs right away. "We are holding a promotional event for Swatch and need four promotion girls to help," said Ms. Kuo. "The requirements are to be at least 160 centimeters [5 feet 4 inches] tall, and have no distinguishable [regional] accent." Amid cheers from the auditorium, dozens of girls swarmed around Ms. Kuo to sign up.

To Ogilvy, which already has about 2,000 employees in China, Red Force is serious business. The agency has developed roots in China since it agreed to a joint venture with the Shanghai government in 1991. Like big clients, including Unilever and Motorola, it wants to extend its reach into China's hundreds of smaller cities.

"If Ogilvy had to build that network on our own, it would take years. But our clients cannot wait—and the market cannot wait," says Ogilvy's Ms. Kuo.

For example, Hong Kong Disneyland, which plans to open China's first Disney theme park in September, hired Red Force to hold six storytelling sessions with children in southern China. Red Force members at the youth league's "youth palaces" read aloud "The Prince and the Pauper" and guided potential Disneyland vacationers to draw pictures of Mickey Mouse, sing Mickey songs, and meet Mickey.

"This is an innovative way to use established infrastructure to reach out to kids in China—like YMCA in the U.S.—to involve the children through community activities and provide a positive learning experience that aims to instill creativity and imagination among kids," says Disneyland spokeswoman Esther Wong.

Ta Lina, a public-relations student at Beijing Communications University, says she sat in the front row of the December Red Force training seminar because she appreciated Ogilvy's prestige. David Ogilvy, the British advertising legend who founded the agency and created the classic "man in the Hathaway shirt" campaign, is a hero in China. Ms. Ta, who is 22, has read three of his books translated into Chinese, all of which were national bestsellers.

Ms. Ta sees marketing as a ticket to opportunity—and away from her backwoods hometown of Hohhat in Inner Mongolia. "I think the PR and advertising industry in China will be very large. I'll have many opportunities to get a good job," she says in perfect English. "I want to be independent, and make my own life."

Finding Target Market Opportunities

PC companies swoop into consumer electronics biz

Consumers win as turf war rages over TVs, cameras

By Michelle Kessler
USA TODAY

LAS VEGAS—The plush Wynn Las Vegas casino will have flat-panel TVs in every guest room when it opens in 2005.

But the 7,000 TVs won't be from leading consumer electronics makers, even though developer Steve Wynn contacted "Sony, Samsung—all of them."

Wynn is expected to announce today that he instead bought TVs from PC maker Gateway, which has been in the electronics business for only a year. Wynn liked Gateway's low prices and flexible designs.

That Sony is expected to lose a deal to Gateway shows how PC-focused companies are changing the consumer electronics industry. Hewlett-Packard, Apple Computer and Dell are plunging into consumer electronics as never before. They're hustling to boost revenue as their traditional businesses mature and to stake out territory as the long-awaited convergence of computing and digital entertainment occurs.

Their entry into new markets is expected to lead to lower prices, more choices for consumers and tougher days for companies pursuing consumer dollars. Although electronics giants such as Sony, Panasonic and Pioneer Electronics have the advantage of experience, they haven't faced significant new competitors in more than a decade. The shakeout "will make the PC battles of the past look like child's play," says Creative Strategies technology analyst Tim Bajarin.

The focus on consumer electronics has been building for months and is culminating at the giant Consumer Electronics Show in Las Vegas.

In a keynote speech Wednesday, Microsoft Chairman Bill Gates announced his company's latest foray into what has been an elusive market for the software giant: Microsoft software that more easily melds PCs and TVs. Other announcements: No. 1 chipmaker Intel, known for PC processors, is expected to announce plans to make chips for digital TVs. Printer maker Epson launched projection TVs.

But those are just the latest moves. In the past year, No. 1 PC maker Dell started selling digital music players and TVs. Hewlett-Packard launched a line of digital

cameras and is expected to get into TVs. Cisco Systems, No. 1 maker of Internet networking equipment, bought Linksys Group, which makes networking gear for homes and small offices. CEO John Chambers called the acquisition Cisco's biggest bet in years.

Luring the new big guns: higher-margin products such as pricey TVs and digital music players; fast-growth markets such as digital cameras and DVD players; and a play to make the previously work-focused PC the center of home entertainment.

Digital electronics, Gates says, are "a new opportunity." They are also a natural extension of PCs, says Gary Shapiro, CEO of the Consumer Electronics Association. In some ways, a digital TV is a closer cousin of a PC than of an analog TV. That's because digital technology turns precise bits of data into pictures and sound, while analog devices convert a less-precise stream of information. Apple's iPod digital music player, which accounts for 6% of its revenue, is basically a computer hard drive with music-playing software. Digital video recorders, such as TiVo, store TV programs on hard drives similar to those in computers.

"The technology of the PC industry has completely taken over consumer electronics," says venture capitalist Roger McNamee of Silver Lake Partners.

CATCHING THE DIGITAL WAVE

It may be harder for some electronics companies to shift to digital than it is for computer companies to get into electronics. But they have little choice. Digital photography is surpassing film, forcing companies such as Eastman Kodak to retool. Digital music sales are expected to reach $200 million this year, taking a chunk out of the CD market. While the U.S. PC market is expected to be worth $59 billion this year, the U.S. consumer electronics market could hit $101 billion.

The fate suffered by Sony's analog TV business illustrates how fast the shift is occurring. It has long been a cash cow because Sony could charge high prices for its finely tuned sets based on bulky cathode-ray-tube technology. But rivals such as Samsung and Sharp

(Cont.)

took the lead in recent years in digital flat-panel TVs. In April, Sony stunned investors with an almost $1 billion quarterly loss. The next quarter, its usually strong TV revenue fell 16%. Sony is now playing catch-up in flat-panel TVs and recently said it will cut 20,000 jobs. Sony isn't the only company feeling the impact of the new entrants, which are affecting:

▶ **Prices.** They're dropping fast for all kinds of products, from TVs to portable music players. "Consumers are the winners here," says Intel Vice President Louis Burns. Example: a 35% drop in price, to $532, for a popular flat-panel TV last year, according to the most recent data from researcher NPD Group.

Computer companies can keep prices low because they're used to running lean. PCs often have profit margins of 5% to 10%, compared with 20% or more for many consumer electronics products.

Gateway shocked the electronics industry in 2002 when it introduced its $2,999 flat-panel plasma TV. At the time, similar sets from electronics players cost about $5,000. "Dell and Gateway are setting the entry-level price point," says Pioneer Senior Vice President Russ Johnston. Pioneer, a leading TV maker, has tinkered with prices to compete and has boosted its advertising budget more than 250%, Johnston says.

Dell this year began offering a powerful digital music player for about $250, when similar players cost $300 or more. That helped spur more affordable high-end players, including Apple's $249 iPod Mini.

▶ **Time to market.** Digital cameras and other electronics are hitting the market faster than ever. One reason is that computer companies are accustomed to developing products quickly. Because computer technology changes fast, most companies refresh products every few months. They also move fast because parts are standardized, and products are quickly assembled in Asian factories. In contrast, electronics companies tend to refresh products just once a year and take longer to design and build.

Even so, electronics makers are trimming design times to keep up. Samsung recently designed a digital music player in four months, a process that once took a year. Pioneer and Panasonic say they're streamlining design to reduce time to market.

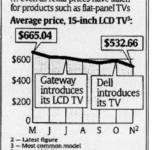

Consumer gizmos boom

Computer companies, trying to boost revenue, are plunging into consumer electronics.

U.S. wholesale revenue for consumer products is expected to rise again this year ...

$96.4 in billions $101.0

1 — estimate
Source: Consumer Electronics Association

... even as retail prices have fallen for products such as flat-panel TVs

Average price, 15-inch LCD TV³:

$665.04 $532.66

Gateway introduces its LCD TV
Dell introduces its TV

M J J A S O N²

2 — Latest figure
3 — Most common model
Sources: NPD Group, companies

By Adrienne Lewis, USA TODAY

▶ **Distribution.** Products once sold only in electronics stores, such as Best Buy and Circuit City, are now sold in all kinds of places. Dell sells most of its TVs and music players online and via phone. Gateway runs its own chain of retail stores. That takes business from traditional retail chains, where most consumer electronics companies peddle their products, says electronics analyst Tom Edwards with NPD.

Electronics makers are responding by increasing their sales channels. Sony is more heavily promoting its five U.S. Sony Style retail stores and boosting its Web offerings. Philips Electronics recently struck a deal with Lane Home Furnishings to sell home entertainment systems in furniture stores. Samsung is running more than 40 online ad campaigns and a promotion with Time Warner Cable.

Still, the different ways to buy can confuse consumers, who are unable to make side-by-side comparisons of many products, Edwards says.

UNPREDICTABLE CONTEST

The computer companies won't necessarily come out on top. Some past forays into consumer electronics have been disasters. Intel made everything from digital cameras to toys in the late 1990s before shuttering the money-losing business in 2001. Gateway, Compaq and Dell made TV-like devices for surfing the Internet that also flopped. And Microsoft's TV set-top boxes never took off.

The PC-focused companies are also accustomed to customers who forgive buggy products. That doesn't work with consumer electronics. "The product has to work 24/7," says Rajeev Mishra, a director at Epson. "Customers won't wait while it reboots."

And the products have to be especially easy to use. That has caught some computer companies off guard. When Cisco bought Linksys, Cisco employees accustomed to handling major crises from technology experts were "unprepared to deal with the consumers when they started to call in," says Cisco Senior Vice President Charlie Giancarlo. Now, Cisco has better-trained staff to handle calls from consumers. The electronics business differs from big business networking gear "in almost every possible way," Giancarlo says. "But it represents a tremendous opportunity."

Medicine

House Calls

Goodbye to long waits, inattentive physicians and all that.
Special treatment can be yours—at a price.

By Peg Tyre

TWO YEARS AGO, FRED PEREN-IC decided the doctors in his health plan weren't worth a dime. "It was hard to get an appointment, and I never saw the same guy twice," says Perenic, 53, the president of a Detroit manufacturing company. At the doctor's office "everyone was always in a rush. It was maddening." So Perenic signed on with Dr. John Blanchard. For a $5,000 annual fee, Blanchard provides Perenic with a yearly three-hour physical, same-day appointments and his personal cell number. Blanchard also calls on Perenic at work to monitor his blood pressure. The price is steep, says Perenic, but for the first time in years, he feels taken care of. Having this much time with a physician, he says, "is almost a guilty pleasure."

Overcrowded offices and overworked physicians have made a trip to the doctor feel like more than a hassle: it's dispiriting. Now, a small but growing number of doctors, clinics and hospitals are offering premium service to elite customers—and affluent baby boomers like Fred Perenic are shelling out big bucks to get it. About 250 so-called "concierge physicians" exist in the United States today: these are primary-care doctors who charge an annual retainer in exchange for same-day appointments, unhurried exams and house calls. The Cooper Clinic in Dallas, whose tab is $3,000 for an eight-hour physical exam, has seen its client base grow 45 percent in the last four years. Baltimore-based Pinnacle Care International charges members between $5,000 and $25,000 a year, in addition to a hefty initiation fee, to keep track of medical records and coordinate health care. Members can get fast-track appointments with overbooked specialists, too.

Health-care experts who fret that too many medical resources are already being spent on too few say the new trend only makes matters worse. Forty-five million Americans live without health insurance. The growth in high-end medicine "is yet another stark inequity in an already unequal system," says David Magnus, a biomedical ethicist from Stanford University. Concierge docs defend boutique care, saying it frees them up to do their jobs right. "I can afford to take the time I need to really listen and get to know each person," says Blanchard. The pay is good, too. While primary-care doctors, on average, make $140,000 a year, Blanchard, who has capped his practice at 100 patients, could make $500,000 before he even picks up a stethoscope. Top specialists find room in their busy schedules for deep-pocketed Pinnacle members, says COO Rick Kramer, because "these patients can pay for their services outright."

There seems to be no limit to what aging boomers are prepared to spend. At Dr. Dan Cosgrove's WellMax clinic in southern California, patients pay up to $9,000 for what may be the most exhaustive physical examination available outside of a medical examiner's office. For three days, WellMax patients get routine tests and blood work, as well as more esoteric exams that measure cognitive function, plaque buildup and genetic vulnerabilities to heart disease or cancer. In three years, Cosgrove's practice has grown from 50 patients a year to nearly 500. "Is it health care for the rich? I guess so," he says. "But when you come to my clinic, I'm not concerned about the national healthcare picture. I'm concerned about you."

One California hospital has even begun leveraging the seemingly insatiable appetite for white-glove care into a fundraising tool. Hoping to turn wealthy patients into big donors, administrators at the University of California, San Francisco, Medical Center founded the Cardiology Council. For $1,500 a year, members get same-day appointments, invitations to lectures and the private cellphone number of the chief of cardiology. UCSF Medical Center CFO Mark Laret says he isn't offering another level of care,

---

Benefits Of Wealth

What money buys:

■ **Concierge Docs:** About 250 nationwide. (Up to $10,000/year)

■ **Health Advisers:** Pinnacle will coordinate with specialists and make appointments. (Up to $25,000/year)

■ **Hospital VIPs:** At UCSF, members get luxe amenities. ($1,500/year)

(Cont.)

only perks that have prompted many council members to make sizable donations. That cash, says Laret, "allows us to hire additional cardiologists who serve all kind of patients . . . Anyone who thinks it is inappropriate for a public hospital to be doing this hasn't taken a hard look at our operating deficits."

While high-end medical care can make you feel pampered, it won't necessarily keep you healthier. Unnecessary medical tests can produce false positives that lead to anxiety—and even more tests.

And almost all carry a small but significant risk of injury and, in some cases, death. What we instinctively know: a doctor's personal attention is a plus. "A primary-care doctor who knows you and has time to treat you," says Barbara Starfield, who studies health care at the Johns Hopkins University, "will keep you healthier."

Joe Polish, 36, a Tempe, Ariz., marketing executive, says the $10,000 initiation and a $5,000 annual fee he paid Pinnacle last year has already made him feel better. So far, Pinnacle helped Polish

change his primary-care doctor, get an executive physical and locate an out-of-town physician for him when he got sick on a business trip. Polish says he joined Pinnacle as an investment in his future. "I'm trying to give myself the greatest possible chance" to live long and live healthy, he says. And for that, Polish says, $15,000 is a small price to pay.

Pampered pooches nestle in lap of luxury

$34 billion a year lavished on food, vet bills, even hair dye

By Mindy Fetterman
USA TODAY

You have a dog. You love your dog.

So you buy good dog food, a special formula if he's an older dog or a little dog, or low-carb if he's chubby, or an organic, vitamin-enriched food if you're into a holistic lifestyle.

You buy a new collar every six months: a bright green one for spring and one with reindeer for Christmas. You buy matching leashes.

You have a dog bed that's not a leftover bathmat. It might have your dog's name embroidered on it. You buy toys and special bones that clean his teeth. You brush his teeth. You might have his picture taken by a professional photographer or painted by an artist.

You have a dog walker. You have a favorite kennel, maybe even one that's a "resort," where dogs lie around on couches and watch TV. OK, maybe that's a bit much. But you'd do it if you could afford it.

When your dog gets sick, you'll pay almost anything to be sure he gets better, including chemotherapy for cancer and hip replacement surgery. You like to take your dog on vacation, and you'll sneak him up the back stairs to the hotel room if they don't allow dogs.

You'd bring your dog to work, too, if they'd let you. Join the crowd.

America has always loved its dogs. But now, you could argue, our obsession is becoming truly obsessive.

In the past 10 years, the pet industry has doubled in size to $34 billion a year in revenue. That includes everything from pet foods and toys to furniture and paying fees for dog walkers, groomers, even pet therapists.

The fastest-growing part of the pet industry is super-high-end luxury items, such as the $5,500 Swarovski crystal doggie vest that is the most expensive item featured so far in New York Dog, a new magazine for that city's dog lovers.

"It's not just Milk-Bones anymore," says Leslie Padgett, editor- in-chief.

Nowhere is this more evident than at the 160 dog shows held around the country every year.

And in particular in New York this weekend, as 2,500 dogs and their owners gather for the 129th annual Westminster Kennel Club Dog Show. About 36,000 show up to watch in person, while about 4 million watch it on TV. Many consider these dogs the nation's most pampered pooches.

Wags call the contest the "sport of grooming."

WHO'S YOUR BABY?

Yet, the Best in Show at Westminster might not really be the most spoiled dog in America. That title might be held by the dog in your house.

Or, maybe in Dana Ujobagy's house in Union Beach, N.J. She spends so much on her Boston terrier, Sophie, that she's embarrassed to tell her boyfriend.

"She's one spoiled prima donna," Ujobagy says. "I don't even look at the price tags. I just say, 'Oh! This would be cute on her.'"

She will admit that her Web site, pawpalaceonline.com, which sells upscale dog clothes, collars and furniture—including a $4,000 bed with matching dresser—is doing great. "Some people don't blink an eye to buy something like that," she says.

Cece Cord of New York City was "horrified" when a friend gave her a miniature Yorkshire terrier after her faithful Labrador died a few years ago. "She looked like a hamster!" she says.

But now, Tiger travels with her everywhere and has inspired Travels with Tiger, her business in high-end luxury goods for dogs, including a $5,700 green crocodile leather travel bag, sold at Bergdorf Goodman on Fifth Avenue in New York. You can buy the matching human purse, too. "It's like playing grown-up Barbie dolls," she says of the little sweaters with fur trim ($295) and other clothes for dogs that she features.

Dog grooming, too, has evolved beyond the occasional flea bath. Padgett reports that dog owners are doing plastic surgery on their dogs and dying their hair when it gets gray. "It's like owners project themselves onto their dogs, and they don't want to look old," she says.

(Cont.)

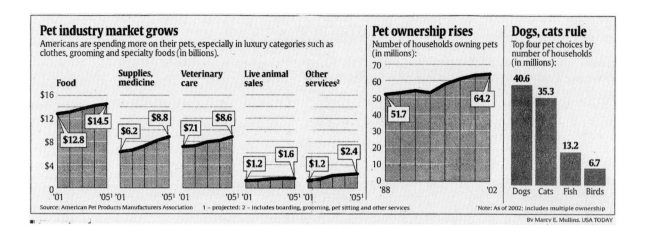

Pet industry market grows
Americans are spending more on their pets, especially in luxury categories such as clothes, grooming and specialty foods (in billions).

Food: $12.8 ('01), $14.5 ('05¹)
Supplies, medicine: $6.2 ('01), $8.8 ('05¹)
Veterinary care: $7.1 ('01), $8.6 ('05¹)
Live animal sales: $1.2 ('01), $1.6 ('05¹)
Other services²: $1.2 ('01), $2.4 ('05¹)

Source: American Pet Products Manufacturers Association   1 – projected; 2 – includes boarding, grooming, pet sitting and other services

Pet ownership rises
Number of households owning pets (in millions):
51.7 ('88), 64.2 ('02)

Dogs, cats rule
Top four pet choices by number of households (in millions):
Dogs 40.6, Cats 35.3, Fish 13.2, Birds 6.7

'Note: As of 2002; includes multiple ownership
By Marcy E. Mullins, USA TODAY

PET INSURANCE: AN EMPLOYEE BENEFIT

Owners are spending tens of thousands of dollars on their dog's veterinary care, too, including kidney transplants and MRIs.

"We've seen invoices that run from $10,000 to $30,000 to treat a variety of conditions," says Peter Weinstein, medical director for Veterinary Pet Insurance in Brea, Calif. The company has sold more than 360,000 pet insurance policies, vs. 157,000 in 2000. And about 1,100 U.S. companies offer VPI's pet insurance as an employee benefit.

"You can't question it, because people need these relationships with their pets," he says. "We know that dogs give unconditional love, they don't go to college, and they never complain. Why not love them? They're better than kids!" he laughs. Of course, he's kidding, but he realizes that his golden retriever, Sundance, is "the most important thing" in his two kids' lives.

The popularity of tiny dogs is growing, spurred by female celebrities who are photographed carrying their Yorkies or Pekingese or Chihuahuas in their handbags, says Padgett, who has a "smart alecky" yellow Labrador retriever named Buck who "runs sideways" when he fetches a ball.

Trends such as later childbirth for married couples, later marriage for singles and more empty nesters with no kids at home are feeding the dog craze, says Bob Vetere, chief operating officer of the American Pet Products Manufacturers Association.

"While the U.S. economy has suffered these last couple of years, the pet industry has not mirrored it," Vetere says. "As Americans have felt more insecure and less sure of the world around them, they're turning to pets for solace."

Vetere has a golden retriever named Dakota who's "a hoot!" he says. "If someone did a lobotomy on him, they'd find a tennis ball. That's all he cares about."

FOUR-FOOTED PEOPLE

The latest trend is for companies that make products for humans to expand into the canine world. "We're seeing the humanization of pets," says Vetere.

OPI, the mainstay of manicurists, has a line of nail polish for dogs. Hasbro makes dog toys. And motorcycle maker Harley-Davidson offers a little leather jacket for dogs.

Two years ago, John Paul DeJoria, the chairman and CEO of Paul Mitchell Systems—the nation's largest privately owned hair-care firm—and some partners launched a line of pet-grooming products that are "tested on humans, so it's safe for your pet."

That human is John Paul himself, who says he's tested every product they sell.

"I even tested the flea and tick shampoo, even though I don't have fleas or ticks," he laughs. You can get "calming moisturizing shampoo" with chamomile and sweet almond oil extracts ($7.99 for a 16-ounce bottle). Or shampoo with natural Australian tea tree oil to control ticks and fleas without chemicals ($9.99 for a 16-ounce bottle). The company's revenue is "in the millions," he says.

Products also are tested for smell by "the coolest dog in the world"—his golden retriever, Jack. "Jack will sniff them," says DeJoria. "If he walks away, that scent is canned."

WORKING LIKE A DOG

On June 24, Pet Sitters International will sponsor its seventh annual Take Your Dog To Work Day. Seven

(Cont.)

years ago, 300 companies participated. Last year, more than 10,000 did.

"The purpose is to celebrate what great companions dogs make in the workplace," says John Long, spokesman for the association, which has nearly 7,000 members worldwide. "They boost morale and productivity and even sales." The goal, though, is to encourage employees to adopt a dog from a shelter and "get the word out" that dogs are great. Long doesn't have a dog, yet. He's in the process of moving and needs space, because, "I'm a Doberman kind of guy."

If we can't take them to work, we hire pet walkers. Laura Vorreyer, 36, makes "six figures, easy," walking dogs in Santa Monica, Calif. "No one raises their hand in the fifth grade and says, 'I want to be a dog walker.' But I can make a good living out here doing this. And I love dogs." She doesn't have one, though. She says she sees enough during the day.

Web sites such as Petswelcome.com and PetTravel.com tell travelers where they can take their dogs along. La Quinta has 300 "dog-friendly" hotels. Some high-end hotels are welcoming dogs the high-end way. The W Hotel in New York offers turndown service including a monogrammed pillow.

Many Ritz-Carltons offer everything from bone-shaped dog pillows and personalized tags to sitters and treats. The policy is "directly in proportion to how many celebrities visit the hotels," says spokeswoman Vivian

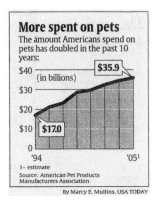

More spent on pets
The amount Americans spend on pets has doubled in the past 10 years:

$35.9
$40 (in billions)
$30
$20
$10 $17.0
0
'94   '05¹
1 – estimate
Source: American Pet Products Manufacturers Association

By Marcy E. Mullins, USA TODAY

Deuschl, who interrupts a conversation to greet Bailey, her black Labrador, who promptly lies down at her feet.

Hotels in New York, Boston, San Francisco, Washington and South Beach in Miami are very welcoming to dogs. At the Central Park South Ritz in New York, "you can borrow a Burberry raincoat for your little dog," says Deuschl. The Ritz in Bachelor Gulch, Colo., has a resident yellow Lab, Bachelor, who's available to be walked, petted and taken on hikes by hotel guests.

At the Ritz-Carlton, Georgetown, in Washington, you can come for a "Tails in the City" weekend that offers your dog a chef-prepared menu and a manicure. Once a month, the hotel holds a "Muttini" hour where you can have a drink while your pooch gets a pet massage or pet aroma-therapy services.

All this pampering, while fun for the dogs and their owners, might seem a little over-the-top to the more practical minded. "To be honest with you, I don't know if anyone really needs a diamond-studded collar for their dog," says Vetere of the pet manufacturers group.

That might be true, says magazine editor Padgett, but dogs give back more than they take. "You can always buy a great purse," she says. "But does it give you a lick on the face at the end of the day?"

Multicultural: Ikea, Circuit City stores go bilingual

Retailers use Census data, targeting software to cater to Hispanics with Spanish signage, expanded offerings

Mercedes M. Cardona. Advertising Age.

AT IKEA's STORE IN Hicksville, N.Y., even the racks of lingonberry jam in the Swedish Shop are tagged in Spanish.

As many big retailers begin spending more marketing dollars to target Hispanics, they are also doing their research to identify and develop Hispanic designated stores. Retailers ranging from home-improvement chain Home Depot and electronics giant Circuit City to department stores like JCPenney and discounters such as Target Stores are adding bilingual signage, collateral materials and staff and tweaking merchandise to appeal to a growing Latino community that accounts for 14% of the U.S. population but shops disproportionately in certain areas.

"We just felt it was the next level of communication for us," said Rich D'Amico, Ikea's regional marketing manager. In September Ikea broke its first original Hispanic TV commercials—and added Spanish-language signage in stores in five markets, Los Angeles, Chicago, San Francisco, New York and New Haven, Conn. At the same time, Ikea did its first Spanish-language catalog and its "How to shop Ikea" video will get a Spanish-language version shortly, said Mr. D'Amico. Anita Santiago Advertising, Santa Monica, Calif., did the ads.

GETTING 'RELEVANT'

Aggressively courting Hispanic shoppers, JCPenney used U. S. Census data and its own market research to identify several Hispanic-designated stores. Changes there include bilingual signage, gift cards and credit applications, plus stocking more colors and sizes Hispanic consumers want, said Manny Fernandez, manager-multicultural and specialty marketing. "It's about providing merchandise that's relevant," he said. He noted some stores stock jewelry appropriate for *quinceaneras,* the 15th-birthday celebration Hispanic families throw for their daughters.

In Hispanic marketing, a little can go a long way, said experts.

"You get great credit for saying 'This store's for you,'" said Randy Curtis, market strategist at consultancy Bueno Curtis Behavioral Marketing and a former Wal-Mart Stores marketer. "There's a story going around here that a Hispanic customer said: 'I speak English quite well, but when I'm talking money, I talk Spanish,'" said Justin Lewis, VP-marketing at Circuit City Stores.

Combing Census data and proprietary research, Circuit City gives any store that is 40% Hispanic or more the full package of bilingual signage, collateral materials and circulars. Below 40%, it varies by store, down to just bilingual bathroom signs and return policy signage near cash registers. All stores also keep handy a Spanish glossary of electronic terms, compiled by Bromley Communications, San Antonio, the Hispanic agency Circuit City hired in January 2004 for its first foray into the Latino market. The first ads, showing a Hispanic family happily shopping in a bilingual Circuit City store, broke in October.

"Obviously, it's a by-market issue," said Mr. Curtis. "If you're looking at return on investment, you're not going to go to the expense of redoing signage for 2% to 3% of the population."

CAREFUL CHOICES KEY

Besides, stores risk alienating other customers who may want their languages represented. So choosing carefully is key. Geography also matters. In Los Angeles, a store in an area where 70% of the population is Latino might be considered Hispanic, but not 20%. In a less heavily Hispanic area, 25% might merit designation as Hispanic.

CVS classifies all its drugstores at one of four different levels that determine the degree of Spanish-language store signage and communications. The levels, based on the Hispanic population in a store's neighborhood, go up to a high of 85%.

Singling out stores with high Hispanic potential has gotten easier with more powerful, cheaper software and detailed Census data, said Marco Vega, head of planning at Ole, New York, Target's first Hispanic shop. It can be as easy as running Microsoft's MapPoint software on a laptop to reveal Hispanic markets a client never knew it could tap. Hispanics will also drive longer to reach a store, on average 15 minutes compared to 10 for the general population, he said. "If you crunch your numbers right, you're going to

(Cont.)

find some nice surprises," said Mr. Vega. For example, a detailed look at not-very-Hispanic Cleveland found a cluster of 300,000 Hispanic consumers in one area, he said.

The fine tuning is important, said Mr. Lewis. He noted Circuit City targeted its stores with input from store managers, who provided key intelligence.

Marketers can also compare the performance of Hispanic and non-Hispanic stores, or set different targets. JCPenney's Hispanic-designated stores, working with Hispanic agency Dieste Harmel & Partners, Dallas, were supposed to grow 2% faster than others. In fact, the HDS stores grew sales by 11.2% from February through September 2004, compared to 6.6% for all JCPenney stores.

CONTRIBUTING: LAUREL WENTZ

Reprinted with permission from the January 3, 2005 issue of *Advertising Age*. Copyright, Crain Communications, Inc. 2005.

These people do make house calls—and business is good
Time constraints, aging population fuel demand

By Stephanie Armour
USA TODAY

As time becomes an increasingly precious commodity, a number of businesses are going mobile—taking their services on the road to make house calls.

In-home service providers will do just about anything: fix a computer problem, string up Christmas lights, X-ray a foot or sharpen rusty garden tools.

In the Seattle area, residents can hire a plant expert who makes horticultural house calls, coming to homes to help prune a plant or perk up a lawn.

As concierge medicine takes off—patients pay extra for 24-hour care and extra attention—doctors are making house calls again, arriving at patients' doors with portable X-ray machines.

In 2002, Best Buy purchased the Geek Squad, specialists who help with computer-related issues. Now available at all Best Buy stores, the specialists will come to a customer's home to do such tasks as setting up a wireless home network or dealing with a computer crash.

"Our agents read the manual so you don't have to," says Kevin Cockett, a spokesman with Best Buy. "People like the convenience of an agent coming to the home. They get one-on-one service in the home."

SERVICES MEETING NEEDS

The emphasis on in-home service is the result of several trends:

▶ Time-strapped Americans are more willing to pay for services that will alleviate stress and cut down on errand running: Combined weekly work hours for dual-earning couples with children rose 10 hours a week, from 81 hours in 1977 to 91 hours in 2002, according to a study by the New York-based Families and Work Institute.

That's one reason nearly 50% of Americans say they "juggle many activities, and it sometimes feels like too much," according to a survey of the luxury consumer market by New York-based communications agency Euro RSCG Worldwide. The higher the income bracket, the more likely people were to agree.

▶ It's also the result of an aging population. Dentists, doctors, even funeral-services providers are trying to serve clients who find it more difficult to leave the home. The number of people 65 and older increased from 31.2 million in 1990 to 35 million in 2000, according to a 2004 U.S. Census report.

Some senior-care pharmacists, for example, now make house calls.

"Among more government programs, health care policies and consumers, there is demand for the notion of 'aging in place,'" says Robert Appel, a spokesman with the Alexandria, Va.-based American Society of Consultant Pharmacists. "More people will be at home alone and at risk, so there will be greater demand for (in-home services)."

▶ And then there is the luxury factor. Consumers will pay to be pampered in their homes. Today's roster of in-home services includes private chefs who will drop off prepared meals that need only to be microwaved before dinner, and pet-waste-removal services that will remove dog droppings from the yard.

Consider one growing service: companies that provide residential holiday decorating. In Omaha, Creative Decorating festoons lights and other holiday displays at several hundred homes and businesses each holiday season. This year, they put up 1 million lights.

Cost runs $400 and up for the exterior of a home, and the prices include a one-time outlay for such equipment as lights. They also come and remove all displays at the end of the season.

"Business is growing. It's out of control," owner Brad Finkle says. "People see what their neighbors are doing and say, 'We better hire somebody.' They're trying to keep up with the Joneses."

And Custom Christmas, based in Alexandria, La., had a client who spent $18,000 this Christmas to have her home decorated—inside and out—for the holidays. The company strung 2,000 feet of lights from the roofline.

(Cont.)

"These trees have become more of a decorator item than a family tradition, and that's part of the trend," says Tom Petrus, who runs the company with his wife, Emma. "It's exploding. We literally have to turn business away."

GROWING BUSINESSES

Many providers of these in-home services say business is booming.

Take Marie McKinsey of Seattle, who will make home visits as part of her horticultural house-call business. Every house-call client receives a packet filled with gardening tips and handouts. The cost for the service is $75 an hour within the greater Seattle area, with a $15-per-hour charge for travel time for calls outside of Seattle.

"I made as much doing house calls as design. It's growing, and we're expanding the house calls," says McKinsey, a co-founder. "It's like stump the expert. We carry reference and resource material in our cars. It can be insect problems, how to plant something."

Many clients who use such services tout the time-saving benefits.

Says Kristina Murti of Seattle, a horticultural house-call client who used McKinsey to help her design a backyard: "She showed us where the plants should go. It was great. I've recommended her to several friends."

SERVICES MULTIPLYING

And the types of services offered also are expanding, from yoga instructors who offer in-home sessions to manufacturers who offer in-home handyman services.

"Consumers value house calls for two reasons: convenience and certainty," says Bruce Judson, author of Go It Alone! The Secret to Building a Successful Business on Your Own. "Some of the best new businesses are created when entrepreneurs see an unmet need for a service."

▶ At Love's Sharpening in Edwards, Miss., owner Tim Love runs a mobile service. He makes house calls to sharpen such tools as scissors, barber tools, saw blades and anything else that can get rusty or dull. The service hearkens back to the 1800s, when sharpening services were routinely provided door-to-door. There is a per-item charge and a $5 travel fee.

"Every year, I see a 10% increase (in business)," Love says.

▶ A growing number of entrepreneurs provide doctors who will make old-fashioned house calls. AM/PM House Calls of Hollywood, Fla., offers 24-hour medical house-call services. Some insurers will cover the cost.

▶ At Herz Financial, based in Farmington, Conn., and Boca Raton, Fla., financial house calls are made for an affluent clientele. Discussions may focus on such topics as estate planning to acquiring insurance products.

"We will meet with clients all over the world," Vice President Randy Herz says. "If you have to meet them at their yacht in Florida, you do that."

Brand Builders: What Yellow Did for Them

Symantec: Where security means never having to live in a yellow submarine

Scott Van Camp. Brandweek.

THINK of a software company with applications on millions of PCs that has pulled off a flurry of acquisitions and weathered the tech downturn better than its rivals. A certain computer giant in Redmond, Wash? Nope. Try Silicon Valley's security software specialist, Symantec.

While Symantec's revenues fall well short of Microsoft's, the company has been on a similar march toward domination ever since former IBM senior exec John Thompson took the reins as CEO in 1999. The upward trajectory reached a zenith last month with the firm's $13.5 billion announced acquisition of storage management software provider Veritas. The merger would transform the company into a one-stop shop for data management and security, and create the world's fourth-largest independent software firm. With Veritas in the fold, Symantec could become the Microsoft of security, boasting products and services that dwarf the competition.

Jumpstarted by post-9/11 cyber terrorism awareness and almost daily threats by hackers worldwide, the security business has never been better. An $8 billion market today, software security is expected to grow to $16 billion by 2008, according to research firm IDC, Framingham, Mass.

Symantec's overall security market share is an estimated 41%, followed by No. 2 McAfee at 21%. Its sub-brand, Norton, owns 70% of the consumer security market. Company stock has grown 766% since 1999—from about $5 to $60 at press time—and gross revenues for fiscal 2004 were $1.87 billion, up 33% from the year before.

"In the past, people have underspent on security," said Sarah Friar, an analyst at Goldman Sachs, San Francisco. "Now they realize it can't be an afterthought. It must be a forethought."

While operating in a burgeoning category, Symantec has consistently found the right marketing formula. Much of the credit goes to Don Frischmann, Symantec's svp-worldwide communications and brand management, another ex-IBMer whom Thompson lured to Symantec in 1999. Together, the two mapped out a plan that hasn't wavered in five years.

The strategy called for growth within the fertile market of corporate (enterprise) customers. At the same time, marketers would continue to offer strong consumer products via the Norton sub-brand, but with the intention of folding it into Symantec within three to five years.

The majority of Symantec's enterprise base consists of small to medium businesses. To maintain its growth, the company needs to sell big-ticket solutions to large firms. Even with the Veritas acquisition, that will not be easy. Symantec faces stiff competition from entrenched players IBM, Hewlett-Packard and Computer Associates. Last May, the company hired HP vet Janice Chaffin as CMO, primarily to spearhead marketing to businesses.

> *Security used to be an afterthought. Post 9/11 and with so many hackers, no more.*

Starting in 2000, Symantec worked with Interbrand, New York, to develop its consumer marketing platform. The resulting set of core values—centering on trust and confidence—continues today. Symantec also jettisoned its old logo of interlaced boxes in favor of a merging yin-yang symbol in yellow and black.

In part because the Interbrand study revealed that customers clearly identified yellow with Norton and Symantec, the company retained the signature color. "Plus, it really popped at retail," said Frischmann. Today, the sunshine hue remains a key branding tool, appearing on the boxes, as background in advertising and in collateral materials.

Symantec earmarked little money for advertising as of 2000, so Frischmann turned to pr to get the message across. "We were able to trade on our expertise by speaking to the media about viruses, and when they got bored with that, we'd talk about security in the enterprise," he said.

While competitors were trading on security fears—depicting deadly snakes and guys with guns in ads—Symantec's message was more subtle.

"Our view was that companies and consumers didn't want to have to think about security; they just wanted to do what they had to do online," said Frischmann. "Our theme was that people want to work and play online with confidence."

(Cont.)

In early 2001 Symantec launched a $40 million campaign via Ogilvy & Mather, Los Angeles, with print and Web ads depicting people dressed in bright yellow suits amid throngs of office workers. "The people were a perfect metaphor for what Symantec stood for: confident, not in the way and there to help," said Brad Fornaciari, then a partner at Ogilvy & Mather who now heads up the account at J. Walter Thompson, Los Angeles.

As a result of the effort, which ran through last October, both Symantec's image and its sales took off. "Our earnings were looking pretty good in a very bad Silicon Valley economy, and we were becoming known as a consumer company that was doing some new things," said Frischmann.

On the corporate side, he noted, CIOs were looking for one or two trusted security vendors. "And that's what we've been doing ever since: integrating security so you don't have to go out and find multiple vendors," said Frischmann.

To that end, Symantec has been on a buying spree, acquiring 16 small to midsize companies in the last five years ranging from network security to e-mail security. Consumer security offerings now cover firewall, antispam, antispyware and intrusion prevention, purchased separately or in a package called Norton Internet Security. Per the company, nearly 25% of its installed base uses the NIS service. Although Symantec still sells the Norton boxes, consumers are offered a $24.95 yearly subscription that provides security updates to their desktops.

The success of Norton has since put a crimp on the company's plans to fold the brand into Symantec. "We figured that, over time, we'd shrink the Norton logo on the box and eventually replace it with Symantec," explained Frischmann. Last quarter, the consumer business accounted for 51% of Symantec's total worldwide revenues, up 63% from the same period the year before. "That's in a quarter without any major virus outbreaks," noted Frischmann.

Along with standard product advertising, the company conducts co-marketing deals with nearly every major computer and consumer electronics retailer, and has relationships with top computers manufacturers to

> **"Consumers don't want to think about security. They want to [go] online with confidence."**

place 60-day trial versions of Norton software on new machines. "We even sell our boxes at gas stations in Germany," mused Frischmann.

CMO Chaffin's first task is fashioning a clear message to the C-level business target. "We're a strong antivirus vendor, but we also have a lot more products and services than that," Chaffin said.

Through surveys of sales teams, customers and industry analysts, Chaffin crystallized the message that businesses want security, but also their data readily available. Hence she introduced a new corporate theme, "Information integrity," along with a print, online and outdoor campaign via JWT that broke last month with the tagline, "Be Fearless."

The yellow-hued ads are meant to express the confidence and trust that comes with Symantec's solutions. One print ad asks: "Regulatory compliance? Is that a problem?," stating that Symantec can help companies deal with the complexities of the Sarbanes-Oxley accounting legislation by making information available and secure.

Thompson himself embodies the "confidence and trust" message. He's an energetic globe-hopper who can reel off security statistics with the best of them. Together with Frischmann, he has fashioned one of the big Silicon Valley success stories. The secret?

"What's been helpful in the building of the brand is that all of the messages were coming through myself and the CEO," said Frischmann. "There is a consistency there, and I don't think that happens in companies very often."

More importantly, the pair has been able to articulate their message to the rest of the company. "There's a belief system in companies that get branding right," said Marty Brandt, a partner at consultancy True-Brand in San Francisco. "Apple has one, and Symantec has also done a great job in building one."

For all its success, however, Frischmann has yet to reach his ultimate goal for the brand. "I'm looking to achieve something along the lines of Harley-Davidson," he said, envisioning, "Symantec logos on everyone's jacket!"

SAND, SUN AND SURGERY
Asian hospitals are luring more patients from around the world

Shaun Reese's Bum Knee had been nagging him for months. He had torn a ligament a couple of years earlier that never healed properly, and the pain was getting worse. But the 48-year-old building contractor from Wyoming didn't have health insurance, so he kept putting off dealing with the problem. Then a friend suggested he fly to Thailand for some sun—and a spot of surgery on the side.

After some investigation, Reese took the advice, and in January he hopped a plane for Bangkok's Bumrungrad Hospital, where he had arthroscopic knee surgery. Total cost: $5,000—half for the surgery and the rest for airfare and three weeks recuperating on the beach. Back home, he would have paid $6,500 for the operation alone. In Thailand, he says, "the people are super nice, and the facilities are nice and clean and convenient." So nice, clean, and convenient, in fact, that Reese says he may return next year for a hip replacement.

Welshman Cyril Parry's problem wasn't the cost of surgery. He had coverage from Britain's National Health Service but had been waiting more than four years for a hip replacement. As his pain increased, he decided to take matters into his own hands. Online, he found the Web site of the Apollo Hospital in Madras, India, and discovered that a doctor there had worked with a pioneer of hip-replacement surgery in Britain. "His credentials were impeccable," Parry says. Although his family thought he was daft, 59-year-old Parry flew to Madras in November and had the operation. Less than two weeks later, he was home. Total cost: $8,300, which he paid out of pocket. He is thrilled with the results. "I could not have gone anywhere better," says Parry. But he notes that, upon his return, "the nurses at the NHS gave me an attitude of near-hostility for going overseas for my operation."

FEARS OF AVIAN FLU

Those NHS nurses—and their counterparts elsewhere in the developed world—may have to shed their attitude. Parry and Reese are among a growing army of patients traveling to Asia for medical care. Thailand's private hospitals treated more than 308,000 patients from abroad in 2002, generating some $280 million in revenue, according to the Thai Private Hospital Assn. And the business is growing. While just around 10,000 international patients checked in to Indian hospitals for everything from hernias to heart surgery last year, health-care tourism in India could become a $1 billion business by 2012, according to a report by McKinsey & Co. and the Confederation of Indian Industry. And Singapore attracted 200,000 foreign patients in 2002 and aims to serve 1 million annually by 2010. Medical care "will be a global business." says C.E. Tan, marketing manager at Parkway Group Healthcare, a chain of hospitals in Singapore that treated 122,000 foreign patients last year.

One potential hitch in the global ambitions of Asian hospitals: The region is seen as a breeding ground for infectious disease. This year's avian flu outbreak will surely cause some would-be patients to check in to local hospitals rather than fly to Asia for treatment. Last year's SARS epidemic took a big bite out of business for many facilities in the region. Although Thailand had no reported cases of the disease, "SARS kicked us quite badly," says Ralf Krewer, marketing manager at the International Medical Center of Bangkok Hospital. "Nobody wanted to get on a plane." And many foreigners are concerned about the safety of the blood supply in developing nations, although officials say those worries are unfounded. The blood used in Thai hospitals is monitored "by the International Red Cross, and every blood-donor clinic is inspected," says Surapong Ambhanwong, a board member of the country's National Blood Donor center.

Those are real concerns. But on price alone, you don't have to be a brain surgeon to do the math. In India or Thailand, a heart bypass costs $8,000 to $15,000, cataract surgery $500 per eye, and a root canal $80 to $225 per tooth. Those prices are a fraction of what U.S. hospitals or dentists might charge. And in both countries, privately run hospitals often provide foreign patients with live video consultations before they arrive, a personal paramedic, airport transfers in either a limousine or ambulance, and a couple of weeks in a hotel to recuperate.

While people have long traveled to far-flung, exotic locales for nose jobs, tummy tucks, and breast enhancements, Thailand wants to woo foreigners in need of nonelective medical treatment. A key catalyst for private Thai hospitals was the financial crisis of 1997-98. With their own middle-class clientele devastated by the economic collapse, the hospitals started courting foreigners to help fill their empty wards. Last year, more than 150,000 international patients (including those seeking outpatient care) from 140 countries came to Bumrungrad, generating 20% of its $112 million in revenue. Now, Bumrungrad is reaching even further afield, with referral offices in Oman, Australia, and the Netherlands.

India has similar ambitions. Naresh Trehan, executive director of the Escorts Heart Institute & Research Centre Ltd. in New Delhi, in August led a mission to Britain to pitch the NHS the idea of sending patients to India for everything from reconstructive surgery to cancer treatment. The NHS says it's not interested, but Trehan says some private insurers are considering the proposal. Although India's public hospitals are often run-down and underequipped, Trehan is confident that private Indian facilities can hold their own in the global operating theater. "We stand tall with the rest of them in the world," says Trehan, who spent 20 years practicing as a cardiac surgeon in New York. "People's impression of India's health care is the 1940s and 1950s," he says. But in recent years, high-end medicine there has "taken a quantum leap."

To ease the concerns of potential patients, some of these hospitals are pursuing accreditation from the same groups that oversee medical facilities in the U.S. and Britain. Escorts is accredited by the British Standards Institute. Both Escorts and the Apollo Group

Cutting Costs
Fees for common surgical procedures requested by medical tourists

	THAILAND/INDIA	U.S.
Heart bypass	$8,000-15,000	$25,000-35,000
Hip replacement	$7,500-8,750	$25,000-35,000
Breast Augmentation	$2,000-2,500	$4,500-8,000
Lasik eye surgery	$1000-1650	$4,000-6,000
Nose job	$1,000-1,750	$4,000-12,000

Data: Bangkok General Hospital, American Society of Plastic Surgeons, Society of Thoracic Surgeons.

(Cont.)

hospitals are seeking certification from the U.S.-based Joint Commission on Accreditation of Healthcare Organizations. Bumrungrad already has accreditation from the Joint Commission. "We are trying to position ourselves as the Mayo Clinic of Asia, to be known as a referral center in this part of the world for patients from all over the world," says Ruben Toral, Bumrungrad's director of international programs.

The facilities are spending big bucks to attract more paying clients from abroad. Bangkok Hospital is building a $7.7 million, 104-bed heart center to be reserved entirely for foreign patients. In December, Escorts inaugurated a $20 million, 170-bed cardiac wing. To keep their customers satisfied, the hospitals often look more like luxury spas than sick bays. Bangkok Hospital offers single

Affordable procedures, excellent doctors—and spa-like facilities

rooms only (with adjoining quarters for family members) and provides in-room Internet access. It serves four different cuisines—Thai, Japanese, and two Western selections—every night. Bumrungrad's soaring lobby features a Starbucks café, a soothing fountain, and dozens of comfortable armchairs where patients and guests can relax. "I would give this five stars," says Yvonne Wilmink, a native of the Netherlands who traveled from her home in

Sri Lanka for knee surgery.

True, even five-star hospitals aren't for everyone if they're thousands of miles from home. Those with decent health insurance will probably stay put for surgery. But Asian medical facilities are betting that for people in developing markets where health care is sub-par, or for those on long waiting lists, or for anyone with inadequate coverage at home, the trip might be just what the doctor ordered.

By Frederik Balfour in Bangkok and Manjeet Kripalani in Bombay, with Kerry Capell and Laura Cohn in London

Reprinted from the February 16, 2004 issue of *Business Week*, by permission. Copyright the McGraw-Hill Companies.

Entrepreneur Joe Semprevivo

Create A Niche—By making cookies a diabetic could love, he pleased himself first

. . . .

By Curt Schleier
Investor's Business Daily

Joe Semprevivo wasn't going to let a little thing like a potentially debilitating disease stop him from enjoying life.

Semprevivo, 32, was diagnosed with juvenile diabetes when he was nine years old. To make his life even tougher, his parents owned an ice cream shop in Deming, N.M. Every day after school, he'd go to the store, help his parents make ice cream and watch other people enjoy his work.

Finally, at age 12, he had enough.

"I went back to the mixing room one day after school and I made a batch of the first-ever sugar-free ice cream," Semprevivo said in a telephone interview.

At first, his parents were less than thrilled when he came running to the front of the store, "my face painted in strawberry ice cream." But when he explained what he'd done, they were as thrilled as young Joseph was.

There was just one problem. It tasted great, but "when we froze it, it came out like a block of ice." So Joseph's father, Larry, worked on the recipe until he came up with a good product.

But this was Joseph's product and he took charge. He knew that customers respond to the personal touch. So he decided to do some research, and went to supermarket freezers to check out the labels on other ice creams. Personalization, he figured, would make his product stand out. So he went with a "square label with a picture of me on it—to add personality to the product line." He even recalled what the label copy said:

"Hello. My name is Joseph Semprevivo. At 12 years old, I created this delicious, sugar-free ice cream for all diabetics and health-conscious consumers."

Semprevivo made sales calls and used every advantage at his disposal.

"I was 12 years old. The supermarket managers thought it was adorable. They waived their fees for using their freezers for me. They asked me, 'Don't you get an allowance?' I said, 'Only if I sell ice cream.'"

Going For Taste

Over the next three years, Semprevivo got his ice cream into about 75 outlets, but young Joseph wanted more. He wanted a snack he could take to school, so he could be just like the other kids. His parents, who used to own a restaurant, secretly worked on coming up with a tasty sugar-free cookie.

"I was at a friend's house. I was supposed to spend the night, but my father called me and asked me to come home. When I got there he gave me this cookie to eat, and I had tears in my eyes. It was the first cookie I'd eaten since I was 9 years

---

Semprevivo At A Glance

Born: 1971 in Cherry Hill, N.J.

Education: B.A in marketing and managerial leadership from New Mexico State University.

Achievements:

▪ Co-founded Joseph's Lite Cookies in 1986 with his parents.

▪ Helped the company become the producer of the top-selling sugar-free cookies in the Western Hemisphere. Sells his products in more than 100,000 stores in the U.S. alone.

▪ Won the U.S. Exporting Award from the Department of Agriculture in 2003 for his products. Also won the Senate Productivity Award for excellence in production and efficiency in New Mexico in 1997 and the Quality Hero Award in 1995.

---

old, and I wanted to share this cookie with everyone in the country."

The ice cream business had drawbacks. Once a customer's freezer broke, and Semprevivo lost 1,000 pints of ice cream that were in the store on consignment. Cookies, however, had a shelf life. The family decided to concentrate on what they could do well, while maintaining some control. Mom and Dad worked on developing more flavors—they developed eight in the first year—and young Joseph tried his hand at marketing.

He got a lot of rejections early on, but, he said, "We were persistent. We wouldn't stop."

Semprevivo built his market one store at a time. His strategy was to go from independent supermarkets to regional chains to national chains. "Not only did I make sales calls, but I did product demos. I opened up the product, handed it out and explained the health benefits of the cookies," he said.

They attended regional food and trade shows to meet buyers and got letters of recommendation from the managers of stores they were already in. Every option was considered, including shipping the cookies on consignment. "I told them, 'I'll ship you product. If it sells, you pay me.' And they did."

He also set up a marketing program with the National Diabetes Outreach, which allows the organization to raise funds by selling Joseph's Lite Cookies. Slowly the company built its presence. Semprevivo estimates that cracking Kroger, a large national chain, took eight years and "1,100 sales calls. Seriously. The buyers kept changing. They have nine regions. My first break after eight years was in Atlanta, Ga. I remember her name: Susan. She was a regional buyer, and she said, 'I'll take a chance with your cookies. I'll take them on.'"

Controlled Growth

Semprevivo's entrepreneurial ability was recognized by the federal government. In 1989, President Bush presented the then-17-year-old Semprevivo with the American Success Award in a Rose Garden ceremony. (When the White House called the company to inform Semprevivo of the award, a secretary hung up, convinced it was a prank.)

(Cont.)

Semprevivo's business is privately held, so it doesn't release financial figures. He does say, however, that since its inception in 1986, he has never seen less than 47% year-to-year growth. But growth has not been pell-mell.

He believes in what he calls controlled growth. "I'll never buy a piece of equipment or move into a larger plant based on one customer," he said. "That way, even if you lose a customer or he files for bankruptcy, you are still protected."

The company first moved from the original ice cream store into a 2,000-square-foot plant, then into a 7,000-square-foot facility. It's now housed in a 48,000-square-foot building in a large industrial park. His production line runs at least 20 hours a day—and sometimes more than that—to keep up with demand.

Part of the reason for the company's success, according to Semprevivo, is an insistence on strict attention to quality. There are five people on duty at any time the line is running who are empowered to shut everything down if they suspect something is wrong with the cookies—their taste, their texture, their color. They are the shift manager, the bagging manager, the assistant manager and the line manager.

The fifth is the quality control manager. His enviable job is to taste a cookie every five minutes and press an emergency button if there's anything he doesn't like. When that happens, "we throw it away," Semprevivo said.

Semprevivo's employees—he calls them team members—get fully paid health and dental insurance and a 401(k) plan. The company also offers them lifetime employment.

"My saying to all my team members is, 'As long as I have a job, you have a job.' It's a real morale booster," he said.

It's a concept he'd like to see spread to other companies. "I want to change the corporate culture as much as I can," he told the El Paso Times. "If a small company can do it, any company can do it."

Evaluating Opportunities in the Changing Marketing Environment

Street Smarts

On the East Coast, Chinese Buses Give Greyhound a Run

Upstarts Rattle the Industry With Cut-Rate Fares; Taking a Tip from JetBlue

Mr. Zheng, Owner and Driver

BARRY NEWMAN. *WALL STREET JOURNAL.*

BOSTON—A bus pulled out of South Station terminal on a Friday morning and headed for New York City. Its windshield was cracked, its speedometer motionless. Orange peel graced its seat trays, and its safety warnings consisted of a single sign: "Watch your step."

The driver said not a word until he stopped the bus outside Cheng's Driving School in New York City's Chinatown. Then, as passengers gathered their bags, he stood up and screamed, "No parking here! You get out!"

The bus, according to the lettering near its luggage compartment, was owned by "Kristine Travel" and operated by "Lucky River," though the sign on its side said "Travel Pack" and its ticket agents called the company "Lucky Star." Its price for the trip from Boston to New York—187 miles in 4 ½ hours—was $15.

That may seem an impossibly low fare, yet another carrier on the Boston to New York run has lately started charging $15, too. The name on the side of its buses is Greyhound.

Greyhound Lines Inc. is a $1 billion company owned by Laidlaw International Inc., a $4.6 billion company. The only national bus network, "big dog" was racing along America's highways even before Clark Gable and Claudette Colbert hopped on a Greyhound in 1934's "It Happened One Night." But today, a dozen or so Chinese-owned bus lines are giving the dog a run for its money.

Immigrant enterprises don't often go head-to-head with huge corporations at critical moments in vital sectors. But partly by using tactics borrowed from discount airlines and online ticket brokers, that's what these little companies are doing to Greyhound. Just as Laidlaw, its parent since 1999, climbs out of bankruptcy, Chinatown buses have sucked Greyhound into a wounding war over its most-traveled runs, from New York to Washington, Philadelphia and Boston.

Two faces of the new Chinese immigration have met along the way: entrepreneurs who don't mind long hours or street fights; and computer engineers who build Web sites. Together, they have broken out of their neighborhoods and gone hunting for customers in what, with few exceptions, have been private Greyhound preserves.

"If Greyhound wasn't a giant, maybe they could beat us," Shui Ming Zheng says through an interpreter. "But because they are a giant, they cannot."

Mr. Zheng, 49 years old, has been in the U.S. 14 years and drives the Washington run himself as part owner of Eastern Travel & Tour Inc. A year ago, Eastern took on David Wong, 38, as a new partner. He has gelled hair, fluent English and an MBA from Indiana State University.

"Common sense tells me that if JetBlue profits on a $79 fare to Buffalo, we can profit on a $15 fare to D.C.," says Mr. Wong, who handles management. "We copied the airline concept to a bus line." Greyhound, he adds, "really feels the pain."

On the Northeast routes that deliver a third of its revenue, Greyhound isn't about to roll over. Conceding that the Chinese lines have reignited bus travel, it has slashed fares to claim new riders for itself.

Greyhound's chief operating officer, Jack Haugsland, says, "We will alter our pricing to protect our market share." In the past year, Greyhound has done more: It sued, trying to bump two Chinese lines out of action by charging they weren't licensed properly, and pushed for a federal investigation of a dozen others.

"The industry is under attack," says Peter Pantuso, who heads the American Bus Association, a lobbying group. Of its 950 members, Greyhound is by far the largest. "People wonder, how can you charge half the price of an established carrier?"

Easily. Eastern Travel, for instance, says its cost for a round-trip to Washington from New York is $700. The driver gets $140. A full busload of 61 passengers, paying $35 each, brings in $2,135.

The first Chinatown buses appeared on Northeastern curbsides about eight years ago, ferrying Chinese workers to restaurant jobs in nearby cities. Chinese students caught on, then other students followed. The business was an underground hit.

But in 2000, as recounted in a New York conspiracy indictment, competition among Chinese bus lines turned nasty. Several people who worked for Farwell Tours, an operator on the Washington run, are accused of brutalizing a rival, D.C. Express. Two people are awaiting trial; the others are at large. Wrecking its buses and threatening ticket agents, they tried to get D.C. Express to either raise its rock-bottom prices or get out of the business, the Manhattan district attorney alleges.

In May 2002, after D.C. Express sold out to another line, a Farwell bus backed into the new owner, crushing his pelvis. The indictment names the driver as Di Jian Chen. Mr. Chen won't be going on trial: He was shot dead on a Chinatown street in May 2003. His murder remains unsolved.

The violence has since ebbed. Yet some Chinese lines, in search of more healthful opportunities, have moved the fight uptown.

"I'm getting Americans to take my bus," says Eastern's Mr. Zheng, meaning anyone not Chinese. He still works in Chinatown, but his partner, Mr. Wong, has moved to 34th Street. Eastern now scoops up travelers near Pennsylvania Station. "The subway is right there," he says. "Everybody comes to us."

The Web is helping. The site most Chinese lines use is IvyMedia.com, launched in 2002 by Jimmy Chen, who came to America from Shanghai for a computer-science doctorate.

"Our model is Expedia," he says. Like the Internet travel service, he offers tickets for several carriers, and sells no more than the empty seats left in inventory. Though Greyhound also sells online, it doesn't limit the number of seats. If it oversells a route, it keeps reserve buses and drivers to absorb overflow passengers. Mr. Chen sees that "wasteful" policy as the big dog's jugular.

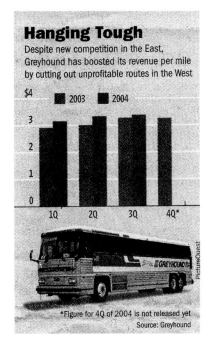

Hanging Tough

Despite new competition in the East, Greyhound has boosted its revenue per mile by cutting out unprofitable routes in the West

*Figure for 4Q of 2004 is not released yet
Source: Greyhound

(Cont.)

An immigrant conquest of the bus business wouldn't be a first. In 1914, a company started carrying Scandinavian miners—not waiters—to Minnesota's iron ranges in modified Hupmobiles. That line evolved into Greyhound. By 1980, its revenue topped $1 billion.

Then came deregulation of the bus industry, a long strike and a bankruptcy in 1990. In 2001, two years after Greyhound merged with Laidlaw, a transportation holding company, it filed for bankruptcy, too. Laidlaw emerged from bankruptcy in 2003. In that year, Bert Powell, an analyst at BMO Nesbitt Burns, pronounced Greyhound, now based in Dallas, Laidlaw's "weakest-performing segment."

Terror fears drove insurance rates up and riders away. Greyhound's results dipped into the red—by $23 million in the first nine months of 2004. Last June, Greyhound charted a course correction: It ended service to 260 Western towns, with more cuts to come. It bet its future on short runs—exactly the ones the Chinese lines are out to snatch.

Greyhound's countermoves began in 2003 on Chinese turf in New York. It offered a shuttle from Chinatown to the Port Authority. Ignored by riders, it was quickly dropped. But Greyhound and the bus industry had higher hopes—in the form of a federal investigation.

"We asked, 'Can you please check this out?'" says Mr. Pantuso of the American Bus Association, which doubted that the Chinese companies were complying with federal insurance and licensing rules. The Federal Motor Carrier Safety Administration formed a task force to look closely. Its head, Annette Sandberg, told the industry in a speech last September: "We'll either bring these carriers into compliance or shut them down."

The investigators ran into language mix-ups, and a muddle of company names and cross ownerships. Hiring an agent fluent in three Chinese dialects, they began picking through the records of 14 companies.

Last fall, they visited the Chinatown offices of Dragon Coach Inc. The line's owner, Edward Ho, made available a copy of his federal compliance review: It lists two "acute" violations—an insurance lapse and a failure to send drivers for drug tests. Mr. Ho put his house in order fast. Dragon Coach scored a federal rating of "satisfactory."

That was the pattern. "Every time we confronted one of these carriers, they did what was necessary to become authorized," says Jim Lewis, a spokesman for the safety administration, a part of the Department of Transportation. The task force has now wound down, but the industry's lobbying group argues that it didn't dig deep enough. Its head, Mr. Pantuso, says, "The feds need to be more aggressive."

Defending its most-traveled corridor, Greyhound already has been: In Massachusetts federal court in last year, it sued two Chinese challengers on the Boston-New York run. With a local partner, Peter Pan Lines Inc., it charged Fung Wah Transportation Inc. and Kristine Travel & Tours Inc. were operating without the proper licenses for scheduled service.

Not even a giant line can "tolerate unauthorized operators cherry-picking business on its busiest routes," Gregory Alexander, a Greyhound vice president, declared in an affidavit. "I wish it were otherwise, but Greyhound's buses are rarely full." Pei Lin Liang, Fung Wah's president, said in his own affidavit that "our buses are packed regularly." The "true purpose" of the suit, he said, was "to drive Fung Wah out of business."

Greyhound and Peter Pan did seek injunctions to close down Kristine and Fung Wah. The court denied them. The Chinese lines soon cleared up the problems with their licenses, and the suit was dismissed. The struggle for Boston, however, didn't end there.

The city's Chinatown is a short walk from South Station, Greyhound's base. Waiting at curbsides, Chinese buses enticed its passengers away. In spring 2003, the lure grew: a new company, Lucky Star, appeared with a $10 fare to New York. The others matched it, and turned Chinatown into a travel hub.

"There'd be hundreds of people," says John Meaney, a chief inspector for the city of Boston. "Suitcases everywhere." This congestion broke traffic laws. Last summer, Boston police went on a ticketing spree, and in September, after Lucky Star and Kristine merged, the Chinese lines were moved off the street and into South Station.

Brian Cristy, head of the state office that oversees the terminal, thinks everybody wins. "If people can't get on Fung Wah, now there's a Greyhound bus and a Peter Pan bus," he says.

Greyhound says business is improving. It set its lowest New York-Boston fare at $15 last year; at times it has been more than twice that. Now ridership (900,000 in 2003) is up. Because of the route cuts in the West, its national ridership (22 million in 2003) is down. That is exactly the kind of efficiency Greyhound says it wants: with more passengers on more profitable routes, its overall revenue per mile is up. "Greyhound," says its spokeswoman, Lynn Brown, "has no objection to competition so long as it is on a level playing field."

Nobody counts overall ridership on the Chinese lines, but they aren't packed any longer. As the Chinese operators see it, the game in South Station isn't on the level at all.

Inside the station, monitors display schedules for Greyhound and Peter Pan. Chinese lines go unlisted, which the station manager blames on "old equipment."

Greyhound and Peter Pan park their buses at the head of the departure hall. Now that the two Chinese lines pay a terminal fee, they also charge $15. But due to space limits, station management says, they must share one parking bay at the hall's far end.

This leads to squabbling as Lucky Star and Fung Wah jockey for one space. And to yelling—"New York City here! Hello! New York City!"—as agents try to snag customers. "In Chinatown, we took passengers from Greyhound," Monique Chow, a Lucky Star agent, said during a shouting break one day. "Now they take from us."

In South Station, perhaps. But lately, another Chinese line has sprouted. It's called Boston Deluxe, and it doesn't stop in South Station or in Chinatown—Boston's or New York's. On a Friday at noon, one of its buses swooped in for a pick-up in midtown Manhattan.

"Next block! Next block!" the driver screamed, rolling past a bunch of passengers who chased him to a loading zone. After a four-hour drive at high speed, he left them in Boston on the doorstep of the First Church of Christ, Scientist.

"Where rich people live," says Jack Ho, owner of Boston Deluxe, explaining his choice of stops. "All we do is American business."

At 28, Mr. Ho has had a painful education in the realities of the Chinatown bus: Di Jian Chen, before being murdered in 2003, was his partner. Today, Mr. Ho has become a student of Greyhound.

He knows that in 1998 it got federal approval for a revenue-sharing deal with Peter Pan, ending an earlier Boston price war. Mr. Ho wonders if Greyhound might try to do even more for him.

"I want to force Greyhound to buy me out," he said with a smile over a plate of dim sum in New York. "Unless they buy me, Greyhound has no chance. Before that, I'm like all American people. I just want to make a buck."

Potent Prescription

In Mexico, Maker of Generics Adds Spice to Drug Business

Using Clinics and Pinups, Mr. Gonzalez Boosts Sales; Now, a Run for President

One 'Chica' Kiss Per Question

DAVID LUHNOW. *WALL STREET JOURNAL.*

MEXICO CITY—Victor Gonzalez has come up with a novel prescription for business success here: cheap drugs, cheap doctors—and a dose of sex.

His Farmacias Similares drugstores, one of Latin America's fastest- growing retail chains, stock only generic drugs, including many that Mr. Gonzalez manufactures. Next door to most of the stores are clinics that he subsidizes, staffed by doctors who charge $2 a visit and write prescriptions for generic drugs.

This arrangement is fine with Lorenzo San Juan, a 40-year-old textile worker. On a recent day, he paid a total of $8 for a doctor to examine his 10-year-old son, and for antibiotics to treat the boy's cough at a Farmacias Similares in Mexico City. "This is the only place that we can afford to buy our medicines," says Mr. San Juan, who, like many Mexicans, earns about $4 a day.

On his way out of the pharmacy, Mr. San Juan made sure to pick up the drugstore's pin-up calendar of the "Simi Chicas." The suggestively dressed models appear on billboards and in newspaper ads endorsing Simi brand condoms, Simi telephone-calling cards, Simi diapers and Simi tequila shot glasses.

Mr. Gonzalez, 57, is shaking up Mexico's health-care system and changing the way drugs are sold here. By spotting gaps in the country's drug market and regulations, he is able to offer low-cost medicines and inexpensive care to millions who lacked both. By raising awareness of generics as an alternative to pricey brand-name drugs, he has revived the fortunes of domestic makers and posed a threat to the U.S. and European pharmaceutical companies that dominate Latin America.

Until Mr. Gonzalez opened his first pharmacy in 1997, generic drugs were available only at government-run hospitals and clinics, not at retail stores. That forced some 50 million Mexicans who aren't covered by the public insurance system—which until recently only covered people who are formally employed—to pay top dollar for brand-name drugs at pharmacies.

While his impoverished customers see him as a champion of the poor, some competitors view him as vaudevillian-style promoter, and have questioned the quality of his drugs. "The products are cheap in every sense of the word," says Julio Portales, head of corporate affairs at the Mexican unit of Eli Lilly & Co. "If I have to buy four times as much of this guy's aspirin to make it work as well as one Bayer, where's my value for money?"

Mr. Gonzalez denies such claims. He says a new Mexican law requiring testing of generics will settle the matter once and for all. But the controversy lingers. Jorge Salas, a doctor who works at a clinic set up by Mr. Gonzalez, says that although most Similares medicines work well, he'll tell a patient facing an emergency to "go take a Pfizer pill instead of the generic."

In building his empire of 2,550 stores, Mr. Gonzalez has made the business a lot more colorful. He has tangled with Mexican anti-abortion groups, Cuban dictator Fidel Castro and his own brother. Now he has launched a long-shot bid for the Mexican presidency in 2006, using universal health care as a rallying cry.

Mr. Gonzalez has created an alternative health-care system. His stores stock mostly older drugs that have lost their patent and can be copied cheaply in Mexico. He subsidizes about 1,900 clinics, catering to those who can't afford the $30 or so that private clinics charge for a visit. Some 800,000 Mexicans visit his clinics every month, according to Mexico's Metropolitan Autonomous University. The clinics are run by a nonprofit group set up by Mr. Gonzalez, and doctors keep the money paid for visits.

In Mexico's $9 billion-a-year pharmaceutical market, the world's ninth largest, branded drugs such as those sold by New York's Pfizer Inc. and the United Kingdom's GlaxoSmith-Kline PLC, make up about 80% of sales by value, according to local drug makers. But Mr. Gonzalez is chipping away at foreign companies' domination. In seven years, his company has gained about a 4% share of drugs sold, compared with Pfizer's leading 8% share, according to Mexico's Pharmaceutical Industry Chamber, a trade group.

"Before we appeared on the scene, poor people in Mexico used to pray to the Virgin to get better because they couldn't afford the medicines," says Mr. Gonzalez. "Now they come to us." He says Farmacias Similares

Cheap Pills

Generic drug sales as a percentage of each total drug market.

	MARKET (in billions)		GENERICS AS % OF ALL DRUG SALES
U.S.	$24.8		9%
Australia	$0.58		10%
Canada	$1.24		11%
U.K.	$4.1		18%
Russia	$4.1		30%
India	$5.7		70%
Mexico	$9		20%

Sources: For Mexico data, estimate by Mexico's National Association of Pharmaceutical Manufacturers; all other country data, Espicom Business Intelligence

had $400 million in sales in 2004, but won't disclose earnings.

Mr. Gonzalez recently opened 11 drugstores and clinics in Argentina and 36 in Central America, where he recruited Guatemalan Nobel peace prize winner Rigoberta Menchu to be a spokeswoman.

The youngest of five children, Mr. Gonzalez worked for years at his family-owned drugstore chain, founded in 1875 by his great-grandfather. But he didn't get along with his oldest brother Javier, who ran the business. Mr. Gonzalez left in the 1980s to run another family firm, Laboratorios Best, which sold generics to the government. Because he has a speech impediment and admits to abusing alcohol in the past, he says his family never expected him to amount to much.

Eventually he bought Laboratorios Best from his family. But he realized the prospects of domestic drug makers were limited because they sold generics solely to the public-health system, at slender markups. Although there was no legal ban on their selling generics, retail pharmacies stocked only branded drugs, which are made by foreign companies and have much fatter margins.

"I realized I was in the wrong business," says Mr. Gonzalez. "I had to sell my generics at the retail level and forget about the government."

Within weeks of opening his first store, sales were so brisk he had to enlist other local drug makers to make medicines. Now, Mr. Gonzalez's Laboratorios Best provides about one-fifth of Farmacias Similares's drugs, with the rest made by local companies.

Six tablets at 20 milligrams of omeprazol, a popular anti-acid drug, goes for $3.50 at Farmacias Similares—versus $20 at a conventional pharmacy for the same dose of Prilosec, the branded drug made by the U.K.'s AstraZeneca PLC.

As sales have grown—he opened 1,248 stores last year alone—Mr. Gonzalez has generated plenty of controversy. In 1999, the National Pharmaceutical Industry Chamber, which represents foreign as well as some domestic drug companies, denounced Similares's drugs as inferior. In response, Mr. Gonzalez erected billboards across Mexico saying multinationals were trying to block access to cheap medicine. "Say no to corruption. Say yes to helping the poor," the billboards read. The trade group soon ceased its attacks.

Mr. Gonzalez focuses his marketing on consumer trust, and created a cartoon character, "Dr. Simi," as the chain's logo. A grandfatherly figure in a white lab coat, Dr. Simi appears regularly in newspaper ads. Every day, there are 2,000 or so workers who dress in 7-foot-tall Dr. Simi costumes and stand outside the stores, gyrating to salsa music and beckoning shoppers. The character stars in his own comic book and a TV show called "The Dr. Simi Hour," hosted by one of the Simi Chicas, Romanian-born actress Joana Benedek.

Mr. Gonzalez's creation of the Simi Chicas give his products a bit of sizzle. Besides arriving at publicity events arm-in-arm with Mr. Gonzalez, the Simi Chicas represent different company themes such as "quality" or "honesty," which they talk up in lectures at schools and clinics. After a speech by Mr. Gonzalez at a trade school in Acapulco, the audience of mostly young men had no questions—until Ms. Benedek offered a kiss in exchange for each question. About 20 hands shot up.

"This guy is a marketing genius," says Eric Hagsater, head of the National Pharmaceutical Industry Chamber. "Dr. Simi appeals to moms and kids, and the Simi Chicas to men."

A new law may resolve questions that have dogged Mr. Gonzalez's company. Until last month, Mexico only required its generic-drug makers to show they used the same active ingredient as a branded medicine. They weren't forced to do testing to ensure the drugs work as well in the human body—a process called "bioequivalency." U.S.- and European-made generic drugs have to undergo such tests.

Mr. Gonzalez says he welcomes the new rule, which requires Mexican companies to also show bioequivalency. He says all of his company's drugs that have been tested so far—about 15% of the medicines he sells— have already passed the tests, which cost about $65,000 each.

Mr. Gonzalez hardly shies from other fights. When Fidel Castro recently denied him permission to open stores in Cuba, Mr. Gonzalez responded with full-page newspaper ads in Mexico attacking Mr. Castro as a "fake" champion of the poor. Rocio Galvez, head of a Catholic anti-abortion group, last year denounced Mr. Gonzalez for selling low-priced condoms, which she said promoted a liberal sexual culture. Mr. Gonzalez shot back with ads thanking her for introducing his product to the public, and featuring a picture of her holding up his condoms at a news conference.

After Ms. Galvez sued him for slander, Mr. Gonzalez tripled the level of advertising using her image and sent dozens of employees to stand outside the courthouse with signs that read "Long Live Condoms!" Ms. Galvez, who declined to comment, later dropped the lawsuit.

Dozens of other Mexican drugstore chains have begun to mimic Farmacias Similares. Among them is Mr. Gonzalez's estranged brother, Javier—who calls Mr. Gonzalez "the Tasmanian devil" because "he picks fights with everyone." Javier, who runs traditional pharmacies, recently opened a chain of drugstores stocking generics, with clinics that offer a checkup for $1.

Mr. Gonzalez is now trying to capitalize on his popularity among the poor to run for president. He publishes his own surveys of Farmacias Similares's customers showing him with 39% support, but most independent polls put him at 2%. At a recent campaign rally in Acapulco, about 4,000 people turned up to cheer Mr. Gonzalez and his entourage of Simi Chicas. "I think the Simi Chicas will make fine first ladies," joked the divorced Mr. Gonzalez, drawing cheers.

Some rivals speculate Mr. Gonzalez will end up endorsing another candidate in return for a deal on health-care policy. Last year, with the help of the Green Party, which is run by his nephew, Mr. Gonzalez led a move in Mexico's Congress to cut the patent on medicines made by foreign companies to 10 years from 20. It narrowly failed. He vows to try again.

Mr. Gonzalez says he's not worried about juggling the demands of a presidential campaign with a fast-growing company. "I'm a businessman in the morning, a politician in the afternoon, and a lover in the evening."

From *The Wall Street Journal,* February 14, 2005. Reprinted by permission of Dow Jones and Co., Inc. via The Copyright Clearance Center.

Latte Versus Latte

Starbucks, Dunkin' Donuts Seek Growth by Capturing Each Other's Customers

BY DEBORAH BALL AND SHIRLEY LEUNG

There's A new brew-haha in Latte-land.

For years, the product lines of the major U.S. brewed coffee sellers have been well defined. On the high end there is **Starbucks** Corp., with 5,439 locations in the U.S. During the past decade, the chain has made its expensive cappuccinos, frappuccinos, espressos and lattes part of the regular lexicon. On the other end, there is Dunkin' Donuts, which has 4,100 stores. Although concentrated in the Northeast, Dunkin' Donuts is the nation's largest seller of regular, nonflavored brewed coffee through fast-food outlets, with a 17% market share, compared with 15% for **McDonald's** Corp. and 6% for Starbucks, according to figures supplied by Dunkin' Donuts that the company said came from the market-research organization NPD Group.

Now, both companies are seeking to stir things up. Starbucks increasingly is looking for growth by opening stores in blue-collar communities where Dunkin' Donuts would typically dominate. Last month, when the Seattle coffee chain reported fiscal first-quarter earnings, executives gave much of the credit to its 10% jump in sales at stores open more than a year to this broadening demographic. Its coffee, explains Howard Schultz, Starbucks chairman and founder, is "an affordable luxury."

At the same time, Dunkin' Donuts, a unit of United Kingdom spirits group **Allied Domecq** PLC, wants to lure Starbucks's well-heeled customers with a new line of Italian brews that it claims it can deliver faster, cheaper and simpler.

"Espresso has become mainstream in America," says Jon L. Luther, chief executive of Allied Domecq's restaurant division, which also includes Baskin Robbins and Togo's. "And who does mainstream better than Dunkin' Donuts?" Its advertisements tout the same idea. One billboard reads: "Latte for Every Tom, Dick and Lucciano."

Last September, Dunkin' Donuts introduced its new cappuccinos and lattes in New England and is now launching the line in other stores in the U.S. A major ad blitz started in New York City last week. The company had expected the espresso products to represent 5% to 10% of store sales, and New England stores are already inside that range.

On average, the new Dunkin' Donut drinks cost at least 20% less than Starbucks's offerings—and an espresso shot is just 99 cents, compared with $1.45 at Starbucks. The Dunkin' Donut drinks are labeled a no-nonsense "small," "medium" and "large" as opposed to Starbucks's "tall," "grande" and "venti." And Dunkin' Donuts has trained its staff to serve them quickly; the company worked with a Swiss manufacturer to develop equipment that makes a real espresso and fresh steamed milk in less than a minute.

"I can order a plain medium caramel latte and not deal with all that fancy stuff," says Kathleen Brown, a 30-year-old Boston lawyer who used to treat herself to a $4 Starbucks Caramel Macchiato but has switched to Dunkin' Donuts, where it costs much less.

To some Dunkin' Donuts regulars, though, the new sophistication is a little too much. Pat Kelly, a 26-year-old Boston police recruit who drinks Dunkin' Donuts coffee daily, refuses to try the new Dunkin' products (and never goes to Starbucks). The only guy in his group of police buddies who tried a Dunkin' latte got a razzing. "I'm not really a latte sort of guy," he says. "Those are yuppie drinks."

"I'm sure there are a number of folks who might be embarrassed" about buying a latte, Mr. Luther admits. "But espresso has gone mainstream, and for us to ignore it would be irresponsible."

So far, Starbucks's Mr. Schultz is taking a high-minded approach to the threat from his downscale competition. In an interview, he says he feels no pressure to lower the chain's famously high prices. "If Dunkin' Donuts is going to spend millions of dollars [in advertising] on coffee and espresso, that is really beneficial to Starbucks business," he says. "I wouldn't be surprised if our business goes up as a result."

Meanwhile, Starbucks, where regular drip coffee starts at $1.50 a cup, is pushing into Dunkin' Donuts' traditional territory. Mr. Schultz says the idea that Starbucks could appeal to any income level came on a visit to a Chicago store several years ago. He noticed limousine drivers running in to pick up coffee for passengers. No surprise there. But he also saw a driver of a United Parcel Service truck running in, too. "I think he's going to make a delivery. No, he gets in line," recalls Mr. Schultz. "He has a 10-year-old thermos. He gets in line and asks, 'Can you fill up my thermos with two double lattes?'"

Starbucks formalized its march to open stores in low-income communities in 1998, establishing a partnership with former Los Angeles Lakers player Magic Johnson to open stores primarily in black and Hispanic communities. Mr. Johnson's **Johnson Development** Corp. operates theaters, T.G.I. Friday's restaurants and other retail businesses in urban areas.

To date, Johnson Development has opened 57 Starbucks, from New York's Harlem and Staten Island to Inglewood, Calif., with plans to open up 68 more over the next several years. Starbucks has already taken lessons learned from the Johnson partnership to apply them across the system, influencing the site selection of hundreds of other stores.

Sales at these Johnson stores mirror the robust performance of the rest of North America, which reported a 12% increase in same-store sales for January. These stores charge the same prices as any other Starbucks.

Marketing focuses on reaching out to local pastors and serving Starbucks at church coffee hours. "When you come into minority communities, church plays a very significant role," explains Ken Lombard, president of Johnson Development in Beverly Hills, Calif.

At a Starbucks that opened in the largely blue-collar South Side of Chicago, the upscale coffee house stands out among its neighbors: a check-cashing outfit, a Dunkin' Donuts, a McDonald's and JJ Fish & Chicken. So rare is a Starbucks in this locale that it's a popular first-date place, says store manager Monica Perez.

The price doesn't seem to be an issue. Last week, Jose Bahena, a 20-year-old Chicago metal shop foreman, plunked down $4.02 for a grande Frappuccino, the chain's signature creamy coffee drink. Mr. Bahena, who says he makes about $20,000 a year, comes to Starbucks four times a week. "It's so good," he says. "You have to pay for something good."

From *The Wall Street Journal*, February 10, 2004. Reprinted by permission of Dow Jones and Co., Inc. via The Copyright Clearance Center.

Grande Ambitions

Upscale drinks from Starbucks and Dunkin' Donuts are going foamy head to foamy head.

Dunkin' Donuts	Starbucks
Espresso Shot: 99 cents	**Solo Espresso Shot:** $1.45
Small Hazelnut Latte: $1.79	**Tall Hazelnut Latte:** $2.85
Medium Caramel Swirl Latte: $2.29	**Grande Caramel Macchiato:** $3.40
Large Mocha Swirl Latte: $2.69	**Venti Caffe Mocha:** $3.55

Source: the companies

Alternative-fuel vehicles star, but wide use is miles away

Costs need to come down before mass sales expected

James R. Healey, Sharon Silke Carty and Chris Woodyard.
USA TODAY.

DETROIT—This is the dawn of alternative automotive power.

HYBRIDS

Automakers are filling the streets of Motor City with fuel-saving and low-polluting gas-electric hybrids, high-mileage diesels and even exotic hydrogen-fueled vehicles, hoping to demonstrate during the high-profile North American International Auto Show that the future is here and that they are its champions, its partisans, its owners.

Ford Motor says it will build more hybrids than announced and do it sooner than planned. General Motors says it is leaping closer to real-world hydrogen fuel-cell power. Volkswagen banged the table at the Los Angeles auto show a few days ago about the need for more diesels.

But each alternative-power vehicle on display at the shows or scuttling around downtown here advertising its maker's prowess is carrying a heavy load of challenges. Before any of the promising alternatives makes a difference in oil consumption or air quality, prices have to come down, reliability has to be proven, consumers have to be sold, and in the case of hydrogen, cheap, safe and convenient ways have to be found to make, transport and dispense the fuel.

A new fuel dawn it truly seems to be. But midmorning might be a long time coming.

"Internal-combustion engines are here for the foreseeable future," says Ford's Mary Ann Wright. That's no small acknowledgment for the enthusiastic director of Ford's hybrid and hydrogen vehicle programs. Still, she swears, "There'll come a time when everything's a hybrid; it's inevitable, because of the fuel economy and performance and (air pollution) benefits."

Hybrids sound like just the ticket. Here now in reasonable numbers at Ford, Toyota and Honda showrooms, you fill the tanks with gasoline and drive normally. A gas engine and electric motor share the workload, saving fuel and polluting less while imposing little or no compromise in performance. It seems pretty mainstream.

Not according to an analysis by the Power Information Network. PIN's Tom Libby notes: "Nearly 42% of hybrid models sold in the U.S. in the last year were in California. Hybrid prices need to drop to the point where they make economic sense for consumers. Until that time, hybrids will successfully appeal only to fringe groups, including Hollywood stars and ultra-environmentalists."

Automakers say they also appeal to upscale college students, long-distance commuters and people who like the cars' high-tech aspects.

Hybrids' $20,000-something prices sound reasonable, but are $3,000-$4,000 more than consumers would pay for similar gas-power vehicles. A driver would have to be a traveling salesman or gas prices would have to about double for a hybrid's lower fuel costs to repay that price premium in the time someone is likely to own the car.

> Hydrogen fuel cells—**GM Sequel**: The technologies embodied in the Sequel concept include hydrogen fuel cells and wheel hub motors.

In contrast, improved technology probably can boost efficiency of the conventional gas engine another 25%, "for a cost of maybe $1,000, and that's a hard target to match," says David Cole, chairman of the not-for-profit Center for Automotive Research.

Wright agrees: "Early adopters are willing to pay a premium. But over time, commercial success requires it to be cost-neutral."

About 84,000 hybrids were sold in the USA last year, automakers report, and J.D. Power and Associates' powertrain expert Anthony Pratt says 220,000 probably will be sold this year. He sees that climbing to 500,000 a year in 2008, then stalling. "We don't think hybrids will appeal to the masses unless gas goes beyond $3.50 a gallon in today's dollars, and we don't

(Cont.)

think that will happen through 2011," he says.

"If you add up every hybrid made from the beginning of time, it doesn't amount to the (annual) output of one auto plant," Cole points out. A big car factory produces 300,000 vehicles a year.

Automakers are divided on hybrids' future: permanent part of the streetscape or way station en route to a hydrogen-power future? At a recent industry conference in Traverse City, Mich., Cole says, "All the guys said that there was some type of mixed strategy, but they had no real percentage on the mix" among gasoline, hybrids, diesels and hydrogen vehicles. "They just didn't know."

Toyota is moving aggressively, planning hybrid versions of most models in the next few years. Honda, which introduced hybrids to the USA when it launched its Insight two-seater in December 1999, is going slowly. It has added hybrid versions of its Civic and Accord sedans, but plans no more until a hybrid SUV that's at least three years off.

GM and DaimlerChrysler plan to jointly develop a hybrid system that both say they'll use widely, but not for several years.

Nissan is not interested in investing in hybrids until it can't avoid doing so, partly to meet clean-air regulations in strict California. Its first will be a hybrid version of a redesigned Altima sedan in 2006.

The big stumbling block for hybrids is the cost issue. They require two complete drivetrains—gas and electric—plus complex transmissions to connect the two and sophisticated computer gear to blend their power output smoothly.

Here's what faces other alternative fuels:

DIESELS

Capable of 20% to 40% better fuel economy than gasoline engines and accounting for about 50% of new vehicle sales in Europe, diesels are about 4% of the U.S. market. Despite improvements, diesel fuel still smells worse than gas, and diesel engines still make a little more noise and smoke a little more than gas engines do.

Now that diesel fuel is more expensive than gasoline, some savings are gone, unlike in Europe, where diesel is cheaper than heavily taxed gasoline.

"There's a hesitancy for North American consumers to buy diesels, but I think you'll see that change"

Hybrid—**2004 Insight:** The Honda two-seater was the first hybrid sold in the USA when launched in December 1999.

Diesel—**2006 Jetta:** Volkswagen's Jetta is the best-selling diesel in the USA.

as cleaner, quieter diesels hit the market, says Brian Ambrose, in charge of the automotive practice at consultant KPMG.

That begins in 2006, when tougher pollution regulations take effect. Regulations also require refiners to begin selling cleaner-burning, low-sulfur diesel fuel that year. The concentration of sulfur, poisonous to pollution-scrubbing catalytic converters, drops to 15 parts per million, vs. 500 ppm now.

Finding fuel can be a challenge. Diesel is available at a significant minority of stations but is not as common as gas. "It's a chicken-egg thing: Does the car come first or does the fuel availability?" says Darran Messem, vice president for fuel development at Shell International Petroleum. Shell is developing a super-clean diesel fuel, but it remains too costly for commercial distribution.

Nevertheless, the two biggest automakers are showing teaser versions of possible future clean-diesel models at the auto show here.

Ford's are the Mercury Meta One and the subcompact Ford Synus sedan. Both envision burning a mix of conventional and bio-mass diesel, made from agricultural or other wastes. Meta One is also a hybrid, teaming the clean-burning diesel with an electric motor to stretch fuel economy. It also has a sophisticated exhaust-treatment system and, Ford says, would be so clean-burning that it would qualify for partial zero-emission-vehicle credits under California's strict rules.

GM's is a two-fer, too: a diesel-electric hybrid. GM is showing off the fuel-efficient powertrain in the Opel Astra, a model sold in Europe.

Neither automaker is promising to deliver the models, or anything like them, for the U.S. market—if at all.

An advantage of diesels is that "drivers don't have to change their lifestyles," says Volkswagen Chairman Bernd Pischetsrieder. Fueling and driving them is similar to using gasoline vehicles. VW sells several diesel models, including Jetta, the best-selling diesel in the USA.

HYDROGEN

It's almost literally everywhere but a little touchy to transport and store. As a gas, its natural state, hydrogen takes up an impractical amount of space. Keeping it as a conveniently compact and energy-dense liquid, though, means chilling it to more than minus-200 degrees Fahrenheit. The alternative is storing it combined with something else—water, for instance, is a mix of hydrogen and oxygen—and that means using a lot of energy to separate the hydrogen when you need it.

"Mass commercialization of hydrogen is maybe 20 years off" because of the challenges, says Ford's Wright.

Hydrogen is useful as fuel in two ways:

▶ Passing the hydrogen through special membranes that create an electro-chemical reaction, resulting in electricity to run a car motor and emitting only water vapor out the exhaust. That's a fuel-cell system.

▶ Burning hydrogen directly as fuel in modified versions of the ordinary internal-combustion gas engine. That's less efficient than a fuel cell and doesn't eliminate as much pollution. But it could keep costs down by continuing to use well-known powertrains and chassis instead of converting to electric drive, as fuel cells require.

Hydrogen typically is obtained from natural gas and is commonly used by refiners to make cleaner fuels and higher-octane gasoline. "It's not an especially expensive or energy-intensive process. Hydrogen can be produced on that scale, in a refinery setting, more cheaply than gasoline. The challenge is transporting it to the retail site, because it needs to be cooled," says Phillip Baxley, vice president for business development at Shell Hydrogen.

Transportation and storage costs would make hydrogen, very roughly, twice as expensive as gasoline, but fuel cells are expected to be at least twice as efficient, making hydrogen no pricier overall.

Shell installed a hydrogen tank and pump at one of its gas stations in Washington, D.C., which GM has been using since October to refuel seven D.C.-based fuel-cell demonstration vehicles.

Baxley says that's the first hydrogen pump at a conventional gas station in the USA and is "a significant step in bringing hydrogen from the research phase to the reality phase."

Convenient fueling will be a major issue because it's hard to store enough hydrogen on a vehicle to go very far. GM is displaying its third-generation hydrogen vehicle here, the Sequel, which has the best range yet—300 miles. Some gasoline vehicles can go more than 400 miles on a tank.

Toyota's 10 prototype fuel-cell vehicles, based on its Highlander SUV, can go 120 miles between fill-ups. Honda's FCX fuel-cell prototypes can go 190 miles. Ford says its fuel-cell Focuses can go nearly 200 miles, double the range of a previous version.

What's out there now and what's coming soon

Here are alternative-power vehicles on sale in the USA now or in the near future:

Hybrids

Toyota
▶ Prius sedan, on sale now.
▶ Lexus RX 400h SUV, to go on sale April 15.
▶ Highlander SUV, to go on sale in June.

Honda
▶ Insight two-seater, Civic sedan, Accord sedan, all on sale now.
▶ Midsize SUV, to go on sale in three or four years.

Ford Motor
▶ Escape SUV, on sale now.
▶ Mercury Mariner SUV, to go on sale this year.
▶ Mazda Tribute SUV, to go on sale within two years.
▶ Ford Fusion sedan, Mercury Milan sedan, both to go on sale within three years.

General Motors
▶ Saturn Vue SUV, Chevrolet Malibu sedan, both to go on sale next year.
▶ Chevrolet Tahoe and GMC Yukon SUVs, to go on sale late 2007.

Nissan
▶ Altima sedan, to go on sale next year.

DaimlerChrysler
▶ Dodge Durango SUV, to go on sale late 2007 or early 2008.

Diesels

Volkswagen
▶ Golf, Jetta, New Beetle and Passat sedans, Touareg SUV on sale now.

DaimlerChrysler
▶ Mercedes-Benz E 320 CDI sedan and Jeep Liberty SUV, both on sale now.
▶ Mercedes-Benz M-class SUV, to go on sale this year or next.

(Cont.)

California and Florida are most active. California has 13 hydrogen fueling stations and about 65 hydrogen-powered vehicles in automaker-backed demonstration fleets, says Robert Hayden, spokesman for the California Fuel Cell Partnership. Gov. Arnold Schwarzenegger hopes for 150 stations by 2010.

In Florida, BP is setting up stations around Orlando to fuel demonstration fleets to be run there by car companies.

GM says it would cost $12 billion to modify gas stations to also sell hydrogen fuel at 12,000 sites in 100 big cities.

Hydrogen filling stations for the public aren't likely until 2015- 2025, Shell's Baxley says.

"We're in the same phase with hydrogen as when cellphones were expensive and large and only available in the largest urban areas."

USA Today. Copyright, January 12, 2005. Reprinted by permission.

Is Fat The Next Tobacco?

For BigFood, the supersizing of America is becoming a big headache ■ *Roger Parloff*

On August 3, 2000, the parody newspaper *The Onion* ran a joke article under the headline HERSHEY'S ORDERED TO PAY OBESE AMERICANS $135 BILLION. The hypothesized class-action lawsuit said that Hershey "knowingly and willfully" marketed to children "rich, fatty candy bars containing chocolate and other ingredients of negligible nutritional value," while "spiking" them with "peanuts, crisped rice, and caramel to increase consumer appeal."

Some joke. Last summer New York City attorney Sam Hirsch filed a strikingly similar suit—against McDonald's—on behalf of a class of obese and overweight children. He alleged that the fast-food chain "negligently, recklessly, carelessly and/or intentionally" markets to children food products that are "high in fat, salt, sugar, and cholesterol" while failing to warn of those ingredients' links to "obesity, diabetes, coronary heart disease, high blood pressure, strokes, elevated cholesterol intake, related cancers," and other conditions.

News of the lawsuit drew hoots of derision. But food industry executives aren't laughing—or shouldn't be. No matter what happens with Hirsch's suit, he has tapped into something very big. Seasoned lawyers from both sides of past mass-tort disputes agree that the years ahead hold serious tobacco-like litigation challenges for the food industry—challenges that extend beyond fast foods to snack foods, soft drinks, packaged foods, and dietary supplements. "The precedents, the ammo, the missiles are already there and waiting in a silo marked 'tobacco,'" says Victor Schwartz, general counsel of the American Tort Reform Association.

Junk food may not be addictive in the same way that tobacco is. But weight, once gained, is notoriously hard to lose, and childhood weight patterns strongly predict adult ones. Rates of overweight among small children—to whom junk-food companies aggressively market their products—have doubled since 1980; rates among adolescents have tripled.

In 1999 physicians began reporting an alarming rise in children of obesity-linked type 2 diabetes. Once an obese youngster develops diabetes, he or she will never get rid of it. That's a lot more irreversible than a smoking addiction.

Though many people recoil at the idea of obesity suits—eating habits are a matter of personal responsibility, they protest—the tobacco precedents show that such qualms can be overcome. Yes, most people know that eating a Big Mac isn't the same as eating a spinach salad, but most people knew that smoking was bad for them too. And yes, diet is only one risk factor out of many that contribute to obesity, but smoking is just one risk factor for diseases for which the tobacco companies were forced to fork over reimbursement to Medicaid. (The industry's share of the blame was statistically estimated and then divvied up among companies by market share.) The tobacco companies eventually agreed to pay $246 billion to the states, and juries are now ordering them to pay individual smokers eight-digit verdicts too.

By the Surgeon General's estimate, public-health costs attributable to overweight and obesity now come to about $117 billion a year—fast approaching the $140 billion stemming from smoking. Suing Big Food offers allures to contingency-fee lawyers that rival those of Big Tobacco, and the implications of that are pretty easy to foresee. While the food industry is not apt to be socked with anything like the penalties that hit tobacco, companies will face consumer-protection suits that might cost them many tens of millions of dollars and force them to significantly change marketing practices.

THE TRIGGERING EVENT OCCURRED in December 2001. That's when the Surgeon General, observing that about 300,000 deaths per year are now associated with overweight and obesity, warned that those conditions might soon cause as much preventable disease and death as smoking. The report prompted journalists to call John Banzhaf III, an antismoking activist and a

law professor at George Washington University School of Law, to see whether tobacco-style litigation might be in the offing. "I said, 'Well, no, there are important differences,'" Banzhaf recalls. But even as he talked, he began to change his mind.

Another key academic strategist in the tobacco wars, Northeastern University law professor Richard Daynard, was soon drawn into the fray. At a conference last April to discuss Marion Nestle's new book, *Food Politics,* he was asked to talk about possible obesity-related litigation. (Nestle, who chairs the nutrition department at New York University and whose name is pronounced NESSel, is not related to the founders of the food company.) Daynard, like Banzhaf, at first saw no analogy to tobacco. But as he read Nestle's book, he, too, began to change his mind.

Here's Nestle's argument. For at least the past 50 years public-health authorities have wanted to deliver a simple, urgent message to the American people: Eat less. They have been thwarted from doing so, however, by political pressure from the food industry. The meat industry alone spends millions a year on lobbying, apparently with great success. Instead of forthrightly saying, "Eat less red meat," government health authorities are forced to say, "Eat more lean meat." Food companies compound the confusion by advertising that their products can be "part of a balanced and nutritional diet," even though they know that their products are not typically consumed that way. Any food can theoretically be part of a balanced diet if you keep the portions tiny enough and eat lots of fruits, vegetables, and grains.

As Daynard well knew, advertising claims that are literally true, but misleading when viewed in a real-world context, can violate state consumer-protection laws. In some states, like California, plaintiffs can force companies to disgorge all profits attributable to advertising that employs such statements, and the plaintiff can win without having to prove that even a single individual was actually tricked by the statement.

(Cont.)

The idea of bringing such suits against the food industry is not unprecedented. In 1983, for instance, the California supreme court greenlighted a suit brought by an advocacy group against General Foods over the way such breakfast cereals as Sugar Crisp and Cocoa Pebbles—which contain 38% to 50% sugar by weight—were being marketed to children. The plaintiffs argued that "although promoted and labeled as 'cereals,'" the products "are in fact more accurately described as sugar products, or candies." The court suggested that ads even implicitly claiming that such products were nutritious or healthful were plausible lawsuit targets. (After the ruling, the case settled.)

Last July, Daynard attended an informal meeting of lawyers and public-health advocates in Banzhaf's office in Washington. "The first question at John's meeting was, 'Is there a there there?'" Daynard recalls. "What persuaded us was, in a sense, the media. This thing is so radioactive in terms of media attention that cases will bring in other lawyers and bring in other cases."

Later that month a lawyer who'd never heard of Banzhaf or Daynard crashed their party. Sam Hirsch, who runs his own small practice in New York City, had become interested in food issues after an overweight associate referred to a burger as a "fat bomb." Though Hirsch, 54, had never brought a class action, he now filed two, one in Brooklyn and another in the Bronx. The suits, brought on behalf of classes of obese people, named McDonald's, Burger King, KFC, and Wendy's as defendants.

The press loved the story. The industry response was ferocious. The Coalition for Consumer Freedom, a trade group of restaurants and food and beverage suppliers (McDonald's is not a member), promptly took out aggressive full-page ads in newsmagazines. One showed a man's bloated, bare gut spilling over a belted waistline. The copy read: "Did you hear the one about the fat guy suing the restaurants? It's no joke."

For plaintiffs lawyers and nutrition activists, the Hirsch suit was a mixed blessing. Some worried that it was such a laughingstock that it might strengthen the forces pushing for tort reform. As a tool of public education, on the other hand, the Hirsch suit was a landmark. Even if the industry was winning the talk-show shout-fests, its arguments about personal responsibility sent a double-edged message, according to Daynard. "'If you're stupid enough to use our products, you deserve to get the diseases our products cause.' That's what it means if you deconstruct it," he says. "This sort of discussion is not good for the lawsuit, but it's very good for public health."

In August, Banzhaf invited Hirsch to the second meeting of his group. Afterward Hirsch decided not to pursue his two lawsuits, which had been filed on behalf of adults, and to bring instead a new class-action suit on behalf of obese children. He focused this suit on McDonald's alone. One prospective class member, 400-pound, 15-year-old Gregory Rhymes, who suffers from type 2 diabetes, stated in an affidavit that he has eaten at McDonald's "nearly every day" since he was 6. Neal Barnard, a doctor who heads a vegetarian advocacy group, submitted a declaration asserting that "the consumption of McDonald's products has significantly contributed to the development of [Rhymes's] obesity and diabetes."

McDonald's has mounted a spirited defense. "Every reasonable person understands what is in products such as hamburgers and fries," McDonald's lawyers argue in their papers, "as well as the consequences to one's waistline, and potentially to one's health, of excessively eating those foods over a prolonged period." The lawyers also warn that the plaintiffs' theories, if accepted, would usher in "an uncontrollable avalanche of litigation against other restaurants and food providers, as well as other industries (such as the pizza, ice cream, cheese, and cookie industries)." In a statement to FORTUNE, McDonald's said that it has long made nutritional information available to customers upon request. "Nutrition professionals say that McDonald's food can be and is a part of a healthy diet based on the sound nutrition principles of balance, variety, and moderation," the statement continues. McDonald's has asked a federal court in Manhattan to take the case away from the state court and then to dismiss it. The court has not yet ruled.

Targeting kids is the food industry's Achilles' heel, says plaintiffs lawyer John Coale, a veteran of tobacco and gun litigation. Fast food, snack food, and soft drink companies focus their marketing on children and adolescents through Saturday morning TV commercials; through cuddly characters like Ronald McDonald (the second most recognized figure among children after Santa Claus); through contracts to advertise and serve soft drinks and fast food in schools; and through ever-changing toys included in Happy Meals.

If misleading advertising can be linked to childhood disease, Coale says, "you've got yourself not only a lawsuit but a movement." Food industry insiders have already come forward to speak to Coale about disturbing marketing practices, he claims. "We're not bringing down the fastfood industry next Tuesday," he says, "but there are legitimate legal issues here."

HIRSCH'S CASE, SAY MANY PLAINTIFFS lawyers, is like the earliest tobacco and asbestos cases, which failed because the damning evidence had not yet come out. But once cases progress into the discovery stage, smoking-gun documents may begin to emerge, showing that the companies knew more than the general public about the impact that their products and advertising were having on children's health. Tort reform advocate Schwartz does not doubt this. "As discovery goes forward," Schwartz explains, "plaintiffs lawyers will be finding documents that, if held up in isolation, make it look like the industry had something to hide. That gives the case heft." Schwartz predicts that it will take about five years to reach that point.

Not everyone on the defense side is as fatalistic as Schwartz. Thomas Bezanson of New York's Chadbourne & Parke, who has defended tobacco, alcohol, and pharmaceutical companies, thinks that what happened to the tobacco industry was unique. "You had a very powerful attack made by the plaintiffs bar, the press, the politicians, and the state attorneys general," he says. "That only works if you are able to use all of those in a coordinated way to persuade society that the object of attack is some kind of pariah. I doubt that kind of attack can be lodged against food companies."

There is another important difference between tobacco and food. The tobacco industry "can't make a safe cigarette," says Banzhaf, "but fast-food companies can do almost everything we want without going broke. They can issue warnings, they can post fat and calorie content on menu boards, they can put more nutritious things on their menus. In fact, they already are." Last year, for instance, McDonald's reduced trans fatty acids in its fried foods and introduced lowfat yogurt and fruit roll-up desserts. A press release touts the yogurt as a "good source of calcium" and says that the fruit desserts provide 25% of the daily recommended value of vitamin C. "As a mom and registered dietician," a McDonald's staffer says in the release, "I know the importance of having this type of nutrient value in a snack food that kids enjoy."

Such gestures are themselves fraught with legal peril, however. Daynard mocks the McDonald's press release on its new healthy desserts, for instance: "We're talking about *desserts* to have *after their Happy Meals!*" protests Daynard. "The suggestion is that a really good mother would order *four* of them, right?"

If companies that produce high-calorie and high-fat foods are worried about future lawsuits, they aren't saying. PepsiCo, Cadbury

(Cont.)

Schweppes, and Kraft all declined to comment. Their trade group was less shy. "We advocate getting good messages to parents to help children develop good eating and exercise habits," says a spokesperson for the Grocery Manufacturers of America. "What we think is counterproductive is finger-pointing, reckless accusations, and lawsuits that won't make anyone any thinner." All the same, prudent food companies might do well to start scrutinizing their advertising and packaging, tweaking product lines, and, yes, squirreling away some reserves for potential judgments.

For at least one industry, though, the new spotlight on fat may be a glimmer of unaccustomed good news. Anecdotally, we've heard that smoking has helped a lot of people lose weight.

21

Food Fight Breaks Out

Industry fears being villainized in obesity flap as Kraft yanks snack ads

Stephanie Thompson. *Advertising Age.*

BIG FOOD is in danger of becoming as vilified as Big Tobacco.

Kraft Foods' pledge last week to stop advertising snacks such as Kool-Aid and Oreos to kids 6 to 11 infuriated competitors in the growth-challenged food industry. Rivals are grumbling that the move plays right into the hands of government regulators and consumer health advocates pushing to end the marketing and even the sale of unhealthy foods, especially to kids. They see Kraft's move as a tacit acknowledgment of guilt in fueling the country's obesity epidemic—and one that damns them by implication.

The $500 billion packaged-food industry's marketing over the last year has already been severely constrained by growing obesity concerns. Kraft, Kellogg Co., PepsiCo, General Mills and others, including fast feeders, have all been clamoring to appease consumers and advocacy groups and meet just-released Food & Drug Administration Food Pyramid guidelines with health-driven products, promotional initiatives and advertising. But Kraft's latest step, which many see as a lawyer-inspired public relations effort driven by its parent, Altria Group, also the owner of tobacco giant Philip Morris, is seen as pushing too far.

Rivals are, for now, holding their ground.

A Kellogg spokeswoman said that the company "has a longstanding commitment to advertising to children in a responsible manner." A PepsiCo spokeswoman mirrored that sentiment, pointing to the increasing shift of PepsiCo's marketing toward its healthier lineup newly designated with a Smart Spot label. General Mills declined to comment. But all the major food marketers are expected to face increased pressure to follow Kraft's lead.

Consumer activists see Kraft's voluntary restrictions on advertising to kids as not nearly enough, but a great first step. "This shows that companies like Kraft are beginning to recognize the harmful impact of marketing unhealthy products to kids," said child and family psychologist Allen Kanner, a member of The Campaign for a CommercialFree Childhood, whose goal is banning all marketing to kids under 8. That's just the kind of reaction Kraft competitors fear.

Credit Suisse First Boston analyst Dave Nelson said Kraft's announcement surely shows that "the industry is going to have to further restrict itself in terms of marketing to avoid criticism and, potentially, regulation." After all, he said, "we have obesity [because] these companies have been extremely successful in getting us to eat their products."

BATTLE OF THE BULGE

A sampling of marketers' top obesity-battling initiatives

- **General Mills:** Converts cereals to whole grain; starts weight-loss program Brand New You

- **Kellogg:** Launches one-third fewer sugar versions of Special K and whole-grain Tiger Power

- **PepsiCo:** Commits to making 50% of new products healthier; Labels 100 products Smart Spot.

- **Kraft:** Labels healthier lines as "Sensible Solution"; pulls kids' ads for un-"Sensible" products.

That success, already severely limited of late for top players including Kraft, is further jeopardized as food marketers shift marketing priorities from a focus on sales and profitability (requiring marketing dollars behind the successful and growing product lines) to self-protection by touting restraint, especially to kids.

APPLE POLISHING

Already over the last year, food marketers have "all been on high alert to make sure their message is about a well-balanced diet and doesn't push their product too heavily," said Leigh Thornberry, executive producer for kids' Web site and advergames developer Circle 1 Network. For its clients, including Kellogg's Keebler brand and the National Cattlemen's Beef Association, that has meant messages, she said, that are less "'Eat our cookies, eat our cookies, eat our cookies'" and more "'have two cookies with your apple and sandwich.'"

But packaged-goods marketers don't make money selling apples.

One executive close to Kraft said, in fact, that despite impressive growth in small better-for-you categories and "a lot of noise from a vocal minority" regarding health issues, the consumers "who make up the bulk of [food companies'] volume are still buying what they've been buying for years and years." Most of it not the healthy stuff.

Kellogg's one-third less sugar varieties of Frosted Flakes and Froot Loops have not been setting the world on fire, according to one Midwest retail executive. And General

(Cont.)

Mills' own 75%-less-sugar items have only skyrocketed since being added to the USDA's supplemental nutrition program for women, children and infants, or WIC, he said.

FUN FUEL

According to Information Resources Inc. data, sales for Kraft's less-than-nutritious Lunchables franchise totaled $519 million, while the 2003 launch of the brand's better-for-you offshoot, Lunchables Fun Fuel, amounted to only $31 million in sales for the 52 weeks ended Dec. 26. But Kraft's Senior VP-Global Health and Wellness Lance Friedmann said in fact that a new lower-calorie, lower-fat Chicken Dunks variety (that will be the type of product bearing Kraft's new Sensible Solution label and advertised to kids 6 to 11) is in fact its "fastest-moving Lunchables variety."

Neuberger Berman analyst Bill Leach said Kraft's decision to focus on the healthiest items in its portfolio is not sales-driven but rather driven by the overwhelming pressure from the lawyers, consumers groups and government agencies looking at the obesity issue. In fact, the news of Kraft's shifts in ad tactics for kids broke first in the *Washington Post*—the Beltway bible for regulators and legislators.

What's clear, however, is that nutrition-focused food marketing efforts are irrevocably the wave of the future.

"All of our companies have nutrition in their minds when developing marketing and new products now," said Stephanie Childs, a spokeswoman for industry association Grocery Manufacturers of America.

The products Kraft claims it will no longer advertise to kids make up 10% of its total product portfolio, or roughly $3 billion in sales. Kraft said that while the type of products being advertised in kids' media will change to focus on better-for-you products, its total spending on the demographic—$80 million, according to *Advertising Age* estimates—remains the same.

Wary media companies aren't taking any chances. Viacom's Nickelodeon issued a statement following Kraft's announcement that the kids' network "has offered promotional incentives to companies who advertise healthy food products on our network, and we look forward to adding additional healthy lifestyle messaging from companies interested in partnering with us."

Nickelodeon will also roll out new "Nicktrition" labels for its licensed foods, the first among them Kraft's Macaroni & Cheese, to include more detailed nutritional information and active lifestyle tips.

22

HISPANIC NATION
Hispanics are an immigrant group like no other. Their huge numbers are challenging old assumptions about assimilation. Is America ready?

Maria Velazquez was born in a dingy hospital on the U.S.-Mexican border and has been straddling the two nations ever since. The 36-year-old daughter of a bracero, a Mexican migrant who tended California strawberry and lettuce fields in the 1960s, she spent her first nine years like a nomad, crossing the border with her family each summer to follow her father to work. Then her parents and their six children settled down in a Chicago barrio, where Maria learned English in the local public school and met Carlos Velazquez, who had immigrated from Mexico as a teenager. The two married in 1984, when Maria was 17, and relocated to nearby Cicero, Ill. Her parents returned to their homeland the next year with five younger kids.

The Velazquezes speak fluent English and cherish their middle-class foothold in America. Maria and Carlos each earn about $20,000 a year as a school administrator and a graveyard foreman, respectively, and they own a simple three-bedroom home. But they remain wedded to their native language and culture. Spanish is the language at home, even for their five boys, ages 6 to 18. The kids speak to each other and their friends in English flecked with "dude" and "man," but in Cicero, where 77% of the 86,000 residents are Hispanic, Spanish dominates.

The older boys snack at local *taquerías* when they don't eat at home, where Maria's cooking runs to dishes like chicken mole and enchiladas. The family reads and watches TV in Spanish and English. The eldest, Jesse, is a freshman at nearby Morton College and dreams of becoming a state trooper; his girlfriend is also Mexican-American. "It's important that they know where they're from, that they're connected to their roots," says

Maria, who bounced between Spanish and English while speaking to *BusinessWeek*. She tries to take the kids to visit her parents in the tiny Mexican town of Valle de Guadalupe at least once a year. "It gives them a good base to start from."

The Velazquezes, with their mixed cultural loyalties, are at the center of America's

> *"Mexicans working in the U.S. sent home about $13 billion last year, more than total foreign direct investment*

new demographic bulge. Baby boomers, move over—the *bebé* boomers are coming. They are 39 million strong, including some 8 million illegal immigrants—bilingual, bicultural, mostly younger Hispanics who will drive growth in the U.S. population and workforce as far out as statisticians can project (charts). Coming from across Latin America, but predominantly Mexico, and with high birth rates, these immigrants are creating what experts are calling a "tamale in the snake," a huge cohort of kindergarten to thirtysomething Hispanics created by the sheer velocity of their population growth—3% a year, vs. 0.8% for everyone else.

It's not just that Latinos, as many prefer to be called, officially passed African Americans last year to become the nation's largest

minority. Their numbers are so great that, like the postwar baby boomers before them, the Latino Generation is becoming a driving force in the economy, politics, and culture.

CULTURAL CLOUT
It amounts to no less than a shift in the nation's center of gravity. Hispanics made up half of all new workers in the past decade, a trend that will lift them from roughly 12% of the workforce today to nearly 25% two generations from now. Despite low family incomes, which at $33,000 a year lag the national average of $42,000, Hispanics' soaring buying power increasingly influences the food Americans eat, the clothes they buy, and the cars they drive. Companies are scrambling to revamp products and marketing to reach the fastest-growing consumer group. Latino flavors are seeping into mainstream culture, too. With Hispanic youth a majority of the under-18 set, or close to it, in cities such as Los Angeles, Miami, and San Antonio, what's hip there is spreading into suburbia, much the way rap exploded out of black neighborhoods in the late 1980s.

Hispanic political clout is growing, too. In a Presidential race that's likely to be as tight as the last one, they could be a must-win swing bloc. Indeed, the increase in voting-age Hispanics since 2000 now outstrips the margin of victory in seven states for either President George W. Bush or former Vice-President Albert Gore, according to a new study by HispanTelligence, a Santa Barbara (Calif.) research group. Bush opened the election year with a guest-worker proposal for immigrants that pundits took as a play for the Latino vote. He will follow up by rekindling his relationship with Mexican President Vicente Fox, who's due to visit Bush at his

Which Scenario For Hispanics?
Experts see three broad possibilities for Hispanics' role in American life:

Melting in - Hispanics follow the path of all other immigrant groups and gradually meld into American life, giving up Spanish and marrying non-Hispanics

Acculturation - Most Latinos speak both languages and retain much of their own culture and ties to their home countries, even as they adapt to U.S. lifestyles

Mexifornia - Many remain in Spanish-speaking enclaves and set the cultural and political agenda in soon-to-be-majority-Hispanic states like California and Texas

Data: BusinessWeek

(Cont.)

As the population of Hispanics explodes...

HISPANICS AND BLACKS AS A SHARE OF THE U.S. POPULATION
NONHISPANIC WHITES
BLACKS HISPANICS

Data: Census Bureau

...they're replacing baby boomers in the workforce...

AS SHARE OF U.S. LABOR FORCE
BABY BOOMERS
HISPANICS

Data: Pew Hispanic Center, Urban Institute, Bureau of Labor Statistics

...and boosting their buying power...

HISPANIC DISPOSABLE INCOME AS A SHARE OF U.S. TOTAL

Data: University of Georgia

...but they lag in school...

2002 GRADUATION RATES, BY RACE AND ETHNICITY
HIGH SCHOOL
COLLEGE

HISPANIC   BLACK   WHITE

Data: HispanTelligence, U.S. Census Bureau

...and may not join the American melting pot

U.S. HISPANIC POPULATION, BY DEGREES OF ASSIMILATION

BICULTURAL, BILINGUAL ISOLATED, MOSTLY SPEAK SPANISH
ASSIMILATED, MOSTLY SPEAK ENGLISH

Data: HispanTelligence, Simmons Market Research, Census Bureau, McKinsey & Co.

LEARNING CURVE
Spanish-speaking kids in Tyler, Tex.

"Of all children under 18, **Latinos are 61%** in San Antonio, **53%** in Los Angeles, **39%** in Miami and San Diego, and **36%** in Houston

Crawford, Texas, ranch on Mar. 5. Democrats, traditionally the dominant party among Hispanics, are stepping up their outreach, too. New Mexico Governor Bill Richardson, a Mexican-American and potential Vice-Presidential candidate, delivered a first-ever Spanish-language version of the Democrat's rebuttal to the State of the Union address.

The U.S. has never faced demographic change quite like this before. Certainly, the Latino boom brings a welcome charge to the economy at a time when others' population growth has slowed to a crawl. Without a steady supply of new workers and consumers, a graying U.S. might see a long-term slowdown along the lines of aging Japan, says former Housing and Urban Development chief Henry Cisneros, who now builds homes in Hispanic-rich markets such as San Antonio. "Here we have this younger, hardworking Latino population whose best working years are still ahead," he says.

Already, Latinos are a key catalyst of economic growth. Their disposable income has jumped 29% since 2001, to $652 billion last year, double the pace of the rest of the population, according to the Selig Center for Economic Growth at the University of Georgia. Similarly, the ranks of Latino entrepreneurs has jumped by 30% since 1998, calculates the Internal Revenue Service. "The impact of Hispanics is huge, especially since they're the fastest-growing demographic," says Merrill Lynch & Co. Vice-President Carlos Vaquero, himself a Mexican immigrant based in Houston. Vaquero oversees part of the company's 350-person Hispanic unit, which is hiring 100 mostly bilingual financial advisers this year and which generated $1 billion worth

(Cont.)

of new business nationwide last year, double its goal.

Yet the rise of a minority group this distinct requires major adjustments, as well. Already, Hispanics are spurring U.S. institutions to accommodate a second linguistic group. The Labor Dept. and Social Security Administration are hiring more Spanish-language administrators to cope with the surge in Spanish speakers in the workforce. Politicians, too, increasingly reach out to Hispanics in their own language.

What's not yet clear is whether Hispanic social cohesion will be so strong as to actually challenge the idea of the American melting pot. At the extreme, ardent assimilationists worry that the spread of Spanish eventually could prompt Congress to recognize it as an official second language, much as French is in Canada today. Some even predict a Quebec-style Latino dominance in states such as Texas and California that will encourage separatism, a view expressed in a recent book called *Mexifornia: A State of Becoming* by Victor Davis Hanson, a history professor at California State University at Fresno. These views have recently been echoed by Harvard University political scientist Samuel P. Huntington in a forthcoming book, *Who Are We*.

These critics argue that legions of poorly educated non-English speakers undermine the U.S. economy. Although the steady influx of low-skilled workers helps keep America's gardens tended and floors cleaned, those workers also exert downward pressure on wages across the lower end of the pay structure. Already, this is causing friction with African Americans, who see their jobs and pay being hit. "How are we going to compete in a global market when 50% of our fastest-growing group doesn't graduate from high school?" demands former Colorado Governor Richard D. Lamm, who now co-directs a public policy center at the University of Denver.

Still, many experts think it's more likely that the U.S. will find a new model, more salad bowl than melting pot, that accommodates a Latino subgroup without major upheaval. "America has to learn to live with diversity—the change in population, in [Spanish-language] media, in immigration," says Andrew Erlich, the founder of Erlich Transcultural Consultants Inc. in North Hollywood, Calif. Hispanics aren't so much assimilating as acculturating—acquiring a new culture while retaining their original one—says Felipe Korzenny, a professor of Hispanic marketing at Florida State University.

It boils down to this: How much will Hispanics change America, and how much will America change them? Throughout the country's history, successive waves of immigrants eventually surrendered their native languages and cultures and melted into the middle class. It didn't always happen right away. During the great European migrations of the 1800s, Germans settled in an area stretching from Pennsylvania to Minnesota. They had their own schools, newspapers, and businesses, and spoke German, says Demetrios G. Papademetriou, co-founder of the Migration Policy Institute in Washington. But in a few generations, their kids spoke only English and embraced American aspirations and habits.

Hispanics may be different, and not just because many are nonwhites. True, Maria Velazquez worries that her boys may lose their Spanish and urges them to speak it more. Even so, Hispanics today may have more choice than other immigrant groups to remain within their culture. With national TV networks such as Univision Communications Inc. and hundreds of mostly Spanish-speaking enclaves like Cicero, Hispanics may find it practical to remain bilingual. Today, 78% of U.S. Latinos speak Spanish, even if they also know English, according to the Census Bureau.

One out of 10 small businesses will be Hispanic-owned by '07, jumping to 2 million from 1.2 million today

---

BACK AND FORTH

The 21 million Mexicans among them also have something else no other immigrant group has had: They're a car ride away from their home country. Many routinely journey back and forth, allowing them to maintain ties that Europeans never could. The dual identities are reinforced by the constant influx of new Latino immigrants—roughly 400,000 a year, the highest flow in U.S. history. The steady stream of newcomers will likely keep the foreign-born, who typically speak mostly or only Spanish, at one-third of the U.S. Hispanic population for several decades. Their presence means that "Spanish is constantly refreshed, which is one of the key contrasts with what people think of as the melting pot," says Roberto Suro, director of the Pew Hispanic Center, a Latino research group in Washington.

A slow pace of assimilation is likely to hurt Hispanics themselves the most, especially poor immigrants who show up with no English and few skills. Latinos have long lagged in U.S. schools, in part because many families remain cloistered in Spanish-speaking neighborhoods. Their strong work ethic can compound the problem by propelling many young Latinos into the workforce before they finish high school. So while the Hispanic high-school-graduation rate has climbed 12 percentage points since 1980, to 57%, that's still woefully short of the 88% for non-Hispanic whites and 80% for African Americans.

MELD INTO THE MAINSTREAM

The failure to develop skills leaves many Hispanics trapped in low-wage service jobs that offer few avenues for advancement. Incomes may not catch up anytime soon, either, certainly not for the millions of undocumented Hispanics. Most of these, from Mexican street-corner day laborers in Los Angeles to Guatemalan poultry-plant workers in North Carolina, toil in the underbelly of the U.S. economy. Many low-wage Hispanics would fare better economically if they moved out of the barrios and assimilated into U.S. society. Most probably face less racism than African Americans, since Latinos are a diverse ethnic and linguistic group comprising every nationality from Argentinians, who have a strong European heritage, to Dominicans, with their large black population. Even so, the pull of a common language may keep many in a country apart.

Certainly immigrants often head for a place where they can get support from fellow citizens, or even former neighbors. Some 90% of immigrants from Tonatico, a small town 100 miles south of Mexico City, head for Waukegan, Ill., joining 5,000 Tonaticans already there. In Miami, of course, Cubans dominate. "Miami has Hispanic banks, Hispanic law firms, Hispanic hospitals, so you can more or less conduct your entire life in Spanish here," says Leopoldo E. Guzman, 57. He came to the U.S. from Cuba at 15 and turned a Columbia University degree into a job at Lazard Freres & Co. before founding investment bank Guzman & Co.

Or take the Velazquezes' home of Cicero, a gritty factory town that once claimed fame as Al Capone's headquarters. Originally populated mostly by Czechs, Poles, and Slovaks, the Chicago suburb started decaying in the 1970s as factories closed and residents fled in search of jobs. Then a wave of young Mexican immigrants drove the population to its current Hispanic dominance, up from 1% in 1970. Today, the town president, equivalent to a mayor, is a Mexican immigrant, Ramiro Gonzalez, and Hispanics have replaced whites in the surviving factories and local schools. It's still possible that Cicero's Latino children will follow the path of so many other immigrants and move out into non-Hispanic neighborhoods. If they do, they, or at least their children, will likely all but abandon Spanish, gradually marry non-Hispanics, and meld into the mainstream.

But many researchers and academics say that's not likely for many Hispanics. In fact, a study of assimilation and other factors shows

(Cont.)

that while the number of Hispanics who prefer to speak mostly Spanish has dipped in recent years as the children of immigrants grow up with English, there has been no increase in those who prefer only English. Instead, the HispanTelligence study found that the group speaking both languages has climbed six percentage points since 1995, to 63%, and is likely to jump to 67% by 2010.

The trend to acculturate rather than assimilate is even more stark among Latino youth. Today, 97% of Mexican kids whose parents are immigrants and 76% of other Hispanic immigrant children know Spanish, even as nearly 90% also speak English very well, according to a decade-long study by University of California at Irvine sociologist Ruben G. Rumbaut. More striking, those Latino kids keep their native language at four times the rate of Filipino, Vietnamese, or Chinese children of immigrants. "Before, immigrants tried to become Americans as soon as possible," says Sergio Bendixen, founder of Bendixen & Associates, a polling firm in Coral Gables, Fla., that specializes in Hispanics. "Now, it's the opposite."

SELLING IN SPANISH

In its eagerness to tap the exploding Hispanic market, Corporate America itself is helping to reinforce Hispanics' bicultural preferences. Last year, Procter & Gamble Co. spent $90 million on advertising directed at Latinos for 12 products such as Crest and Tide—10% of its ad budget for those brands and a 28% hike in just a year. Sure, P&G has been marketing to Hispanics for decades, but spending took off after 2000, when the company set up a 65-person bilingual team to target Hispanics. Now, P&G tailors everything from detergent to toothpaste to Latino tastes. Last year, it added a third scent to Gain detergent called "white-water fresh" after finding that 57% of Hispanics like to smell their purchases. Now, Gain's sales growth is double-digit in the Hispanic market, outpacing general U.S. sales. "Hispanics are a cornerstone of our growth in North America," says Graciela Eleta, vice-president of P&G's multicultural team in Puerto Rico.

Spanish-language TV is likely to see the largest revenue gains this year, climbing 16%, vs. 8% for the industry as a whole

Other companies are making similar assumptions. In 2002, Cypress (Calif.)-based PacifiCare Health Systems Inc. hired Russell A. Bennett, a longtime Mexico City resident, to help target Hispanics. He soon found that they were already 20% of PacifiCare's 3 million policyholders. So Bennett's new unit, Latino Health Solutions, began marketing health insurance in Spanish, directing Hispanics to Spanish-speaking doctors, and translating documents into Spanish for Hispanic workers. "We knew we had to remake the entire company, linguistically and culturally, to deal with this market," says Bennett.

A few companies are even going all-Spanish. After local Hispanic merchants stole much of its business in a Houston neighborhood that became 85% Latino, Kroger Co., the nation's No.1 grocery chain, spent $1.8 million last year to convert the 59,000-sq.-ft. store into an all-Hispanic *supermercado*. Now, Spanish-language signs welcome customers, and catfish and banana leaves line the aisles. Across the country, Kroger has expanded its private-label Buena Comida line from the standard rice and beans to 105 different items.

As the ranks of Spanish speakers swell, Spanish-language media are transforming from a niche market into a stand-alone industry. Ad revenues on Spanish-language TV should climb by 16% this year, more than other media segments, according to TNS Media Intelligence/CMR. The audience of Univision, the No.1 Spanish-language media conglomerate in the U.S., has soared by 44% since 2001, and by 146% in the 18- to 34-year-old group. Many viewers have come

from English-language networks, whose audiences have declined in that period.

In fact, Univision tried to reach out to assimilated Hispanics a few years ago by putting English-language programs on its cable channel Galavision. They bombed, says Univision President Ray Rodriguez, so he switched back to Spanish-only in 2002—and 18- to 34-year-old viewership shot up by 95% that year. "We do what the networks don't, and that's devote a lot of our show to what interests the Latino community," says Univision news anchor Jorge Ramos.

The Hispanicizing of America raises a number of political flash points. Over the years, periodic backlashes have erupted in areas with fast-growing Latino populations, notably former California Governor Pete Wilson's 1994 effort, known as Proposition 187, to ban social services to undocumented immigrants. English-only laws, which limit or prohibit schools and government agencies from using Spanish, have passed in some 18 states. Most of these efforts have been ineffective, but they're likely to continue as the Latino presence increases.

For more than 200 years, the nation has succeeded in weaving the foreign-born into the fabric of U.S. society, incorporating strands of new cultures along the way. With their huge numbers, Hispanics are adding all kinds of new influences. Cinco de Mayo has joined St. Patrick's Day as a public celebration in some neighborhoods, and burritos are everyday fare. More and more, Americans hablan Espanol. Will Hispanics be absorbed just as other waves of immigrants were? It's possible, but more likely they will continue to straddle two worlds, figuring out ways to remain Hispanic even as they become Americans.

By Brian Grow with Ronald Grover, Arlene Weintraub, and Christopher Palmeri in Los Angeles, Mara Der Hovanesian in New York, Michael Eidam in Atlanta, and bureau reports

23

India Is Becoming Powerhouse; Growth Expanding Middle Class

Size, pace rival China's; English-speaking MBAs and gov't fuel takeoff.

. . . .

By Marilyn Alva
Investor's Business Daily

Move over, China. Here comes India. With a population of 1.1 billion, the second most populous nation after China is becoming the next emerging economic powerhouse.

Job growth in tech services is already fueling a rapidly growing consumer class much like China's economic miracle is minting a new yuppie class. Sales of autos, computers and cell phones are mushrooming.

More than 2 million cell phone connections are sold every month, making India the second fastest mobile phone market after China. And the mobile phone penetration rate is still below 3%. Car sales are tracking to hit 1 million a year by 2005, thanks in part to low interest rates.

If you follow the money, a lot of it seems to end up in India these days.

Foreign direct investment alone totaled $6 billion in 2003, says David Darst, chief investment strategist of Morgan Stanley's individual investors group. That compares with an average $2.5 billion a year from 1995 to 2002.

India's arrival as the developed world's biggest back office isn't the only reason it's coming on so strongly.

Robust growth in other sectors such as manufacturing, agriculture and consumer goods are fueling strong GDP growth—an estimated 8% this fiscal year, which ends in March. GDP might slow to 6.5% next year, but it's still among the top growth rates worldwide.

And this is just the start. A widely touted report by Goldman Sachs says India will eventually become the world's third largest economy after China and the U.S.

That might not happen for a few decades, but as Ashish Thadani, senior vice president at Brean Murray & Co., put it, "There is a sense that this is a very sustainable upswing."

Goldman Sachs says India's GDP growth starting in 2010 will equal and then surpass China's, which is now a sizzling 8% to 9%, but is expected to eventually slow. India's population also will likely pass China's.

India is still largely a nation of have-nots. Average per-capita income is $500 a year. About 35% of the population live in poverty.

But because of its enormous population, India's growing middle class assumes formidable weight.

"Even if the middle class is just 5% or 10%, any percent of a billion is substantial," said Michel Leonard, chief economist of Aon Trade Credit, which maps risk for companies that want to do business in foreign countries.

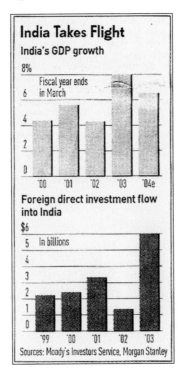

India Takes Flight
India's GDP growth

Fiscal year ends in March

Foreign direct investment flow into India

In billions

Sources: Moody's Investors Service, Morgan Stanley

Government Reforms

Like China, India's government is making strides to improve creaky infrastructure and privatize government-dominated industries.

The government plans to soon sell off in an initial public offering about 10% of its oil and gas giant, Oil & Natural Gas Corp. The deal, valued at nearly $3 billion, would put it in the same ballpark as last year's biggest IPO: China Life Insurance Co.

"It would be a landmark offering," said Darst.

If demand is brisk, he says, it could lead to more government-sponsored IPOs.

In a recent report, he estimates the government owns $50 billion in listed holdings as well as stakes in several large unlisted concerns such as National Thermal Power Corp. and Life Insurance Corp. of India.

Foreign institutional investors own 17.5% of the top 50 Indian companies and 31% of the top 10, writes Darst. Capital inflow the last 12 months is 50% higher than any other 12-month period in India's history, he contends.

India's stock market rose about 80% in 2003. Some sectors with the best returns: auto, steel and financial services.

Of the hundreds of Indian public companies, only 10 trade in the U.S. via American depositary receipts (ADRs). But more are expected to list this year.

Indian ADRs include two banks, HDFC Bank Ltd. and ICICI Bank; a telecom services firm, Videsh Sanchar Nigram; and generic drug maker Dr. Reddy's Laboratories. Three are software outsourcers: Infosys Technologies Ltd., Satyam Computer Services Ltd. and Wipro Ltd.

India's foreign exchange reserves mushroomed $30 billion in the last year to $100 billion, leading Moody's Investors Service in late January to upgrade India's long-term foreign currency ratings to investment grade for the first time.

Insular India is giving rise to an open India. Over the last decade, India's unwieldy democratic government—with its socialist bent—has gradually loosened its

(Cont.)

grip over business and industry, easing regulations and opening its doors to foreign investors.

The government lowered import tariffs and granted tax breaks to outside investors.

Just recently, India agreed to ease foreign ownership limits in some sectors such as oil.

The government also is addressing infrastructure problems, such as poor roads and power outages. After the government decided last year to reform its power markets, foreign investors have been building several hydraulic electric plants.

New gas discoveries in the Bay of Bengal by India's Reliance Industries will likely help fuel what could be the world's largest power station, to be located in the poor northern state of Uttar Pradesh.

"Government efficiency and infrastructure in the last four years has gone from a level four to a level six on a scale of one to 10," said Partha Iyengar, vice president for Gartner India, based in Pune, India.

"Right now it's a good period to go into India," said Aon's Leonard. "People are making money in India. There are few people that have made money in China yet."

Morgan Stanley projects that leading Indian companies will post earnings growth of nearly 25% in fiscal 2004 ending in March, but slow to 14% in fiscal

"India has liberalized its trade before it's liberalized its capital markets. There's been some stock market reform, but buying and selling stocks is still archaic, about 20 years behind."

Mike Leonard, *Aon Trade Credit*

2005. Darst cites slower industrial growth and a widening trade deficit.

Business process outsourcing is India's fastest growing industry. It's no secret that India's large pool of educated and English-speaking professionals make India the preferred low-cost outsourcing destination of American companies for an ever-expanding list of services, from call centers to strategic solutions.

Leonard says 90% of Aon's clients who want to outsource services consider India first. China, he says, is fourth on the list.

Despite the euphoria over India's prospects, some experts are starting to raise caution flags. They fear India's financial system won't be able to handle all the money that's flowing in.

"India has liberalized its trade before it's liberalized its capital markets," Leonard said.

He added, "There's been some stock market reform, but buying and selling stocks is still archaic, about 20 years behind."

Leonard notes the political situation is less volatile than in previous periods and that tension with Pakistan has recently eased. But those problems won't disappear.

He compares India to China, which opened it borders to foreign direct investment before it had liberalized its capital markets.

"(China) is trying to get its books in order and make it more appealing to investors," he said. "Whenever you have a liberalization, the banks are the last to go."

Economists believe India's banking system is in better shape than China's, especially in terms of non-performing loans and modernizing various transactional systems.

"This was an agricultural and cash-based economy," Darst said. "Large advances have been made with the deepening of the middle class."

24

THE WORLD ACCORDING TO EBAY

The online auction giant is on a spectacular international growth tear. Here's Meg Whitman's master plan for global domination.

Erick Schonfeld. Business 2.0.

What is it about Frank Oltscher that makes him a dream customer for eBay chief executive Meg Whitman and her managers? He's an avid trader—he's even bought a marble fireplace online—but that doesn't exactly explain it. After all, some hard-core eBay customers buy more in a single day than Oltscher bought in the past two years. And true, his personal computer homepage is eBay, which is fairly intense. But it still pales next to other expressions of addiction to the site, like the eBay tattoo a woman in Louisiana had inked onto her ankle not long ago.

No, what makes Oltscher special—what, until recently, set him apart from most other eBay users—is this: He does his trading from his Berlin apartment through eBay's German auction website. That makes him the kind of customer Whitman & Co. lust after today, the validation of a strategic thrust that is poised to propel eBay, already one of the fastest-growing companies in history, into a new phase of turbocharged global expansion.

Five years ago eBay had virtually no international operations. Today its global business is surging. The company has 31 sites straddling the globe, from Brazil to Germany to China. They generated an estimated $1.1 billion in 2004 sales—46 percent of eBay's overall trading revenues—and are growing twice as fast as the company's domestic operations. International trading revenues are likely to surpass domestic in 2005. "International is a very important part of the future growth," says Whitman, sitting in a conference room at eBay's San Jose headquarters. "We're entering new countries that are at a much earlier stage of e-commerce development than the U.S. They should provide higher levels of growth for the foreseeable future."

Of eBay's 125 million registered users, roughly half are outside the United States. These international online shoppers buy a garden gnome every six minutes in Germany, a soccer jersey every five minutes in Britain, a bottle of wine every three minutes in France, and a skin-care product every 30 seconds in China. All told, they're estimated to have traded at least $16 billion worth of goods in 2004. "At the most basic level," says Matt Bannick, president of eBay International, "this concept travels pretty well."

That much is clear. But eBay's international advance is not merely a matter of breezing into foreign territory and throwing up some signs saying "Electronic flea market today!" eBay appears to have cracked the code for one of the toughest tasks in the increasingly interconnected global economy: transplanting a hit business concept into places with vastly different cultures and allowing it enough flexibility to adapt to local conditions without losing the core elements that made it a phenomenon in the first place. How has eBay done this? Gregory Boutte, the country manager for eBay France, provides a simple answer: "The eBay playbook explains the success of eBay."

He's not speaking metaphorically. There is an actual playbook. It consists of several hundred webpages of the collective wisdom of all of eBay's worldwide managers. The playbook is constantly updated and covers topics ranging from online marketing and category management to community outreach. It is the how-to manual by which every eBay country manager lives—or dies. And if eBay executes on that playbook, Bannick says, "Europe alone will be bigger than the U.S. for us."

eBay already has so many signal achievements that it's easy to forget that the company is only nine years old. It hit $3 billion in annual revenue faster than Microsoft, faster than Dell, faster than Cisco. But eBay's global ambitions were more thrust upon it than planned. Whitman, who became CEO in 1998, remembers the first inkling she got about the potential for global growth: "I knew when I got here that we had users from well over 50 countries, and they were using eBay.com in English—a completely American site." But Whitman was focused on perfecting eBay's concept at home before mucking around abroad, and she and her team had real questions about whether eBay would translate internationally. By the summer of 1999, however, mini eBays were springing up all over the world, and Whitman realized that eBay

(Cont.)

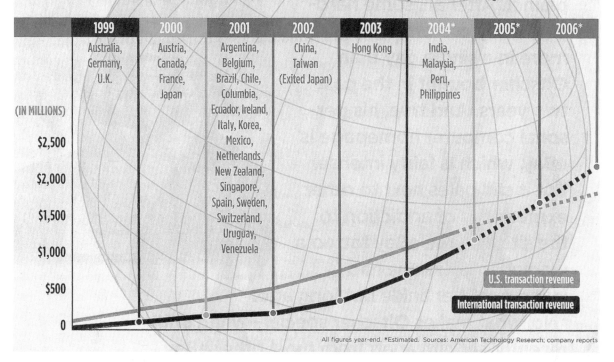

Not So Small, After All

eBay has transplanted its online auction model to 31 countries, beginning with Australia, Germany, and the United Kingdom in 1999. Now, roughly half of eBay's 125 million registered users are overseas, and international revenues are expected to outstrip domestic by the end of the year.

	1999	2000	2001	2002	2003	2004*	2005*	2006*
	Australia, Germany, U.K.	Austria, Canada, France, Japan	Argentina, Belgium, Brazil, Chile, Columbia, Ecuador, Ireland, Italy, Korea, Mexico, Netherlands, New Zealand, Singapore, Spain, Sweden, Switzerland, Uruguay, Venezuela	China, Taiwan (Exited Japan)	Hong Kong	India, Malaysia, Peru, Philippines		

(IN MILLIONS)

U.S. transaction revenue

International transaction revenue

All figures year-end. *Estimated. Sources: American Technology Research; company reports

had to turn its attention to global markets or cede them to Amazon, Yahoo, or local startups.

The company's first foreign stop: Germany. Whitman likes to tell the story of how her 84-year-old mother, a veteran Asia traveler, encouraged her back then to take on the Chinese market first, to which Whitman replied, "Mom, there are 40 million Internet users in Germany. There are 1 million in China. Forty million. One million." Sorry, Mom—Germany it would be.

The opening moves established what has become a fixture of the eBay playbook. eBay bought a Berlin-based copycat site called Alando for an estimated $47 million in June 1999, four months after some young German business students founded it. Philipp Justus, a German-born Boston Consulting Group alum brought in by eBay to head up the site, was taken aback by his first visit to Alando's headquarters in a Berlin loft. "It was 50 people," he says. "Half of them were interns."

But personnel was the least of Justus's problems. Haim Mendelson, co-director of Stanford University's Center for Electronic Business and Commerce, says that in Germany, eBay "didn't understand, when they went in, what needs to be local and what needs to be controlled from headquarters." Indeed, the German website was quickly migrated to eBay's technology center in San Jose, which saved money but also made it more difficult for Justus to respond rapidly to local needs. For instance, a popular feature of Alando's site was its ability to sort auctions by which would end the soonest. But in the United States, you could sort only by which items had been listed most recently, regardless of when an auction would end. Justus implored Web developers in San Jose to create a new sorting feature and other functions for the German site—to no avail. "We were not making our point about how important it was to get this," Justus recalls. He was bombarded by angry e-mails from irate

(Cont.)

International Players

Matt Bannick, a former State Department diplomat who runs eBay's overseas operations, emphasizes putting locally born execs in charge of the company's international sites. One top lieutenant is Philipp Justus, a German who now runs eBay Europe; he pioneered much of eBay's approach to new global markets at the company's German site. Another is Korean Jay Lee, who runs eBay Asia. Lee was once told by his own local managers that Koreans would never warm to eBay's auction model; now Korea is the company's third-largest overseas market.

MATT BANNICK
President, International

PHILIPP JUSTUS
Senior VP,
Europe

JAY LEE
Regional VP,
Asia

German sellers; trading volume on the site was lagging. Finally, Justus hopped a plane to California, showed up practically unannounced at headquarters, and pleaded his case to a group of startled engineers.

Within a week, many of the problems were fixed—and the German way of listing auctions was eventually adopted by the U.S. site as well. "The U.S. is not the only center of innovation," Whitman notes. "New ideas pop up all over." And all of these ideas get folded into the playbook. In Germany, a lot of work was done on figuring out how to structure categories of goods. Managers would focus on specific categories to learn how sellers wanted to list their products. The category manager for, say, stamps would go to stamp fairs and try to persuade sellers there to try eBay. "We had to make it relevant, category by category," Justus says. "That was pioneered in Germany, then exported."

Today, Germany is by far eBay's largest international site, with an estimated $7 billion in annualized sales. (That compares with $20 billion for the United States.) And it boasts a far higher percentage of active users than any other country site, with roughly three-quarters of

registered users trading on a regular basis.

Success in Germany spurred eBay to expand farther afield. Shortly after buying Alando, eBay launched its own sites in the United Kingdom and Australia. Then, in 2001, it went on a buying spree, investing in Korea's Internet Auction Co. and grabbing Europe's iBazar for about $130 million, which put eBay into Italy, the Netherlands, and Spain. eBay also acquired a minority stake in Latin America's leading auction company, MercadoLibre. In all, eBay has spent more than $1.6 billion on international acquisitions.

Once eBay sets up operations, managers rely heavily on the playbook. In reality, each function within eBay has its own playbook. There's a product management playbook, a Web development playbook, an Internet marketing playbook, and many others. And simply being able to tap into the collective experience of other country managers gives each new country site a huge leg up on competitors. At eBay France, for instance, the Internet marketing techniques pioneered in the United States and Germany proved crucial. The playbook details how important it is to drive traffic to the local eBay site through online ads on a given country's most popular websites and search engines. "This was very new to us," says eBay France manager Boutte. Before it was purchased, his French site built awareness primarily through expensive TV ads, as did its competitors. Some of those competitors are no longer in business. "About 65 percent of the people in France don't have Internet connections, so when you spend on TV ads, you're wasting a lot of money," Boutte says. He learned from the playbook that it doesn't make sense to start general TV branding until the number of users on a site reaches critical mass; in Germany and the United Kingdom, for instance, eBay didn't launch TV ads until those countries' sites reached more than $1 billion in annual merchandise sales.

The playbook wouldn't be nearly so valuable if not for eBay's ability to infinitely tailor a common technological and business platform to local markets. This flexibility is built in, since all the products, information, and chat boards on eBay's country sites are created by the buyers and sellers on those sites. "The users of eBay Germany are primarily German citizens, the site is German, and all the conversations are in German," says Bill Cobb, the former head of international operations who now runs eBay North America. Ditto for India, Italy, and elsewhere. "So it doesn't feel like an American brand. It feels like that community's brand. Yet they have this opportunity to access a global trading platform."

In essence, the playbook describes how to set the right conditions for electronic trading to flourish in a particular area. In the more nascent countries, for instance, it's important to focus on Internet marketing and bringing new customers to the site before perfecting detailed category management or rolling out PayPal. Says Bannick, "You don't apply it cookie-cutter to every country."

The playbook hammers home one point above all others: Success is not foreordained, despite eBay's record to date. "If all markets were not essentially local," Wharton Business School professor Eric Clemmons explains, "everyone would just trade on eBay's U.S. site." As it happens, only 12 percent of eBay's total gross merchandise sales are cross-border transactions. Each country is a self-contained battlefield that must be won by slugging it out with rivals.

And eBay doesn't always triumph. In Japan, eBay was aced out by a joint venture between Yahoo and Softbank. Yahoo had only a five-month head start, but it took control of the field and never let go. Yahoo now sees more than $5 billion in transactions a year in Japan. eBay gave up on the country entirely in 2002.

Whitman says the main lesson from that experience was to "go early and go fast." That doesn't necessarily mean going all in; in China and Korea, eBay acquired minority stakes in existing sites and gradually upped the ante as it learned more about the market. In Korea alone, eBay spent $733 million over several years to buy up Internet Auction Co., one of the country's early e-commerce sites.

Today, Korea is eBay's third-largest international market. But when Jay Lee was installed as country manager there in May 2002, he inherited a catastrophe. The business was bleeding cash. Lee discovered that the founders were distracted by trying to move into unrelated areas like real estate listings and insurance. Lee set about refocusing the operation on online auctions, but his own local managers warned him that Korean consumers would never accept the auction concept.

A Korean himself, Lee understood that in Asia there's a stigma against buying used goods. "In Korea," he notes, "even among siblings, you don't pass down your clothes." But he believed that the need to trade is a basic human urge. (Indeed, Whitman often cites a universal primal

What Sells

eBay's global markets are highly individualized, as a sampling of local favorites demonstrates.

Brazil — SOCCER JERSEYS National hero Ronaldo's Real Madrid shirt has been in particular demand.

Britain — ROYAL FAMILY MEMORABILIA Princess Di teacups remain a favorite.

China — SKIN-CARE PRODUCTS Olay's Regenerist moisturizing lotion is a brisk seller.

France — WINE A 1959 Petrus goes for about $1,300, roughly half the brick-and-mortar price.

Germany — GARDEN GNOMES One sells roughly every six minutes.

Italy — COMIC BOOKS Bonelli Comics's Dylan Dog and Il Comandante Mark are huge sellers.

need to trade as eBay's great ace in the hole.) Lee focused on building up categories to auction off newer items like digital electronics, computers, and fashion. He encouraged enthusiasts to meet on the site's chat boards, where they organized into groups like the Digital Camera Mania Club and the Inline Skating Club that would organize outings and lessons—and talk up online trading. Today, eBay Korea is on track to produce $1 billion in annual online sales. And the stigma against buying used goods is fading, at least online. Such items, Lee says, currently make up 40 percent of eBay Korea's sales.

Lee is now trying to transplant his success to the rest of Asia. But the region is still anyone's gold mine. In addition to Japan, Yahoo is also the leading auction site in Taiwan and has operations in China, Hong Kong, and Singapore. "I think it is a country-by-country race," says Allan Kwan, Yahoo's regional vice president for North Asia.

At eBay, the defeat in Japan still stings, and the company is determined not to lose again. Lee thinks his advantage is eBay's all-consuming focus on auctions and nothing else. He's transferring a lot of the tricks he learned in Korea to China, including offering escrow accounts to build trust in e-commerce. He's also working with Chinese officials to create a "job garden" where potential eBay merchants can learn how to sell online. Today, China is one of eBay's fastest-growing markets; it now has 90 million Internet users. The United States has 200 million. Whitman believes that within five years, there will be more people on the Web in China than in America.

Given the vast potential for eBay in places like China and India, it's not hard to see why some analysts think the company could be entering a phase of enormous profitability. Analyst Mark Mahaney of American Technology Research predicts that international sales will account for 65 percent of eBay's total revenue growth this year, up from 60 percent in 2004. Mahaney estimates that by 2006, fueled by foreign growth, eBay will earn $1.5 billion on revenue of more than $5 billion. It took Microsoft two decades to hit those figures.

Whitman and her team will have to work to make those gaudy numbers, of course. One challenge is how to get global markets to adapt readily to PayPal, eBay's payment mechanism. In much of Asia, for example, such electronic payment systems remain a mystery, and many eBay deals are sealed only with face-to-face cash payments. Another issue: the uncertainty of different countries' laws.

Recently, eBay's top manager in India was busted after a pornographic video was offered on the site. But for Whitman, whether eBay can sustain its international march will turn on a more basic question: Can the company continue to create markets where none existed before, and to find the inner electronic trader in people who never imagined that they had one?

People like Michel Suret-Canale, for instance.

For 30 years a struggling French artist who had difficulty selling his work, Suret-Canale began listing his experimental "robotic paintings" and classic nudes on eBay five years ago. Since then he's sold 4,000 works of art directly to collectors as far away as the United States and Asia, for about $100 a painting. He just quit his day job as an art teacher. He feels he has finally found his audience. "I am like a singer, and for 30 years I have been singing in an empty room," he says. Now, thanks to eBay, he's on a global stage. And eBay has a fresh entry for the playbook.

Buyer Behavior

American Demographics:

Families spend less on food as they pursue house, car dreams

Labor Bureau stats also show decline in share spent on apparel

Bradley Johnson. Advertising Age.

THE AVERAGE AMERICAN family spent $40,817 on goods and services in 2003. Where'd the money go? More than half of the budget went for the house (33¢ of every dollar) and car (19¢). After paying for food (13¢), medical bills (6¢), a little booze (1¢) and more, families had a nickel left to spend on entertainment.

Household spending has increased tenfold since 1950, according to the Bureau of Labor Statistics. Factor in inflation, and the increase is less dramatic. Spending, adjusted for inflation, rose from about $29,000 in 1950 to $37,000 in 1972. Since then, spending has seen smaller real increases.

Viewed over the long term, statistics prove a point:

OFF THE CHARTS

18%/41%

Share of household food budgets spent on out-of-home meals in 1950 and 2003

$198/$237

Average spending on alcohol and tobacco in 2003 for households in bottom 20% of income

$902/$281

Average spending on alcohol and tobacco for top 20% of households

3.1%/2.6%

Share of budget spent on education for bottom and top 20% of households

Source: Bureau of Labor Statistics' 2003 Consumer Expenditure Survey

Americans' real income has increased, which leads to more consumption, which leads to changing priorities. A primer on consumer spending patterns over the decades and a closer look at 2003, based on labor statistics data:

FOOD

The most dramatic change in consumer spending is food's shrinking share of wallet. Food accounted for 13¢ of each consumer dollar in 2003, down from 32¢ in 1950 and 43¢ in 1901. A big change—and fully expected as the nation's income grew. It confirms Engel's Law, the observation by 19th century German statistician Ernst Engel that the proportion of income spent on food falls as income rises.

Rising income also means more dining out. Restaurant dining and takeout food accounted for 41% of food spending in 2003, up from 21% in 1960.

Rich and poor allocate the same amount of spending—about 5.5¢ of each dollar—on away-from-home meals, according to the bureau's latest Consumer Expenditure Survey. But share of food budget devoted to dining out increases with wealth. The poorest fifth of families spent one-third of food budgets on away-from-home meals in 2003. The top fifth spent slightly more dining out ($4,535) than eating at home ($4,503).

HOUSING

The drop in the food budget frees up income. Much of the extra money has gone into the American dreams of house and car.

Americans are buying more—and bigger—homes. The Census Bureau says 69% of families own homes today, vs. 63% in 1965. The average new house today is 2,300 square feet, vs. about 1,500 square feet in the mid'60s and below 1,000 square feet in 1950, according to the National Association of Home Builders. Those rooms need to be furnished. Add it up, and housing accounted for 33¢ of every dollar of consumer spending in 2003, up from 26¢ in 1950.

(Cont.)

TRANSPORTATION

Transport costs took 19¢ of every consumer dollar in 2003, up from 15¢ in 1960. The reason is more—and more expensive—cars. One in 17 Americans bought a new car in 2004, vs. one of 25 in 1960, according to census data and sales figures from *Automotive News*. In 1960, a basic Ford sedan cost $2,257, or $14,000 in 2003 dollars. In 2003, the average transaction price for a new vehicle was about $25,000.

The annual Consumer Expenditure Survey shows how reliant auto marketers are on upper-income buyers. In 2003, households in the bottom three quintiles of income spent more money on used cars than new. The second-highest income group spent only a little more on new cars. Only the top 20% overwhelmingly splurged for that new car smell. The top fifth of households spent almost as much on new cars as the bottom 80% combined.

Rich and poor drive different wheels. Simmons' spring 2004 National Consumer Survey found lower-income households are 70% more likely than the average household to drive a Mercury, not good news for Ford Motor Co.'s ailing upmarket brand. The rich favor lux brands BMW, Infiniti and Lexus.

APPAREL

The average household spent 12% of its budget on apparel and shoes in 1950, but that fell to 8% in 1972, 6% in 1984, 5% in 1993 and 4% in 2003.

Inflation has been held in check by the rise of low-cost foreign production and discounters like Wal-Mart; $100 of clothing in 1984 would have cost $116 in 1993—and the same $116 today, according to Consumer Price Index data. Households tend to allocate a similar share of the budget to clothes—4% to 5%—regardless of income.

ENTERTAINMENT

The share of money spent on entertainment has hovered around 5% since 1950, but priorities have shifted. Spending on consumer electronics has soared; spending on newspapers, magazines and books has plummeted. The average household apportioned just 0.3% of spending ($127) for reading materials in 2003, down from 1% ($51, or $317 adjusted for inflation) in 1960.

The rich, who also are more educated, spend more money on print media and books than the poor do. But don't read too much into that. It turns out households in every quintile of income spent the same average 0.3% of budget on reading in 2003. For publishers, that doesn't make cents.

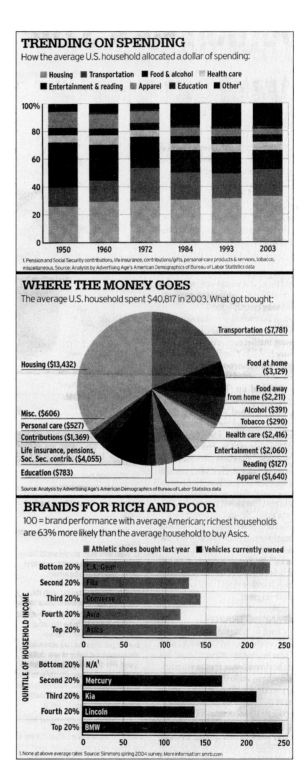

In iPod America, legions in tune
Apple's hip music player inspires fanatical devotion

Marco R. della Cava
USA TODAY

SAN FRANCISCO—With its high-tech decor and clubby feel, Apple's flagship store here doesn't look like a creepy cult headquarters. But there's some kind of mind-noodling going on: Everyone exiting its glass doors is ready to spout the gospel of iPod.

"I love the sound quality and how many songs I can carry around," says real estate agent Paige Baron, 25, running her fingers over a pink iPod Mini. "My friends all have one, and I just felt it was time to catch up."

She has just joined the iPod nation. Apple may have introduced its innovative digital music player in 2001, but of the 10 million iPods sold to date, 8.2 million of the $249 to $399 gadgets were purchased in 2004. Nearly 5 million were bought over the holiday season alone. With its new $99 Shuffle, Apple expects the streets to soon sprout even more iPod people.

"This is all part of the shift from mass media to personalized media," says Paul Saffo, research director of the Institute for the Future, a tech think tank in Palo Alto, Calif. "With the iPod, the Buddha is in the details. The finish and feel are such that you want to caress it."

"And when you do, wonderful things happen."

For the gizmo-impaired, an iPod is a white plastic rectangle the size of a deck of cards. It allows you to cart around up to 10,000 of your favorite songs and navigate through them with the flick of a thumb. All of which makes its cultural predecessor—Sony's cassette-based Walkman—seem like a relic of the Flintstone Age.

Befitting a contraption that has captured the fancy of everyone from working stiffs to head-bopping celebrities like Nicole Kidman and Leonardo DiCaprio, the iPod has created its own:

▶ **Economy.** Dozens of new companies cater to the faithful, including accessory manufacturers that turn your iPod into a digital audio recorder; fashion firms making clothes with iPod-ready pockets; and companies that will load your entire CD collection onto your iPod.

▶ **Cultural trends.** Some nightclubs are offering patrons the chance to DJ via their iPods, while even bolder owners practice iPod "jacking," momentarily swapping units with a stranger to tap into another devotee's musical soul.

▶ **Naysayers.** Some consumers still balk at the top-of-the-line iPod's cost, and others have yet to be convinced that Apple's version of the MP3 player will ultimately dominate the category. Recently, Dell CEO Kevin Rollins dissed the iPod as a "one-product wonder" that his and other companies would top soon.

Tell that to iPod's legions and get ready to duck. All you need to know is that one woman calls hers My Precious after the prized *Lord of the Rings* talisman.

THIS DEVICE 'HAS CHANGED MY LIFE'

Interviews with owners of various ages tell the same unsolicited tale. They shun today's radio programming (too much talk, not enough good songs) and resent buying CDs that are full of songs they don't want (they gladly spend 99 cents a song at Apple's iTunes online music store, where 1.2 million songs are snapped up daily).

"This is no fad—the iPod has changed my life," says Andrea Kozek, 29, a health care professional from Milwaukee and owner of, yes, My Precious.

Between hours on planes and at the gym, Kozek is rarely iPodless.

"When I need to block out the rest of the world, I turn it on," she says. "Forget about radio stations. Do I really want to hear Britney Spears doing Bobby Brown's *My Prerogative?* It wasn't a good song the first time around."

Such paeans spell good news for anyone in the portable digital music market. One innovative success story belongs to New York-based RipDigital, which offers busy people quick entry into the iPod world.

Say you've collected hundreds of CDs but cringe at the thought of loading—or "ripping"—those discs into your computer for transfer to an iPod. In fact, at roughly 10 minutes of ripping time per CD, a collection of 150 would take "four weekends of your free time," RipDigital founder Richard Adams says.

For roughly a dollar a CD, Rip Digital and competitors such as Get Digital and LoadPod will send you packing material for your collection, transfer that

(Cont.)

collection either onto a DVD or an external hard drive, and ship it back in a comparative wink.

"We've been making hay since Christmas, thanks to the iPod," Adams says. "People who never adopt tech gadgets seem to have adopted this one. It looks great and isn't intimidating."

Rival MP3 makers hoping to chase down Apple's runaway hit have their work cut out: Maverick CEO Steve Jobs has his foot to the company's floorboard.

Newer offerings include both the already popular Shuffle, which can hold up to 240 songs and is the size of a stick of gum, and the iPod Photo. In its 60-gigabyte incarnation, the iPod Photo will swallow up to 15,000 songs and as many as 25,000 photos, which can be viewed on a full-color screen.

The Cupertino, Calif.-based company also is expanding on its work with BMW—which offers an iPod-ready vehicle—in an effort to get automakers from upmarket Mercedes to Toyota's populist Scion brand to provide iPod owners a seamless transition from home to dashboard.

"We had no idea this thing would get this huge, but now that we do, we just plan to innovate faster than any of our competitors," Apple Senior Vice President Phil Schiller says.

Even with the right gee-whiz hardware, other MP3 makers still have to contend with Apple's *coup de grace*. Simply put, the iPod is the king of cool.

How cool? Consider that last year, Jonathan Ive, the iPod's British-born designer, took the BBC's title of Britain's most influential cultural figure, beating out *Harry Potter* creator J.K. Rowling and *The Office* star Ricky Gervais.

'It's what everyone wants'

When you literally rock the world, folks notice.

"When I was a teen, I went everywhere with my AM transistor radio," says Linda Iroff of Oberlin (Ohio) College's information technology department. "Then, that was the coolest thing. Now the iPod is. It's what everyone wants."

Iroff should know. Oberlin, which is renowned for its music conservatory, allows its students to share their music—listening only, no copying—via Apple's iTunes software, which is networked throughout the campus.

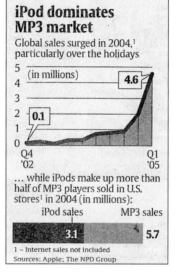

iPod dominates MP3 market

Global sales surged in 2004,[1] particularly over the holidays

(in millions) 4.6 ... 0.1

Q4 '02 — Q1 '05

... while iPods make up more than half of MP3 players sold in U.S. stores[1] in 2004 (in millions):

iPod sales 3.1 — MP3 sales 5.7

1 – Internet sales not included
Sources: Apple; The NPD Group

"I'll get an instant message from a friend saying, 'I have a song you should check out,' and that's been a great way to listen to artists I've never heard of," says junior Ethan Baldwin, 20. "And, of course, everything gets zipped to my iPod. It goes everywhere, the car, the gym, to work, everywhere."

Students at Duke University in Durham, N.C., can be seen clutching their iPods for another reason.

This past fall, the school decided to issue nearly 2,000 iPods to incoming freshmen, as well as some upperclassmen and professors. Dubbed the "iPod First-Year Experience," the program is meant to make language classes and lecture-heavy courses easier by providing students with the handy audio tool.

"The iPod is such a pop-culture phenomenon that we wanted to see if there was a way to use it to enhance the academic experience," says Tracy Futhey, Duke's vice president for information technology. "There are more uses for this thing than you can imagine."

That includes the nascent practice of Podcasting, essentially an audio version of blogging. Instead of posting your thoughts to a personal Web log, imagine recording anything from a movie review to chats with a friend and making that session available for download to an iPod (hence the name) or any other MP3 player.

iPods also are turning the average clubgoer into a tastemaker for the masses. Cafe Saint-Ex in Washington, D.C., hosts a monthly party in its Gate 54 lounge during which iPod owners are allowed to plug their devices into the sound system and give fellow revelers a taste of their own collections.

"We've found that everyone wants to be a DJ for 15 minutes," general manager John Snellgrove says. "Most of the music people play is pretty modern. Sometimes things are a bit off, but nobody boos or anything. A lot of times people wind up posting their set lists on Web sites so people can see what music they heard."

That sense of sharing musical passions is behind the quirky custom of iPod-jacking, which requires an openness usually not found in today's fast-paced world. When Steve Crandall started spotting other iPod listeners during his ritual walk around his condo complex in

(Cont.)

Basking Ridge, N.J., he began to make eye contact.

"One day, a girl made eye contact back with me, pulled her headphones out of her jack and offered me her iPod. I took it, gave her mine, and not a word was said," says Crandall, 51, the technology chief at a design research company. "After a few minutes, we swapped back, nodded, and moved on."

What was on her iPod? "Very cool stuff, specifically modern versions of Sami music from Lapland," Crandall says. After that encounter, he found himself—perhaps unwisely—approaching strangers in New York with his iPod proffered. "People don't always seem that social there," he laughs. "But you know, when I did that, a lot of people responded in kind."

Russell Miller knows the feeling. While riding the local train one day, the 19-year-old sophomore at the University of Miami approached a woman with an iPod and asked what she had playing.

"She had Radiohead on, which I love. And she was very cute," Miller says. He didn't get a date, "but I got to listen to that song, and that was pretty cool."

There's that word again: cool. It pops up time and again in conversations with iPod faithful.

Not long after Lauren Fix bought her green iPod Mini, she took it on a flight. Someone thought it was "so cool they offered to buy it from me on the spot, and I told him he was crazy," the auto journalist and mother of two says. Every member of her family has an iPod.

"We'll all be listening to our own music at the same time: I'll be connected to iTunes on my laptop, my kids will have the iPods on, and my husband likes to listen to his while he's surfing around on eBay," says Fix, 40, of Williamsville, N.Y.

The combination of a plane ride and an iPod helped Bruce Carroll reconnect with an old friend he didn't see much anymore.

After "counting the minutes until 10,000 feet, when I could turn on my iPod," Carroll, 36, of Chantilly, Va., heard a song in his random mix of personal tunes that reminded him of his buddy. When he landed, he e-mailed the friend, simply putting a choice lyric from the song in the "Subject" field.

"He was in the middle of a business meeting, but he burst out laughing," Carroll recalls. "That song triggered memories of our strong friendship. I absolutely love my iPod."

Yes, there are naysayers

But rest assured, not everyone is a devoted follower. In fact, some have yet to see the appeal of digital music at all.

"While I love music, I don't have an iPod and don't really have an interest in one," says Jason Andracki, 30, of Meadville, Pa. "I feel music loses something when it's removed from the album format and doesn't include liner notes and artwork."

Fair point, Jason. Stick to those old-school guns. Just don't wander by an Apple store, where a cooing salesman might show you how the new iPod Photo allows you to download album art to your tiny full-color screen. For Apple, there are no disinterested consumers—just nonbelievers to convert.

Advertising

China's Cultural Fabric Is a Challenge to Marketers

By Geoffrey A. Fowler

STRIKING A PATRIOTIC chord might not help you win customers in China, but offending national pride is a surefire way to lose them.

It is a lesson that **Toyota Motor** of Japan learned the hard way. In December, the auto maker had to pull and formally apologize for 30 magazine and newspaper advertisements depicting stone lions—a traditional sign of Chinese power—saluting and bowing to a Prado Land Cruiser sport-utility vehicle.

"These ads were intended to reflect Prado's imposing presence when driving in the city," says Julie Du, account manager with **Publicis Groupe's** Saatchi & Saatchi, which made the ads.

"You cannot but respect the Prado," the ad says.

But Chinese words often hold multiple meanings. Prado translates into Chinese as *badao,* which also means "rule by force" or "overbearing."

Consumer critics who called Toyota and posted scathing—occasionally profane—messages in Internet discussion groups said the lions resembled those flanking the Marco Polo Bridge, the site near Beijing of the opening battle in Japan's 1937 invasion of China.

The Toyota fiasco highlights the tricky cultural and historical pitfalls that afflict marketing for even the savviest China-based foreign companies. On one hand, the ad industry increasingly agrees that despite rampant nationalism, patriotism doesn't build brands. But Toyota and others recently have discovered that they can't ignore how strongly politics shapes Chinese consumer sentiment.

As China's economy grows at breakneck pace and it prepares for the 2008 Olympics in Beijing, Chinese people may be growing more nationalistic. An October 2003 survey by **WPP Group's** Ogilvy & Mather advertising firm found that 34% of young people in prosperous southern China found patriotism to be "extremely important"—a 10 on a scale of one to 10.

"Young people are indoctrinated from very early on in school to be patriotic," says

Toyota's **Prado** campaign hit a nerve with some Chinese consumers. Critics say the lions resemble those at the site of the opening battle during Japan's 1937 invasion of China.

Joseph Wang, Ogilvy's group managing director for Hong Kong and southern China.

Some Chinese brands such as **Coca-Cola** competitors **Jianlibao** and **Fei Chang Kele** try to tap that patriotism in ads. "The Chinese people's own Cola!" exhorts ads for Fei Chang Kele.

But an increasing number of ad agencies are finding that a patriotic appeal doesn't lure Chinese shoppers to sportswear brands such as homegrown favorite **Li-Ning Sports Goods** over **Nike** just because it originates in China.

Indeed, the Ogilvy survey found that the strongest patriots were just as likely to buy foreign brands as shoppers who claimed to be indifferent. Ninety-four percent of the "more patriotic" drank Coke, compared with 100% of the "moderately patriotic." Only 19% considered country of origin a factor in brand choice.

"Brand-buying today is a personal activity. Patriotism is [a] collective activity," Ogilvy's Mr. Wang explains.

As a result, agencies are dumping patriotic pitches in favor of pragmatism. "It's the same as in politics: A political party can go only so far on a patriotic platform. Ultimately, if they don't deliver the goods, voters give them the boot," says Mickey Chak, planning director of DDB Worldwide Communications Group Inc. China.

Foreign sportswear makers who sponsor local Chinese teams often receive a lukewarm response. As a result, brands increasingly are highlighting their global significance instead. "Many sports fans in China aren't just interested in a sport because there are Chinese players in it," Mr. Chak says. "Long before Yao Ming, basketball enjoyed popu-

larity, and Chinese consumers bought into the NBA."

But even though they are dumping patriotism, advertisers such as Toyota have bungled by going too far and ignoring it.

Despite longstanding wartime antagonisms, the Chinese have become major consumers of Japanese products—which carry a high-quality cachet—even as they complain about accidents involving Japanese products, or Japanese service manuals that make political gaffes by identifying Taiwan as separate from China.

Bayerische Motoren Werke of Germany faced weeks of negative publicity in state-run newspapers during October after a woman in the northeastern Chinese city of Harbin crashed into a crowd with her BMW X53.0 Diesel Sport. Marketed to China's elite upper-class, the BMW brand became a target of populist resentment from millions of laid-off former state workers left behind by China's economic boom.

Many agencies have implemented "disaster checks" before their campaigns go live to make sure that they haven't been blinded to a political sore spot.

Toyota will establish a "supervisory system" for its marketing, a public-relations officer in charge of its Chinese office says.

Saatchi & Saatchi, which declined to discuss the role of patriotism in advertising, is working on new Toyota Prado ads but doesn't yet have a release date for them.

From *The Wall Street Journal,* January 21, 2004. Reprinted by permission of Dow Jones and Co., Inc. via The Copyright Clearance Center.

Top Online Chemical Exchange Is Unlikely Success Story

BY JULIA ANGWIN

IN 1999, John F. Beasley bragged that his Web start-up **ChemConnect** Inc. was likely to become the "largest business-to-business exchange on the Internet, period." Now, his assessment is a bit different: "It's better to own a smaller piece of a watermelon than an entire grape," he says.

Times have changed since the heady days when online business-to-business exchanges like ChemConnect thought they could revolutionize the world. Most of the entrepreneurs who built online trading platforms for industries ranging from steel to auto parts failed. The Old Economy companies that were supposed to be crushed by the upstarts have generally prevailed with their own online exchanges.

ChemConnect, however, is an unlikely success story. It is now the biggest online exchange for chemical trading, with volume of $8.8 billion in 2002, the latest figure available. Customers like Tom Garner, president of **Vanguard Petroleum** Corp. in Houston, have come to rely on ChemConnect for their business.

Mr. Garner says about 15% of his spot purchases and sales of natural-gas liquids are conducted on ChemConnect's commodities trading site. "Before, I would have had to beat the phones to death," he says. Now, "I'll post it online and 150 people are seeing it. It would take me all day to canvass that many people."

One key to ChemConnect's survival was speed. It was first to market, launching an Internet bulletin board in 1995. It was also the fastest and best fund-raiser among its dozens of competitors—bringing in $105 million by the time the stock-market bubble burst in 2000, compared with $50 million for its chief competitor, **CheMatch.com.** Mr. Beasley also realized that the only way to persuade traditional chemical companies to trade online was to allow the industry to

profit from ChemConnect—so he sold about one-third of the company to more than 40 chemical companies.

ChemConnect still isn't profitable, although it expects to break even this year. And while it is used by about 44% of the industry, many sellers wish there were more buyers online, according to a survey of 250 chemical buyers and sellers by AMR Research. "The key now is to basically be as patient as you can, but to continue to push the adoption curve," Mr. Beasley says.

When he founded ChemConnect in 1995, Mr. Beasley was 31 years old and a vice president of mergers and acquisitions at First Physician Care, an Atlanta physician-management practice. Bored with that, he decided to become an entrepreneur. He had no computer and knew nothing about the chemical business. But when he went to the library to search for ideas, he was intrigued by books about a giant network of computers called the Internet. So he asked his friend Jay Hall, who had some computer experience, to meet him for pizza.

Over beer and thin-crust pies, Mr. Beasley proposed some ideas he thought might work on the Internet, such as selling motorcycles or jeans overseas. But Mr. Hall had other ideas. Although he was an electrical engineer by training, he had been drafted to help sell his father's chemical business. "I said, 'The chemical industry is the most backward industry in the world,'" Mr. Hall recalls. (He says his view has changed since then.) Messrs. Beasley and Hall decided to set up a way for chemical companies to find suppliers online.

Together, they invested $10,000 in computer equipment and set up shop in Mr. Hall's spare bedroom—a loft that was "blistering hot and very cramped," Mr. Hall recalls. After work and on weekends, the two taught themselves Web programming and typed in lists of chemical suppliers to create an online directory. Within a month and a half, they had built an Internet bulletin board and were accepting classified advertising from chemical companies. Each listing cost $100.

In the spring of 1996, the partners hired Patrick van der Valk, a Dutch chemist, to build a Web site that would allow buyers and sellers to electronically post their listings, and eventually they made him a partner in the business. Their first customers were Indian and Chinese companies aiming to sell chemicals in the U.S. By 1998, they had 10,000 customers.

Competitors also were popping up. "We knew if we didn't raise money we'd be dead," Mr. Beasley recalls. So the team made the rounds of investors in Silicon Valley, eventually raising $4 million from Institutional Venture Partners and relocating to the San Francisco Bay area.

The pressure to get big fast was intense. More than a dozen chemical exchanges had emerged by 2000, led by CheMatch.com, which had lined up support from **DuPont** Co., while ChemConnect had backing from **Dow Chemical** Co.

Mr. Beasley launched himself into a frenzy of fund-raising, flying around the world to meet with chemical companies. In the spring of 2000, he raised $72 million from 38 of them. To keep the exchange neutral, he limited each company to, at most, a 5% stake. His success scared his rivals. "His ability to raise money was constantly sticking in my side," recalls Dave Tabors of Battery Ventures, who was an investor in CheMatch.

Mr. Beasley had his own moment of panic when CheMatch filed for an initial public offering before ChemConnect did.

"It was a pretty scary moment," Mr. Beasley recalls. "Had they been successful, they would have had a very significant amount of capital." Ultimately, neither firm went public because each failed to launch an IPO before the dot-com bubble burst.

With its hefty cash hoard, ChemConnect took the opportunity to buy competitors, including CheMatch.com and an industry-owned exchange. Mr. Beasley also recruited a seasoned chemical executive, John Robinson, to run the company as chief executive, while Mr. Beasley remained chairman.

The company has since moved from its flashy San Francisco offices to more modest quarters in Houston. Its staff has shrunk to 60 from about 190 during the boom era. And Mr. Beasley, who still lives in San Francisco, has more time for his hobby of motorcycle racing.

On a clear San Francisco day, he takes a visitor for a ride on his limited-edition Italian motorcycle. The sign overlooking the Golden Gate Bridge says "15 MPH," but he takes the hairpin turn at about 50 miles per hour. "The faster you go, the more intensely you have to focus," he says.

Material Effect

For Caterpillar, Commodity Boom Creates a Bind

Lofty Prices for Metals, Oil Lead to Soaring Sales But Large Tab for Supplies

Searching for Really Big Tires

TIMOTHY AEPPEL. WALL STREET JOURNAL.

PEORIA, Ill.—All over the world, high commodity prices have more companies digging for iron ore, copper and coal. They need new roads to move these materials, and new warehouses and port equipment. That's all good news for Caterpillar Inc., which has seen demand rise sharply for its familiar yellow tractors, trucks and bulldozers.

As the increase in commodity prices ripples through the world economy, Caterpillar is just one of a broad array of companies—from heavy-equipment makers to steel mills to chemical plants—finding it can raise prices more than at any time since the 1970s. Behind the surge: rebounding industrial growth, especially the voracious demand for commodities from burgeoning China and India.

For Caterpillar and other companies benefiting from the commodities boom, there is also a down side: Manufacturers, like everyone else, have to pay more for many supplies. With demand raging, just finding enough metal parts has become a challenge for Caterpillar.

Caterpillar, which almost never adjusts prices more than once a year, imposed an extra increase in July that averaged 3% and has announced another 3% boost for this month. "A bit of inflation is actually the optimum," the company's chief executive, Jim Owens, says, but nobody at Caterpillar anticipated the ferocity of the commodities surge that began about a year ago.

The world's largest producer of construction and mining equipment and diesel and natural-gas engines, Caterpillar sells machines to mine coal in Australia and build gas pipelines in Siberia. It also benefits from the broader economic growth that accompanies

a commodities boom: Workers at busier factories earn more money, which allows them to buy new houses, requiring builders to buy more bulldozers.

The commodity-price increases have been striking. Aluminum rose nearly 25% in 2004, copper by more than 37% and lead by more than 40%. Oil soared to $55 a barrel but has moderated recently, ending the year up almost 34%. Caterpillar's biggest material cost by far is steel. The spot price of steel plate, which it uses to make its machines, shot up 106% last year. Caterpillar, one of the world's largest consumers of steel plate, uses its heft to negotiate better deals, but the prices it has paid rose sharply, too.

Higher commodity and energy prices have helped push up overall inflation, although in the service-heavy U.S. economy, that translates into relatively modest changes. Consumer prices in the U.S. rose a seasonally adjusted 3.7% in the first 11 months of 2004, compared with 1.9% for all of 2003. Federal Reserve officials predict this won't lead to long-term higher inflation. But they are raising interest rates anyway, in part to try to prevent commodity-price increases from sparking corporate and individual expectations of greater inflation.

Daniel Meckstroth, an economist at the Manufacturers Alliance/MAPI, an association of manufacturing companies in Arlington, Va., says the latest upswing in commodity prices was heightened by the length of the slump that preceded it. Things were so grim for so long, many companies shuttered mines and steel mills, curtailing their ability to respond when demand finally snapped back.

"In June 2003, the whole world's manufacturing sector started to recover at the same time," says Mr. Meckstroth. That combined with the emergence of huge, low-wage economies—especially China's—to create a ravenous appetite for steel, copper, iron ore and oil. Mr. Meckstroth predicts that the supply of commodities will eventually catch up with demand and that commodity prices could start falling later this year.

Caterpillar reported the highest sales in its history for the nine-month period that ended Sept. 30, 2004: $21.68 billion, up 33% over the comparable period a year earlier. The company ordinarily makes impressive profits on its expensive machinery, and net earnings for the nine-month period rose 98%, to $1.48 billion, or $4.19 a share. But Mr. Owens says the company didn't even pass along to customers all of its steep supply-cost increases. Profits would have been even higher were it not for material costs and supply-chain bottlenecks, he told investors when announcing the results. Still, he predicted Caterpillar "will deliver record sales and profit" for 2004.

Caterpillar stock closed yesterday at

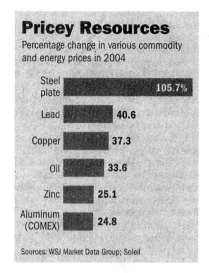

Pricey Resources

Percentage change in various commodity and energy prices in 2004

Steel plate	105.7%
Lead	40.6
Copper	37.3
Oil	33.6
Zinc	25.1
Aluminum (COMEX)	24.8

Sources: WSJ Market Data Group; Soleil

$95.07, down $2.44, in 4 p.m. New York Stock Exchange composite trading.

Tractor Innovation

Caterpillar was founded in 1925 by the merger of two equipment companies. Benjamin Holt, the head of one, developed one of the first commercially successful tractors that moved on tracks rather than wheels, making heavy vehicles better able to negotiate muddy, uneven terrain. Those machines' lumbering motion inspired the Caterpillar name.

Commodity prices have always helped dictate Caterpillar's fortunes, which have been prone to powerful swings up and down. In 2004, nearly every Caterpillar market skyrocketed, and the company expects to grow overall an additional 10% in 2005.

"We've had businesses go up dramatically before, but never like this," says Daniel Murphy, the company's head of global purchasing. He has one of the toughest jobs in a company vulnerable to supply bottlenecks.

Caterpillar's 16.5-acre assembly plant for track-type tractors in East Peoria illustrates how it is straining to meet huge demand. Every nook is filled with machinery, and 11 giant machines are parked near the back doors, waiting to be shipped. Most are so large they have to be disassembled to be put on trucks or fastened to railcars.

Two workers in one construction bay are busily attaching parts to a 22,000-pound metal frame, already painted Caterpillar yellow. The label on the frame shows it is destined for a coal-mining operation in Australia. The problem here, as elsewhere, is that the company's suppliers have struggled to fill parts orders.

"Cat wants 40% more product, but I

(Cont.)

can't make 40% more product," says James Griffith, chief executive of Timken Co., a Canton, Ohio, manufacturer of bearings and specialty steel. Mr. Griffith explains that he has other customers demanding more from him, too.

Even with sharply higher demand, Mr. Griffith and most other suppliers aren't building new plants. That's an example of the kind of cautiousness that has persisted in a range of industries, despite the overall economic upturn.

Caterpillar is no exception. The company has added thousands of workers world-wide, including 1,300 new members of the United Auto Workers at its big Midwestern plants. It now employs a total of 76,200. The company has also persuaded union workers to accept changes that allowed it to add more workers not covered by union agreements. Caterpillar managers say these shifts add enough capacity for now and that they are mainly hampered by supply shortages.

For example, the company says its usual suppliers haven't kept up with its hunger for more of the enormous tires that go on its machines. In response, Caterpillar has gone to new tire makers in China and Eastern Europe, a potential long-term threat to its traditional suppliers.

One of Caterpillar's long-term suppliers, Goodyear Rubber & Tire Co., based in Akron, Ohio, says through a spokesman that it doesn't comment on relations with customers. But Goodyear notes that there are natural constraints on making heavy-equipment tires. A 57-inch off-the-road tire, for instance, takes half a day just to cure, the last step of the production process in which a raw tire is heated and pressed into its final form. Goodyear produces only three of these huge tires a day. Caterpillar won't say how many it needs, but in 2004, it bought 240,000 tires of all kinds.

Japan's Bridgestone Corp., another Caterpillar supplier, announced in April a $100 million expansion at its Hofu plant in Japan to make more large tires. But that project won't be finished until the end of 2007. "We've increased our supply to Caterpillar and other major [equipment makers] in order to respond to their increased demand," says Christine Karbowiak, a Bridgestone spokeswoman.

Advising Suppliers

In some cases, Caterpillar has dispatched its own experts to help suppliers raise output. A foundry in Indiana nearly doubled its output of steel castings, to 115 tons a day, by reshuffling its manufacturing process with Caterpillar's assistance. One change involved cleaning castings before shipping, a time-consuming process that requires workers with blow torches and grinders. Caterpillar guided the supplier to outsource the grunt work to another company, freeing workers at the foundry to make more parts.

Caterpillar executives say they could probably raise prices for their machines even more, but they don't want to be accused of employing "rape and pillage" tactics. That could create openings for competitors, and it could sour relations with customers. Caterpillar's chief global competitor, Japan's Komatsu Ltd., announced price increases on April 1, the start of its fiscal year, including a 5% increase on mining equipment sold in North America.

Some heavy-equipment makers in specialty niches have more muscle to raise prices because they have few rivals. Bucyrus International Inc., the U.S. manufacturer that built the excavators used to dig the Panama Canal a century ago, has seen its raw-material prices soar 25% to 40% over the past year. The company has raised equipment prices enough to cover the higher costs and take some additional profit, as well, says Tim Sullivan, Bucyrus's chief executive. He declines to provide more detail on how much the commodity boom has contributed to the bottom line. He does say, "We're looking at a decade of higher inflation approaching, and it's starting with commodities."

Workers in Bucyrus's factory in South Milwaukee are assembling a massive metal platform that will replace the base on an existing dragline, a five-story-tall machine used in open mines to move vast amounts of earth. The customer, a multinational mining company that doesn't want to be named, agreed to pay $2.3 million for the dragline base in the fourth quarter of 2003. Bucyrus recently sold a similar part to another customer at $3.5 million, a 52% increase. Mr. Sullivan attributes the increase almost entirely to raw materials, above all steel. Labor costs rose only about 3.5% in 2004, as dictated by a contract with the United Steelworkers.

Overall, the company said its sales rose 32% in last year's third quarter, to $111.5 million. Bucyrus reported a net loss of $1 million for the quarter, down from a loss of $1.5 million in the comparable period in 2003. "Any time there's price turmoil in the marketplace, it's an opportunity," Mr. Sullivan says.

Donald Roof, chief financial officer of Joy Global Inc., another mining-equipment maker in Milwaukee, notes that 70% of his business is with coal mines that have seen coal prices double over the past year. "Our sale prices are going up faster than they have in a decade," Mr. Roof says. Joy's customers, including Consol Energy Inc., Massey Energy Co., and Phelps Dodge Corp., are pushing back on prices, Mr. Roof says, "so it'll still be a challenge."

But in a commodities boom, customers such as mining companies understand that rising raw-material prices can force equipment makers to raise their prices, too. "We've had health care, pension costs [and] regulatory costs going up for a long time, but it's definitely easier to make a case to a coal mine why we should be passing along a price increase for steel," says Richard White, executive vice president of Flexible Steel Lacing Co. in Downers Grove, Ill.

His company, which makes fasteners used to connect conveyor belts used in mines, instituted two price increases last year, each for between 5% and 6%. Aided additionally by a weaker dollar, which has made the company's products less expensive for foreign buyers, Flexible Steel has seen a strong upturn, Mr. White says. The closely held company has annual sales of more than $60 million, he adds, but it hasn't taken more profit as a result of recent price increases.

Caterpillar says it has offset some of its increased costs with productivity gains and other economies. The company three years ago instituted unified purchasing of steel and other materials for all of its plants. That gives it more leverage with suppliers. Caterpillar also buys large amounts of steel on behalf of its suppliers, effectively giving those smaller companies purchasing muscle they wouldn't have on their own.

Gerard Vittecoq, the group president responsible for Caterpillar's business in Europe, says the company has received strong support from its foreign suppliers, particularly those eager for more business. One supplier in Romania, for instance, wasn't getting enough electricity to increase production of castings for Caterpillar's plant in Grenoble, France. So the supplier, Uzinele Mecanice Timisoara, Romania's largest maker of lift and transport equipment, cut a deal with the city of Timisoara: It shifted more power to the plant at the expense of more electricity disruptions for residents.

30

A 'CHINA PRICE' FOR TOYOTA
The auto giant is taking its cost-slashing drive to a new level. Can its suppliers match China's cheaper parts?

Five years ago, Toyota Motor Corp. stunned the auto world by embarking on a plan to slash costs 30% across the board for the car parts it buys—from air-conditioning ducts and door-assist grips to windshield wipers. The bold plan to squeeze its own network of traditional suppliers, known as a *keiretsu,* was designed to make sure the Toyota group would retain its competitive edge against a spate of global auto alliances such as DaimlerChrysler, which promised gigantic synergies from their bigger size.

DaimlerChrysler is still struggling to make its merger pay off. But Toyota's cost-cutting program—dubbed CCC21, or Construction of Cost Competitiveness for the 21st Century—has been a remarkable success. With just one year to go, the plan is on track to save the auto maker some $10 billion over its five-year time frame. Not only is CCC21 sourcing components more cheaply but Toyota has also improved the parts' quality. The program has even bested archrival Nissan Motor Co., whose chief executive, Carlos Ghosn, kicked off the savings scramble in 1999 by pledging 20% cuts in procurement costs.

But where does Toyota go from here?

Even after putting its supply network through the wringer, Japan's No. 1 carmaker can ill afford to rest easy. Toyota may be under more pressure now to cut costs than when it began CCC21. So the drive is on to replace expensive materials, benchmark Toyota's auto parts against Chinese-level pricing, and squeeze its Japanese suppliers further by relying more on non-*keiretsu* parts makers. "We need to adjust our cost-cutting drive to meet a whole new set of challenges," says Katsuaki Watanabe, 62, the executive vice-president who helped devise and supervise CCC21. In a sign that streamlining is still a top priority, the company announced on Feb. 9 that Watanabe will take over as president of Toyota from Fujio Cho in June.

STEEL SHORTAGE

Watanabe is a demon at spotting costs that no one even knew existed and eliminating redundancies that few had noticed. Under his prodding, one Toyota CCC21 team disassembled the horns made by a Japanese supplier and found ways to eliminate six of 28 components, resulting in a 40% cost reduction. No part has been too mundane to escape the Watanabe squad's notice. His favorite example: interior assist grips above each door. There once were 35 different grips. Now, Toyota's entire 90-model lineup uses just three basic styles. Toyota gearheads call this process *kawaita zokin wo shiboru,* or "wringing drops from a dry towel." It's an unending, excruciating process, but essential to Toyota's bottom line.

But even Watanabe needs a new game plan to counter what's coming. Among the most pernicious threats: the surge in prices of crucial items such as sheet steel due to higher costs for raw materials like iron ore and coal. Blame China's voracious demand for steel and a shortage of Asian blast furnace capacity—factors that are unlikely to go away anytime soon. What's more, the strong yen means Toyota's reported profits from outside Japan come in lower, increasing the pressure to cut expenses.

These burdens come just as the automotive giant's latest cost-cutting push has started to run out of steam. On Feb. 3 the company acknowledged its cost cuts will likely total just $1.7 billion for the fiscal year ending in March, 15% short of its annual target, in large part because of the surge in sheet steel prices. Nikko Citigroup Ltd. notes that the pace of cost cuts has slowed to $388 million in the most recent quarter, down from $582 million a year earlier.

To cope, Watanabe is pushing Toyota to winnow down the number of steel parts it uses in an average vehicle from 610 to about 500, although it won't say by when or how much savings that will net. Toyota will probably turn to more steel substitutes such as aluminum and heavy-duty advanced plastics and resins. Moving away from steel goes hand-in-hand with the company's longer-term goal of cutting the weight of its vehicles to increase fuel efficiency and rust-proof durability.

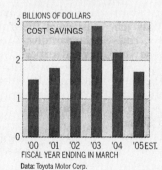

Toyota's **Cost Cutting**

Since 2000, the Construction of Cost Competitiveness for the 21st Century— CCC21—has helped Toyota cut procurement costs by nearly a third. But as the program winds down, Toyota is looking for new places to trim the fat.

SAVINGS SO FAR...

BILLIONS OF DOLLARS

COST SAVINGS

'00 '01 '02 '03 '04 '05 EST.
FISCAL YEAR ENDING IN MARCH

Data: Toyota Motor Corp.

...AND WHAT'S NEXT

■ Cutting steel parts in cars from 610 to 500 to deal with the soaring cost of steel

■ Forcing some component makers to meet or beat rock-bottom prices offered by suppliers in China

■ Buying from more parts manufacturers not affiliated with Toyota's *keiretsu,* or corporate fraternity

(Cont.)

That said, there's a limit to how many steel parts Toyota can replace. There's also no guarantee that prices of aluminum and petrochemicals won't skyrocket to the point where those materials are no longer cost-effective substitutes.

Something more is needed—and that's the China benchmark. Under CCC21, Watanabe's lieutenants identified about 180 key parts, then figured out who the world's most competitive suppliers of those parts were—companies like Robert Bosch of Germany, Delphi Corp., and the Toyota Group's own Denso Corp. The Toyota cost-cutters used this information as the "benchmark" against which Toyota's *keiretsu* suppliers had to compete. The *keiretsu* outfits must learn how to meet the benchmark—or risk losing the business. Toyota worked with affiliate Denso, for example, to consolidate production of air-conditioning vents to just four key styles, down from 27 previously. That resulted in a 28% cost reduction. Watanabe still wasn't happy: He had wanted just three.

Now the exercise goes to a whole new level. The boom in auto production in China is nurturing a car-parts industry—with both multinational suppliers and local companies—providing new data on how low prices can go. For now, that's mostly limited to commodity-type components such as assist grips, not high-end modules and core parts like brakes. Toyota officials say the rise of China has raised the bar for its *keiretsu* suppliers. They increasingly must push their prices toward the Chinese level to keep Toyota's business. "China has become an important new benchmark for us," says Watanabe.

This doesn't mean Toyota will soon start importing all its parts from China for use in its Japanese and U.S. factories. Analysts say it may be a decade before the parts makers in China can go toe-to-toe with components made in Japan, South Korea, and the U.S. The ultralow defect rates for parts made in Japan, for example, can be as important to cutting prices as cheap fixed costs. Even so, benchmarking against the Chinese price forces suppliers to come as close as possible to matching it without sacrificing quality. That involves rethinking everything, from the number of designers assigned to making any one part, to the supply chain involved in sourcing components, to the utilization rates of equipment at a parts factory.

The China benchmark will increase the pressure on Toyota's traditional suppliers. But so will the company's efforts to court more non-Japanese suppliers to find the best price. And parts makers like Bosch and Delphi, which turn out everything from air bags to transmissions, are now more willing to meet demanding specifications. Bosch, for example, supplies the complete brake system for the Toyota Avensis sedan and the diesel-injection system for the Toyota Yaris subcompact, both made in Europe. Toyota won't say how much of its parts purchasing comes from its *keiretsu* versus outsiders, but non-Japanese suppliers are eager to win a bigger share. No wonder: The auto maker expects its global sales to hit 8.5 million vehicles by next year, about 1 million more than in 2004. That will put it on par with General Motors Corp., the world's largest carmaker. "Toyota is an important customer for Bosch," says Bernd Bohr, chairman of the company's automotive group. "We maintain a close cooperative relationship with Toyota and in development projects."

Non-*keiretsu* suppliers see their best chance in markets where Toyota is expanding fastest, especially China, where the Japanese auto maker is eager to catch up with established rivals like GM and Volkswagen. "This is a great opportunity for outside suppliers to increase their business with us," says Watanabe. Those suppliers would love ultimately to win orders on a global basis—including in Japan, where local suppliers account for all but a fraction of the auto giant's parts purchases.

PART OF THE FAMILY

To show the depth of its commitment, Delphi now sends technicians to Toyota headquarters in Toyota City to collaborate on the blueprints for new parts, and invites Toyota execs to tour its plants and offer suggestions for improving productivity and increasing quality. Although Delphi won't disclose how much business it does with Toyota, less than 10% of its roughly $1 billion in Asian revenue comes from the Japanese. The company, however, says it has high hopes for supplying more to Toyota from its 13 plants in China. "We are becoming part of Toyota's extended *keiretsu* family," says Choon T. Chon, president of Delphi's Asia Pacific unit. And part of Watanabe's ruthless drive to cut costs to the bone.

Chester Dawson in Toyota City, with Karen Nickel Anhalt in Berlin. Business Week.

31

Wal-Mart's Low-Price Obsession Puts Suppliers Through Wringer

Duct tape manufacturer welcomes efficiencies that Wal-Mart requires.

. . . .

By Marilyn Much
Investor's Business Daily

Remember the rush on duct tape after the Homeland Security Department raised the terror alert to orange last February?

If you don't, Bill Kahl, executive vice president of marketing at Henkel Adhesives, can clue you in. As the maker of Duck brand duct tape, Henkel saw a spike in demand following the announcement.

During that time, Kahl and his team worked hard to keep a steady flow of the product in stores. Key customer Wal-Mart helped ease the burden. Using Wal-Mart's online Retail Link system, which gives its suppliers daily point-of-sale data, Kahl's team tracked inventory levels in the discount chain's regional warehouses.

When Wal-Mart centers in peak selling areas ran low, Henkel was able to fill the void by diverting shipments from other regions. The result? Henkel kept Wal-Mart stores fully stocked with duct tape even in the face of huge demand.

Wal-Mart's relentless pursuit of lower prices reaches well beyond creating efficiencies for its suppliers. The chain has helped drive down prices of goods, which benefits consumers. And through improvements in technology, it's bolstered the nation's productivity rate, economists say.

It's no secret that in its quest to create cost efficiencies throughout the retail supply chain, Wal-Mart helps its suppliers become leaner and more efficient.

"Working with Wal-Mart has made us a better company," Kahl said.

But Wal-Mart's pricing power is a double-edged sword. Smaller discount chains such as Caldor and Ames couldn't compete, and have gone out of business. And Wal-Mart's size and efficiency were key factors in

Kmart's filing for bankruptcy in 2002.

Wal-Mart is the world's biggest retailer. It has close to 3,500 stores in the U.S. and 4,844 worldwide. In fiscal 2004, it boasted an estimated $253.5 billion in sales. Wal-Mart accounts for about 10% of total U.S. retail sales, excluding autos. It holds between a 25% and 30% share of sales of most consumer staples—everything from detergent and batteries to toothpaste.

It's also the nation's No. 1 retailer of groceries, toys, DVDs, CDs and entertainment software, apparel and home textiles.

Pricing Pressure

Pricing is the most obvious effect Wal-Mart has on retailing and the economy, says Frank Badillo, senior economist at consulting firm Retail Forward Inc.

"Its (impact) is like a ripple in a pond," Badillo said.

With its huge negotiating power and economies of scale, Wal-Mart boasts retail's lowest cost structure. It passes those savings on to consumers. Though Wal-Mart has an impact on all retail prices, it's been exerting the most pressure in segments where it competes directly—discount chains and department stores, Badillo says. In 2003, prices in these segments fell at more than a 3% annual rate, on top of a more than 2% drop the year before.

> "By going back to a supplier and saying, 'Lower your costs by say 5%,' Wal-Mart is shifting (pricing pressure) downstream."

The effect of Wal-Mart's pricing power has rippled throughout the economy.

When Wal-Mart enters a new geographic market, general merchandise, food and apparel prices fall in that area by 2% to 10% in the course of a year, says Carl Steidtmann, chief economist at Deloitte Research.

Mapping Out Costs

Similarly, when Wal-Mart lowers prices in a product category, other stores typically follow suit. For instance, since Levi Strauss debuted its Signature brand of clothes for the mass merchandise channel in Wal-Mart stores last July, the entire basic denim category has experienced a big price reduction, says analyst Jeffrey Klinefelter of Piper Jaffray & Co. Overall, U.S. consumer goods prices fell by 2.5% in 2003 from 2002. Analysts say Wal-Mart played a roll in that decline.

As Wal-Mart has grown, it's had a direct impact on the total retail supply chain, says Michael Niemira, chief economist for the International Council of Shopping Centers.

Wal-Mart executives wouldn't comment for this story. But here's how Wal-Mart might work with a vendor, says James Allen, a Bain & Co. consultant: During negotiations, a Wal-Mart rep maps out how much the store intends to lower prices for consumers. If the supplier wants to do business with Wal-Mart, it has to bring its yearly costs down the same amount, says Allen.

"By going back to a supplier and saying, 'Lower your costs by say 5%,' Wal-Mart is shifting (pricing pressure) downstream," Niemira said.

For suppliers, working with Wal-Mart is a mixed bag. On the plus side, Wal-Mart will agree to large-scale, long-term contracts in return for lowered costs. That can motivate firms to seek ways to cut costs and improve their productivity.

But there are minuses. Wal-Mart's relentless cost pressure can lead vendors to cut corners, Allen says. For instance, in an effort to pare labor costs, a maker might end up sourcing through countries that have low safety and environmental standards and poor labor conditions.

U.S. firms have been outsourcing production to lower-cost nations for years. But the growth of Wal-Mart has accelerated that trend.

"With its scale and competencies, Wal-Mart has made the need greater for brand

(Cont.)

owners to (lower) costs because the prize is distribution at its stores," Allen said.

In its quest to pare costs, Wal-Mart has been one of the leaders in sourcing goods directly from China.

"This creates a chain reaction and forces other companies to follow.... We're seeing the pattern more and more," said Badillo of Retail Forward.

He notes that No. 2 discounter Target set up a sourcing center in Shenzhen, China, in September. Chris Huber, Target's director of sourcing services, told China Daily that the retailer expects to double procurement from China this year over last. Badillo also cites the fact that early this month, Levi Strauss closed its last two U.S. sewing plants, and this spring it will shut its three plants in Canada, completing a shift to production in China and other countries with cheaper labor.

Then there's the effect Wal-Mart has on other retailers. Not only is the store making it tough for discounters to compete, but as the nation's No. 1 grocer it's also creating headaches for supermarkets.

A lot has to do with Wal-Mart's low-cost structure. It's more efficient than traditional supermarkets in terms of logistics and distribution. It's also a nonunion shop that pays lower wages and offers fewer costly benefits than supermarkets, which are unionized.

When you combine all its efficiencies, Wal-Mart has a 20% to 30% cost advantage over supermarkets, says Sandy Skrovan, a vice president at Retail Forward.

Wal-Mart charges 15% to 20% less on core items like beverages and paper towels. In so doing, Wal-Mart has increased its share of total consumer spending on consumable goods to 8% of the total in 2002 from 5% in 1997, Skrovan says.

As Wal-Mart has expanded its share of the grocery market and made the field more competitive, it's helped drive 13,000 mom and pop stores out of business in the last decade, Skrovan figures. She expects another 2,000 stores to close in the next five years, due largely to Wal-Mart's competitive stance.

32

BlackBerry Maker Finds Friend In Uncle Sam

Targeting Public Sector.

. . . .

By **PATRICK SEITZ**
Investor's Business Daily

For Research In Motion Ltd., the daily scene on Capitol Hill is a dream come true. Practically everywhere, congressmen, staffers and lobbyists are using RIM's BlackBerry handheld e-mail devices.

A few years ago, RIM focused its sales efforts on New York City and the financial community. But the world changed after 9-11, and so did RIM's business.

Government customers, such as Congress and the Defense Department, have become in aggregate the largest category of BlackBerry users, says Don Morrison, chief operating officer of RIM. Government officials are using "tens of thousands" of the palm-sized devices with their distinctive thumb keyboards.

"Since 9-11, because of BlackBerry's performance under crisis situations, the government market has eclipsed the finance market in terms of actual number of users," Morrison said.

He estimates government users account for 10% of the more than 1 million subscribers to BlackBerry's wireless data service.

One question facing RIM is whether the widespread use of BlackBerry devices in Washington, D.C., is a unique situation or something it can replicate elsewhere.

After 9-11, Congress spent $6 million to buy 3,000 BlackBerrys for members and their staffs and to set up secure wireless messaging.

The move was criticized because RIM is a Canadian firm and Congress rushed ahead with the purchase. U.S.-based rivals such as Palm Inc. didn't get a chance to bid.

As chairman of the House Administration Committee, Rep. Robert Ney, R-Ohio, made the decision to buy BlackBerrys for all 435 members of the House and their staffs and link them to the emergency communications network. Ney was sold on BlackBerrys because they worked on Sept. 11, 2001, when cell phone networks were overloaded, says Ney's spokesman, Brian Walsh.

At the time, the BlackBerry was the only device available that met Congress' data encryption and communications needs, Walsh says. The House network now supports 3,700 BlackBerrys, Walsh says. BlackBerrys aren't as widespread or coordinated on the Senate side, he says.

On Feb. 2, after the discovery of the poison ricin in the Dirksen Senate Office Building, House members and their staffs were alerted on their BlackBerrys, while many Senate staffers were left in the dark because they don't have a comparable messaging system.

For House members, that was an improvement over the poor showing for the emergency communications system last Halloween. That's when two staffers' costumes and a plastic gun prompted an office lockdown while SWAT teams searched House offices. A message didn't go out over the BlackBerry network until almost an hour after the incident became known,

Picking BlackBerrys

The government market makes up roughly 10% of RIM's subscribers

BlackBerry subscribers, in millions

'02	0.32
'03	0.53
'04e	1.06
'05e	2.53
'06e	3.94

Source: ThinkEquity Partners

according to The Hill newspaper. Staffers had to get updates by watching TV news. The BlackBerry messaging system was improved soon afterward.

Congress' purchase of BlackBerry devices worked like an endorsement for the firm. Soon, federal agencies and branches of the armed services signed on too, Morrison says. The Canadian government became a big user around the same time as Congress, he says. Plus, state and local governments have become converts to BlackBerry.

Government use of BlackBerry devices has helped RIM sell to commercial customers, Morrison says. Corporate buyers have a higher comfort level knowing that government users are satisfied when it comes to security, he says.

"The inside-the-Beltway customers are very high-profile customers," he said.

RIM has doubled its subscriber count in the past year. In early March 2003, it had 534,000 subscribers. It reached 1 million subscribers on Feb. 3. "It's really taking off," Morrison said.

By year-end, RIM could have 2.2 million subscribers, says Tom Sepenzis, an analyst with ThinkEquity Partners. "They really do have a wonderful platform for delivering e-mail," he said.

The Waterloo, Ontario-based company is getting a boost from new BlackBerry phones that merge a cell phone with a RIM e-mail device, he says. And RIM is gaining subscribers in Europe and Asia, he says.

Coming soon are devices from other hardware makers, such as Nokia, that will use RIM technology. RIM doesn't have much competition today, but small, privately held Good Technology Inc. could give it a run for its money, says Todd Kort, an analyst with Gartner Inc. Sunnyvale, Calif.-based Good has signed up hardware makers Dell and PalmOne to use its technology.

RIM wants to move beyond e-mail, giving customers wireless access to information stored behind firewalls in server computers. For example, salespeople can use their BlackBerrys to update customer

(Cont.)

records, check on the status of an order or get information before a sales call. "Principally today it's a communications medium," Morrison said. "Increasingly it also will be an information medium."

RIM can see Congress and other government customers finding similar uses for BlackBerry devices.

House members and their staffs originally got BlackBerrys for emergencies, but now mostly use them for routine communications.

"A lot of members have become dependent on them," Walsh said. Some admit being addicted to the devices, calling them "crack berries."

In the nation's capital, you'll see congressmen and their support people using them in restaurants, theaters and at committee hearings.

Washington has a love-hate relationship with BlackBerrys, says Abraham Genauer, a staff writer for The Hill. "Members love it because they can bother their staffs any time, no matter where they are, whether they're in the district or on the road. And the staffs don't like being bothered all the time," he said. "It used to be if the con-gressman was away, you may not hear from him for a day or two. Now there's no getting away from them."

Getting Information for Marketing Decisions

33

MAKING MARKETING MEASURE UP

The pressure is on to take the guesswork out of ad spending

For years, corporate marketers have walked into budget meetings like neighborhood junkies. They couldn't always justify how well they spent past handouts or what difference it all made. They just wanted more money—for flashy TV ads, for big-ticket events, for, you know, getting out the message and building up the brand.

But those heady days of blind budget increases are fast being replaced with a new mantra: measurement and accountability. Armed with reams of data, increasingly sophisticated tools, and growing evidence that the old tricks simply don't work, there's hardly a marketing executive today who isn't demanding a more scientific approach to help defend marketing strategies in front of the chief financial officer. Marketers want to know the actual return on investment (ROI) of each dollar. They want to know it often, not just annually. And increasingly they want a view of likely returns on future campaigns. "Marketing has gone from being a cost or expense to an investment," notes Martyn Straw, chief strategy officer of ad agency BBDO Worldwide, who says honing an ROI system for clients is his main job. "Call marketing an equity investment, and suddenly there's lots of accountability in the room."

The push is coming from the top ranks. CEOs, CFOs, and even board directors, have relentlessly cut costs in every corner of their companies except marketing and are fed up with funneling cash into TV commercials and glossy ads that they say cost more and seem to do less. That's especially true at a time when profits are under attack and consumers of all ages are zapping ads and spending more time playing video games and surfing the Internet. The bean counters know that marketing matters. But they're hazy about how much or what kind.

That's one reason companies are increasingly shifting their dollars from TV and print ads to the Net and direct marketing. They can get a swift and accurate measure of the impact of their efforts for a fraction of the cost of advertising in traditional media. DaimlerChrysler, for example, is relying less on 30-second TV ads in favor of events where names, profiles, and addresses of prospects can be collected and tracked. It's also pushing

direct marketing and online advertising where response rates are easily measured. "You better believe my money is chasing media and marketing outlets that can prove their return in hard data," says Jeff Bell, vice-president-Chrysler/Jeep marketing.

DASHBOARD DATA

Companies in every segment of American business have become obsessed with honing the science of measuring marketing performance. Consumer-products giants such as Procter & Gamble, Kraft Foods, and Gillette are further along this path, having long chased statistics to link different forms of marketing to sales and brand awareness. But the desire to construct a comprehensive set of performance measures—what many call a marketing "dashboard"—is fast extending to marketers in other industries as well. Xerox Corp. uses the measurement techniques of Six Sigma to analyze marketing's impact on a range of measures, from leads generated to cost per sale. Home Depot Inc. has a proprietary computer model with sophisticated algorithms that correlate marketing investments with product sales and regional variations that have led the retailer, for example, to push paint using radio spots in some markets and newspaper inserts in others. "Marketing ROI is one of the most difficult things

to measure in retailing because of all the details," says John Costello, executive vice-president for merchandising and marketing. But, he adds, the ability to do it right is fast becoming a competitive advantage.

For many, the goal is to identify and cultivate potential buyers—and then track whether they respond to marketing efforts by ultimately making a purchase. Mark R. LaNeve, head of North American marketing and advertising for General Motors Corp., cites customer tracking as the carmaker's top priority. "We do less and less advertising simply because it feels right," says LaNeve. There are no more sponsored golf tournaments, for example, unless the sponsoring brand collects a healthy number of customer profiles through test drives. Those people are then tracked every time GM runs into them through a similar event or mailing and again when they buy a GM vehicle. Such measures have helped GM halve Cadillac's marketing spending over the last three years while increasing sales, market share, and awareness. Although marketing giants such as GM know they have to be on TV to launch models and blitz airwaves with a new rebate deal, the share of the marketing budget going to network TV is steadily declining. LaNeve says he knows with 98% certainty what the payoff of a direct-marketing campaign will

A Madison Avenue **Makeover**

Frustrated over their inability to measure the bang they get for their marketing bucks, advertisers are trying new methods of gauging advertising effectiveness:

GENERAL MOTORS	GM is shifting more dollars into "addressable" media: direct marketing, online, and events through which it can collect names, profiles, and e-mail addresses. This gives a clearer sense of which messages inspire people to actually buy a car.
PROCTER & GAMBLE	P&G is an early subscriber to Apollo, a joint Arbitron/VNU project that will track the media habits of 70,000 people. Apollo should yield ad effectiveness using that data plus home scanning of groceries, Internet usage, and frequent surveys.
HOME DEPOT	Sophisticated computer modeling matches media plans to sales. The data allow smarter, more localized spending decisions: Newspaper ads may drive paint sales in one region, for instance, while radio works better in another.

(Cont.)

be before committing a cent. Yet the impact of image-building TV and print ads—as opposed to those pitching rebates—remains mostly "a mystery or educated guess."

Indeed, the Holy Grail of measurement is to figure out the impact of traditional mass advertising, especially the 30-second TV commercial. One of the most elaborate efforts involves a joint venture between Arbitron Inc., a media and marketing research firm, and VNU, the Dutch media company that owns Nielsen. "Project Apollo" next year will begin tracking the media habits of 30,000 households representing 70,000 consumers. "Panelists" wear a pager-like device that picks up all the electronically coded TV and radio they consume. That data, plus online usage and grocery purchases scanned in half the households, and frequent surveys of attitudes and lifestyle choices should help advertisers figure out which of their marketing tactics really pay. Procter & Gamble Co., which spent $4.4 billion on advertising in the last fiscal year, has already signed on as a subscriber. P&G is looking for the system to tell it whether it's better off funding an end-aisle display in 2,000 grocery stores or increasing its radio ad buy for a month in the same markets. "It's not perfect," admits Arbitron's project head Linda Dupree. "But the information they get will be the best they have ever had."

PERFORMANCE ANXIETY

Because advertisers work with multiple ad agencies there's a push to establish some benchmarks and standards for measuring ROI. The CMO Council, a Silicon Valley network of close to 1,000 chief marketing officers at tech companies, released an extensive report of marketing performance measurements in October. Merely counting eyeballs no longer seemed enough once the tech bubble burst, says the report's editor-in-chief, William Glazier. Yet fewer than 15% of council members have a comprehensive model in place.

For all the effort to bring science to marketing, the art component will never go away. Figuring out how much of a product's appeal is due to marketing and how much stems from innovative features or quality is often hard to pin down, even for individual consumers. They don't know why they like it, they just do. That's the human factor—and so far, no one has found a way to measure that.

Diane Brady, with David Kiley and bureau reports. Business Week.

34

New Penney: Chain Goes for 'Missing Middle'

ELLEN BYRON. WALL STREET JOURNAL.

IT'S NO SECRET that as **Wal-Mart Stores** Inc. thrives on low prices and **Neiman Marcus Group** Inc. prospers on luxury, stores in the middle are being squeezed. To cope with such a competitive retail environment, many department stores either are cultivating a tonier image to lure the affluent or moving down-market.

But **J.C. Penney** Co., long synonymous with middle-market tastes, is taking a different approach: to stay that way.

In its latest strategy, which the company plans to announce tomorrow, the 1,020-store chain will set out to better target a part of the closet it calls "the missing middle," or casual clothing that suits the tastes of middle-income women between ages 35 and 54. "The core of America is up for grabs in terms of their heart and soul," says Mike Ullman, Penney's new chairman and chief executive officer, who comes to the job with extensive experience in luxury retailing. "This customer is underserved."

To appeal to this demographic, Penney is launching two lines of moderately priced, casual women's clothing, including one from designer Nicole Miller. It will broadcast its new attitude in ads to run during the Academy Awards, a largely female-viewing event that its marketing team calls the "Super Bowl for Women."

Penney's sharpened focus marks the latest phase in an aggressive, four-year-old turnaround strategy mapped out by recently retired chairman and CEO Allen Questrom. He closed underperforming stores and centralized back-office operations. His plan is beginning to pay off: After years of dismal results, Penney recently reported an 86% climb in third-quarter earnings. And its January sales beat even the company's expectations, rising 3.3% for stores open at least a year.

The latest initiative may be the Plano, Texas, company's most important. Penney is attempting to shed a persistently dowdy image that has turned off many shoppers and pushed them away—to mass merchants such as Target Corp. or to more-upscale stores such as those of Nordstrom Inc. Most old-style department-store chains are grappling with similar competitive pressures, prompting a flurry of merger activity.

In recent years, department-store chains have done plenty of soul-searching in a bid to win over more middle-income women. Last year, companies such as **Federated Department Stores** Inc. and **May Department Stores** Co. carved up their apparel floors to display new, gently priced career offerings from name-brand designers including Michael Kors, Ralph Lauren and Tommy Hilfiger.

As part of its turnaround strategy, Penney, meanwhile, lured away behind-the-scenes designers from competitors to overhaul and upgrade its private-label collections, particularly in its Arizona jeans brand, which targets juniors and young men, and it added exclusive home-furnishing lines by Chris Madden and Colin Cowie. While the company already sells contemporary sportswear labels such as Bisou Bisou and Bongo, which aim to deliver the latest fashion trends, Penney realized it didn't resonate with its missing middle customer.

While its competitors with their new designer lines sought to dress women in more formal clothing for the workplace, Penney found that its target women had a more casual lifestyle, and wanted separates that offered a more laid-back but trendy feel that was missing from the careerwear suits of its Worthington private label. Penney executives felt that female customers faced a big apparel void: in-between, pulled-together styles suitable for relaxed office dress codes, eating out, parties, luncheons and their children's school events. They even gave this category a name, "dressy casual."

From its own research, the company already knew that its typical customer was married with children, and had a median household income of about $69,000. While many shopped the chain for their homes and families, they still tended to go elsewhere for many of their own fashions. Penney's past efforts to court them—by going more upscale—failed when high-end brands balked at the retailer's pedestrian image and refused to let Penney carry their clothes.

Beginning in January of last year, Penney conducted an in-depth research blitz to better define its target and understand her needs. The first step was a telephone survey of 900 women that asked them about casual clothes. To drill down further, Penney researchers videotaped interviews, lasting up to six hours, with 30 women, recording everything from their feelings about fashion to what is hanging in their closets as well as a shopping trip at J.C. Penney and a competitor. The women also clipped words and images from magazines and glued them to posters to express their feelings about what casual clothing meant to them.

During the interviews, which took place in the women's homes, the participants delivered on-camera, heartfelt soliloquies about their posters. Pointing to a photo of Sponge Bob SquarePants, with his typically strung-out expression, one woman told the camera, "This is me, my stress with shopping." Explaining a cluster of words glued to her poster, she continued, "These are the things to stop—short shorts and skirts, exposed midriffs or cleavage, spaghetti straps on tank tops."

But the women said that being alluring is still important—to a degree. "You could still be a mom, but you still want to be cute and a little bit hip," another subject said. "You're not dead yet, and you're not a grandma—you still want to be in the game."

Two big no-nos: matronly and sex-kitten looks. Even though they are beginning to feel their age, these women say they want to look stylish and crave options that hint at sensuality, without being too tight. Quality also is crucial, and something for which they are willing to pay a premium. Participants in the Penney survey study told the chain that they study clothing labels and feel garments to assess fabric and construction. They prefer a touch of Lycra, interesting buttons, good stitching and styles that let women make a personal statement.

Armed with this information, Penney approached designer Nicole Miller. While Ms. Miller is best known for her cutting-edge fashions, working with Penney offered a chance to tap a huge market and build her

---

The 'Missing Middle' Woman

Who J.C. Penney's core female shoppers are . . .

- ■ **35-54** years old
- ■ **$69,000** median household income
- ■ **Married,** with children
- ■ **Buy many of their casual clothes** elsewhere

. . . and the casual clothes they look for.:

- ■ **Stylish,** but not overly trendy
- ■ **Form-fitting,** but not too tight
- ■ **High-quality fabrics,** stitching and buttons

Source: the company

(Cont.)

brand into more of a household name. To prepare, Ms. Miller and Bud Konheim, CEO of **Nicole Miller** Ltd., watched the videotaped interviews.

"We neglect these people because they're not flashy or celebrities," Mr. Konheim says. "This is about the democratization of design."

Ms. Miller, whose new nicole by Nicole Miller styles range from $26 camisoles with "bra-friendly" straps to $100 coats, notes that inexpensive apparel need not be poorly made. "With resources today, you can make good quality clothes at a good price," she says.

Penney also is launching a private-label brand called "W—Work to Weekend," catering to the same audience. Private-label brands make up 40% of Penney's sales.

In another bid to differentiate its new looks, Penney will market Ms. Miller less as a designer/celebrity and more as a working woman. The Nicole Miller section of the stores features a photo of her face with no-nonsense quotes from her, such as "Great designs shouldn't be limited to those who can afford it." Indeed, one of the reasons why Liz Sweney, Penney's executive vice president

and general merchandise manager for women's apparel, chose Ms. Miller for the line revolved around the fact that Ms. Miller would be directly involved in designing it, rather than just lending her name to it. "She's a mom, too, and leads a busy lifestyle," says Ms. Sweney. "It was clear she understood what this woman needed."

From *The Wall Street Journal,* February 14, 2005. Reprinted by permission of Dow Jones and Co., Inc. via The Copyright Clearance Center.

35

How to Measure Product Placement

Research tools evolve, but dollar values remain a big question mark

Todd Wasserman. Adweek.

In the dot-com era, there was a mania for linking Internet sales to TV based on a simple premise: Wouldn't it be cool if you could see Jennifer Aniston wearing a sweater on *Friends* and then—just like that—log on to the Internet to buy it?

In 2005, *Friends* is ancient history, and the industry is no longer preoccupied with selling Aniston's sweater. However, it is grappling with a related issue. If in the old days the question was how to buy the sweater, the new query is: What is the value of a scene in which it is worn?

The relevance of the question is the result of two major trends: the growth of product placement as a key component of marketing programs in a TiVo era; and the increasing pressure on businesses to show a return on investment for all marketing activities.

John Wanamaker once famously observed that 50 percent of the money spent on advertising is wasted, but no one can figure out which 50 percent. Now, the industry is "trying to make that a better equation," says Martyn Straw, chief strategy officer at BBDO in New York. "The marketing investment has, to a certain extent, been allowed to go down a black hole. Now you've got people scrambling to generate growth, whether on the top line or the bottom line."

Previous attempts to estimate the value of product placement in television have been conducted informally by dedicated placement agencies like NMA, Los Angeles, which has had a ranking system for years. Other firms provide measurement systems for product placement in films and videogames.

As the TV deals have grown in size and scope, a cottage industry has formed to address the value question in more concrete terms. Currently, several firms offer tools that rate product placements in terms of both viewer impact and dollars and cents. Though some marketers are using internal measurement systems, more are outsourcing the job to an independent agency.

General Motors is one of them. The automaker has enlisted the services of Intermedia Advertising Group, New York, to gauge the effectiveness of its numerous placements, including the huge Pontiac giveaway last September on *The Oprah Winfrey Show* and the ongoing GMC Yukon Denali integration on Bravo's *Queer Eye for the Straight Guy*.

"We're going through a lot of effort to try to quantify placement and integration," says Steve Tihanyi, general director of marketing alliances and regional operations at GM. "Not only do we track some major GM initiatives, but we track how we are comparing to others. One thing we do know for certain is that the right kind of integration does have a significant positive impact."

> **EARLY ADOPTERS: Coca-Cola and Crest were out of the gate quickly, linking with 'American Idol' and 'The Apprentice.'**

Gisela Dawson, president of the Entertainment Resources Marketing Association, Los Angeles, says that initially, marketers were starstruck by getting their products onscreen. But now that it's more of a business, "most of our members have been looking for ways to quantify it," she says.

TV networks are eager for such tools, as they would mean another revenue stream, says Laura Caraccioli-Davis, svp at SMG Entertainment, Chicago. "They would love to have Coke or Pepsi decide: Will the [sitcom] family have Coke, or will they have Pepsi?"

She cautions, however, that a standard measurement might lead to lower fees for product placement: "Once you quantify [product placement], you will commodify it."

Chris Eames, svp of sales, sponsorship and marketing at Turner Broadcasting System, agrees. "It's difficult to create a standard. Clients have different goals and challenges going in," he says. "If you're Coke, you have 100 percent awareness, so just getting awareness isn't as valuable as it is for a new product launch. Those factors aren't put into a [third-party firm's] formula."

Nuts and bolts: the measurements

Given all the variables involved in a placement—foreground or background, oral or visual, main character or sidekick—developing an adequate methodology can be daunting. Whether there will ultimately be a rate card or an exact value for a 20-second flash of Aniston's sweater is anyone's guess. But that hasn't stopped the mobs of chart-toting researchers from making their case.

Among the firms is Nielsen Media Research (which, like *Adweek,* is owned by VNU). Nielsen began monitoring prime-time programming for instances of product placement on the six major networks in September 2003. Employees in Shelton, Conn., monitor every minute of shows and jot down instances where a brand gets screen time or a verbal mention. The information is logged into a database where subscribers can search placements using various criteria (brand, category, show, etc.), and then matched to the show's rating in that minute.

Thus, a subscriber can see that on the Dec. 3, 2003, episode of the WB's *The Gilmore Girls,* Poland Spring bottled water got 85 seconds of screen time as the show was garnering a 2.2 rating—i.e., 2.2 percent of the nation's 108 million households with TV sets were tuned in at that moment.

What may help to differentiate Nielsen's service is the company's sheer size: The firm has tracked 100,000 product placements since the fall of 2003.

Dave Harkness, svp of business development at Nielsen, says no one else has the manpower to track and provide ratings for the vast number of TV placements. He envisions Nielsen's rating system as an algorithm that could be automatically applied to 90 percent of placements. Thus, he argued, Nielsen's system would become the industry standard. "We'd like to take 90 percent off the table," he says.

Still, Nielsen's service makes no attempt to parse the data or draw conclusions, and some marketers may balk at those limitations.

Chris Monaco, director of entertainment marketing at Allied Domecq, says he doesn't really care how much airtime his competitors are getting. "This isn't something where it's keeping up with the Joneses," says Monaco, who has developed product placement deals for Domecq brands Stolichnaya, Malibu and Beefeater on Spike TV's new reality series *The Club.*

"Why should I care if [my competitors] are getting 10 times as many placements as us?" he adds. "Who says a shotgun approach works in that situation?"

In response to such criticism, Nielsen is in the process of creating a tool that would produce a product placement rating. As a step toward establishing its methodology, the firm expects to release a study next month analyzing the variables that increase viewer recall of

> **'This isn't keeping up with the Joneses. Why should I care if my competitors are getting 10 times as many placements?'**
> —CHRIS MONACO, ALLIED DOMECQ

product placement. Harkness says he's briefed five of the major media-buying agencies and all have expressed interest. He declines to elaborate on the rating system, except to say that focus groups will not be used.

Harkness expects that marketers, media agencies and others will continue to use their own methods to attempt to find a value for placements. "I'm not sure there will be one definitive standard," he says. "Agencies want some flexibility in the model."

Nielsen is not the only game in town. At least a dozen others have established unique methods of measuring product placement. They include BrandAdvisors (which measures film placements), NextMedium, Delivery Agent, Image Impact and Millward Brown. The "big three" at the moment, however, are Nielsen, iTVX and IAG.

Deutsch in New York has partnered with iTVX, a New Rochelle, N.Y., firm that compares the value of a product placement to the cost of a 30-second ad through an elaborate grading system. Founder Frank Zazza is a product placement veteran who previously established AIM Productions in Astoria, N.Y. Zazza fondly recalls the days when a handshake with a propmaster scored onscreen mentions for Junior Mints and Pez on *Seinfeld*— not to mention his greatest coup: Reese's Pieces' cameo in 1982's *E.T.,* considered by many observers as the birth of modern product placement. "Product placement was relationship marketing with set decorators up until the early '90s," says Zazza. "It was beautiful. We'd do things with producers, set dressers."

Times have changed. Media firms (UMD, MediaVest), product placement agencies (NMA), talent firms (William Morris) and reality producers such as Mark Burnett (*Survivor, The Apprentice*) and David Collins (*Queer Eye for the Straight Guy/Girl*) have all muscled in on the action. "If you're a branding executive, you get five proposals—one from William Morris, one from your product placement agency," says Zazza. "It's the Wild West."

Zazza might have seen an end to his livelihood, but in fact saw an opportunity. Marketers, after all, want to have something to show for their placements. They especially want to know if they paid too much to get their brand on *According to Jim.* As a rule of thumb, clients pay a relatively small fee—usually about $10,000 per month—as retainer to a placement agency. The deals themselves, of course, can run into the millions.

Can you put a price tag on that?

Regardless of how finely tuned the new measurement systems become, there will always be differing opinions as to whether product placement gets a marketer bang for its buck. M&M's, for example, paid relatively little for its placement on *ER* in October 2002—a few thousand dollars at most, according to industry sources—yet Masterfoods executives were relatively unhappy with

> **'Part of this is intuitive. You understand when it's a good placement. It's gut instinct.'**
> —ERIC KORSH, SCOUT PRODUCTIONS

the effort. In particular, they wanted to know why the bag was shown backward.

According to Zazza, a 30-second ad during that timeslot would have cost $242,720. The total time that the characters talk about M&M's or are in the shot with the bag is about 30 seconds. Yet iTVX estimates that the placement was worth $430,613, or about 1.8 times the price of the ad.

Why? This placement, which is divided into three segments, over-indexes on various parameters. The audio clarity is better than average and the awareness factor is high, meaning that someone watching the show is more likely to remember it.

The awareness scale progresses from commercial TV to premium cable to IMAX, with the latter proving most memorable. *ER* apparently beats other prime-time shows on commercial TV in this respect. People also tend to remember a placement at the end of a show better than one at the beginning.

Finally, iTVX takes into account the fact that the M&M's segment is self-contained and has a beginning, middle and end. The placement starts with Dr. Gregory Pratt (Mekhi Phifer) and Dr. Jing-Mei "Deb" Chen (Ming-Na) sharing a moment by a vending machine. Pratt asks her, "Plain or peanut?" Chen responds, "Huh?" He clarifies: "M&M's." At the end of the segment, she finally answers him. "I want plain M&Ms." He takes out

the bag—he already chose the plain—and she playfully taps him on the head with it.

All of this leads to a product placement/commercial cost ratio of 1.75, which, when multiplied by the price of a spot during the show, results in the $430,613 valuation.

As another example, iTVX estimates that Procter & Gamble's integration of Crest on an early second-season episode of *The Apprentice* has a PP/CC ratio of 10.8. The high rating arose in part from the fact that the placement had a beginning, middle and end (the brand appeared on-screen for most of the hour) and was held by the main characters in the show.

The episode featured a competition to see which team could best promote the launch of new Crest Whitening Expressions Vanilla Mint toothpaste. After one group entertained a few wild ideas (such as pumping the New York subway system full of vanilla aroma), another conducted a demonstration with baseball's Mike Piazza during a sampling event.

According to Zazza, P&G paid about $2.5 million for the deal. A 30-second ad would have cost $350,000 in that NBC timeslot. Given the PP/CC ratio, iTVX estimates the value of the placement at $3.8 million. "They did very, very well," says Zazza.

The matrix that iTVX developed is one method of tackling the cost issue. Another is to measure viewer response by asking audience members what they think.

That's the tack taken by IAG, which tracks audience response to marketing activities, including TV ads and sponsorships. About three years ago, marketers began asking co-CEO Alan Gould about measuring product placements.

Gould, who got into advertising by working on the 1992 Clinton-Gore campaign, among others, says marketers are most interested in not screwing up. "It's like the Hippocratic oath," he says. "First, do no harm."

That issue is addressed in what he calls the "fit" question: Did the placement fit—i.e., was it delivered in an appropriate context? IAG counts on some 800,000 people to fill out online surveys about their favorite shows. Though the firm dangles $5 and $10 coupons to reward respondents, Gould says most are happy to answer questions about those shows, including whether viewers recall the content of the show in addition to the specific brand.

In the case of IAG client American Express and its tie-in with NBC's first season of *The Restaurant,* the "Does it fit?" answer was no. The overcooked placement—which had chef Rocco DiSpirito intoning, "Get me the representatives

(Cont.)

for American Express Open"—was widely panned and AmEx did not reappear during the second season. At the time, the company said the first season worked for Open because it involved starting up a business, and expressed satisfaction in the deal.

> **GUEST STARS: The Ford F-150 was central to an episode of '24'; Macintosh mingled with the castaways on 'Survivor.'**

Gould says other brands have received low "fit" scores, but nevertheless considers the placement successful. The key, he says, is that the placement achieves its marketing objectives. P&G, for example, may not be too concerned if the Vanilla Crest/*Apprentice* tie-in achieved a low score if its marketers were chiefly concerned about building awareness for the brand, which, in all likelihood, it did.

That's a common sentiment. The object of a placement, after all, could be to build buzz for a new product or reposition an existing brand. Still, marketers often come into a placement deal looking specifically for airtime.

"They want to know: 'How many seconds [will my brand get]?'" says Robert Reisenberg, CEO of Full Circle, New York, an Omnicom unit charged with developing and producing TV programs to meet the needs of advertisers. "But when you sit them down and tell them it doesn't work that way, they're responsive."

DIY measurements

Even as they look to outside help, marketers are trying to become more sophisticated about measuring product placement. Boost Mobile, the teen-focused wireless firm, uses a five-point scale to determine whether a placement makes sense, though it is also soliciting bids for a third-party product placement agency.

Tricia Bouzigard, senior entertainment marketing manager at Boost Mobile, says she uses a checklist that includes reach, sales-driving opportunities and other goals to evaluate the brand's efforts, which include placement on MTV's car makeover show *Pimp My Ride*. "Clearly [the show] is our target audience," she says. "It's people taking it to the next level in their lives."

Whether the strict placement/commercial cost ratio developed by iTVX and others becomes a standard, many observers argue that allowing for those other variables is important.

"Having your brand written into the script is more effective than just having your brand sitting there in a shot," notes Kristin Petersen, whose new role as vp of brand exposure and promotions at the Gap signals the retailer's intent to bring a higher profile via branded entertainment to its stores, including Old Navy and Banana Republic.

"Part of this is intuitive," adds Eric Korsh, chief operating officer at Scout Productions, producer of the *Queer Eye* shows. "Creatively, you understand when it's a good placement. It's gut instinct."

Allied Domecq's Monaco cautions that marketers should ask whether the placement uses the brand in a credible manner—and meets its long-term marketing strategies. Invariably, he believes doing placements involves a leap of faith. "In some ways, it can be measured, but in other ways, it has to be something that's done because you believe in it," he says. "If you don't believe in it, you might as well be running regular TV spots."

36

Spying on the Sales Floor

'Video Miners' Use Cameras Hidden in Stores to Analyze Who Shops, What They Like

JOSEPH PEREIRA. WALL STREET JOURNAL.

Braintree, Mass.—STEPPING INTO a Gap store at the South Shore Shopping Plaza on a recent evening, Laura Munro became a research statistic.

Twelve feet above her, a device resembling a smoke detector, mounted on the ceiling and equipped with a hidden camera, took a picture of her head and shoulders. The image was fed to a computer and shipped to a database in Chicago, where **ShopperTrak RCT** Corp., a consumer research firm, keeps count of shoppers nationwide using 40,000 cameras placed in stores and malls.

ShopperTrak, whose profile has risen this holiday season as appetite grows for more real-time shopping data, is a leader in "video mining"—an emerging field in marketing research enabled by technology that can analyze video images without relying on human eyes.

ShopperTrak says it doesn't take pictures of faces. The company worries that shoppers would perceive that as an invasion of privacy. But nearly all of its videotaping is done without the knowledge of the people being taped.

"I didn't even know there was a camera up there," says Ms. Munro, a public-transit manager who popped into the mall on her way home from work to find a gift for her 12-year-old daughter.

Using proprietary software to gauge the size of the images of people, a ShopperTrak computer determined that Ms. Munro was an adult, not a child, and thus a bona fide shopper. Weeding out youngsters is critical in accurately calculating one of the valuable bits of data ShopperTrak sells—the percentage of shoppers that buys and the percentage that only browses. It arrives at this data, including the so-called conversion rate, by comparing the number of people taped entering the store with the number of transactions.

Ms. Munro's visit was tallied up twice: once as a visitor to the Gap and once in a national count of shoppers. **Gap** Inc., of San Francisco, pays ShopperTrak for the tally of Gap shoppers. ShopperTrak sells the broader data—gleaned from 130 retail clients and 380 malls—to economists, bankers and retailers.

ShopperTrak takes into account how much shoppers spend, data that it gets from credit-card companies and banks, and extrapolates outward to the entire retail landscape. "We can get sales and traffic figures that are identical to the government's, two months before they can issue their report," says Bill Martin, ShopperTrak's founder and president.

Of the millions of shoppers videotaped daily in the U.S., many are aware that security cameras are watching to detect shoplifting. In some cases, stores post signs to disclose such monitoring. But there is far less awareness by consumers that they are being filmed for market research.

ShopperTrak discloses its clients—a list that includes Gap and its Banana Republic unit; **Limited Brands** Inc., of Columbus, Ohio, and its Victoria's Secret chain; **PaylessShoe Source** Inc., of Topeka, Kan; **American Eagle Outfitters** Inc., of Warrendale, Pa.; and **Children's Place Retail Stores** Inc., of Secaucus, N.J.

Several other research companies that videotape shoppers say they sign agreements with clients in which they pledge not to disclose their names. They say their clients want the taping to be secret—and worry shoppers would feel alienated or complain of privacy invasion if they knew.

Katherine Albrecht, founder and director of Caspian, a Cambridge, Mass., consumer-advocacy group, says consumers have "no idea such things as video tracking are going on" and should be informed. When she tells them about such activities, she says the response she often hears is, "Isn't this illegal, like stalking? Shouldn't there be a law against it?" There aren't any state laws forbidding retailers from videotaping shoppers for research—although in New Jersey last week, Caesars Atlantic City Hotel Casino was fined $80,000 for videotaping the breasts and legs of female employees and customers with cameras intended for security.

Some research companies' cameras, with lenses as small as a quarter, can provide data on everything from the density of shopping traffic in an aisle to the reactions of a shopper gazing at the latest plasma TV set. The cash register is a popular spot for cameras, too. But cameras can be found in banks, fast-food outlets and hotel lobbies (but not guest rooms).

Video miners say their research cameras are less invasive than security cameras, because their subjects aren't scrutinized as closely as security suspects. Images, they say, are destroyed when the research is done.

Robert Bulmash, founder of the Private Citizen Inc., of Naperville, Ill., which advocates for privacy rights, says that being in a retailer's store doesn't give a retailer "the right to treat me like a guinea pig." He says he wonders about assurances that images are destroyed, since there isn't any way to verify such claims. The pictures "could be saved somewhere in that vast digital universe and some day come back to haunt us," he says.

Already, video images can be subpoenaed from retailers for law-enforcement purposes. Technology capable of matching a photo with an individual's identity, say from credit-card transactions, "has certainly arrived," says Rajeev Sharma, a Penn State University computer science professor who has launched a company that is creating shopper-monitoring systems. It isn't certain whether retailers are availing themselves of the know-how. Credit card companies currently aren't sharing individuals' financial information with retailers, he adds, but retailers have their own customer databases as the result of loyalty cards, store credit cards and other in-house programs. Theoretically, they could link a transaction at a cash register with the face of a shopper appearing on the videotape.

Dr. Sharma's start-up, **Advanced Interfaces** Inc., of State College, Pa., is expected this week to launch a Web site, videomining. com, highlighting the company's patented "computer vision" technologies.

In a pilot project conducted last year in the Philadelphia area, Advanced Interfaces set up nine cameras in each of two **McDonald's** Corp. restaurants to find out which consumer types would find a new salad item most appealing. The research was done without consumers' knowledge, says Dr. Sharma, who is Advanced Interfaces' chief executive.

Seven of the cameras were already in place for security purposes and needed only to be reconfigured using Advanced's sensors. Two additional cameras were positioned in the ceiling directly over cash registers. By measuring the shapes of people's faces, the sensors were able to provide a breakdown of the fast-food customers by race, gender and age group, he says. The videos also revealed the length of time customers spent waiting in line or looking at the menu before ordering. Mr. Sharma declined to discuss the findings.

All of the video was subsequently destroyed, he says. "Only the computers and no humans saw the pictures of the customers," Mr. Sharma says. Advanced is conducting similar consumer-behavior analysis this holiday season for three other retailers that Mr. Sharma declined to identify.

Video mining is being spurred by digital video cameras. Unlike their analog counterparts, digital video cameras can be programmed so that the images can be quickly read by computers—taking only hours to complete tasks that might have taken weeks for humans to do.

(Cont.)

In a recent assignment that **Kahn Research Group,** of Huntersville, N.C., completed for **American Express** Co., computers took only a couple of days to sift through 64 hours of tape. Kahn researchers hid four cameras near the checkout counter at a couple of supermarkets in Southern California to study whether American Express gift cards should be displayed off in a spot by themselves, or lumped with competing brands near the cash registers.

Researchers were interested in customers' facial expressions and eye movements as they spotted the gift cards, and whether they walked to a display to pick up a card. Kahn cameras, each the size of a golf ball, were hidden behind the displays. The devices were programmed to detect fast-eye movement, smiles and frowns, says Greg Kahn, the company's CEO.

The research, which involved filming 2,000 shoppers, was "really not invasive," Mr. Kahn says. "Nobody knew they were being recorded and our work didn't interfere with the store environment. Had we tried to interview people, the process would have taken much longer."

And had people known they were being taped, he says, "I know many of the shoppers would have stuck their hands in front of the camera lens and refused to be recorded."

A spokeswoman for American Express described the project as a "pilot program . . . that's not for public consumption" and declined to comment further.

It isn't clear whether the American public will be as tolerant of secret market research using videotape as they are of security cameras. There are 29 million cameras videotaping people in airports, government buildings, offices, schools, stores and elsewhere, according to one widely cited estimate in the security industry.

37

Never Heard Of Acxiom?
Chances Are It's Heard Of You.

How a little-known Little Rock company—the world's largest processor of consumer data—found itself at the center of a very big national security debate. ■ *by Richard Behar*

Last summer a sheriff in Cincinnati stumbled onto what may have been the biggest security breach of consumer data ever. Searching the home of Daniel Baas, a 24-year-old computer-systems administrator at a data-marketing firm, detectives found dozens of compact discs containing the personal data of millions of Americans. The information, it turned out, had been hacked by Baas over a period of two years from a giant server in Arkansas belonging to a company called Acxiom.

Never heard of Acxiom? The publicly traded, politically connected Little Rock company is the world's largest processor of consumer data, collecting and massaging more than a billion records a day. Its customers include nine of the country's top ten credit-card issuers, as well as nearly all the major retail banks, insurers, and automakers. It's a business that generates $1 billion in sales annually and, after a few bumpy years, is expected to produce $60 million in profits. Analysts project earnings to grow 15% annually over the next five years.

For most of its life, Acxiom (the "c" is silent) has kept a low profile—its corporate customers like it that way. But lately it has found itself at the center of a white-hot swirl of anti-terrorism, national security, and consumer-privacy issues. Remember the flap about JetBlue giving passenger records to a government contractor? And the one about John Poindexter's terrorism futures exchange? They all touched Acxiom.

And in the middle of all that, it now turns out, Acxiom itself was getting hacked. While there's no evidence that Baas—who pleaded guilty in December to federal cybercrime charges—used the stolen data for any commercial purpose, the case raises serious questions about the vulnerability of databases at companies like Acxiom, which should be the most secure.

Indeed, another electronic break-in was discovered during a self-audit by Acxiom following a tip-off from authorities about another intrusion. Acxiom reported the second incident to government investigators.

The group of hackers in Boca Raton, Fla. who had penetrated the same Acxiom server for three months last year also accessed data on millions of Americans. Once again, it doesn't appear that consumers were defrauded, but indictments aren't expected before March. "We dodged a howitzer with that one," admits Charles Morgan, Acxiom's longtime chairman and CEO. "It was a whole company—a bunch of crooks. If it had been the Russian mafia, we would have been in a hell of a mess."

Such embarrassments come at a bad time, not just for Acxiom but for America. Since 9/11, the company has been campaigning for crucial federal contracts in homeland security.

> "We dodged a howitzer," says Morgan. "If it had been the Russian mafia, we would have been in a hell of a mess."

Retired general and presidential candidate Wesley Clark and the Clintons have helped. But until recently, Acxiom officials were unaware that their own homeland had been breached. Baas easily cracked Acxiom's passwords, helping himself to unencrypted data belonging to 10% of Acxiom's customer base—upwards of 200 large companies. "This is a wake-up call for us and our industry," says Morgan.

As Morgan knows, the stakes go way beyond the privacy of consumers. Since 2001, Acxiom has engaged in research with the Pentagon and other agencies to find ways to consolidate, link, and share data. The federal Transportation Security Administration recently announced that this summer it will roll out its controversial second-generation Computer Assisted Passenger Prescreening System, or CAPPS II—a scheme that color-codes airline passengers in terms of their likelihood to be terrorists. The project will rely heavily on Acxiom's data and its identity-matching logarithms. Privacy advocates worry that systems such as CAPPS will hurt the innocent by producing streams of false positives. But the opposite may be the case. In late December several flights from Paris to the U.S. were grounded because intelligence intercepts misidentified a half-dozen people as possible threats, including a 5-year-old child mistaken for an al Qaeda pilot. Had Acxiom's identity-resolution system been in place, that probably wouldn't have happened.

Many say the use of private-sector data is critical in the fight against terrorism. "Government must have access to that information," concludes a recent report by the Markle Foundation, which focuses on technology policy and whose 36-member security task force includes Clark. "The travel, hotel, financial, immigration, health, or educational records of a person suspected by our government of planning terrorism may hold information that is vital."

By most accounts, nobody does a better job of identity verification than Acxiom, which is rapidly expanding its reach in Europe and Asia. "The Acxioms of the world—these are citizen patriots in this new war," says David Aufhauser, the Treasury Department's recently departed general counsel. "It's as if it's 1776 all over again. A great deal of the intelligence that we receive in the shadow war on terror is suspect—the product of capture, interrogation, bribery, deceit, false feints, or, abroad, torture. Information in financial or personal databases provides a measured counterpoint."

(Cont.)

But as much as the country may need Acxiom, the hacking incidents could be rocket fuel for those who oppose CAPPS and similar programs. Clark, for one, appears to be distancing himself from his lobbying for the data giant. "Had I still been on that [Acxiom] board when all this was going through," Clark said in a presidential candidates' debate last month, "I would have insisted that ACLU and others be brought in to preapprove CAPPS II." (In fact, Clark was on the board through most of the process.)

Acxiom itself has been downplaying the hacking breaches—it hasn't said anything publicly about the Florida attack—as it tries to maintain the confidence of both its corporate clients and its federal benefactors. Even so, an Acxiom team is beefing up the company's computer security in ways that may also become a model for Washington. That need is pressing: A recent government report concludes that many federal agencies, including the Department of Homeland Security, are failing in computer security.

To grasp what is at risk, one need only take a walk through Acxiom's five-acre data center in Conway, Ark. Thousands of servers and storage units—a city of blinking six-foot boxes —quietly process the billions of data bits that flow into the company each second. As silent as Mars, Planet Acxiom has few signs of life beyond a handful of geeky traffic controllers monitoring the liftoffs and landings of data in cyberspace on NASA-sized screens. "Think of it as an automated factory, where the product we make is data," says a manager. In a separate, locked glass room known as the shark tank, black plastic fins jut from the tops of some of the 70 servers and storage units. "Some clients don't work well in the same sandbox," explains Jeff Kauble, who co-manages the complex. Citigroup? Allstate? Homeland Security? He won't say. Another client insists its data be stored miles away, in the sealed underground vault of a former government building.

Once upon a time in America a savvy store clerk knew that you had, say, three kids, an old Ford, a pool, and a passion for golf and yellow sweaters. Today Acxiom is that store clerk. It manages 20 billion customer records, has enough storage space to house all the information in the Library of Congress 50 times over, and maintains a database on 96% of U.S. households that gives marketers a so-called real-time, 360-degree view of their customers.

How? Acxiom provides a 13-digit code for every person, "so we can identify you wherever you go," says the company's demographics guru, Bruce Carroll. Each person is placed into one of 70 lifestyle clusters, ranging from "Rolling Stones" and "Single City Struggles" to "Timeless Elders." Nearly one-third of Americans change their clusters annually as a result of a "lifestyle trigger event," Carroll says. Acxiom's catalog also offers hundreds of lists, including a "pre-movers file," updated daily, of people preparing to change residences, as well as lists of people sorted by the frequency with which they use credit cards, the square footage of their homes, and their interest in the "strange and unusual." Says Carroll: "We're pushing a new paradigm."

The man behind the paradigm is Morgan, who joined the company in 1972 and built the industry's first large-scale, multisourced database in 1978. Although he just turned 61, the IBM-trained engineer still drives a Harley to work, pilots the company plane, and until last year drove in NASCAR races. "Charles is the guy you want to have flying the airplane if something goes wrong," says Acxiom's general counsel, Jerry Jones. "He can take in lots of information and make decisions. He tweaks algorithms in his spare time and loves to drill down into the data."

A decade ago Morgan got rid of most titles

"This is very powerful data," Clark said— "absolutely what the government needs to be aware of."

at Acxiom and sardined top executives, himself included, into ten-by ten-foot offices. The moves have paid off: For five of the past seven years, Acxiom was among FORTUNE's 100 best places to work in America. Morgan is two years ahead of the marketplace in using grid-based processing—replacing expensive servers with cheap, interconnected PCs to dramatically drive down costs and improve processing speeds. He's also critical of the government's anti-terror infrastructure. While the two-year-old Patriot Act sanctions the sharing of data between the government and private parties, Congress only recently approved the FBI's expanded power to demand records from securities and car dealers, travel agencies, and currency exchanges. But operators of ships, trains, and planes still don't have the ability or authority to verify a simple driver's license. "Homeland Security has done a poor job of doing just about anything," Morgan says.

When America was attacked on 9/11, Acxiom was in a unique position to help. Shortly after the FBI released the names of the 19 hijackers on Sept. 14, Acxiom located 11 of them in its databases. "Call the FBI," suggested company director Mack McLarty, former chief of staff in Bill Clinton's White House. By day's end, subpoena in hand, a team of FBI agents had moved into Acxiom's headquarters. "Isn't there something you guys can be doing to help?" former President Clinton, a friend of Acxiom counsel Jones's, asked in a call to the company a few days later. "We are," said Jones.

Clinton visited the company's Little Rock offices on Oct. 5, 2001, and phoned Attorney General John Ashcroft to encourage him to use Acxiom for passenger ID verification. Clark, too, was impressed when he was given a demonstration. "This is very powerful data—absolutely what the government needs to be aware of," Clark said at the time. Clark, who had declined to join Acxiom's board a year earlier, started working as a consultant and lobbyist. He joined the board in December 2001, and, according to Acxiom, was paid $460,000 in fees by the company. (Clark refused to talk to FORTUNE about his activities on behalf of Acxiom.)

Morgan was dumbfounded, he recalls, when the FBI arrived at Acxiom. "Their technology was unbelievably bad," he recalls, "and the international terror experts were computer illiterate." For one thing, the agents were toting laptops with Intel 286 processors—slow, low-memory computers that went out with the 1980s. "I thought, 'This has to be a joke,'" he says.

The FBI-Acxiom collaboration lasted for months. Morgan won't provide details, but he says current and former addresses helped identify housemates of the hijackers, as well as suspects with whom they may have been in contact. "We were always paranoid about people looking at the data in that way—as an investigative tool," says Morgan, who wrote much of the software code for the FBI. "It was a slow-going, laborious discovery process, with some amazing moments."

Acxiom's work led to "deportations and indictments," says an executive, as well as thank-you calls from Ashcroft and FBI boss Robert Mueller. In one case, Morgan says, Acxiom was enlisted after the capture in Texas of two Muslim immigrants with expired visas who had boarded planes on 9/11 with box cutters. The two were never linked to the hijackings, but Acxiom's data helped convict them of involvement in the sale of fraudulent credit cards, which led to their deportation.

Meanwhile, Clark began opening doors in Washington, looking to convert the good will toward Acxiom into business opportunities. He arranged and attended meetings at the CIA, Treasury, the State Department, and the Pentagon. By all accounts, officials from Paul O'Neill to John Poindexter were impressed, as was Health and Human Services Secretary Tommy Thompson, who met with Clark in October 2002 and agreed to initiate a test using Acxiom data to help reduce fraud. Beyond tracking terrorists, connecting the government's disparate and archaic databases can help drive down identity theft, the nation's fastest-growing crime. In one test, Acxiom found more than 100 people using the same Social Security number.

Morgan recalls joining Clark for a meeting at the Pentagon, where they made their way to the front of a long security line. As soon as guards spotted the retired general, they whisked the two inside under armed escort. "A lot of the headway we have made lies in the access that General Clark has provided," states a memo from Morgan in 2002. "Here's the approach he takes to helping position Acxiom: 'IT has a role to play because we'll never be safe enough if we try to build walls and conduct searches and screenings. We have to really know who our neighbors are and what their interests are.'"

The highest-ranking official Clark and Morgan visited was Vice President Dick Cheney. Clark led the July 2002 presentation, which laid out the firm's capabilities in a 40-page white paper that cited the example of American Airlines hijacker Waleed Alsheri—Acxiom consumer No. 254-04907-10006. Cheney was "very positive," recalls former Arkansas Senator Tim Hutchinson, who arranged the meeting. "He said he would 'ring the bell'—as he put it—and try and let people know about it."

One of Acxiom's biggest cheerleaders was Hillary Clinton. According to Morgan, Clinton expressed support for a system that would gather detailed data on every passenger during the ticketing process. After a visit with Clinton in November 2001, Morgan reported to his staff: "It was very gratifying when the president of one of Lockheed Martin's companies approached Jerry [Jones] and me after one meeting and said she had heard from Senator Clinton that Acxiom was a company she really needed to get to know." Clark also played a significant role with Lockheed, and in February 2003, when the TSA named the company as its prime contractor on CAPPS II, Acxiom got a key subcontract.

Just when things were looking up for Acxiom's government business— which accounts for less than 1% of the company's annual revenue— the wheels came off. Hutchinson says the company got "bogged down" in federal bureaucracy. Others at Acxiom wonder if politics might have been at play. Certainly Clark's harsh attacks on the Bush administration throughout 2003 didn't help. Nor have Clark's post-Acxiom diatribes against the two-year-old Patriot Act, which sanctions the sharing of data between government and the private sector.

And the timing of the computer hacks couldn't have been worse, occurring just as Acxiom's key government projects were coming under fire. In September the Senate wiped out funding for the Terrorism Information Awareness project (TIA), a global surveillance database launched in January 2002 by DARPA, the Pentagon's advanced research agency. Clark had gotten Acxiom in the door. But before it could land a contract, the project was shut down—and its director, John Poindexter, forced out—when a TIA subcontractor posted information on its website about a proposed futures market in terrorism and assassination.

Jones, Acxiom's lawyer, says killing TIA was an overreaction. For one thing, it was purely a research project using artificial data, not a mandate to build and implement a product. "You can't create a system on the fly to

> It was a colossal oversight. "So often the thing you don't think about comes and bites you," says Morgan.

make it useful," Jones says. "You must at least build the infrastructure and have things running in the background." A public debate in advance would have been better, he adds: "Starting the debate afterward, the outcome is certain."

Acxiom was also caught in the blowback over CAPPS II. Last February, Torch Concepts, a Pentagon subcontractor, included the real Social Security number of a passenger in a PowerPoint presentation to a trade group. The information came from Acxiom, which had been asked by one of its customers, JetBlue, to provide detailed information on two million passengers to Torch for an Army study. A privacy activist eventually found out about the breach and posted the Social Security number on the Internet. In September, Congress blocked funding for implementing CAPPS II until the GAO issues a report on privacy concerns, which is expected this month.

Today the situation is as complicated as the hunt for terrorists. The Federal Trade Commission is examining Acxiom's role, JetBlue is fending off class-action lawsuits, and one of Clark's former campaign rivals, Senator Joseph Lieberman, has requested that the Secretary of Defense investigate whether the Army violated the Privacy Act by not informing JetBlue's passengers. "There wouldn't be politics in that, now would there?" asks Morgan about the Lieberman effort. Adds Jennifer Barrett, Acxiom's chief privacy officer: "We're not having a thoughtful and deliberative debate. Shut down the funding and you don't fix the problem."

That Acxiom was caught snoozing by hackers is ironic. Despite its Big Brother capabilities, the company gets praised—even by critics—for being a pioneer on privacy issues. Every employee undergoes regular and rigorous training about privacy. Morgan often butts heads with his trade group, the Direct Marketing Association, on everything from e-mail spam to the federal do-not-call list. He understands that agitated consumers are bad for business. "The first time I brought up privacy policy at the DMA was 1992, when I joined the board," he recalls. "Everyone looked at me like I was an idiot. It wasn't on the agenda." Acxiom was among the first in any industry to appoint a chief privacy officer with power to nix unethical projects like selling data linked to Social Security numbers to marketers. Yet it was only in the wake of the hacker intrusions that Acxiom created the post of chief security officer, with full-time responsibility for preventing cybercrime and mandating encryption.

The lack of encryption was a colossal oversight. "So often the thing you don't think about comes and bites you," says Morgan. "Most of our customers didn't want to go through the trouble of encryption." Yet that seems reckless at a time when the credit card industry is under siege by hackers and identity thieves. "The losses [to business] are in the billions," Morgan says. Acxiom maintains that its two breaches were the only ones in its history. How can the company be sure? Baas was nailed almost by accident, after investigators examined the computer of another hacker they were probing. And he had taken up residence inside their server for two years.

If Acxiom expects to hold itself up as the gold standard for technology linking and processing, Morgan has to seal his own leaky roof. Investigators say Baas offered Acxiom's data to other hackers if they would help him organize the information into his own database. Luckily he found no takers. "Large

(Cont.)

> "Large corporations need to realize they are the trustees of the personal information of millions of Americans."

corporations need to realize that they are the trustees of the personal information of millions of Americans," says Robert Behlen, a federal prosecutor in the Baas case. "Had the defendant chosen to post the stolen information on the Internet or used it to open credit card accounts, the amount of damage would have been significantly higher."

Last June, in an appearance before the FTC, Morgan said that Acxiom conducted "risk assessments and regular audits on all internal and external information systems to ensure the integrity of client data and Acxiom data." And Morgan's clients have for years performed their own security audits of Acxiom's network, testing it for penetration weaknesses. But the file transfer protocol (FTP) server penetrated in both computer hacks had miserable protection.

Think of an FTP server as an electronic mailbox sitting outside the firewall—a landing spot used by customers and vendors to send and receive files. Baas used a password issued to his employer, an Acxiom vendor, to access the server. From there he managed to crack hundreds of passwords, including one that acted like a master key to the internal systems, letting him scoop up unencrypted data on millions of consumers. "Once you're in the family, so to speak, we're probably more trusting and not as careful as we probably should be," explains Morgan. "We must change that."

In October, Acxiom told securities analysts that new projects and contracts were largely on hold as the firm scrambled to improve its security. It put a SWAT team in place, hired two independent auditing firms, and bought third-party tools to detect intrusions. The company also changed its access and password procedures, and is rapidly moving toward full and automated encryption. Jones held a conference call with 100 general counsels of the affected companies, while other firms flew to Arkansas to see for themselves what had happened. But publicly Acxiom has tried to play down the breaches. "I think this was a much bigger deal than the company let on to investors," says analyst Brad Eichler, who follows Acxiom for Stephens, the Little Rock investment bank that took Acxiom public. "They spent a lot of time that quarter patching things up with customers who were really ticked off."

Acxiom executives say the breaches haven't resulted in any customer defections. Nor have they affected the company's stock price, which recently hit a 52-week high of $19.32.

The larger question is whether the hacking incidents and the concerns about privacy will derail efforts to create a linked infrastructure of databases to help in the war on terrorism. In the debate between privacy and national security, Congress should not lose sight of its own joint congressional inquiry into 9/11, which concluded that law enforcement was unable to connect the dots before the attacks because technology "has not been fully and most effectively applied" in terror prevention. The hijackers followed patterns that could have been detected: purchasing tickets with cash, sharing residences and post office boxes, even using the same frequent-flier number. One terrorist had an expired visa. Another went to a travel agent to buy his ticket, only to discover that his debit card had insufficient funds. He paid in cash and offered a fake Virginia driver's license for ID. Asked for a telephone number, he gave one that was disconnected and had never been his. Acxiom's database could have provided real-time data to connect those dots.

The World on a String

P&G's Jim Stengel is willing to bet $5.5 billion that marketing must change

By John Galvin, Point (supplement to Advertising Age)

Jim Stengel is sitting at a conference table in his Cincinnati Procter & Gamble office, waxing on about a tiny little product made from the essence of yeast used in ancient Japanese sake production.

Legend has it that a monk discovered and isolated the "age-defying liquid" after noticing what soft hands the sake-factory workers had. Today, the good monk's work is manifested in a Procter & Gamble skin-care line called SK-II, and it includes everything from "facial-cleansing cream" to "anti-aging emulsions" and "revitalizing eye-contour serum." SK-II practically promises to turn back the aging clock on your skin, and to get it you don't even have to sell your soul—just your stock portfolio.

Despite prices ranging from $100 to $300 for a magical little bottle, SK-II is the high-end skin-care market leader in Asia, and Procter & Gamble is rolling it out to Saks Fifth Avenue stores in the U.S.

But it isn't the high cost that has Stengel excited. It's how the product is positioned that has him thinking of new ways to sell everything from Folgers coffee to Head and Shoulders shampoo. It's a good way, in fact, to highlight what is (very rarely) right and what is (more often than not) wrong about most marketing.

"SK-II has taken a tremendously holistic view of their brand and consumer experience," say Stengel. "We have tremendous knowledge of the consumer. We have tremendous aesthetics and sense of design. We have great packaging, and great in-store experience."

"We [also] have great permission marketing. Many consumers buy SK-II directly from a consultant in a store, so there's follow-up with replenishment. We'll follow up with a spa experience so the customer can try new products. We reach out to them outside the store, through email or hard mail, and that's been one of the pillars of that brand's success."

Within this marketing effort are the secrets to a global marketing strategy that Jim Stengel believes will carry Procter & Gamble into the future.

GLOBAL VISION

Stengel is, of course, the Global Marketing Officer of Procter & Gamble. Like many in P&G's top ranks he's a lifer, having started in 1983 as a brand assistant on Duncan Hines cookies. After graduating to brand manager of Jif, he went on to head the European and global baby-care units until he was promoted to the senior marketing post in 2001.

In this era of lofty titles, GMO must be one of the loftier ones. But, in this case, it's entirely appropriate. Stengel oversees an annual marketing budget of $5.5 billion, and manages a global work force of 3,500 marketers who, in turn, run more than 300 brands. Together, they sell Ariel in Yemen, Charmin in Chicago and Crest in Beijing.

And, as of late, they are doing it quite well. Last year, the company had $51 billion in sales—more than the entire gross domestic product of many countries, including the

> **STENGEL'S CHALLENGE:**
>
> If he can't re-educate an entire industry to this new way of thinking about marketing—if the whole industry doesn't get what he's talking about—then none of the changes will work for P&G.

United Arab Emirates, Guatemala and the Dominican Republic. Add to that an impressive 25% growth in net income over the previous year, with 16 brands—from Bounty to Pampers—ringing in over a billion in sales last year.

Yet, as Stengel is the first to point out, and as most marketing professionals already know, these are scary times in the marketing business. The consumer is increasingly elusive. But in times of stress and change, old habits die hard. "We are trying to get away from having TV story boards in our first pitch meetings," says Stengel. "It's really ridiculous when you think about it, but it still happens all the time." If it's happening at P&G, it's happening everywhere.

Call it a kind of industry-side cognitive dissonance. Everyone is aware of the problem, but too many are still acting—and billing—as if they aren't. "The industry isn't there yet," say Stengel. "But the days of pounding people with images, and shoving them down their eyeballs are over. The consumer is much more in control now, and if people don't believe that, they just need to spend some time with the consumers."

(Cont.)

FOUR STANDARDS

In the most basic terms, there are four concepts underpinning Jim Stengel's global marketing strategy for 2005: holistic marketing; permission marketing; better measurement; and experimentation. Stengel is developing these concepts as tools for the rest of Procter & Gamble. And here's his challenge: If he can't re-educate an entire industry to this new way of thinking—if the whole industry doesn't get what he's talking about—then none of the changes will work for P&G.

In Stengelese, holistic marketing is code for "know your customer, and know how she wants to receive information from you." In years past at P&G, agency a concept—most universally delivered via a series of TV spots—and media planners figured out how to get the message in front of P&G prospects. "Now," says Stengel, "we think much more upfront about *who* is the consumer. We do a lot of deep consumer understanding, and we do it with the communications-planning agency. We try to figure out how she consumes entertainment, how she lives her life, and what are the right ways to be part of that life."

A favorite "holistic" example of Stengel's is the successful Tampax tampons relaunch. After years of research, P&G decided the principle consumers of Tampax were teens, and teens had different ideas about how, and where, they wanted to learn about feminine hygiene. It wasn't through TV. "So, we radically changed our approach," says Stengel. "There was a large investment in Internet, and a large investment in print. We totally changed the brand's attitude, and the entire creative product that came out of it."

"It was a profound change. There were new people on the team from the beginning—communication planners, designers. It was a different process, and we got a very different approach to marketing. The business turned around, and it would not have happened without that process."

Indeed, the idea seems to be embraced by P&G's agencies. Kevin Roberts, the CEO of Saatchi and Saatchi, which handles several P&G brands, believes P&G is changing the industry for the better: "The first seismic shift came four years ago, when P&G changed how we are compensated. Now we get paid if sales increase. It was liberating because we could come up with *any* idea, not just TV."

Working under the new communication-planning strategy, Saatchi and Saatchi and P&G are turning Pampers into a baby health-care line, not just diapers that keep your baby dry. "With Pampers we came up with the idea—it's in the U.K. and Sweden now, and coming to the U.S.—of looking at the world through a baby's eyes," says Roberts. "In one park—because that's a place where parents take their children—we placed these giant park benches around. So, instead of TV we are reaching parents in stores, hospitals, and on the Net." Likewise, for Tide, you'll soon start seeing the orange bull's-eye in places where people get dirty—places like ballparks and, perhaps, even restaurant bathrooms.

STENGEL'S THEORY:

CMOs who are most successful in driving their company's growth, innovation, and brand building are those managers who have the same agenda as the CEO.

The second Stengel strategy is permission marketing, a program that flows directly from holistic marketing. The idea is that if your know your customer intimately, you will use marketing tools to create a connection that is so interesting, and so compelling, that consumers will ask for more. In effect, they will give you permission to market to them, just as the ladies buying SK-II freely give up their phone numbers so they can talk about upcoming SK-II products.

Measurement is perhaps the biggest laggard in Stengel's strategy. At the moment, he says, there aren't any decent tools to measure how events like in-store experience, or Internet exchanges, are working. "Most of the industry's tools today measure TV, a single variable of a marketing plan," says Stengel. "We need to measure the impact of the total approach to the consumer."

No such impact-meter exists at the moment, but P&G has been an early (and substantial) supporter of the VNU/Arbitron Apollo. Together, the two are developing a pager-size receiver to monitor what information a consumer receives throughout the day. Did going to a Website such as Tampax's beinggirl.com lead to a purchase later in the day? Did seeing a Tide bull's-eye on a baseball stadium's Jumbotron lead to a detergent purchase after the game? These are questions the Apollo project hopes to answer, and P&G has brought other multi-tiered advertisers to their Cincinnati headquarters to learn about the project. "It's in test markets right now," says Stengel. "They have bold plans but it has to be right for the consumer. We are going to be quality driven on this, not time driven. We are impatient for it, but we will go forward when they think it's right."

For his part, Stengel is an obsessive measurer, and has turned the measurement campaign inward. He commissions annual surveys to assess marketers' morale, job satisfaction, training effectiveness and how much time marketers spend on their core work. "Marketing is defined a bit differently at different companies," says Stengel. "Unless you are vigilant, and unless you are extremely clear as a leader about what is important in marketing, it gets diffuse. One area I look at is: How consumer-centric are we? Are we spending adequate time on it? I'm not talking about just sitting in a focus group, but serious time understanding consumers. That means being experientially involved with consumers and customers. It means living the life of consumers where, in some markets, their lifestyle and income level are radically different from ours."

(Cont.)

Herein lies the role of the GMO, as Stengel sees it: Making sure that a worldwide marketing organism is thinking the same way, motivated by the same things, and working towards the same goals. "If that happens it's a powerful dynamic," says Stengel. You certainly have to have the right culture to do that, but it's leadership's challenge to make that happen."

NEW TEST FOR NEW MARKETS

Early this year, in the midst of a multi-week tour through Asia, Jim Stengel will broadcast live over the Web from Guangzhou, China. It's part of an ongoing series called the Stengel Marketing Hour and the audience will be Procter & Gamble's global marketing force. It's one-part group-strategy session, one-part marketing variety hour. Guangzhou is a 6.6 million-person metropolis at the mouth of China's Pearl River—a place where P&G would like to sell a lot of products. The meeting's setting also highlights that China is not Europe, and not the U.S., and a new market dynamic is likely to require a different marketing perspective.

It's a natural segue to this quarter's Marketing Hour theme: experimentation. Indeed, if you had to crystallize Stengel's 2005 global marketing strategy in three words, they would be experiment, experiment and experiment.

"I'm not talking about wild experimentation," says Stengel. "I'm talking about strategic consumer-based experiments. We introduced a test product called Mr. Clean AutoDry and it's been an incredible success. We experimented with a lot of direct-television selling before that went to retail. We did a lot of influencer marketing with passionate car buffs before product was out, so we did a lot of seeding of the idea. That's very different from how we normally would have marketed."

Timothy Calkins, clinical associate professor of marketing at Northwestern's Kellogg School of Management, thinks Stengel is taking the right approach. "The trick is to continue doing what you know how to do well, and then experiment with all of the new stuff," says Calkins. "The flip side is that you can really get into trouble by investing everything in new ideas and projects. It can absorb all of your resources, and if it doesn't work then you've tanked the business."

Enabling much of this experimentation is, of course, technology. Mobile phones now get spam text messages. Music-only cable channels, which originally only identified the musician and the album, now carry advertisements. Pop-up ads, which some marketers might call inventive—but which most consumers call annoying—are everywhere.

Twenty P&G products showed up on last season's "Survivor" including one contest that offered Pringles as a reward. Competitors on the most recent *Apprentice* series designed an ad campaign for Crest. It drove more than 100,000 dentalphiliacs to a Crest Website for some honest-to-goodness permission marketing.

OVERKILL?

There is, however, a risk of alienating consumers with so much marketing overkill. People tune in to "The Apprentice" to watch fledgling megalomaniacs and celebrity-wannabes scheme against each other, not because they want to learn abut the new M&M M-Azing candy bar.

The threat is that perhaps people don't want to be marketed to everywhere and every way. With TV commercials, at least everybody knows what the game is. TV, as fragmented as it is, is still quite powerful. "If you want to reach every household in the country," says Northwestern's Calkins, "there's only one way to do it: Super Bowl commercials. If you want to launch a product nationally in four weeks, you need to advertise on network television."

For his part, Stengel shares the alienation concern, arguing that at some point in the future marketers will have the ability to reach any consumer, anytime on a personal device—be it a phone, computer or PDA. The trick is figuring out where and when it's OK to market.

"This test that Google is doing with G-mail is very interesting," says Stengel. "They give you storage on their server, and very subtly link up some advertising based on what your interests in your emails show. Now that might be getting pretty close to the privacy line, but actually if the consumer says that's a helpful service, and the approach is very low key, a lot of consumers will see it as a great service. At Amazon, if you buy a few books they recommend some others, and most people find that helpful, and even stimulating and enjoyable."

Proximity to the target audience is a vital part of Stengel's plan. "If you are close enough to the consumer, you will get that understanding, and if we keep marketers in their assignments longer, in order to develop knowledge in the category and with the consumer—like I was talking about earlier with SK-II—then I think we will be able to deliver that."

CMOs who are most successful in driving their company's growth, innovation, and brand building are those managers who have the same agenda as the CEO. At least that's Stengel's theory on why he has met with success in the job. "I'm very happy to say we have the same agenda

> **STENGEL'S CONCERN:**
> At some point in the future, marketers will have the ability to reach any consumer, at any time on a personal device—be it a phone, computer, or PDA. Yet no consumer will want this.

(Cont.)

here," says Stengel. "A.G. [Lafley, P&G president-CEO] and I both came out of marketing, as did most of our senior management. Our offices are just a few meters apart and the doors are always open. We sit down with the top 15 franchise leaders once a quarter. We do a once a year health check on our top brands. He participates in our training."

THE GMO CHALLENGE

Being a GMO, by definition, makes it difficult for Stengel to personally fulfill one of the key components of the corporate agenda: getting to know consumers. It's a struggle he regularly engages. On his Asia swing, Stengel will go on an in-house visit. He will sit in a customer's home, listen to her stories—even get a chance to see what her bathroom looks like. The visit will bring him closer to his far-flung customers, but also set the tone for his team of worldwide marketers: It is imperative that they understand the life of their customers.

In Tokyo he'll visit retailers and ask how they feel about P&G products. Could they be packaged better? Could they be placed better? Could they be better? In Singapore he'll visit one of SK-II's spas so he can understand those customers—and yes, he'll get a facial too.

"A lot of our breakthrough innovations have come from people who are passionate about the consumer, people who want to make their lives better, and who found unusual ways to uncover insights and learning. We have that living and breathing in our culture right now and we need to continue to be all over that because it will be the difference between success and failure," says Stengel.

According to Calkins at the Kellogg School of Management, P&G is "asking all the right questions. They are pushing the agencies, pushing the researchers, and experimenting with new ideas," says Calkins. "Nobody knows what's going to happen over the next few years, but they've put themselves in a good place to figure it out when it happens."

Stengel agrees. "I can't sit here—no GMO can—and say which way marketing is going to unfold in the next 10 years," he continues. "I can encourage a culture of experimentation and testing and creativity. Because 3,500 P&G marketers working with all their agencies will come up with some new approaches and some innovations that I can then recognize and transfer much of that learning—or the principles behind it—to other brand franchises and across country and regional lines. That is a huge power of the role I'm in: To create the conditions and culture for positive change and then share the learning across our organizations."

Jim Stengel is, himself, a fanatic. Ask him to talk about Procter & Gamble, or the woes of modern marketing and he'll take you up on your offer—at length and in detail. It's a passion that—outside the world of P&G—probably doesn't make him a great dinner guest, but so far makes for a successful

THE BACK ROAD TO THE HIGH ROAD

As second-in-command in the P&G marketing hierarchy, Ted Woehrle engineers strategy and tactics.

Ted Woehrle began his Procter & Gamble career in 1983 as an engineer managing energy conservation at the century-old plant that makes Ivory soap in Cincinnati. Today, he engineers two very different kinds of projects—P&G's drive to boost marketing return on investment and the implementation of its new communications planning model.

"He's understated yet effective," says Pete Blackshaw, chief marketing officer of online feedback tracker Intelliseek, who worked under Mr. Woehrle in P&G's interactive marketing unit in the late 1990s. "He has a consistent track record of getting things done without rattling the cage or shaking the boat, which is amazing."

Jim Stengel paved the way for Mr. Woehrle's move to marketing when, as brand manager of Jif peanut butter in 1989, he brought the engineer in as assistant brand manager. Their career paths then diverged until last year, when Mr. Woehrle assumed a newly created position as VP-Marketing North America, reporting to Mr. Stengel and to Rob Steele, group president-North America.

"It's the first time my responsibilities have rolled up under one person in North America," says Mr. Woehrle, who's also charged with training and retention of more than 500 marketers across P&G's business units.

He comes to his task of reengineering marketing with P&G entrepreneurial credentials. His last position was VP overseeing the launch of the Tremor online buzz marketing venture, which uses a group of more than 200,000 highly connected teens to spread the word about new products for P&G and other clients. Previously, he was the marketing director who spearheaded the Agency Relationship Renewal process that replaced media commissions with sales-based compensation, loosened conflict rules and simplified advertising development.

"Innovation has been a theme," Mr. Woehrle says. "All of these experiences help me be a more effective change agent."

—Jack Neff

management strategist. Marketing, for Stengel, is not about selling a product; it's about letting a consumer know that you've got something that just might change her life.

It's a lot to ask of Mr. Clean, or even SK-II. But if nobody believes in it, then how do you expect somebody to buy it?

39

Nielsen's Search For Hispanics Is a Delicate Job

Miriam Jordan. Wall Street Journal.

Los Angeles—**JORGE DELGADO** pounds the pavements of this city's blue-collar neighborhoods, knocking on doors if he thinks someone is home. Mr. Delgado is often mistaken for an immigration officer, a missionary or a swindler. He has been chased away by jealous husbands.

But the 57-year-old Peruvian-American isn't selling encyclopedias, proselytizing or looking for love. As a recruiter for market-research company AC Nielsen, he's trying to persuade one of the nation's fastest-growing consumer groups—Hispanic immigrants—to cough up information about their shopping habits.

It isn't particularly easy. Mr. Delgado pleads, cajoles and applies some gentle arm-twisting. He tells the people who answer the door that he isn't interested in their immigration status. He tries appealing to community spirit, to the Latino sense of family. "You will make Hispanics count," he tells potential recruits. "Companies will know what we like and better serve our people."

Mr. Delgado, who has been a recruiter for three years, once knocked on 208 doors before signing up a single participant. A more typical success rate is one in 40. "It's a tough job just getting them to open the door," says Mr. Delgado, who knows tough jobs. He used to sell health insurance.

AC Nielsen, a unit of **VNU** NV, in 1989 launched its Homescan Consumer Panel to track consumers' purchases of packaged goods, and by year end it is expected to cover 90,000 U.S. households, most of them recruited by mail. People who sign up get a device to use at home to scan the bar codes of the products they buy. AC Nielsen collects the data for clients such as **Procter & Gamble** Co. and **Kraft Foods** Inc. The companies like the survey because it aims to track consumers' actual purchases rather than their reported preferences.

But recruiting Hispanic households presents difficulties for market researchers, even in Los Angeles, where Hispanics make up about 40% of the population. (Another VNU unit, Nielsen Media Research, which tracks consumers' television-viewing habits, was named in a lawsuit, filed by Spanish-language broadcaster **Univision Communications** Inc., alleging that Nielsen's "people meter" undercounts Hispanic homes.)

Hispanics are the most mobile of all groups, according to the U.S. census. About half of AC Nielsen's Hispanic panel has to be replenished every year. "There goes my household," says Isabel Valdes, a consultant who helped AC Nielsen design the Hispanic project, every time someone disappears. The scanner, which is worth about $350, often goes with departing families.

Some immigrants who may be in the U.S. illegally are nervous or skeptical when contacted by strangers. Even if their immigration status isn't in question, they often have little experience with consumer research and a good deal of exposure to crooks and fraudsters.

Given these difficulties, AC Nielsen outsourced the job of Hispanic recruiting to Cultural Access Group, Mr. Delgado's employer and a company that specializes in multicultural market research. It's taken three years to enlist 1,500 households in the Los Angeles program. The cost to recruit one of those households is at least five times the cost of recruiting non-Hispanics, industry experts say.

Juana Castillo says suspicious spouses often stymie her work as a recruiter for Smart Hispanic Services, a Santa Ana, Calif., firm that arranges focus groups for packaged-goods and pharmaceutical companies. When Ms. Castillo asked one woman about birth control, her husband called back and shouted at her for asking personal questions. Another woman followed her husband to a focus group about motor oil and threw a fit when she couldn't get into the interview room, Ms. Castillo recalls. The woman calmed down when she was allowed to watch through a two-way mirror.

Mr. Delgado dresses neatly, but not too neatly, lest someone mistake him for a door-to-door missionary. His first task is overcoming the fundamental obstacles in door-to-door sales. On a recent trip to Los Angeles's Huntington Park area, he spotted some evangelists who had arrived ahead of him. He made a U-turn and headed back. "Nobody was going to listen to me anymore around there," he says.

If Mr. Delgado gets a foot in the door, he tries to explain that Homescan participants can accumulate points to claim prizes. And Nielsen usually offers new participants a free mug, a key chain or a pen. But Hispanic households dismissed those inducements as insignificant. Instead, Nielsen sends $5 to Hispanic families as a welcome gift and then another $5 every month they participate.

When a recruiter tried to persuade Maria Nava to join, the Mexican housewife was suspicious. "I was almost certain that I would have to pay something in the end, or that he would try to sell me something," says Ms. Nava, 36, of La Mirada, Calif., who became a devoted panelist.

Since Sept. 11, 2001, the scanner and its red beam have unnerved some people. After muttering under his breath about undercover cameras, an East Los Angeles man told Mr. Delgado he didn't want anything to do with the scanner.

Even after Mr. Delgado manages to find someone to *empanelar*—his Spanglish term for signing someone up—another hurdle arises: teaching participants how to use the scanner. The lesson can take more than two hours. He leaves his cellphone number behind, in case of emergencies.

One enthusiastic participant called almost every time he used the scanner, Mr. Delgado recalls. Once, the panelist called to ask which button to press for a shoe store. Mr. Delgado always helps out, even if a call interrupts his Sunday nap. His wife suggested Mr. Delgado tell the man to read the manual. "He's my panelist and I have to help him," says Mr. Delgado.

Silvia Perez, 32, quit the panel after about a year, because the small Mexican grocery stores where she shopped—unlike big chains—weren't preprogrammed in the scanner. Ms. Perez had to enter most items manually. "If I bought a toothpick at the corner store, I had to punch it in," says the Santa Ana resident.

AC Nielsen blames husbands for many of its difficulties getting into Hispanic homes. Maria Vasquez, a 37-year-old who lives in Corona, Calif., says her husband, Jesus, developed scanner envy. Mr. Vasquez complained the scanner, which he dubbed *la maquina,* or "the machine," wasted electricity (it runs on batteries) and detracted from his wife's cooking time, the couple says.

To appease her husband, Mrs. Vasquez waited until her husband wasn't around before she would take the groceries out of the cupboard and scan them. She recalls picking through the garbage to find an empty bottle of sparkling water to scan. One day, Mr. Vasquez ordered his wife to get rid of the scanner. She hid it. Eventually, the Vasquez family dropped out of the program. "This machine caused domestic problems," Mrs. Vasquez says.

Not all of Mr. Delgado's encounters are such hard work. If he gets inside, Mr. Delgado is sometimes offered something to eat and drink. If he overcomes all suspicion, he is treated like a friend. AC Nielsen recruiters say they often are invited to parties thrown by participants.

But after investing hours explaining the scanner, sometimes Mr. Delgado has to reject willing participants if it's clear they don't really understand how it works. "I feel bad when I have to turn people down," he says.

Product

40

WELCOME TO PROCTER & GADGET
The consumer giant is leading the way in building brands with mechanical gizmos

It looks as cool as an iPod and costs nearly as much: a sleek, handheld device that sprays ionized particles of makeup foundation on the face. But the company that will launch the $200 appliance in the U.S. within a year is hardly perceived as a cutting-edge gadget maker. It's Procter & Gamble Co., the Cincinnati consumer-goods company best known for household staples such as Pampers, Crest, and Tide.

The SK-II Air Touch, already selling in Japan and Britain, is leading a P&G strategy to jazz up those humdrum brands by placing them inside nifty new delivery devices. Not coincidentally, that also allows the company to boost pricing. It's a lesson P&G learned from watching Gillette's well-worn razor-and-replacement-blade strategy and its own runaway success with its $14 Swiffer mop (and $5.75 replacement pads) and the $7.69 SpinBrush electric toothbrush. P&G is spreading the strategy to multiple categories, redefining how it interacts with consumers and using the experience that is created through a device to foster greater loyalty to its brands. Says longtime P&G consultant Gary Stibel of New England Consulting Group: "It's a substantial shift in how P&G is thinking about brands."

Rivals such as S.C. Johnson & Son Inc. and even blade king Gillette Co. are also placing bigger bets on gadgets. But P&G is stepping on the gas. In the past year it has launched at least eight mechanical or electric gizmos. They include Febreze Scentstories, an electric air freshener machine that plays CD-like scent disks; Tide Buzz Ultrasonic Stain Remover; and Tide StainBrush,

a battery-powered brush. It also introduced Swiffer Sweep + Vac, a device that combines a Swiffer electrostatic dust mop with a vacuum, and Mr. Clean AutoDry, a water-pressure-powered car-cleaning system that dries without streaking. Sales of all P&G's gadget-related items grew 16% last year and now total about 8% of its $54 billion in annual sales. That's up from 2% in 2000, estimates Lehman Brothers Inc. analyst Ann Gillin Lefever.

COFFEE PADS

Consumer-products companies need new growth wherever they can find it. Sales in packaged goods are crawling ahead at just 3% annually. Gadgets not only create new sales but also drive future sales through replacement items. P&G is advancing that strategy by partnering with appliance makers who make hardware to support unique P&G products. Last year, home-appliance maker Applica Inc. launched the Home Café, a one-cup coffee maker that uses distinctive Folgers and Millstone coffee pads from P&G. Royal Philips Electronics introduced a Sonicare electric toothbrush that calls for specially formulated Crest toothpaste.

These profitable devices are lifting otherwise stagnating profit margins of soaps and household cleaners, thus offsetting margin pressure on sales in developing countries. And while consumer-products companies typically struggle to win any price increases these days, P&G is launching a $34 higher-powered premium version of AutoDry that also works inside the car and costs 70% more than the original. That beats a

22-ounce bottle of Mr. Clean for $2.99. By signing up contract manufacturers to make the devices, P&G gets to share capital costs. Profit on these devices is one reason P&G has been able to absorb rising costs of raw materials better than rivals Unilever Group and Colgate-Palmolive Co., which haven't followed the gadget strategy, says Banc of America Securities analyst William Steele.

P&G Chief Executive Alan G. "A.G." Lafley believes the most important aspect of his gadget approach is its potential to increase brand loyalty. Since taking the top job in 2000, Lafley has expanded the definition of P&G's big brands. Instead of just toothpaste, for instance, Crest now includes whitening products and the low-price electric SpinBrush line. The cheap, fun-to-use brush, Lafley says, has created a new and positive vibe around the whole Crest brand. "People remember experiences," Lafley notes. "They don't remember attributes."

Competitors are taking note. Last year, Gillette launched its M3Power battery-powered wet shaver after a first-time collaboration among the company's razor group, its Braun appliance division, and its Duracell unit. Clorox Co. introduced Swiffer competitor ReadyMop. S.C. Johnson rolled out Scrubbing Bubbles Fresh Brush, a toilet cleaning brush with a flushable disposable head that requires refills, and is testing a gadget under the same brand that hangs in the shower and automatically cleans the tub and tile.

Are companies creating demand by inventing new categories or responding to consumers' wants? Both, say executives and

Batteries Required
Consumer-products companies see gadgets as a way to hook consumers—and raise prices.

ORAL-B HUMMINGBIRD	TIDE BUZZ	VENUS VIBRANCE	SK-II
Gillette's undulating Oral-B Hummingbird flosser is riding a wave of oral care products. From whitening systems to flossers and tongue scrapers, consumers are more into their smiles than ever. Price: $7.29, $2.99 for floss refills.	P&G's stain-removing gadget, which uses an ultrasonic wand and special Tide cleaner. Price: $29.99, plus $4.88 for refills at Target. Stain-removing sprays and sticks run about $2.99.	The women's version of Gillette's battery-powered M3Power razor and blade system hits the market this spring. Price: About $10 for the starter kit—50% more than the nonpulsating shave.	Procter & Gamble's electric applicator for makeup foundation. Designed to replace the trusty (and cheap) sponge, the Air Touch is already selling in Britain and Japan and should arrive in the U.S. within a year. Price: About $200.

(Cont.)

consultants. "Inexpensive personal care gadgets is where the desire to self-pamper meets the gadgeting of our briefcase, belt, and car," says independent marketing consultant Dennis Keene. Add a willingness to spend more on personal grooming by baby boomers and Generation X, plus a growing distaste and lack of time for housecleaning by the same consumers, and it adds up to a huge opportunity for new devices, Keene says. Gillette's M3Power did little else but make the disposable razor head vibrate, but that was enough to grab 35% of the U.S. razor market in dollar terms and 6% of the disposable blade market within a short seven months of launch. "This has the potential to be the biggest-selling product ever in the blade and razor market," says Peter K. Hoffman, president of blades and razors at Gillette.

MR. CLEAN AUTO DRY:
Items like this car cleaner
help P&G boost margins

But there is clearly a fad worry to the gadget boom. As consumer-products companies generate new devices, margins inevitably will contract, predicts William A. Sahlman, a Harvard Business School professor who has studied the success of SpinBrush. Consumer demand for such devices, too, is difficult to gauge. And execution isn't always on target. Drug chain Walgreen Co., for example, reports that sales of P&G's $7.49 Dawn Power Dish Brush have eased since its launch in

2003. And some Procter & Gamble managers worry about the quality of devices, which can ultimately hurt the overall brand. P&G recently had to recall the Swiffer Vac because of electrical problems.

Lafley acknowledges there's no telling when consumers will max out on gadgets. "We have to be careful we don't push it too far," he admits. But for now, P&G is determined to find new ways to pack consumers' cabinets with nifty gizmos.

Robert Berner in Cincinnati, with William C. Symonds in Boston. Business Week.

41

Care, Feeding and Building of a Billion-Dollar Brand

Pringles manager Niccol mounts Stax defense

By: Jack Neff

It's Friday morning at Procter & Gamble Co., and while you'd never know it by his demeanor, Brian Niccol is under attack.

Not personally. But Mr. Niccol is North American brand manager for Pringles at a time when his potato-crisp brand faces its biggest-ever direct challenge in the form of Lay's Stax from PepsiCo's Frito-Lay. Stax launched in the U.S. in September and crossed the border in January to open a second front in Canada.

In a company known for its stiffness, particularly under fire, Mr. Niccol isn't showing it. He's relaxed and quick with a wisecrack, belying a P&G stereotype of unpersonable managers. At one point, he mentions his plans to host a "Survivor" party on a Sunday night when most of America will be at Super Bowl parties. The reason: His athletic-themed spoof ad for Fiery Hot Pringles lost out in P&G's internal Super Bowl derby to Charmin, but its runner-up status won time on the premiere of "Survivor 8" following the Super Bowl.

Mr. Niccol is a rare under-30 brand manager at P&G. Even before he took the Pringles job in December 2002, he had spent two years as brand manager launching Therma-care heat wraps. That stint is commemorated by a ballcap and other brand memorabilia that liven his cubicle—one of many cube farms throughout the very cubic P&G "central building" in Cincinnati.

WUNDERKIND

Already managing one of P&G's billion-dollar brands at 29, Mr. Niccol has the markings of a wunderkind. He also has the added bonus, according to one former P&G executive, of working on a snack business considered "non-core," and thus relatively free of senior management meddling.

But his day is quite typical of the grindstone sharpening that noses get around here. Mr. Niccol gets in around 7:45 this morning, typical for him and many other P&G brand managers who trickle in before 8, despite snow-snarled traffic. The time before 9 will be one of the few quiet, meeting-free segments he'll spend alone in his cubicle as he catches up with e-mail, voicemail and reading. The rest of his day, which ends around 7 p.m., is filled mainly with meetings, both scheduled and impromptu.

Besides his 55-hour-plus workweek, Mr. Niccol takes his work home on the weekend. From Chairman-CEO A.G. Lafley and Global Marketing Officer James Stengel comes the drive to spend more time with consumers. For Mr. Niccol, that usually means taking his wife on a Saturday shopping trip that spans four stores, representing the gamut of classes of trade, so he can check displays and chat up consumers.

He's been married three years. And while he didn't meet wife Jennifer at work, like many office-bound P&Gers do, he was introduced to her by a colleague. "I was complaining that I hadn't had any dates," Mr. Niccol recalls. "And at P&G, a culture of action, they took care of it for me."

His Friday morning starts with *The Wall Street Journal.* An article makes him wonder whether Pepsi's "It's the Cola" campaign reflects a broader shift by PepsiCo, including Frito-Lay, to focus on products and advertising ideas rather than celebrities.

Mr. Niccol's mind is on the competition a lot these days. His first meeting, around 9 a.m., is with Jason Thacker, assistant brand manager in charge of "Stax defense" and new-product initiatives. It's a natural combination in Mr. Niccol's mind: "Obviously, I'm cognizant of what my competitors are doing," he says later. "But I strongly believe the best defense is a good offense."

With Mr. Thacker, he's reviewing the weekly sales and share data from ACNielsen Corp. Stax recently has lowered its retail price under $1 at a major store account, and now P&G is tracking a wide array of other retailers starting to follow.

Pringles' cheddar-flavor version—comparable to a cheddar version of Stax—is 7% below forecast, but Mr. Thacker chalks it up to lingering effects of a tornado that shut down Pringles' Tennessee factory for several weeks last summer and made it miss out on back-to-school promotions.

CONFERENCE CALL

Mr. Thacker also passes on what he learned at a bar over the weekend from an acquaintance—that another package-goods company has been working up plans for a co-branded flavor to pitch to Pringles. But the same marketer already has a deal with a regional competitor, Mr. Niccol notes.

Mr. Thacker is one of five ABMs who report to Mr.

(Cont.)

Niccol, along with a marketing specialist in retail design and a clerical support staffer. Mr. Niccol tries to meet with each daily, and his next stop is a conference room at 9:45, where he pulls ABM Nate Lawton to go over the comprehensive business review he'll present in the next few weeks to Jamie Egasti, VP-North American snacks.

Around 10, Mr. Niccol starts a conference call with two executives from his ad agency, Grey Global Group's Grey Advertising, New York. He goes over a laundry list of issues big and small—how music royalties are keeping them from getting extra mileage for the "Athlete" ad on CBS.com; an ABM's maiden voyage to a commercial shoot planned for Los Angeles the next day; plans to "on-board," in P&G-speak, African-American shop Carol H. Williams Advertising, Oakland, Calif., on marketing plans.

Mr. Niccol notes a corporate goal of spending 10% to 15% of media dollars on African-American ads for the top 10 to 15 brands, including Pringles. "It's got to be qualified copy [in other words, hit minimum copy test scores] to release the funds," he says.

Then he gets to the bigger picture. "In the mid-'90s, we had better advertising," he tells Grey's Lynn Janovsky, VP-group management supervisor, and Liz Mason, account supervisor. That was a period when now-defunct Wells, Rich, Greene handled the business. But, he adds: "I think we have a lot of momentum now coming out of the 'Athlete' spot" set to break on "Survivor."

'GET ON BOARD'

Talk shifts to work being done by Grey's Canadian agency team. "They need to get on board with the pace we want to go in," he says. "The pace is only going to go faster."

By 10:45, Mr. Niccol's focus has shifted to the store and a different conference room, as he meets with two sales managers and a finance manager to go over promotion plans. Item one: a promotion with a nontraditional retailer that has spun out of control, with prices so low they're upsetting other retailers.

"Does Jamie know about this yet?" Mr. Niccol asks, referring to Mr. Egasti. A sales executive shakes his head, somewhat sheepishly. They talk over ways to structure a new trade deal to help combat the more aggressive pricing on Stax in a way that treats all the classes of trade fairly, but they need more data to reach a conclusion.

Lunch arrives, to the same room, about 10 minutes ahead of the "Stax defense" meeting, which Mr. Niccol and crew will eat their way through.

From meeting to meeting, Mr. Niccol is spending as much time influencing decisions as making them. By the end of the day, he'll have had input on almost every aspect of the brand.

"The brand manager job is becoming a place where it's about influencing your cross-functional counterparts," Mr. Niccol says later. "I feel accountable to raise the red flag when we're saying we want to achieve X but we haven't resourced correctly to do it. . . . I view it as carrying the torch of the brand equity."

He continues to carry that torch in two new-product initiative meetings, and regroups at the end of the day with his ABMs.

Then it's off to the weekend and that party themed to "Survivor," where the reality show's own torch-carrying tribe members are constantly reminded that "Fire is life."

With Names Like These . . .

By Laura Shanahan

"WHAT'S IN A name?" pondered Shakespeare, famously noting that a rose by any other appellation would smell as sweet. Good thing William could spin sonnets and speeches, because marketing clearly wouldn't have been his calling. Sure, a rose or a hose would be the same by any other name; but the $64,000 question is: Would it sell? Sorry, Will, but the pay, not the play, is the thing here.

Increasingly, it seems names are noteworthy, for better or worse, for products as diverse as four-wheelers and films.

"Nearly as unwatchable as it is unpronounceable," the *Los Angeles Times* critic clearly enunciated about the motion picture Gigli, in which the titular character had to repeatedly advise "Jee-lee," while audiences got restlessly jiggly and inappropriately giggly. Would a less-annoying name have saved this turkey? Probably not, but it unnecessarily added yet another target for critics' and talk-show hosts' tossed tomatoes.

Volkswagen recently rolled out the well-received luxury SUV Touareg, which is so patently pronouncement-challenging that various reporters added something rarely seen in reviews: a phonetic spelling, so consumers wouldn't feel like total nimrods in front of car dealers. One particularly diligent reviewer noted that while "toor-egg" seems to be the way to go, he's also heard "ter-egg," "twor-regg," "twahr-reg," "too-reg" and even "twah-ray," concluding "suit yourself."

Ah, but the problem is, consumers don't like to risk looking like unschooled fools in front of sales and service staff. That's why we point to what we want on French menus. Sometimes on English ones, too. Or we order something else. Or nothing else. As the saying goes, better to stay silent and seem stupid, than to open one's mouth and confirm it.

Then there are the names we can pronounce all too well; we're just not comfortable saying 'em. At least not to folks we don't know very well.

"I'd like to get 'extra close,'" is at least one variant of what I'd have to say to philosophy's sales associate, in order to indicate a desire to purchase a shaving kit. (And yes, the company's name and products are lowercased, making the statement even more ambiguous in print.)

Alternately, I could say, "I need 'extra help,'" if I wanted to purchase a men's zit-zapping kit. Dunno about you, but I'm always fearful that if I feed people a straight line like that they'll turn into Triumph the Insult Comic Dog: "Lay-dee, tell me sahmtheeng I don't know—before I poop on you!"

Then there's the cosmetic cream by Fresh (now, that's a *great* name for a toiletries company; short, vividly descriptive, modern and, um, fresh!). Alas, in nearly stark contrast is the product's name: Crème Ancienne; shades of the French menu, with a *soupçon* of unfortunate association. No, the cream won't make you ancienne, but your wallet might look the worse for wear, having $250 extracted.

Speaking of unfortunate associations, I recently bought a sweater in a shade I'd call pale lime. "Frozen Frog," ribbit'd the hangtag, which I read *apres*-purchase. Now every time I wear it, I have visions of being trapped in a frigid school lab. I also liked a Coach pistachio-green suede bag, until I read the catalog description of "pear." Prickly. As sounds Cactus Club orange juice—yeah, that's what you want for liquid refreshment; associations of aridity and sharp needles.

> *Prickly. As if Cactus Club orange juice is what you'd want for liquid refreashment.*

Of course, much association is idiosyncratic; Smucker's, a fine brand, famously acknowledges the potential pitfall of a less-than-elegant moniker: "With a name like Smucker's, it has to be good." But my friend Jon loves the name. "It actually has the word 'muck' in it," I point out, but all Jon hears is a sound that smacks of smacking one's lips, which he does when he eats the make's jams.

What can we conclude? Other than that Jon is an idiot? Avoid names that evoke moribund animals, or are hard or embarrassing to say—and opt for the pithy and the positive.

Unless you're pitching to rebel youth, of course. Or selling hot sauce. I hear Screaming Sphincter is doing real well.

FAKES!

The global counterfeit business is out of control, targeting everything from computer chips to life-saving medicines. It's so bad that even China may need to crack down.

A year and a half ago, Pfizer Inc. got a disturbing call on its customer hotline. A woman who had been taking its cholesterol-lowering drug Lipitor complained that a new bottle of tablets tasted bitter. She sent the suspicious pills to the company, which tested them at a lab in Groton, Conn. The white oblong tablets looked just like the real thing—and even contained some of the active ingredient in Lipitor. But Pfizer soon determined that they were counterfeits. Over the next two months, distributors yanked some 16.5 million tablets from warehouses and pharmacy shelves nationwide.

An isolated case? Hardly. Last October, Brazilian police got a tip-off about a hoard of bogus Hewlett-Packard Co. inkjet cartridges and seized more than $1 million worth of goods. Chinese police last year conducted raids confiscating everything from counterfeit Buick windshields to phony Viagra. In Guam, the Secret Service in July uncovered a network selling bogus North Korean-made pharmaceuticals, cigarettes, and $100 bills. In June, French customs seized more than 11,000 fake parts for Nokia Corp. cell phones—batteries, covers, and more. In January, U.S. Commerce Secretary Donald Evans blasted the Chinese on a visit to Beijing, demanding they step up efforts to police intellectual-property violations. Evans singled out the case of a General Motors Corp. subsidiary that is suing Chinese carmaker Chery Automotive for ripping off the design of its Chevrolet Spark minicar. The uncanny resemblance between the two cars, said Evans, "defies innocent explanation."

CRITICAL MASS

Kiwi shoe polish, Callaway Golf clubs, Intel computer chips, Bosch power drills, BP oil. Pick any product from any well-known brand, and chances are there's a counterfeit version of it out there. Of course, as anyone who has combed the back alleys of Hong Kong, Rio, or Moscow knows, fakes have been around for decades. Only the greenest rube would actually believe that the $20 Rolex watch on Silom Road in Bangkok or the $30 Louis Vuitton bag on New York's Canal Street is genuine.

But counterfeiting has grown up—and that's scaring the multinationals. "We've seen a massive increase in the last five years, and there is a risk it will spiral out of control," says Anthony Simon, marketing chief of Unilever Bestfoods. "It's no longer a cottage industry." The World Customs Organization estimates counterfeiting accounts for 5% to 7% of global merchandise trade, equivalent to lost sales of as much as $512 billion last year—though experts say this is only a guess. Seizures of fakes by U.S. customs jumped by 46% last year as counterfeiters boosted exports to Western markets. Unilever Group says knockoffs of its shampoos, soaps, and teas are growing by 30% annually. The World Health Organization says up to 10% of medicines worldwide are counterfeited—a deadly hazard that could be costing the pharmaceutical industry $46 billion a year. Bogus car parts add up to $12 billion worldwide. "Counterfeiting has gone from a local nuisance to a global threat," says Hanns Glatz, DaimlerChrysler's point man on intellectual property.

The scale of the threat is prompting new efforts by multinationals to stop, or at least curb, the spread of counterfeits. Companies are deploying detectives around the globe in greater force than ever, pressuring governments from Beijing to Brasilia to crack down, and trying everything from electronic tagging to redesigned products to aggressive

> Counterfeiters are now so proficient that forensic experts are sometimes needed to spot bogus products

pricing in order to thwart the counterfeiters. Even some Chinese companies, stung by fakes themselves, are getting into the act. "Once Chinese companies start to sue other Chinese companies, the situation will become more balanced," says Stephen Vickers, chief executive of International Risk, a Hong Kong-based brand-protection consultant.

China is key to any solution. Since the country is an economic gorilla, its counterfeiting is turning into quite the beast as

CALLAWAY GOLF CLUB

PROBLEM:
Fiberglass shaft rather than graphite; head made from steel rather than titanium

RESULT:
Shaft may break; head may rust; may cause golfers to slice or hook their shots

REAL: $1,600*   FAKE: $1,200*

*Price per set of irons

well—accounting for nearly two-thirds of all the fake and pirated goods worldwide. Daimler's Glatz figures phony Daimler parts—from fenders to engine blocks—have grabbed 30% of the market in China, Taiwan, and Korea. And Chinese counterfeiters make millions of motorcycles a year, with knock-offs of Honda's workhorse CG125—selling for about $300, or less than half the cost of a real Honda—especially popular. It's tales like this that prompt some trade hawks in the U.S. to call for a World Trade Organization action against China related to counterfeits and intellectual-property rights violations in general. Such pressure is beginning to have some effect. "The Chinese government is starting to take things more seriously because of the unprecedented uniform shouting coming from the U.S., Europe, and Japan," says Joseph Simone, a lawyer specializing in IPR issues at Baker & McKenzie in Hong Kong.

Yet slowing down the counterfeiters in China and elsewhere will take heroic efforts. That's because counterfeiting thrives on the whole process of globalization itself. Globalization, after all, is the spread of capital and knowhow to new markets, which in turn contribute low-cost labor to create the ideal export machine, manufacturing first the cheap stuff, then moving up the value chain. That's the story of Southeast Asia. It's the story of China. Now it's the story of fakes. Counterfeiting packs all the punch of skilled labor, smart distribution, and product savvy without getting bogged down in costly details such as research and brand-building.

The result is a kind of global industry that is starting to rival the multinationals in speed, reach, and sophistication. Factories in China can copy a new model of golf club in less than a week, says Stu Herrington, who oversees brand protection for Callaway Golf Co. "The Chinese are extremely ingenious, inventive, and scientifically oriented, and they are becoming the world's manufacturer," he says. The company has found counterfeiters with three-dimensional design software and experience cranking out legitimate clubs for other brands, so "back-engineering a golf club is a piece of cake" for them, he says. And counterfeiters are skilled at duplicating holograms, "smart" chips, and other security devices intended to distinguish fakes from the genuine article. "We've had sophisticated technology that took years to develop knocked off in a matter of months," says Unilever marketing boss Simon.

The ambition of the counterfeiters just keeps growing. In China, recent raids have turned up everything from fake Sony PlayStation game controllers to Cisco Systems router interface cards. "If you can make it, they can fake it," says David Fernyhough, director of brand protection at investigation firm Hill & Associates Ltd. in Hong Kong. Don't believe him? Shanghai Mitsubishi Elevator Co. discovered a counterfeit elevator after a building owner asked the company for a maintenance contract. "It didn't look like our product," says Wang Chung Heng, a lawyer for Shanghai Mitsubishi. "And it stopped between floors."

Many fakes, though, are getting so good that even company execs say it takes a forensic scientist to distinguish them from the real McCoy. Armed with digital technology, counterfeiters can churn out perfect packaging—a key to duping unwitting distributors and retail customers. GM has come across fake air filters, brake pads, and batteries. "We had to cut them apart or do chemical analysis to tell" they weren't real, says Alexander Theil, director of investigations at General Motors Asia Pacific. The parts might last half as long as the real thing, but that's not apparent until long after the sale.

The counterfeiters even ape the multinationals by diversifying their sourcing and manufacturing across borders. Last August, Philippine police raided a cigarette factory in Pampanga, two hours outside of Manila. What they found was a global operation in miniature. The factory was producing

fake Davidoffs and Mild Sevens for export to Taiwan. The $6 million plant boasted a state-of-the-art German cigarette-rolling machine capable of producing some 3 billion fake smokes, worth $600 million, annually. The top-quality packaging came from a printer in Malaysia. The machinery itself was manned by 23 Chinese brought in by a Singapore-based syndicate, says Josef Gueta, director of Business Profiles Inc., a Manila firm that tracks counterfeit rings for multinationals. "They have shipping, warehousing, and the knowledge and network to move things around easily," he says.

As such counterfeiters get more entrenched and more global, they will be increasingly hard to eradicate. Financing comes from a variety of sources, including Middle East middlemen, local entrepreneurs, and organized crime. Sometimes the counterfeiters are fly-by-night operations, but just as often

LOUIS VUITTON MURAKAMI HANDBAG

PROBLEM: Cheaper leather, rivets, and fasteners; no lining

RESULT: Wears out faster

REAL: $1,200   FAKE: $70

. . . And The Key Steps To Faking It

The tricks of the trade are growing highly sophisticated

FINANCE

Seed capital comes from varied sources. Middle East businessmen invest in facilities in China for export. Local Chinese entrepreneurs provide capital. Criminal networks invest as well. Sometimes multinationals that finance licensees unwittingly support counterfeits when the licensees make fakes on the side.

EXPERTISE

Current and former employees of licensed manufacturers of branded goods can disassemble products and reengineer them. Licensed factories may add another shift to crank out counterfeits, using cheaper materials. Sophisticated packaging equipment is acquired to give the appearance of authenticity. In the case of memory chips, discards from real chip plants are smuggled to counterfeiters, who then etch brand names such as Intel into them.

DISTRIBUTION

The most important step. Authorized licensees who decide to counterfeit can tap legitimate channels to enter retail outfits, auto shops, and more. Some counterfeiters mix real items with fake ones. Containers loaded with fakes are deliberately shipped through so many ports that it becomes impossible to determine their origin.

they're legitimate companies that have a dark side. In fact, many are licensed producers of brand-name goods that simply run an extra, unauthorized shift and sell out the back door. Or they are former licensees who have kept the molds and designs that allow them to go into business for themselves. Shoemaker New Balance Athletic Shoe Inc. is suing a former contract manufacturer in Guangdong province for selling unauthorized New Balance sneakers that have turned up as far away as Australia and Europe. In the Philippines, semiconductor distributor Sardido Industries says it has been burned by counterfeiters that have sold it microprocessors rejected by inspectors from the likes of Intel and Advanced Micro Devices. These are doctored with logos and serial numbers to look like genuine parts and sold off cheaply as returns or production overruns. Other counterfeiters

are generic manufacturers who moonlight as makers of fakes. Yamaha Corp. has licensed five plants in China to make its motorcycles, but almost 50 factories have actually produced bikes branded as Yamaha.

It's easy to find the counterfeiters, too. The Ziyuangang market in the sprawling city of Guangzhou, two hours north of Hong Kong, looks pretty much like any recently built Chinese shopping mall. But venture inside, and you'll find row upon row of shops offering bogus Gucci, Versace, Dunhill, Longines, and more. Each shop has just a few dozen samples but offers vast catalogs of goods that can be made and delivered in less than a week. At one outlet, a clerk offers counterfeit Louis Vuitton bags in various sizes. "Even fakes have many grades of quality, and these fakes are really, really good," she boasts. Exports? She's happy to arrange shipping to the country of your choice.

Once those goods leave China, they can sneak into the legitimate supply chain just about anywhere. Sometimes, phony components get used in authentic products. Last year, for example, Kyocera Corp., had to recall a million cell-phone batteries that turned out to be counterfeit, costing the company at least $5 million. Unscrupulous wholesalers will fob off fakes on small auto-repair shops, office-supply stores, or independent pharmacies by saying they have bargain-priced—but not suspiciously cheap—oil filters, printer cartridges, or bottles of shampoo that another retailer returned, or which are close to their sell-by date. Some traders mix phonies in with authentic goods. "It's easy to slide a stack of fake Levis under the real ones," says one investigator based in Shanghai. "Most inspectors and buyers can't tell the difference."

Counterfeiters can also disguise their wares before they reach their final destination. Some ship unmarked counterfeit parts in several consignments to be assembled and labeled at their destination.

And last May, Shanghai customs officials were inspecting a Dubai-bound shipment of 67 100cc motorcycles labeled with the brand name Honling. But when they peeled back stickers on the machines' crank cases, they found "Yamaha" engraved on the casting. "They are very sneaky and cunning, and that's very frustrating," laments Masayuki Hosokawa, chief representative of Yamaha Motor Co. in Beijing.

STRATEGIC DEFENSE

They are also making big bucks. Counterfeiting has become as profitable as trading illegal narcotics, and is a lot less risky. In most countries, convicted offenders get off with a slap on the wrist and a fine of a few thousand dollars. Counterfeiters, after all, don't have to cover research and development, marketing, and advertising costs, and most of the expense goes into making goods look convincing, not performing well. Fake Marlboros that cost just pennies a pack to make in China could end up selling for $7.50 in Manhattan. Phony New Balance shoes can be stitched together for about $8 a pair and retail for as much as $80 in Australia, while real ones cost between $11 and $24 to make, and sell for up to $120. Gross margins for knockoff printer cartridges are north of 60%. Counterfeiters "use low-paid employees and cut corners on safety," says Richard K. Willard, general counsel for Gillette Co., which turns up hundreds of thousands of imitation Duracell batteries every week. "If they can push them off as a high-quality product, there is a big margin for them."

While the counterfeiters are piling up profits, the multinationals are spending ever more on stopping them. Luxury house LVMH Moet Hennessy Louis Vuitton spent more than $16 million last year on investigations, busts, and legal fees. GM has seven full-time staffers sleuthing the globe, and Pfizer has five people working in Asia alone. Last September, Nokia started making batteries with holographic images and 20-digit identification codes that can be authenticated

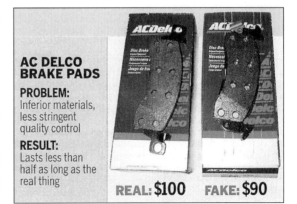

AC DELCO BRAKE PADS

PROBLEM:
Inferior materials, less stringent quality control

RESULT:
Lasts less than half as long as the real thing

REAL: $100   FAKE: $90

(Cont.)

online. Cigarette maker JT International has boosted its anti-counterfeiting budget from $200,000 to $15 million in the past six years, spending the money on a network of investigators, lawyers, and informants in factories suspected of making fakes.

Pfizer will soon introduce radio-frequency ID tags on all Viagra sold in the U.S., which will enable it to track drugs all the way from the laboratory to the medicine cabinet. Other companies simply try to make life as difficult as possible for manufacturers and distributors by raiding factories and warehouses or by slightly altering the look of products, making it tough for counterfeiters to keep up with the changes. JT International—which sells Camels and Winstons outside the U.S.—sometimes digs through dumpsters at suspect factories looking for counterfeit packaging. Callaway patrols the Web looking for suspiciously cheap clubs bearing its brand—though as soon as it shuts one dealer down, another is sure to pop up. "Getting rid of the problem altogether is too much to ask," says Callaway's Herrington. "We just try to do our best and give the counterfeiters a really bad day."

One tactic is to outwit the counterfeiters in the marketplace. Anheuser-Busch Cos., for instance, was plagued by knockoff Budweiser in China. A big problem was that counterfeiters were refilling old Bud bottles, so the company started using expensive imported foil on the bottles that was very hard to find in China. The company also added a temperature-sensitive label that turned red when cold. The result: "We've been able to keep [counterfeiting] at a pretty low level," says Stephen J. Burrows, chief executive and president of Anheuser-Busch International. Yamaha, meanwhile, overhauled the way it manufactures and designs motorcycles to lower costs. Now it charges $725 for its cheapest bikes in China, down from about $1,800. To stay competitive, counterfeiters have since lowered their prices from around $1,000 to roughly half that.

The biggest challenge is getting cooperation from China. For years, Chinese authorities turned a blind eye to the problem, largely because most of the harm was inflicted on foreign brand owners and most counterfeiting was seen as a victimless offense. The only time China got tough on counterfeiters was when there was a clear danger to Chinese. Last year, for example, 15 infants died from phony milk powder. The ringleader was sentenced to eight years in prison. But when the victim is a company not an individual, the courts are far less severe. Last June, a Guangdong businessman was found guilty of producing fake windshields under 15 different brand names, including General Motors,

DaimlerChrysler, and Mitsubishi Motors. He was fined just $97,000 and given a suspended sentence. It's unclear just how much he made selling fakes, but GM gumshoe Theil says "there is no way the fine is commensurate with the profits he made."

But more Chinese corporate interests have seen profits hit because of counterfeiting—which may lead to a tougher response from Beijing. Li-Ning Co., China's No. 1 homegrown athletic footwear and apparel company, has gotten the ultimate compliment from counterfeiters: They're faking its shoes. So today, Li-Ning has three full-time employees who track counterfeiters. The state tobacco monopoly is conducting joint raids with big international tobacco companies, since counterfeiters have started cranking out Double Happiness, Chunghwa, and other Chinese smokes. The crackdown, investigators believe, has forced some cigarette counterfeiters to decamp to Vietnam and Burma. And piracy—which accounts for 92% of all software used in the mainland—isn't just setting back the likes of Microsoft Corp. "Piracy is a big problem for the development of the local software industry," says Victor Zhang,

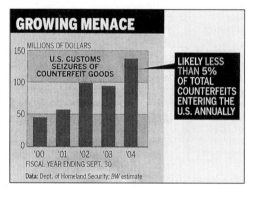

GROWING MENACE

MILLIONS OF DOLLARS

U.S. CUSTOMS SEIZURES OF COUNTERFEIT GOODS

150
100
50
0

'00 '01 '02 '03 '04
FISCAL YEAR ENDING SEPT. 30

LIKELY LESS THAN 5% OF TOTAL COUNTERFEITS ENTERING THE U.S. ANNUALLY

Data: Dept. of Homeland Security; BW estimate

senior representative for China of the Business Software Alliance, an industry group. Some fear that Western companies may cut research spending in China if the mainland doesn't crack down.

Now, China is toughening its legal sanctions. In December, Beijing lowered the threshold for criminal prosecution of counterfeiters. Prior to the changes, an individual needed to have $12,000 worth of goods on hand before police could prosecute. It was easy to skirt that rule by spreading the wares around. Today, that threshold stands at $6,000 for counterfeiters caught with one brand and $3,600 for those with two or more. And in late January, Beijing began the trial of two Americans who are accused of selling $840,000 in knockoff CDs and DVDs made in China over the Internet. The two could

face up to 15 years in jail if convicted.

One big problem: Too many scammers have ties to local officials, who see counterfeit operations as a major source of employment and pillars of the local economy. "Two or three of our raids have failed because of local protection," says Joseph Tsang, chairman of Marksman Consultants Ltd., a Hong Kong-based company that has helped conduct raids on behalf of Titleist and Nike Golf. Take the example of a raid last August in Fujian province. The police found a dirt-covered hatch hiding a stairway that led into a pitch-black cave. Inside was a rolling machine, cigarette paper, and a die for stamping Marlboros and Double Happiness packaging. But the counterfeiters themselves had cleared out and taken the smokes with them. "They knew we were coming," sighs a Hong Kong-based investigator who participated in the raid.

EMBATTLED BEIJING

Beijing says it's doing what it can. The government has raised intellectual-property issues to the highest levels: Trade czar and Vice-Premier Wu Yi, for instance, has held regular meetings with the Quality Brands Protection Committee since 2003. "China customs is taking the fight seriously," says Meng Yang, director general for the Policy & Legal Affairs Dept. of the General Administration of Chinese Customs. The agency in November held a conference in Shanghai with brand owners and customs officers from around the world to map out strategies. But delegates acknowledged their biggest challenge is finding the funds to fight counterfeiting, as most governments are more concerned with preventing the smuggling of drugs and arms.

Could the U.S. apply stronger pressure to get China to crack down? "The answer is for the Administration to bring a WTO case against the Chinese," says one leader of the intellectual-property bar in Washington. The challenge is to secure evidence from U.S. companies, which desperately want relief but don't want to anger Beijing. More calls for a WTO action may come soon, after the U.S. Trade Representative's office finishes a review of IPR in China in March.

Hard as it is, there's every reason to try to keep up the fight to stop counterfeiting. One is safety. Novartis says counterfeiters have used yellow highway paint to get the right color match for fake painkillers. And in some African countries, counterfeit or illegal medicines account for as much as 40% of the drugs on the market. "You even have antibiotics without the ingredients," says Daniel L. Vasella, chairman of Novartis. Pfizer says police and regulators in Asia uncovered

(Cont.)

more than 1.5 million counterfeit doses of its hypertension drug Norvasc in 2003. "You are seeing counterfeiters exploit a loose supply chain and moving from lifestyle drugs to life-saving drugs," says Pfizer's vice-president for global security, John Theriault. "That should make people nervous."

The other reason to mount an offensive against the counterfeits is, obviously, the hit to corporate profits—and the likelihood developed markets will one day be seriously contaminated. It's already happening. In June, 2003, Tommy Hilfiger Corp. successfully sued Goody's Family Clothing Inc. for $11 million for carrying fake shirts. The incidence of fake prescription drugs in the U.S., though small, is rising sharply. The U.S. Food & Drug Administration began 58 investigations of counterfeit drugs in its fiscal 2004, up from 22 in 2003.

More alarming, say police, is counterfeiting's connection to the underworld. "Organized crime thrives on counterfeiting," says Ronald K. Noble, Secretary General of Interpol. So does terrorism. Noble says profits from pirated CDs sold in Central America have funded Hezbollah in the Middle East. One cigarette executive estimates North Korea earns $100 million per year in fees from pirates producing there. That kind of activity proves that buying fakes "isn't innocent, and it's not a game," says Bernard Arnault, chairman of luxury goods maker LVMH.

The counterfeiting scourge, meanwhile, continues to spread. Pakistan and Russia are huge producers of fake pharmaceuticals, while in Italy an estimated 10% of all designer clothing is fake, much of it produced domestically. Gangs in Paraguay funnel phony cosmetics, designer jeans, and toys from China to the rest of South America. Bulgarians are masters at bootlegging U.S. liquor brands. This is one fight that will take years to win.

Frederik Balfour, With Carol Matlack in Paris, Amy Barrett in Philadelphia, Kerry Capell in London. Business Week.

44

Don't Devour The Company's Sales

Branding—Roll out new items without cannibalizing existing product lines

. . . .

By Kirk Shinkle
Investor's Business Daily

In November, Sharper Image Corp. unveiled an entertainment system that has pretty much everything.

The Personal Entertainment Center is a portable DVD/CD/radio/TV system, replete with 20 or so "soothing sound" environments (from church bells to rain). The device, which sells for about $600, also has an alarm clock and temperature readout.

But the gadget retailer already sells dozens of versions of all of those electronics.

Wouldn't its other product lines suffer with the introduction of the combo unit?

"The personal entertainment center was a great product for the holidays," said Aimee Cooper, the firm's head of public relations and human resources. "We didn't see a lot of cannibalization."

Cannibalization is an ugly word, but it's a problem companies regularly face. Keeping new offerings from cutting into existing sales is an inexact science.

Unfortunately, firms can't always innovate fast enough when competition comes knocking at the door. From DVD players to breakfast cereal, firms have to keep their brands fresh or risk getting trounced.

They also must face the fact their latest idea is probably going to steal some thunder from products they already have on the shelves.

But companies have ways of making sure innovative products steal market share from rivals, not from their own bottom line.

> It's a good anti-cannibalization strategy: Introduce brands at different price points, and also get more shelf space."
>
> **John Lister,** *brand consultant*

Cooper says Sharper Image customers were asking for a product with all the features found in the Personal Entertainment Center.

The retailer held focus groups to zero in on what features customers most wanted.

Defensive Pricing

Sharper Image stays cautions when it introduces a product that competes with existing wares. It manufactures about 20% of its products, so initial orders can be small—5,000 to 15,000 units to start. Those sales are a gauge of how well the new product will sell overall.

Cannibalization can also be a problem when a firm rolls out a new version of an existing product. For instance, each year Sharper Image introduces an update of its signature Ionic Breeze air purifier.

For the 2003 holiday season, it put out a desktop version of its filter. The new unit carried a cheaper price and extra features.

"There was zero cannibalization. These are people who wanted to buy it for the office," Cooper said, noting that earlier sales patterns showed Ionic Breeze customers were likely to be repeat buyers.

Pricing is another key defense against cannibalization.

The $600 tag on the do-everything DVD player is higher than most of the firm's other electronics. Most of its other combination audio-products go for between $100 and $300. Sharper Image also sells a 20-inch Toshiba TV/DVD/VCR that sells for $400.

Other firms combat cannibalization using a host of tactics, depending on the nature of their products.

John Lister, a branding expert with New York-based Lister Butler, says while many companies try to figure out how much cannibalism will occur, most go out of their way to avoid it.

"The strategy many people are taking is to minimize cannibalization as opposed to quantifying it," he said.

One way to do that: Created a separate brand image. That's what big consumer product companies continue to do.

"Consumer goods companies like Kraft have a smart strategy," Lister said. "They have their own barbecue sauce, but then they have the Bull's-Eye line at a different price point. It's a good anti-cannibalization strategy: Introduce brands at different price points, and also get more shelf space."

Another example: "How does Kellogg's justify having 18 breakfast cereals next to each other? I guess they don't really care as long as you pick one of them," Lister said. "And why are there six versions of Ritz crackers? Well, somebody's buying them all."

Some companies avoid cannibalizing their own products by offering just one product at a time.

Harman International Inc. is known for high-end speakers like Harman Kardon and JBL. Joe Milano, director of strategic accounts at the firm's multimedia unit, likes to keep it simple.

He introduced in January the JBL Creature II, a small, three-piece computer speaker system. The first version was unveiled in 2002. Harman cut the price by $30 on the new version and added new features, and Milano opted to discontinue the old line.

"We don't plan to have both on the market at the same time," he said. "We try not to have products that compete with each other on performance."

No Stuffing Allowed

Milano likes to keep products priced at least $50 apart, and keep technical

---

> The firm unveils a version of Ionic Breeze each year, but positions is so as not to steal sales from earlier models.

(Cont.)

specifications decidedly disparate. Other offerings—the JBL Duet and the JBL Invader—go for about $60 and $180, respectively. That strategy has kept cannibalization to a minimum, he says.

Brand consultant Lister notes that Procter & Gamble employs a similar strategy by keeping just one or two market-leading products in each of its segments, rather than stuffing a category full of competing products.

He says different approaches at different companies are just part of everyday business, and says there's still a fair bit of guesswork when it comes to fighting cannibalization.

"I'm not sure you're always going to get numerical data or even clear-cut strategies. A lot of stuff might boil down to common sense marketing," Lister said.

Put Some Pizzazz in Your Packaging

Consumers shopping for deodorant, cereal, snacks or soft drinks come up against a virtually impenetrable wall of bottles, boxes and bags in retail aisles. The gaudy blur of packaging makes it increasingly difficult to tell products apart.

Gary Grossman. Brandweek.

The seemingly infinite selection of look-alike products comes at precisely the point where shoppers make seven out of 10 purchase decisions. And retailers, forced by "everyday low price" category killers, must look beyond pricing if they hope to find ways to stand out to shoppers.

The answer? Eye-catching products that connect with consumers—ones with pizzazz, a stylish, high-aesthetic look and feel that magnetize attention, no matter how cluttered the environment. But there must be substance to pizzazz and the "wow factor" must be integral to the core values of the product, its essence, something consumers want, need and simply cannot get from other products.

In this context "product" also means "package" and smart marketers are learning to start the product development process with the consumer's viewpoint using five key strategies:

Structural innovation. Rethink the total structure of a package—especially its shape. The Coca-Cola bottle, designed in 1915 by Raymond Loewy and called "the most perfectly designed package in the world," thrives on differentiation. In those days soft drinks were typically chilled in tubs of ice water. Paper labels slid off when wet and customers had to fish around for the brands they wanted. The solution: a distinctive shape that could be easily identified even underwater. And so the world's best-known package was born.

Functional innovation. Functional innovation means designing packages that introduce new value for users in terms of convenience. A classic example is the "Serv-a-Tissue" box, introduced by Kleenex Tissues in 1929, offering the unique dispensing package. The POP-UP® box opened a new range of new uses, taking it from a basic handkerchief function to wiping windshields, cleaning kitchen pans and draining fried foods.

Structural and functional innovation. More recently, Kraft added value to its mayonnaise products by replacing its old round glass jar with a "big-mouth" plastic package in a racetrack shape with a flip-top lid. Functionally, the wide opening reduces mess on hands and utensils, the oblong cross section makes it easy to grip, and the plastic lid is easy to open.

Telling the product story via graphics. Colorful graphics carries the sales message to the point of purchase. This was Kellogg's strategy for its Eggo Filled WafFulls—"for children on the go who love waffles but don't like the mess without a plate." Kellogg tells the story of inventing its special waffle with jelly already filled in on the box itself.

Freeing the product to sell itself. Another bold strategy was adopted by the developers of a $5 electronic toothbrush in a category where rivals charged $50. Born of necessity because the small entrepreneurs could not afford national ads, the packaging invited trial by allowing the consumer to turn on the brush in the store. In year one, some 10 million SpinBrush units have been sold, more than three times the then-U.S. electric toothbrush market. That got the attention of P&G, which now sells the product worldwide and has made it the No. 1 selling electric toothbrush.

> **Allowing consumer trial in stores got Spin Brush 10 million unit sales in year one.**

Breaking through at retail takes the R&D team out of its natural environment and throws it into the customer's reality-at home, at work, in the store, wherever the product touches the customer's life. That's the real source of effective design strategies for products with pizzazz: products that stand out on the shelf and compel purchase.

Published in *Brandweek*, January 17, 2005. Used by permission of the author, M. Gary Grossman.

'Whole Grain': Food Labels' New Darling?

SARA SCHAEFER MUNOZ.
WALL STREET JOURNAL

NEW DIETARY GUIDELINES from the federal government are expected to rock the world of baked goods when they are released today.

Recommendations for 2005 are expected to call for five to 10 servings of grain products, cutting out as many as two servings a day from the guidelines last issued in 2000. And for the first time, the government is expected to call for three of those servings to be whole-grain, rather than refined-grain, products. The changes, first proposed in August following months of debate and lobbying, are prompting the Food and Drug Administration to weigh labeling rules for whole-grain content.

After years of low-carb dieting, baked-goods makers are pouncing on the advice about whole grains, seeing a chance to recoup lost sales and prestige. Companies are saying, "Wait a minute, this is going to get us back into the game," says Cynthia Harriman, a manager at Oldways Preservation Trust, a Boston think tank on food issues,

In recent months, **Sara Lee** Corp. has launched four whole-grain breads, Campbell Soup Co.'s Pepperidge Farm, Inc. rolled out a line of whole grain breads and English muffins and **Nestle** S.A.'s U.S. unit added Spa Meals, a line of whole-grain rice and pasta dishes, to its Lean Cuisine frozen-meal line. **ConAgra Foods** Inc. is introducing Ultragrain, a whole-grain flour designed to look like white flour but retaining all of the grain kernel, including the fiber-rich bran and germ.

Kellogg Co. is selling Tiger Power, a new whole-grain cereal. And **General Mills** Inc. says it has reformulated Trix, Lucky Charms, Golden Grahams and the rest of its cereals to use whole grains and will have them in stores by the end of the month. **PepsiCo** Inc.'s Frito-Lay unit is revising Sun Chips packaging to tout the snack food's whole-grain content.

Some makers of whole-grain products say they already detect an increase in demand. **RiceTec** Inc., of Alvin, Texas, said sales of the brown rice items in its RiceSelect lines, which include Texmati rice, grew 18% in 2004, compared with less than 10% in 2003.

Some whole grains, such as oatmeal and brown rice, are familiar; others are exotic, such as small, round quinoa from South America and gluten-free sorghum. The bran and germ found in whole grains contain fiber and many nutrients. Fiber is needed for proper bowel functioning; vitamins B and E are thought to promote heart health; and folic acid reduces neural-tube defects in fetuses. In refined grains, the bran and germ have been removed, leaving only the starchy endosperm.

Unlike the dairy industry, which lobbied hard to promote milk to the federal advisory committee drafting the new guidelines, makers of grain products didn't make a united push for the emphasis on whole-grain products.

In fact, makers of refined-flour products aren't entirely happy about the emphasis on whole grains. The North American Millers' Association and the Foundation for the Advancement of Grain-Based Foods urged the government to clarify that refined products are fortified with important nutrients such as folic acid. Meanwhile, the Grocery Manufacturers of America decried the increased focus on whole grains, saying it creates "the impression that refined grains are expendable."

Some baked-goods companies already had whole-grain products in the pipeline. But after the federal advisory committee released its proposed guidelines in August, many companies put whole-grain offerings on a fast track. "They are doing it defensively," says Walter Willett, head of the department of nutrition at the Harvard School of Public Health.

Still, an onslaught of whole-grain products could leave many consumers bewildered. The FDA hasn't figured out the rules for labeling whole-grain content. And there are plenty of confusing labeling terms out there: Crackers and cereals labeled as "multigrain," "stone-ground," "cracked wheat" or "seven grain" usually aren't whole-grain products, as one Agriculture Department pamphlet points out. PepsiCo's Quaker Oats unit, meanwhile, is quick to note both its oatmeal and instant oatmeal are whole grains.

Some consumer advocates worry marketers will use the phrase "whole-grain" to hype products of dubious nutritional value. Snack foods made from whole grains, for example, may also be laden with salt and fat, nutritionists warn. And while dark breads usually are made from whole grains, some are made from refined flour darkened with food color or molasses. "Consumers need to read the fine print," says Michael Jacobson, executive director of the consumer-advocacy group Center for Science in the Public Interest. "If a breakfast cereal contains some whole wheat and 50% sugar, it's junk."

The FDA is reviewing a petition from General Mills asking that products be allowed to call themselves a "good source of whole grain" if they contain eight grams of whole grain, and an "excellent source" if they contain 16 grams. "Consumers understand that whole grains have various health benefits, but they do not fully understand what whole grains are and where they can be found," General Mills said in a comment on the dietary-guidelines committee's report.

Without clear guidelines, nutrition experts say the "whole grain" designation has tremendous potential to confuse. "I'm an expert in the area, and of all the [packaged] cereals, I couldn't tell you which are whole grains and which aren't," says Joanne Lupton, professor of nutrition at Texas A & M University and a member of the dietary-guidelines committee.

The government updates dietary guidelines every five years. The 2000 guidelines' recommendation to eat six-to-11 servings of "bread, cereal, rice and pasta" has been widely cited in connection with the widening of America's waistlines. The advisory committee cited research linking whole-grain consumption to lower risk of heart disease and diabetes when it proposed reducing the bread and cereal group to five to 10 servings and that three of them be whole grains. The updated guidelines will help determine the content of the school-lunch program and other federal food programs. In a parallel effort, the Agriculture Department is redesigning the nation's food "pyramid" to illustrate the guidelines. The revamped pyramid is due out in February.

More Fruits, Veggies

As proposed in August, new dietary guidelines would trim the recommended servings of breads and cereals. A look at recommendations for a 2,200-calorie diet:

		2005	2000
Breads, cereals, rice and pasta*	SERVINGS	7	9
Fruits	SERVINGS	4	3
Vegetables	SERVINGS	6	4
Milk	SERVINGS	3	2
Meat and beans	OUNCES	6	6
Oils	GRAMS	27	n.a.
Discretionary	CALORIES	235	n.a.

*New guidelines suggest at least three servings of whole grains
Source: U.S. depts of Health and Human Services, Agriculture

Let There Be L.E.D.'s

Tiny, Glowing and Efficient, Chips Take On the Light Bulb

BY IAN AUSTEN

It started innocently enough. Marcel Jean Vos, an interior and commercial designer in London, bought some light-emitting diodes to create a small lighting system in the kitchen of his apartment. Now, four years later, Mr. Vos has transformed a neighboring one-bedroom apartment into a space lighted entirely with L.E.D.'s, the solid-state technology more commonly associated with the tiny lights on electronic gadgets.

The apartment has 360 L.E.D. arrays, and about 20 yards of plastic ribbons embedded with the glowing semiconductors. The lighting effects include a kitchen counter that changes color, an illuminated shower stall, a candle that has chips instead of a wick, and a light sculpture.

"Everyone is looking for an excuse to ditch the incandescent light bulb," said Mr. Vos, the chief executive of Vos Solutions, his design consultancy. "And it is about time. We are using extra energy for nothing."

But his project demonstrates both the advantages and the drawbacks of replacing incandescent light, a technology that has not changed substantially since Thomas Edison developed his first successful bulb in 1879.

Despite its enormous number of light fixtures, Mr. Vos's apartment uses no more electricity than four 100-watt incandescent bulbs would, he said. ("And what kind of fun can you have with just four light bulbs?" he asked.)

But offsetting the frugality is the staggering cost of the installation. Mr. Voss estimated that he spent $50,000 to create the apartment's lighting system.

"Right now it's something that's only for the rich and famous," said Mr. Vos.

While Mr. Vos's apartment is unusual—he makes the unverifiable claim that it is the world's first residence entirely lighted by chips—he is not alone in his thinking that L.E.D.'s may help end the reign of the conventional light bulb. Major manufacturers like G.E. Lighting and Philips Lighting, along with some much smaller newcomers, want to find a place in every home for L.E.D. illumination.

What began with Christmas tree lights and under-the-cabinet lights may eventually lead to inexpensive, solid-state lighting systems. Researchers are promising lights that will be more like wallpaper than bulbs.

The research into solid-state lighting is motivated by light bulb makers who want to create new and profitable products. But saving energy is a consideration, too. About 20 percent of all electricity in the United States is used for lighting. A shift from bulbs to L.E.D.'s and other more efficient kinds of lighting could cut that percentage in half, easing the strain on power systems and reducing the chances of a blackout like the one that affected the northeastern United States and Canada last August.

"What we're looking at here is really changing the way people think about their environments," said Mark Roush, a former lighting designer who is now a senior marketing executive at Philips Lighting. "And there's nothing that drives awareness of lighting more than not having it."

In the incandescent bulb, it would seem that Mr. Roush and his counterparts at other companies have an easy target. "The standard by which we judge all light sources is the incandescent," he said. "But the incandescent has very poor color rendering."

The incandescent bulb, which works by heating a thin metal filament so that it emits light, is also inefficient. About 90 to 95 percent of the electricity that goes into most incandescent bulbs is converted to heat rather than light.

"It's absolutely the least efficient light bulb you can buy," said Anil R. Duggal, the manager of G.E.'s light energy conservation program. And you don't have to be an engineer to know how little it takes to shatter an incandescent bulb or how frequently the filament burns out.

But one factor sweeps all those considerations aside when most household users go shopping: incandescent bulbs are very inexpensive. Standard bulbs commonly sell for as little as 50 cents each, and even brighter and longer-lasting halogen incandescent bulbs can be had for a few dollars. That makes more efficient alternatives like compact fluorescents, at $10 or more, seem extravagant, and leaves little or no room in the market for the even more expensive lights that use L.E.D.'s.

L.E.D.'s are tiny devices, made of semiconductor material, that allow an electric current to travel in only one direction and produce light as a byproduct of current flow. Like fluorescent lights, L.E.D.'s do not have filaments, so they run cooler and last longer. Their higher prices might be offset by longevity and lower operating costs, but few consumers do those calculations while pushing a shopping cart. "I know that when I go into a store, I mostly look at what's in my wallet," said Gert Bruning, a lighting researcher at Philips Research.

Plug It In

Something New Under the Counter

Aside from some Christmas lights, L.E.D. lamps designed for consumers are scarce. The first consumer offering from GELcore, an L.E.D. lighting company partly owned by General Electric, has more than a little commercial lighting in its genetic makeup.

The GELcore Flexible L.E.D. Accent Lighting System is an 18-inch cord dotted with five light-emitting diodes, each about a half-inch high.

Scott Hearn, the president and chief executive of GELcore, said the flexible lighting was descended from a system that the company sells as a replacement for neon tubes. Retail stores using the product, known as Tetra lighting, noted that its flexibility and low heat level would make some variation of it ideal for use inside display counters, he said.

The consumer version—which costs about $25 and is available at several retail stores, including Wal-Mart—was introduced in the fall.

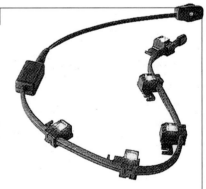

Mr. Hearn said it had been particularly popular with hobbyists who light display cabinets filled with their handiwork.

For installations with little room to spare, the compactness of the lamps may be offset by the electrical power converter attached to its plug. Also, phosphors applied to the L.E.D.'s are designed to create a bluish light similar to a florescent fixture. While ideal for department store cabinets, that cold light may seem out of place in the home. *Ian Austen*

(Cont.)

For now, that has made L.E.D. lighting mostly of interest to the commercial world, where energy use and maintenance costs are carefully watched. The vast video screens and animated signs that cover buildings in Times Square are the most dramatic commercial use of the technology. But the most common applications tend to be prosaic. Many traffic signals, Walk/Don't Walk signs and indicator lights on trucks and buses use L.E.D.'s.

GELcore, an L.E.D. lighting maker owned by G.E. and Emcore, a semiconductor company, recently unveiled an L.E.D. technology for illuminated street signs. Similarly, what appear to be neon tubes on new buildings are often plastic ribbons embedded with L.E.D.'s.

The major barrier to creating inexpensive L.E.D. lights for homes is not the semiconductors themselves. The real obstacle is the cost of overcoming several basic limitations of the chips.

The first is the nature of their light. Incandescent or fluorescent bulbs diffuse their glow over a wide area. L.E.D.'s, in contrast, are very bright only at a single point. That's handy for showing that a cellphone is charged or for making up one subpixel in a huge video billboard, but a drawback for filling rooms with light. "L.E.D.'s are very good at lighting effects," Mr. Roush said. "Now they are coming across the threshold to effective lighting—delivering the light where you want it."

Most of the bulbs in Mr. Vos's apartment, which are the kind used for signs, achieve that result by combining several L.E.D.'s under a plastic lens.

Light color is also a problem. Currently no L.E.D. produces light of a color that is suitable for everyday household use. The best produce a white light that has a pronounced and very unflattering blue tinge.

At the moment there are two ways around the color problem. Many L.E.D. bulbs create white light by blending the output of separate red, green and blue diodes.

Scott Hearn, the president and chief executive of GELcore, said his researchers were developing an alternative in which the L.E.D.'s generate invisible ultraviolet light. That light in turn causes phosphors on the chip to glow. As with fluorescent lights, producing a specific color becomes a matter of adjusting the phosphors' chemical recipe.

GELcore began selling a $25 under-cabinet accent light this fall that uses a variation of the concept. The light has a series of blue L.E.D.'s that have been coated with yellow phosphors to improve their light color.

Most people in the L.E.D. lighting industry have already conceded the business of replacing standard incandescent bulbs to efficient compact fluorescent lamps. They're hoping to use the technology to introduce entirely new kinds of household fixtures.

Replacing incandescent lights with chips can save electricity, but the cost of installation is steep.

"Having these flat things is a totally different way of looking at lighting," Mr. Roush said. "All of a sudden I have dynamic color, color that can change. Inside spaces can be illuminated to match the whiteness of daylight outside, while buildings can change their colors outside."

The most successful L.E.D. lighting product for consumers so far emerged from a desire to overcome a common seasonal annoyance. Frustrated by the need to climb a ladder to replace burned-out Christmas lights on his house in Yardley, Pa., David Allen began looking into alternatives.

At first Mr. Allen looked at developing fiber-optic systems. But along the way he discovered that, contrary to industry assumptions,

it was possible to assemble strings of L.E.D.'s that could be plugged into wall outlets without a power converter. The lights are rated for up to 200,000 hours of use.

This holiday season was the second that his Forever Bright lights were widely distributed in North America. While Mr. Allen declined to give sales figures, he said that sales of the lights increased by 500 percent over 2002, partly because of promotions by some electrical utility companies.

But even if more houses start to resemble Mr. Vos's futuristic apartment, the glory days for L.E.D.'s may be cut short by their younger sibling, organic light-emitting diodes, or O.L.E.D.'s. Because they are based on plastics, O.L.E.D.'s do not have to be manufactured in semiconductor factories. Nor are they limited to relatively small sizes.

"Organic L.E.D.'s can potentially be made with a low-cost printing line, much like you print a newspaper," said Dr. Duggal of GE.

More important, they could be created on flexible materials, leading to new forms of lighting. Rolls of O.L.E.D.'s could be produced as a kind of luminous wallpaper. Table lamps could exchange their bulbs for shades that provide both light and decoration. But O.L.E.D.'s are in their infancy and so far have few applications. Phillips uses them in an electric razor, and they are found in some small displays in car dashboards. They are not very energy efficient, and the light output tends to decrease over time.

Dr. Duggal said that much work remained to be done to improve the technology. "How this gets adopted is going to be interesting," he said. "But making all this work is still a big challenge. It's not a done deal."

48

Makers Of Child-Tracking Technology Find Big Potential Market

Trackers Evolving, Shrinking
....

Kidnapping fears also are driving sales of cell phones, which parents give to kids.
....

By Patrick Seitz
Investor's Business Daily

Recent high-profile kidnapping cases have raised interest in technology for tracking and locating children.

Privately held Wherify Wireless Inc. soon will begin selling a pendant-sized device that combines a global-positioning-system receiver and cell phone, which kids can wear or put in their pocket.

The company says it's a big advance over its first-generation product—a bulky wristwatch.

Cell phone companies in general are benefiting from child safety concerns as parents buy mobile phones for their children at younger ages than a year or two ago, analysts say.

Steve Wozniak, co-founder of Apple Computer Inc., also has designs on the kid-tracking market with his venture called Wheels of Zeus Inc.

"It's likely to become a crowded space," said Keith Waryas, an analyst with market research firm International Data Corp.

Wherify sold thousands of its first product, but hopes to sell millions of the new product after it becomes available this summer, says Timothy Neher, chief executive of the Redwood Shores, Calif., company.

The new device is about the size of an Oreo cookie. It includes a cell phone with a two-way speaker. It comes with a panic button for calling 911 and a programmable button for calling home. It has "aided GPS" capabilities for locating people inside buildings. Normal GPS devices can't penetrate buildings.

"We've gone light years ahead of where we were," Neher said.

The original Wherify wristwatch bracelets were similar to the first cell phones in that they were brick-sized and expensive, he says.

That first Wherify product can't be used for voice communications, but works as a GPS locator, pager and watch. The company is both a service provider and product maker. That first product now sells for $199, with service plans starting at $20 a month.

"It was more of a technology statement than anything else," Neher said. "Any first-generation product is going to be limited. We sold thousands of them, but not hundreds of thousands. We think with this next generation we can get to millions of units."

Wherify expects the pendant device, called the GPS Locator Phone, to sell for less than $149, with service plans starting at $10 a month. The basic service would include three "locates"—times when people can go online and locate their child—and 15 minutes of talk time. More expensive plans would offer more locates and talk time.

Wherify also plans to sell a new version of its watch starting in the fourth quarter or the first quarter next year, Neher says. It will be 80% smaller than the current

Locating Your Kids

Wherify's first wristwatch bracelet for tracking children was fairly large and expensive. Its new locator product, which also can be used for voice communications, fits in the palm of a hand.

version, Neher says. The first wristwatch locator weighs 3.9 ounces and has been sold since fall 2002.

The new model, he says, will come with "Dick Tracy stuff" like two-way voice communications and downloadable games. The expected price is $149.

"It targets a market that has a huge amount of potential," said David Hilliard Williams, an analyst with E911-LBS Consulting in Wilton, Conn.

But many parents aren't waiting for special tracking and communications devices for children. They're buying regular cell phones for their kids, analysts say.

A few years ago, the generally accepted minimum age for cell phone usage was 16. Today it has fallen to 12 or even younger, IDC's Waryas says. The Columbine school shootings and frequent Amber alerts have raised awareness about the need to track kids and communicate with them in emergencies, he says.

"It's not just limited to tracking. It's the ability to get in touch with your kids in this increasingly connected society," Waryas said.

Surveys show that people want family tracking capabilities with their cell phone service, Waryas says. At 11 p.m. or midnight, when a kid has missed curfew, parents want to be able to go to their PC, push a button and find out where their child is, he says.

But that sort of service raises legal and privacy concerns, Waryas says. It raises questions such as: Who has rights to access the data, and how long will the data be stored? Can law enforcement agencies get the data, especially given the scope of the Patriot Act?

The child-tracking services raise liability concerns, such as what happens when the device fails to locate a missing child, Williams says.

All cell phones soon will come with a location-tracking ability to meet the Federal Communications Commission's wireless Enhanced 911 requirements. About 60% of cell phones sold today have E911, which can be used to locate a caller in an emergency, Waryas says.

Giving children cell phones is a tough call. He says it can be expensive, especially if they lose or break their phones. Plus, parents want to place limits on usage.

(Cont.)

Wozniak says one benefit of his WozNet system is it will be low cost. He envisions his system being used to track small devices on kids, pets and Alzheimer's patients, and also used to track assets like cars and briefcases.

But Wozniak is counting on homeowners and communities to put in place a new local wireless infrastructure for his system to work. That's a drawback. "That's reinventing the wheel," Wherify's Neher said. "There's going to be a lot of dead spots with that concept."

An early use for WozNet will be home security, Wozniak says. The system can notify users remotely when something happens, such as a break-in at the house, he says.

WozNet is still in development, but the firm has signed up Motorola Inc.'s broadband communications unit as a partner.

49

Wi-Fi Changes Virtually Everything

Users say they'll never go back

By Michelle Kessler
USA TODAY

Watching football on TV doesn't cut it anymore for John Furrier and his son, Alec, 8.

Broadcasters can't spew enough statistics to satisfy the two. So the Furriers rely on a laptop with wireless Internet, called Wi-Fi, to get the latest data from the living room couch while watching the game.

Wi-Fi sends Web pages and other information through the air via radio waves. The Furriers' Wi-Fi laptop receives up-to-the-minute scores and trivia from ESPN.com, though it's not plugged into a phone line. That allows father and son to swap stats without missing a minute of the game.

Hankering for some nachos? They can take the laptop with them to the kitchen and not miss a play. John Furrier, 38, even admits to surfing the Web from the bathroom.

Wi-Fi is catching on fast—and changing the way people use the Internet. Fans say it leads them to do more things online: They pay bills from the living room, search recipes from the kitchen and check e-mail on the go. Tech analysts say that's just the beginning of what Wi-Fi can do. In the future, it will connect all kinds of devices—lamps, stereos, computers—and, for the first time, truly integrate the Internet into daily life.

"It's going to connect all kinds of things that need to be connected together," says Matt Peterson, cofounder of a San Francisco-area Wi-Fi users group. "It could really make your life easier."

Wi-Fi has been in the mainstream only about four years, but it's already causing a rise in laptop computer sales. Laptops made up 22% of PCs sold in the USA in late 2002. By the end of 2003, they made up 30%, says researcher Gartner.

Now, Wi-Fi is starting to appear in consumer electronics. Gateway, Microsoft, Samsung and others are building TVs, DVD players, stereos and other gadgets that can talk to one another—and to nearby PCs. That makes it possible to download a movie or song from the Internet and send it wirelessly to your home entertainment system.

That's just the beginning. Researchers are working on a tiny version of Wi-Fi that can be used to send very simple commands to household appliances. You could use it, say, if you wanted to turn on your lights remotely, via the Internet. Or adjust your thermostat. Or check whether you left the iron on. There are thousands of possibilities, Peterson says.

That means big opportunities for enterprising companies, says Nielsen/NetRatings analyst Charles Buchwalter. Six million people buy something online each day, and millions more use the Web for research and reservations, according to the Pew Research Center's Internet & American Life Project. As Wi-Fi makes the Web more convenient, those numbers will rise, he says. Companies that sell online goods and services—and adapt quickly to Wi-Fi—could have a huge, new customer base, he says.

Wi-Fi will prompt companies "to take the Internet much more seriously," Buchwalter says. "It's revolutionary."

FROM COUCH TO KITCHEN

Wi-Fi is taking off fast. More than 64 million Wi-Fi systems are expected to be sold this year, up from 24 million in 2002, says researcher IDC.

Already, Internet companies such as ESPN.com are tailoring features to customers with Wi-Fi. In September, ESPN.com launched a host of features. Among them: live chats with sports experts, more video clips of big plays and tools to help fantasy football fans track their teams.

It's a big change from ESPN.com's initial design, based on targeted users who watched the game in the living room and dashed to an office PC to check scores or stats. ESPN launched the redesign after focus groups said they were using Wi-Fi to take the site into the living room.

The new interactive features "give a little bit of a sports bar feel, even though you're sitting alone on your sofa watching the game," says General Manager John Kosner. ESPN.com is considering additional interactive features, such as instant messaging during games, he says.

Cooking Web site Allrecipes.com underwent a similar overhaul. The site's original users were people who browsed recipes at a desk and printed them to

(Cont.)

What you need for Wi-Fi

▶ Wi-Fi antenna. Found in most electronics stores for $50 to $150. Often called an "access point."

▶ Broadband Internet connection. The most common types are a digital subscriber line (DSL) or cable modem.

▶ Laptop equipped for Wi-Fi. Most new ones are. Wi-Fi attachments are available for most older laptops for about $80.

take to the kitchen. Now, anecdotal evidence suggests, users are sorting recipes in the kitchen on a laptop with Wi-Fi, says marketing director Esmee Williams.

In November, Allrecipes redesigned its site, in part to make it easier for Wi-Fi users. They've simplified navigation and made it easier to view a whole recipe on one screen, without a flood of ads.

Epicurious, another cooking site, boosted its offerings of how-to videos that users can watch while cooking. It also enhanced its online "recipe box" feature, which stores favorites for users, and is continually adding recipes to the site.

Entertainment portal Yahoo TV caters to Wi-Fi users, too. Customers are starting to use a Wi-Fi-equipped laptop while watching TV for interactive viewing, says Director Doug Hirsch. When a big show is on, traffic on the Yahoo site jumps, he says.

To capitalize on the trend, Yahoo TV recently signed a partnership with Television Without Pity, a TV gossip site that features real-time chats about shows as they air. "This is convergence. You're talking about your show while you're watching," Hirsch says.

And customers keep coming up with ways to use Wi-Fi. Rajesh Vasireddy, a graduate student at the University of Illinois at Urbana-Champaign, hates using

his remote to navigate program listings that come with cable TV. So he uses a Wi-Fi laptop to breeze through the listings online. Anna-Marie Claassen, who works for a Wi-Fi company, likes to do crossword puzzles online from her couch. Tim Pozar, another co-founder of the San Francisco Wi-Fi group, uses it to check his e-mail from a personal digital assistant while following his 4-year-old son around the house. "It's handy," he says.

WI-FI IN THE WAREHOUSE

Wi-Fi is also transforming the way businesses use the Internet. The technology first was used by business travelers, who needed an easy way to go online while on the road. Some businesses use Wi-Fi to replace costly wires or provide connectivity in hard-to-reach places, such as warehouses. By making it easier for employees to work wherever, whenever, Wi-Fi often boosts productivity and provides a return on investment of 200% or more, says Bill Clark, a wireless analyst with researcher Gartner.

Myrtis Smith, who runs a career-coaching service from her Cincinnati home, worried that a new baby would make working tough. She installed a Wi-Fi network just before her son was born. Now, Smith, 30, can check e-mail while watching her 8-month-old son play. "I'm free from my desk," she says.

Unique ways to use Wi-Fi are expected to flourish as it gets cheaper and easier to use. Two years ago, a home Wi-Fi antenna, sometimes called an access point, cost $300. Now it's less than $100, says IDC technology analyst Abner Germanow.

Wi-Fi fans say they'll never go back. "I'm addicted to it," John Furrier says. "I can't imagine life without it."

50

A High-Definition Showdown

To bring DVD players into the HDTV age, two rival formats are on their way. But an upstart is already on the scene!

MICHEL MARRIOTT. NEW YORK TIMES.

JORDAN GREENHALL sat before a flat-panel television that glowed with remarkably crisp, bright images, offering it as evidence that he could put a full-length movie in high-definition quality on a standard DVD, with room to spare.

Neat trick.

So neat, in fact, that it would seem to upstage the efforts of the biggest consumer electronics companies and Hollywood studios, which are choosing sides in a battle between two high-definition DVD formats, Blu-ray and HD DVD. Those formats, expected to reach North America late this year, will require ultra-high-capacity DVD's and a new class of expensive players.

The advent of Blu-ray and HD DVD may give rise to a format war reminiscent of the Betamax-VHS contest in the early days of videocassette recorders. At stake are potentially billions of dollars in hardware and discs as the demand for high-definition content grows.

In the midst of the battle, for which the two sides mounted elaborate floor displays this month at the Consumer Electronics Show in Las Vegas, Mr. Greenhall is asking, Why wait for the giants to sort it all out? There's a little guy, he said, with a high-definition solution right now: his own company's DivX 6 software.

"We're just going straight to market," said Mr. Greenhall, the 33-year-old co-founder and chief executive of DivXNetworks. "It's cheap. It's great, and it's going to be in the DVD players."

The first DivX-capable DVD player is the $250 Avel LinkPlayer 2 by I-O Data. Mr. Greenhall and his DivX team, based in San Diego, said the company hopes to see DivX high-definition players for as little as $100 by late fall. (Toshiba, in contrast, recently announced an HD DVD player to be brought to market late this year for about $1,000.)

In short, Mr. Greenhall said, he wants high-definition DivX to be to video what the MP3 audio format was to music: a "grass-roots movement that breaks above ground." But if you're thinking about joining the movement, there is a major vulnerability: no major studio is marching along. That means those buying DivX players, for now at least, will lack prerecorded high-definition discs—like major Hollywood movies—to play in them.

All the talk of high-definition DVD's, no matter which approach ultimately prevails, may seem premature in a marketplace saturated with standard-definition DVD's. According to industry analysts, most consumers indicate that they are satisfied with the picture and audio quality of standard DVD's, and they are growing accustomed to finding the players an inexpensive commodity, priced as low as $40.

Nonetheless, as television picture quality evolves with high definition, many consumer electronics makers expect substantial demand for DVD's and players that can use that quality to advantage.

Consider, for example, the consumer who just spent thousands of dollars for the latest big-screen high-definition television, only to find that a Bon Jovi concert on a high-definition cable television service looks vastly better than a standard DVD of Zhang Yimou's color-drenched "Hero."

Besides, said Andy Parsons, senior vice president for advanced technology at Pioneer Electronics, a major backer of Blu-ray technology, consumers are already outgrowing traditional DVD's, which were first introduced in 1996.

"If you look at most of the 'A' titles coming out now—'Spider-Man 2,' these sorts of things—they're two discs," Mr. Parsons said. "There's one for the movie and there is usually one for the bonus features."

Mr. Parsons said next-generation DVD's must offer much more storage than today's five to nine gigabytes. HD DVD, backed primarily by Toshiba, NEC and a number of studios—including Paramount Home Entertainment, Universal Pictures, Warner Brothers and New Line Cinema—is capable of storing 15 gigabytes of data on a single-layer disc. A Blu-ray DVD can store up to 25 gigabytes on a single layer and 50 gigabytes on a dual-layer disc. Both formats use blue lasers rather than the regular red one.

"It would be, I think, foolish to limit ourselves in terms of capacity unnecessarily," Mr. Parsons said. "Why not do the very best we can do as far as today's technology?"

Backers of HD DVD say making discs in their format will be much less difficult and expensive than Blu-ray DVD's, which are supported by Sony, Samsung, Hewlett-Packard, Panasonic, LG Electronics, Sharp, Mitsubishi, Dell, Walt Disney Pictures and Television, 20th Century Fox and others.

For Mr. Greenhall of DivXNetworks, much of the debate between Blu-ray and HD DVD misses the immediate point.

"The essence is that DivX makes you realize that high definition and blue laser are not linked at the hip," he said. "Blue laser means lots of storage; high definition means good quality. With DivX you don't need lots of storage to get quality."

Blu-ray and HD DVD partisans would disagree. In all these approaches, a significant factor is the way the video file is compressed to make it fit on a disc. While DivX can compress video to a greater degree—hence its use of conventional DVD's—it makes compromises in picture quality, its rivals say.

Mr. Greenhall said his company was pursuing an aggressive DivX certification program to help more DivX-capable players get to market this year. It has also received an investment from Samsung.

But, he added, he has no illusions. While DivXNetworks says that more than 160 million people worldwide have downloaded and used its video-compression software since the company was founded in 2000, the lack of studio support is a major handicap. "Very frankly," he conceded, "the studios are tough to crack on the high-definition front. They're kind of standing away."

Meanwhile, he said, DivX is "concentrating on all the other content in the universe," notably independent movies. He also noted that consumers with high-performance personal computers could record high-definition television broadcasts in DivX 6, then burn the broadcasts onto blank DVD's. High-definition home movies can also be burned onto DVD's using DivX, available as a free download at www.divx.com.

"They have begun to build a significant presence among PC users," P.J. McNealy, an analyst for American Technology Research, said of DivX. "They have become a nice alternative to HD DVD and Blu-ray, and more readily available. But the question is, can they get significant content from the major studios and television networks?"

The reputation of DivX (which is unrelated to a defunct video-rental format of the same name) has also suffered because of its early use for pirating. And after having

(Cont.)

their content on commercial DVD's illegally copied and distributed, studios have said they are less willing to take additional risks with next-generation DVD's.

So far, the studios have entrusted DivX-Networks with a few high-definition movie trailers, available from the DivX site; they can be played on a PC if a free DivX software player is downloaded and installed.

Mr. Greenhall said he was aware of whispers of the use of DivX as a piracy tool, but said it would take time to distance DivX from that image. "Dastardly deeds were done," he said, adding that such incidents happened long ago. "We've been getting away from that image for almost five years now."

He said DivX 6 provides strong digital-rights-management safeguards. He attributes the studios' caution to DivX's late entry into standards talks that gave way to the adoption of the Blu-ray and HD DVD technologies. Blu-ray players are being sold in Asia.

"We were very late to the game," Mr. Greenhall said of DivXNetworks. "A lot was going on before we matured enough to know what was going on in this world. They were in the endgame by the time we were ready."

Nonetheless, he said, as DivX high definition becomes more available in players there will be more content, and more content will help usher in more DivX-capable players. "Ten million people later," he said, pausing, the studios will have little choice but to take DivX seriously.

But Ross Rubin, director of industry analysis at the NPD Group, a research firm, said there was probably no rush to adopt any of the formats. For consumers to play high-definition DVD's, they need high-definition-capable televisions.

"The installed base right now is quite small, certainly under 10 percent of the population," Mr. Rubin said. "Consumer electronics makers probably don't want to confuse the marketplace, which is already confused enough."

Place

E-commerce Report

In the pursuit of face-to-face sales and Web site traffic, Expedia and Travelocity.com open shops in tourist areas.

BOB TEDESCHI. NEW YORK TIMES.

VIRTUAL travel agents are virtual no more.

After years as online-only brands, Expedia and Travelocity.com will begin selling vacation activities the old-fashioned way. Both companies are opening kiosks and small retail shops in major tourist areas this month.

The companies said the change would help them reach customers who had not yet purchased travel services online and would strengthen the companies' bonds with hotels, where many of the kiosks will be located. The new locations will also help the companies get a much bigger slice of the lucrative vacation activities business, selling services like helicopter tours, luau outings and show tickets. The activities market has no dominant player, with most tourist destinations relying on regional companies to market local tours and services.

"We felt we could make a pretty good business here by bringing our credibility to a space where there is no brand," said Jamie McDonald, vice president of destination services at Expedia, a unit of **IAC/InterActiveCorp.** "At the same time, we felt we could help our customers while they're in a destination."

The kiosks underscore the latest trend among online travel agencies, which have been trying in recent years to evolve into travel retailers, rather than simply Web sites that quote published air and hotel rates and pass orders on to suppliers, according to Henry Harteveldt, an analyst with Forrester Research, a technology consultant.

The moves come as travel sites fight to maintain their profit margins. Airlines have cut the commissions they pay to travel agencies and now market their own sites more aggressively. Hotels are also directing customers to their own sites by reducing the number of discounted rates available to online agencies. Mr. Harteveldt estimated that kiosk sales generate profit margins of about 20 percent, compared with 10 percent to 18 percent profits for hotel sales online and 5 percent to 10 percent margins for rental cars.

"Kiosks are a core plank to their future foundation," Mr. Harteveldt said. "It makes them less reliant on selling airline tickets and individual products, and more about selling vacation packages, destination services, etc. These guys are all about becoming a new form of retailer, much like L.L. Bean."

But Expedia clearly hopes that the kiosks will attract new customers to the online business as well. The kiosks, which will begin carrying the "Expedia!Fun" brand this week, have been operating in about 55 hotel lobby areas for years, under various brand names, serving customers who walk in or call. At one Activity World kiosk that Expedia began managing last spring in the Aston Waikiki Beach Hotel, about 80 percent of the customers had not used Expedia for their vacation booking.

"So our hope is, if it's your first experience with the Expedia brand, maybe you come back to the site and we'll see some sort of boomerang effect," Mr. McDonald said.

Expedia's retail kiosk effort began in earnest last spring when it bought, for an undisclosed sum, Activity World, which sells luau outings, bike tours and other activities on behalf of vendors in Hawaii. The company has since invested in similar companies in other destinations, including Mexico and New York, and will probably expand to London, Paris and other "key destinations where consumers spend money on tourism activities," Mr. McDonald said.

Mr. McDonald added that the kiosks, which are typically staffed by two employees at hotel lobby desks or within small retail spaces, did not signal a large shift toward full-service storefront travel agencies, with all the attendant costs in labor, rent and office expenses. He said that Expedia!Fun customers who want help booking airfare or hotels would be advised to log on to Expedia.com.

"We still feel good about it as a small retail operation," Mr. McDonald said, adding that he expected the kiosks to be less profitable than Expedia's core online business.

The kiosk initiative of Travelocity, owned by **Sabre Holdings,** also began with an acquisition—the 2004 purchase of Allstate Ticketing, which sells Las Vegas show tickets, Grand Canyon and Hoover Dam tours and other activities in more than 20 kiosks in and around Las Vegas. The kiosks will this month begin bearing signs that read: "ShowTickets.com, a Travelocity company."

According to Michelle A. Peluso, Travelocity's chief executive, the retail booths will help the company improve its relationships with hotels in Las Vegas in particular. "When we sell their show they get a percentage of the revenue, so they can make a lot of money with those shows. So this helps us provide more value to them than just selling hotel rooms," she said. "This clearly depends on our relationship with our customers."

ShowTickets.com's print advertising campaigns, which involve millions of brochures in Las Vegas, will also incorporate the Travelocity brand, Ms. Peluso said, giving the company greater exposure to future online bookings. Given the benefits of the kiosks and the fact that the business is already profitable, Ms. Peluso said the company was "actively looking at expansion plans."

Part of the travel sites' shifting retail strategy, according to Mr. Harteveldt of Forrester, can be seen in how online travel agents are changing the ways they market airline seats. Travelocity, for instance, will introduce a new feature tomorrow called Flight Navigator, which will display a range of attributes about flights, including the availability of meals on board, whether the seats offer extra legroom and the number of seats available for a certain rate.

"They're helping customers understand why there might be a difference in price, which is absolutely the mindset of a retailer," Mr. Harteveldt said.

That effort is critical in helping attract more business from customers while also improving relationships with suppliers, Mr. Harteveldt added. "If Travelocity can help customers understand the value in an airline ticket that might cost $30 more, then both Travelocity and the airline has a more profitable sale," he said. "The airline might say, 'Well, because I can advertise my product more effectively on Travelocity and I'm getting a higher average ticket sale there, I'll give them first dibs the next time I've got a promotional fare to distribute,'" he said.

Ms. Peluso of Travelocity said that Flight Navigator and other recent Web site improvements were a signal that the company no longer thought of itself in purely travel-related terms.

"When we're in the office tossing around the names of companies we aspire to be, we talk about Williams-Sonoma, Target, Home Depot," she said. "We're not talking about American Express."

The Almighty Dollar

Christian bookstores go bust after chains find religion.

Peg Tyre. Newsweek.

AFTER NEARLY A DECADE of steady sales, Richard Ellingsworth, co-owner of GreenLeaf, a Christian bookstore in Towson, Md., started feeling the squeeze. In 2000, Barnes & Noble moved nearby and began selling Christian books for less. Ellingsworth started discounting, but a short time later, Wal-Mart and Best Buy moved into the affluent Baltimore suburb, too. After three years of dismal sales, Ellingsworth is closing his store in March. He's trying not to be bitter. "The good news is that more people are being exposed to Christian ideas," he says. While it's bad news for him personally, "I'm not in this just for me."

That kind of selfless attitude seems almost quaint in what is rapidly becoming the dog-eat-dog world of Christian bookselling. The titles have never been hotter: "The Prayer of Jabez," "The Purpose-Driven Life" and the "Left Behind" series have carved out a permanent berth on best-seller lists from coast to coast. But that success has attracted big book chains and discount retailers that are aggressively taking over the market, selling Christian books often at a steep discount. In 2003, 271 of the 2,700 or so Christian retailers closed their doors. Bill Anderson, president of the CBA, the Christian booksellers trade association, estimates that 200 more are sputtering. The independents, says Anderson, "have been thrust from a protected specialty niche into an open

field with a price-driven market." The retail climate, says Anderson, is "the worst it's been in 30 years."

Christian booksellers say that Christian publishers are partly to blame. Enticed by the prospect of turning Christian-community favorites into household names, Christian publishers arc undercutting the independents in favor of the chains. Jo Panter, co-owner of the Rainbow Bookstore in Traverse City, Mich., says she's found top Christian titles retailing at her local Sam's Club for just a dollar more than she can buy them wholesale. "I think there's an element of greed at work here," she says.

Christian publishers say they're sympathetic—to a point. Don Jacobson, head of Multnomah, which publishes "The Prayer of Jabez," says independent booksellers need to "quit griping" and begin promoting their better service, wider selection and more-knowledgeable salespeople instead. Zondervan's publisher Scott Bolinder, whose company has made millions on "The Purpose-Driven Life," says that while they're launching new marketing schemes to help bolster the little guys, they're also ramping up the competitive climate by selling bound chapters of their best-selling titles in grocery stores for $1.49. The fate of Christian bookstores, says Bolinder, rests with customers. "Wherever the consumer wants to buy our books," says Bolinder, "that's where we want to be."

Christian booksellers have grown

General retailers
$100 MILLION
Increase in sales of Christian products, '00-'02

Christian retailers
$100 MILLION
Decrease in sales of Christian products, '00-'02

tired of turning the other check. The CBA is running commercials on Christian TV. Family Christian Stores opened its doors on Sunday. And Chris Childers, owner of Macon Christian books in Macon, Ga., says he's found a way to take on these modern-day Goliaths. Shortly before the DVD release of "The Passion of the Christ," Childers matched Wal-Mart's deeply discounted price, then threw in a free Christian book and a $10 coupon to his store. He lost money on the DVD, but overall sales jumped 20 percent. "I run this store because I want to do something that's good for the Lord," he says. "But in order to do it, I realized I had to become a better businessman." Now he's trying to think up another way to beat back Wal-Mart. He knows that unlike David, he won't be able to defeat this behemoth with a single shot.

The Lessons of Isaac

What Mr. Mizrahi Learned Moving From Class to Mass; Battle of the Hot Pink Blazer

TERI AGINS. WALL STREET JOURNAL.

WHEN HE RAN his own fashion house in New York from 1988 to 1998, Isaac Mizrahi had little patience for the minutiae of business.

In the mid-1990s, retail buyers begged him to repeat his popular "paper bag waist" pants—cotton trousers with a cinched waist—to meet strong demand. But the designer refused.

"I just got bored with them," Mr. Mizrahi said at the time. "Look, it is all I can do to make fabulous collections. I can't imagine how it will translate at retail."

Today, Mr. Mizrahi is no longer oblivious to the machinations of retail. After almost two years of designing $19.99 tops and $29.99 dresses for **Target Stores** Inc., he's gone through a midlife, bottom-line epiphany.

"I used to think my job was about coming up with a new, bold, crazy look every six months, making something fabulous and pretty for my friends and the models," he says. Now, he gets giddy over how well his clothes sell to masses of ordinary women. "I did this blended wool toggle coat with a pink quilted lining for $50 and Target sold something like 17,000 of them!" Mr. Mizrahi says. Indeed, his business manager, Marisa Gardini, says he gets unexpected satisfaction from tracking sales of individual items. "He knows how many weeks of inventory we have," she says.

How Mr. Mizrahi, 43 years old, went from elite designer to purveyor of sensible style for the masses is a tale of timing and necessity. It also reflects major shifts in American fashion and retailing today. With luxury-goods conglomerates losing patience with money-losing lines, designers can no longer simply whip up outlandish creations with little thought to how many women buy them. With sophisticated shoppers increasingly mixing pricey and mainstream fashions, couturiers are being forced to pay more attention to customers' needs. And with

discounters adapting high-fashion runway looks immediately as well as creating their own trends, the mass market is no longer a vast wasteland of style.

Mr. Mizrahi hasn't left the high-fashion game. Tomorrow, during the New York runway shows, he plans to reveal an exclusive couture line of $10,000 gowns and fancy frocks sold at Bergdorf Goodman and made to order for clients such as Sarah Jessica Parker. Playing both ends of the spectrum has taught him some valuable lessons that the rest of the fashion world is still learning. And as the two worlds converge, his deal is a harbinger of others between mass and class. Swedish retailer Hennes & Mauritz hired Chanel designer Karl Lagerfeld to design a collection of $49 blouses and $89 dresses last fall. **Bed Bath & Beyond** has an exclusive deal with New York designer Nicole Miller for home furnishings. **J.C. Penney** Co. is about to announce a deal with a high-end designer as well.

Mr. Mizrahi learned the importance of profits the hard way. After launching his fashion house in 1988, he quickly became famous for his colorful, original take on classic clothes, paraded on the runway by supermodels Naomi Campbell, Linda Evangelista and Kate Moss. Ebullient and canny, he was known for never listening to anyone, a feature captured in the 1995 documentary "Unzipped."

Yet despite his fame, the Isaac Mizrahi business remained small with estimated sales of under $10 million and no profits during its peak years in the 1990s. When Parisian fashion house Chanel SA stepped in to become Mr. Mizrahi's financial backer in 1994, fashion insiders hoped the brand would finally reach a critical mass with the launch of Isaac, a line of $150 dresses and sportswear.

But Isaac didn't catch on and Chanel pulled the plug in 1998, forcing the business to close. Mr. Mizrahi still bristles at the memory of his company closure splashed across the front pages of newspapers. But he insists he was never crushed by the event. "It wasn't a failure," he says. "It was an opportunity."

After a period of artistic experimentation—as an actor in a one-man play called "Le Miz," a nightclub cabaret singer and a wacky TV talk show host—Mr. Mizrahi got a call from Target with an offer for a licensing agreement in 2002. It was a move some advised against but Mr. Mizrahi and his business partner, Ms. Gardini, agreed he should take it. "It's not like it was Kohl's or J.C. Penney," he says. Given Target's experience with (sportswear designer) Mossimo and (architect) Michael Graves, Target "gets it," he says.

The mass merchant introduced him to Middle America in TV commercials, where the hammy designer cavorted among models, while belting the tune "I Believe in You,"

from, ironically, "How to Succeed in Business Without Really Trying."

Some critics warned that designing clothes for Target could tarnish his image, but instead, the deal has boosted Mr. Mizrahi's career. His designer line was far from reaching the heights of a Ralph Lauren or Giorgio Armani. But in the mass-market world, he is hailed as a hero. "Target just enhances Isaac's cool factor," says designer Peter Som, who says he would consider doing a budget line after firmly establishing his signature collection.

The Minneapolis discounter and Greenwich Village designer didn't always see eye to eye. Early on, Mr. Mizrahi had to talk Target into doing a pink corduroy blazer, insisting that it would be a hot look that would punctuate the collection, Ms. Gardini recalls. Target balked at the wild color. But the pink blazer turned out to be a runaway best seller. Now when he designs every new group he asks, "what's going to be our pink corduroy blazer?"

Mr. Mizrahi learned fast that the key to success at Target was sales. For his first collection, which debuted in August 2003, he flew to Target's Minneapolis headquarters and toured a mock-up of a sales floor with T-stands—four-sided metal display fixtures holding about six garments on each side—to see how his collection would look. "Isaac walked in there and styled the merchandise on the rack the way that he would put it together," Ms. Gardini says. He didn't display any of the artistic fits that he made famous in "Unzipped."

Today he uses terms like "hanger appeal"—industry lingo with how styles look on the racks—without blinking an eye. His line gets about six T-stands in the average Target store displaying 24 different looks as well as a smattering of accessories such as shoes, handbags and sunglasses. "It comes down to what it will look like on a rack," he says. "You don't want to throw the customer off."

Mr. Mizrahi insists that his agreement with Target—to design clean-lined sportswear—wasn't such a big leap since his studio collection had featured a lot of boxy jackets and basic silhouettes. The biggest creative compromises lie in the choice of fabrics and the inability to do intricate detail work at budget prices. "Isaac said, 'we aren't going to have things made in Italy, but I've got to adjust,'" recalls Ms. Gardini.

Target finds the fabrics for the collection, including some that only resemble the look of fine fabrics. For example, Mr. Mizrahi can't do fabulous leathers at Target. "We can do pigskin jackets for $39.99," he says, but not rich leathers. And instead of doing sequins, he has to do sequin prints. "My concept is still there," he says.

Target's high-volume production has brought unexpected creative opportunities,

(Cont.)

he says. One of the first things Mr. Mizrahi designed after arriving at Target was a pointed toe tennis shoe. Because the rubber mold necessary to manufacture such shoes is cost prohibitive for an independent designer, Target's ability to produce thousands and sometimes tens of thousands of an item allows him to make products he wouldn't otherwise attempt.

In terms of production, "They are experts," he says. "They know how to make something on the cheap—that if you stitch the jacket this way instead of another way, you can save money." He points out the seams, lining and buttons on an orange paisley corduroy blazer, "At $29.99, how cute is that?" he exclaims.

Mr. Mizrahi has incorporated some of those lessons in his couture collection of about 18 looks, Ms. Gardini says. "He has a lot more self-discipline in the process," she says. While the made-to-order collection provides an outlet for creative ideas that can't be incorporated into the Target collection, the main difference between the lines is fabric and workmanship. The budget versions are likely to have less stitching, cheaper buttons and trim, and fewer details such as pockets and darts. And the volume production allows for economies of scale and therefore much lower cost.

Since he's not trying to impress fashion critics or fashion-store buyers, Mr. Mizrahi no longer has qualms about using his ideas from past collections. For example, a giant colorful poppy print that he splashed all over a dress in a memorable high-end collection in the mid-1990s is now being recycled for his debut home furnishings collection at Target launching next month. The red poppy, among other designs, will appear on bedding, shower curtains and china for Target.

Mr. Mizrahi's sensibilities have helped the line—sold in all 1,304 of Target's stores—"exceed our initial expectations," says John Remington, vice president of communication and event marketing at Target. While the company declines to reveal sales of the line, it says many of his pieces sell out fast with few markdowns. Neither Target nor Mr. Mizrahi will disclose the designer's royalty payments he receives based on sales of his brand. But to get an idea of how big the Isaac brand could be, Mossimo Gianulli, the Los Angeles-based designer who also has a design deal with Target, disclosed in a filing that Target would pay him guaranteed royalties on cumulative sales of $1 billion over three years starting in 2001.

While some in haute fashion circles have criticized his commercial turn, Mr. Mizrahi is sanguine about his creative efforts, considering himself both an artist and an entrepreneur. "Target has an image—a humor and a freedom that is more cutting-edge than anywhere," he says enthusiastically. "You're not selling out, you're reaching out."

When Exclusivity Means Illegality

Stores' 'Exclusives' Are Routine—and Sometimes Flout the Law

ELLEN BYRON AND TERI AGINS.
WALL STREET JOURNAL.

AS LONG AS there have been sellers and merchants who supply them, there have been exclusive deals. Target Corp. has exclusive rights to sell Isaac Mizrahi's line of trendy budget clothes. And **Bed Bath & Beyond** Inc. has exclusive rights to market Nicole Miller bedding.

In today's cutthroat retail environment, dominated nationwide by brutally efficient mass-market giants, it is more critical than ever for stores to differentiate themselves with merchandise unavailable elsewhere. But when New York Attorney General Eliot Spitzer charged the former chief executive of **Federated Department Stores** Inc. with perjury Tuesday, the entire idea of "exclusives" came under closer scrutiny.

James M. Zimmerman, who stepped down as chairman of Federated last year, was indicted by a grand jury on charges he allegedly lied under oath to conceal evidence of possible antitrust violations. The charge stems from an investigation by Mr. Spitzer's office of whether Federated and **May Department Stores** Co. conspired to dissuade **Waterford Wedgwood** PLC and **Brown-Forman** Corp. unit Lenox Inc. from selling products to Bed Bath & Beyond in 2001. The four companies agreed to settle the antitrust allegations last August, paying $2.9 million in civil penalties, without admitting any wrongdoing. Mr. Zimmerman is accused of lying to Mr. Spitzer's investigators in connection with the case. He pleaded not guilty and was freed on bail of $50,000.

Mr. Spitzer has built part of his reputation by shining a light on what some call "open secrets," industry practices that, while widespread and routine, could be harmful to certain constituencies or downright illegal. The brokerage and mutual-fund industry found this out, with Mr. Spitzer arguing that certain behavior was victimizing ordinary investors; his probes have also roiled the insurance business.

The New York attorney general's office declines to comment on whether it has other retailing investigations under way. But the Federated case raises questions about whether there may be broader implications for retailers holding exclusive deals with vendors.

Summing up the widespread drive for exclusives, Allen Questrom, former head of J.C. Penney Co. as well as Federated, says: "It's not unusual for people to try to prevent a competitor from getting a product, but there's a legal way to do it, and an illegal way to do it."

Exclusives, which engender shopper loyalty and offer crucial differentiation between retail competitors, have been a basic tenet of retailing for decades. During the 1980s designer boom, big chains such as May Department Stores' Marshall Field's, **Saks** Inc.'s Saks Fifth Avenue and **Neiman Marcus Group** Inc. competed to lock up fragrance launches and fashion shows for big names such as Yves Saint Laurent and Donna Karan. Today's versions are more likely to be smaller deals—Barneys New York has exclusivity agreements with designers Dries van Noten and Lanvin so that no other big specialty chains sell those brands in America.

"This is retailing 101, in which legal counsel has always told buyers what you can say during a business negotiation," says New York retail consultant Philip B. Miller, a former chief executive of Marshall Field's and Saks Fifth Avenue. "You can ask for exclusives and you can maintain exclusives as long as you don't identify specific retailers who you don't want to be sold to."

The area is "a very fine point of law where you have to be careful," Mr. Miller says. "It can be a timing issue, an introduction, a franchise agreement that crosses a broad range of merchandising actions . . . and most people in the industry are very careful about this."

According to legal experts, retailers and vendors have the right to establish exclusive arrangements where a vendor's goods are only available through one retailer—so long as that vendor has made a unilateral decision to do so. But such an arrangement becomes legally murky, and likely to catch the attention of antitrust investigators, if any one of three scenarios arise, according to Lloyd Constantine, former chief of antitrust enforcement for the New York attorney general's office.

The first scenario would be if such an agreement occurs between "horizontal" competitors, or businesses that compete directly against each other. Two retailers, for example, can't form their own exclusive arrangements, nor can two vendors agree to act together. Secondly, legal issues can arise if one of the parties is the exclusive producer, distributor or retailer of a dominant product.

Finally, exclusives face scrutiny if any part of the arrangement suggests that they exist in order to fix prices. If a product is sold at a number of retailers, including discounters, and then suddenly there is an agreement to sell exclusively through full-price outlets, the inference of price fixing arises.

While the legal guidelines are clear, the practice of restraining trade of certain brands has been a murkier area with vendors purposely restricting their distribution. "What manufacturers will often say is we need exclusivity to protect our brand image," says a spokesman for the New York attorney general's office. "There's an intangible image there, which nevertheless is very commercially valuable."

In the mid 1990s, **Costco Wholesale** Corp. wanted to start selling a leading national pet food brand and approached **Colgate-Palmolive** Co. to sell its Hill's Science Diet pet food, which is the nation's leading pet-food brand sold in specialty channels. Colgate denied the request, preferring to keep its distribution out of mass channels like Costco and **Wal-Mart Stores** Inc. In response, Costco stopped stocking Colgate toothpaste. Several years later, however, Colgate launched Colgate Total toothpaste, which quickly became the leading toothpaste brand in the country. At that point, Costco relented and started selling Colgate Total.

In 2000, Calvin Klein Inc. and its jeans and underwear licensee **Warnaco Group** Inc. sued each other after Warnaco began selling goods to warehouse clubs such as Costco and **BJ's Wholesale Club** Inc. Calvin Klein was also angered when Warnaco announced plans to sell CK underwear to **J.C. Penney** Co.—a revelation which caused fancier department stores to say that they would cut back their orders on CK underwear. The 2001 settlement between the parties was said to give Calvin Klein more control over where its goods could be sold.

In 1991, when Barneys New York was preparing to open a new flagship on Madison Avenue in New York—in the same neighborhood where many designers operate their own shops—designer Giorgio Armani decided to stop selling his upscale "black label" collection to Barney, where it had been sold since the 1970s.

But before the store opened in 1993, an arbitration panel in Geneva ruled against Mr. Armani, forcing him to continue to sell to Barneys.

Retailers Rely More on Fast Deliveries

BY ELIZABETH SOUDER
Dow Jones Newswires

NEW YORK—When **Nintendo** Co. shipped its new "Mario Kart: Double Dash" videogame to stores in November, most retailers agreed to pay a little extra to have the games sent directly to the stores within nine days.

For about 60% of the stores, the games went from a packaging plant near Seattle straight to the retail-store shelves, no stops at warehouses or distribution centers, which can increase the time a product gets to the shelf to as long as six weeks.

As it turned out, speed was crucial. The game, which features characters racing go-carts while throwing things at each other, was out of stock by the first week of December, after sales of almost 500,000 games. Nintendo was able to restock shelves in time for the critical pre-Christmas rush—thanks to Atlanta-based **United Parcel Service** Inc.—and Nintendo sold more than 900,000 games in the U.S. by the end of the year.

This past holiday season, retailers turned to shipping companies to help maintain supply lines. That demand has prompted transport companies such as UPS and Memphis, Tenn.-based **FedEx** Corp. to offer new services directed at retailers and to use their transport networks differently, bringing in new sources of revenue.

The trend toward just-in-time retail shipments has been growing over the past decade. Nintendo began shipping videogames that way 10 years ago. But in 2003, with the economy sputtering, retailers strove to keep inventories low. So when an item like "Mario Kart" sold well, some retailers were in a bind, and relied on faster shipping of merchandise to stores to accommodate customers.

"Really the biggest time of year for us is November and December," said George Harrison, senior vice president of marketing for Nintendo of America Inc., the U.S. unit of the Japanese company. "If it goes out of stock for a while, customers tend to lose interest in it."

Quantifying the trend is slippery, but experts across the industry agree the amount of direct-to-store shipping is growing, and will continue to grow until most retailers receive at least some of their merchandise that way.

"We're moving more to a continuous replenishment of inventory," said Adrian Gonzalez, a logistics expert with ARC Advisory Group.

The retail industry is moving away from the cycle of building up inventory and letting it decline when the economy hits a rough spot, he said. "The inventory build will not be as great as it was in the past" as the economy improves, Mr. Gonzalez said.

UPS and FedEx have beefed up their services for retail shipments, not only delivering packages to stores on a tight schedule, but also handling customs or packing the goods exactly as the retailer wants. UPS goes so far as to inspect goods for retailers and to put clothes on hangers.

UPS spokeswoman Lynnette McIntire said the company's supply-chain services unit makes up about 8% of UPS's total business. And the unit's revenue is set to increase by a double-digit percentage this year, she said.

Other transport companies are using their extensive delivery networks in new ways to handle direct-to-store shipments. Closely held truckload carrier **Schneider National** Inc., Green Bay, Wis., sees itself as a "rolling warehouse," delivering goods to retail stores as they are needed, said Tom Nightingale, vice president of marketing for the carrier.

Schneider uses the same equipment to load goods on trucks or on trains, which has turned out to be one of the company's strengths as a retail-goods carrier. A shipment in the Schneider network can change its destination without having to be reloaded on different equipment, he said.

Mr. Nightingale said most of the direct-to-store shipments Schneider handles are for one-time promotions or special sales, rather than as a constant method of replenishing shelves.

Gus Pagonis, head of logistics for **Sears, Roebuck** & Co., Hoffman Estates, Ill., said he sometimes sends full truckloads of goods directly to stores for special promotions. He said that is among the cheapest methods of direct-to-store delivery. But he doesn't like to inundate stores with so much inventory all the time.

"The backroom of a store is like a quagmire," said Mr. Pagonis, who as a lieutenant general in the U.S. Army ran logistics during the Gulf War.

For smaller loads, retailers often turn to less-than-truckload carriers to ship directly to stores. Bill Zollars, chief executive of **Yellow Roadway** Corp., said the Overland Park, Kan., less-than-truckload carrier has seen an increase in direct-to-store shipments in the past year, benefiting Yellow's expedited service.

"It's the same amount of goods, probably shipped a little more frequently," he said. Where Yellow captures more revenue is when a shipment must be expedited to meet a deadline, he said.

One deadline Yellow was asked to meet was the release of the latest Harry Potter book. Beth Ford, a senior vice president with New York-based **Scholastic** Corp., which published the book in the U.S., said 94% of the shipment went directly from the presses to book stores on trucks operated by Yellow and **J.B. Hunt Transport Services** Inc., of Lowell, Ariz.

Last June, Scholastic shipped 8.5 million copies of the book, the fifth of the bestseller series, within two days in order to meet the launch deadline. By planning the loads carefully, the shipping costs per book actually dropped below those of the fourth Harry Potter book, which hit stores in 2000, Ms. Ford said.

Direct-to-store deliveries don't always make sense for Scholastic, which also publishes textbooks that are stored in a warehouse and sent out a few at a time.

Ms. Ford said Scholastic has been focusing in the past few years on improving its logistics system to cut overall costs. She said it is also a priority for many of Scholastic's bookstore customers, who want to keep less inventory in the stores and are returning unsold books to Scholastic more quickly. "Logistics companies are becoming more sophisticated with their offerings, and we're looking at what we can use," Ms. Ford said. "I might pay more for the logistics side" if it means cutting costs elsewhere or keeping a commitment to customers.

Working closely with retail stores to reduce inventory requires implementing expensive technology to track where products are selling the best. Transport companies must have the technology to track shipments and get them to the retailer at a specified time, and manufacturers must install their own tracking systems to match that of the retailers.

Suppliers such as Scholastic and Nintendo tend to bear most of the costs of getting goods to the retailer, and in some cases that means paying to store inventory on behalf of the retailers.

Mike Peters, a vice president for warehouse operator ProLogis, said he has seen a shift in the company's customer base toward more manufacturers than retailers, as retailers demand that manufacturers handle more inventory.

Retailers have been "very cautious about investing in inventory" of late, said Mr. Peters, who runs the consulting business of the Aurora, Colo., company. "Some of that inventory will be pushed upstream and held by manufacturers."

The question for retailers: "Are they willing to share in that risk, or are they just pushing the goods upstream?" he said.

As for Nintendo, a 10-year veteran of direct-to-store deliveries, the game maker has managed to pass along some of the shipping costs to retail customers.

Marketing head Mr. Harrison said retailers that participate in the direct-to-store shipping program must pay extra, amounting to about 2% of total sales, allowing Nintendo and retailers to share the costs.

"We try to show them the benefits" of cutting down on their own inventory and cycling fresh products on the shelves more quickly, he said.

From *The Wall Street Journal,* January 14, 2004. Reprinted by permission of Dow Jones and Co., Inc. via The Copyright Clearance Center.

66,207,896 Bottles of Beer
on the Wall

Every time a six-pack moves off the shelf, Anheuser-Busch's top-secret nationwide data network knows. Here's how BudNet gives the company its edge.

By Kevin Kelleher

When Dereck Gurden pulls up at one of his customers' stores—7-Eleven, Buy N Save, or one of dozens of liquor marts and restaurants in the 800-square-mile territory he covers in California's Central Valley—managers usually stop what they're doing and grab a notepad. Toting his constant companion, a brick-size handheld PC, the 41-year-old father of three starts his routine.

"First I'll scroll through and check the accounts receivable, make sure everything's current," he says. "Then it'll show me an inventory screen with a four-week history. I can get past sales, package placements—facts and numbers on how much of the sales they did when they had a display in a certain location." After chatting up his customer, Gurden "walks the store, inputting what I see." What he sees, that is, about his *competitors'* product displays, which goes into the handheld too. "It's no extra work to get the competitive info," he says. "You always want to walk the store."

All done, Gurden jacks the handheld into his cell phone and fires off new orders to the warehouse, along with the data he's gathered. "Honestly? I think I know more about these guys' businesses than they do," he says. "At least in the beer section."

What makes Gurden so smart? He's a sales rep for Sierra Beverage, one of about 700 U.S. distributors that work for Anheuser-Busch. Gurden and several thousand reps and drivers serve as the eyes and ears of a data network through which distributors report, in excruciating detail, on sales, shelf stocks, and displays at thousands of outlets.

Called BudNet, it the King of Beers's little-known crown jewel, and the primary reason that Anheuser's share (by volume) of the $74.4 billion U.S. beer market inched up to 50.1 percent from 48.9 percent during the past year—a huge gain at a time when a week economy, lousy weather, and the threat of higher state taxes and tighter drinking laws have kept sales of Coors, Miller,

and other brewers on ice. No wonder Anheuser-Busch is so tight-lipped about its data-mining operation. (Only one executive agreed to be interviewed for this story.)

According to dozens of analysts, beer-industry veterans, and distributor execs contacted for the article, Anheuser has made a deadly accurate science out of finding out what beer lovers are buying, as well as when, where, and why. The last time you bought a six-pack of Bud Light at the Piggly Wiggly, Anheuser servers most likely recorded what you paid, when that beer was brewed, whether you purchased it warm or chilled, and whether you could have gotten a better deal down the street.

Anheuser uses the data to constantly change marketing strategies, to design promotions to suit the ethnic makeup of its markets, and as early warning radar that detects where rivals might have an edge. "If Anheuser-Bush loses shelf space in a store in Clarksville, Tenn., they know it right away," says Joe Thompson, president of Independent Beverage Group, a research and consulting firm. "They're better at this game than anyone, even Coca-Cola."

As recently as six years ago, the beer industry was a technological laggard. Distributors and sales reps returned from their daily routes with stacks of invoices and sales orders, which they'd type into a PC and dial in to breweries. They, in turn, would compile them into monthly reports to see which brands were the hottest. But Anheuser changed the rules in 1997, when Chairman August Busch III vowed to make his company a leader in mining its customers' buying patterns.

While most brewers were experimenting with Internet-based record keeping, Anheuser began amending its contracts with wholesalers to demand that they start collecting data on how much shelf space their retailers devoted to all beer brands, which ones had the most visible displays, and the locations of those displays. At first, it was left up to the distributors to figure out just how to amass the data and deliver reports to Anheuser; many resorted to sending in Excel spreadsheets, a method that grew cumbersome as Anheuser demanded more data. A cottage industry quickly emerged for software developers who, working with Anheuser execs, simplified the process for distributors. It then fell to Joe Patti, Anheuser's vice president for retail planning and category management, to fine-tune the system into BudNet. "Wholesaler and store-level data has become the lifeblood of our organization," Patti writes in an e-mailed statement.

Understatement is more like it: Collecting the data in a nightly nationwide sweep of its distributors' servers, Anheuser can draw a picture each morning of what brands are selling in which packages using which medley of displays, discounts, and promotions. Anheuser then sends its distributors out with new marching orders.

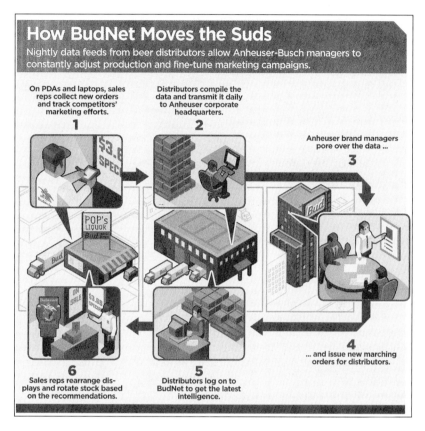

How BudNet Moves the Suds

Nightly data feeds from beer distributors allow Anheuser-Busch managers to constantly adjust production and fine-tune marketing campaigns.

1 On PDAs and laptops, sales reps collect new orders and track competitors' marketing efforts.

2 Distributors compile the data and transmit it daily to Anheuser corporate headquarters.

3 Anheuser brand managers pore over the data ...

4 ... and issue new marching orders for distributors.

5 Distributors log on to BudNet to get the latest intelligence.

6 Sales reps rearrange displays and rotate stock based on the recommendations.

"Since Michelob Light (an Anheuser brand) serves as an official sponsor of the LPGA Tour," Patti explains, "if someone asks how the brand is distributed on golf courses, we can quickly calculate our distribution and develop plans to address the courses that don't carry Michelob Light."

That's an advantage Anheuser enjoys for two reasons. First, the company wields Wal-Mart-like clout with wholesalers and insists on exclusive deals with as many as possible, offering incentives for those that comply, IBG's Thompson says. Second, none of the other brewers approaches Anheuser's data-mining savvy. "It's not just collecting data," says Harry Schuhmacher, editor of *Beer Business Daily*. "It depends on brainpower. Anheuser-Busch is the smartest in figuring out how to use it."

The trick has served Anheuser beautifully since Busch III announced the company's tech blitz. Anheuser has posted double-digit profit gains for 20 straight quarters, while its nearest competitors, Coors and Miller, have flatlined. Today it's the only major brewer to rely heavily on data from Information Resources Inc.—which tracks every bar-coded product swiped at checkout and per-

forms Nielsen-style consumer surveys—and to conduct its own monthly surveys to see what beer drinkers buy and why. Parsing the aggregate data tells Anheuser what images or ideas to push in its ads, and what new products to unveil—such as low-carb Michelob Ultra, Anheuser's most successful launch since Bud Light.

This data, crossed with U.S. Census figures on the ethnic and economic makeup of neighborhoods, also helps Anheuser tailor marketing campaigns with a local precision only dreamed of a few years ago. The data reveals trends by city (Tequiza may be hot in San Antonio, but Bud Light plays better in Peoria), by neighborhood (gay models appear on posters in San Francisco's Castro district, but not on those in the Mission), by holiday (the Fourth of July is a big seller in Atlanta, but St. Patrick's Day isn't), and by class (cans for blue-collar stores, bottles for white-collar). "They're drilling down to the level of the individual store," Thompson says. "They can pinpoint if customers are gay, Latino, 30-year-old, college-educated conservatives." Anheuser's most sought-after demographics? Twenty-somethings and Latinos. Not only are both more likely to drink beer than the overall

(Cont.)

population, but these groups are also projected to grow by more than 3 percent a year through 2010, according to Census Bureau estimates.

BudNet hasn't just added efficiency into the beer chain, it's changed the dynamics of the industry. The data juggernaut has turned the beer wholesaling business from an unruly network of mom-and-pops into an industry in which only the most tech-savvy survive. (Three of the six biggest distributors in the country—Ben E. Keith Beers, Silver Eagle Distribution, and Henley & Co.—handle only Anheuser suds.)

According to the Independent Beverage Group, operating income for the average Anheuser wholesaler is $2.2 million—five times greater than the average for Miller or Coors distributors. And wholesalers that don't perform to Anheuser's ever stricter standards are unceremoniously dumped. One distributor, founded by former Yankees slugger Roger Maris after his 1968 retirement, sued Anheuser in 1997, winning $50 million in damages after arguing that the beer company unfairly cut it loose. "Anheuser-Busch keeps their distributors under its thumb," says Madison

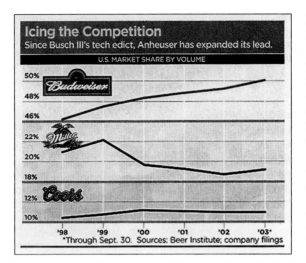

Icing the Competition
Since Busch III's tech edict, Anheuser has expanded its lead.

U.S. MARKET SHARE BY VOLUME

*Through Sept. 30. Sources: Beer Institute; company filings

McClellan, an attorney for Maris Distributing.

The case is under appeal, but Anheuser shows no signs of letting up. At a recent gathering of beer distributors, August Busch IV, president for domestic operations, promised his audience that "brewers and wholesalers with a clear data-driven focus will have a distinct competitive advantage." According to Bal Maraj, president of MIT Systems, which makes software for devices used by several Anheuser distributors, the company will soon require all of its drivers and sales reps to carry handheld computers for wireless data uploads, just as Gurden does.

Three years ago, still toting around clipboards and invoices, Gurden didn't even bother keeping track of the Coors and Miller displays in his customers' stores. Today those are among the most important data fields in his handheld. And Coors and Miller are paying dearly for what he knows.

57

RETAILING:
YOUR NEW BANKER?
Wal-Mart can't be or own a full-fledged bank—yet—but its partnerships and in-store financial services are giving the industry jitters

Wal-Mart Stores Inc. didn't get to be the world's biggest retailer by giving up easily. So despite being twice thwarted by lawmakers in its efforts to buy a bank, it has quietly but tenaciously expanded its foothold in financial services. In its latest move, announced on Jan. 21, the retailing giant is introducing a no-fee Wal-Mart Discover credit card that offers 1% cash back, which it will launch with GE Consumer Finance in March.

The retailing giant's relentless push into financial services is starting to send shivers through the banking industry. Few believe Wal-Mart will stop with basic services as it applies its low-price, high-volume formula to yet another business category. And while other companies, from Nordstrom to General Motors, have bank and thrift charters or hybrid Federal Deposit Insurance Corp.-insured industrial loan companies (ILCS) in tow, no one trips alarms like Wal-Mart. Many community bankers are convinced the behemoth won't rest until it has obtained full banking powers. "It's not a question of if Wal-Mart's going to be a bank, it's a question of when," says D. Anthony Plath, a finance professor at the University of North Carolina at Charlotte.

Clearly, Wal-Mart is on the move. Over the past three years, the giant has steadily built alliances with financial-service providers, such as MoneyGram International and SunTrust Banks, enabling it to offer services such as bargain-priced money orders and wire transfers. It has bank branches operated by, partners in nearly 1,000 of its massive supercenters. And it has stepped up the pace. SunTrust is experimenting with nearly 45 in-store bank branches co-branded as "Wal-Mart Money Center by SunTrust," with plans to expand to about 100 of them by early 2006.

Already, Wal-Mart customers are reaping the benefit. They can cash payroll checks for just $3, transfer money to Mexico for $9.46, and buy a money order for 46 cents. Some competitors charge twice as much. These are mostly high-margin, highly fragmented businesses in which the poor and immigrants are sometimes at the mercy of unscrupulous operators. "Traditionally, nonbank vendors of financial services have charged an arm and a leg," says David Robertson, publisher of *The Nilson Report,* a newsletter about credit and debit cards. Adds Gary Stibel of New England Consulting Group in Westport, Conn.: "Wal-Mart is giving people in lower-income brackets opportunities in financial services they never had before."

Financial services could open a rich new vein of profits for Wal-Mart as it seeks to remain a growth company. By one rival's estimate, the market for services that Wal-Mart already offers is worth about $5 billion a year in fees, leaving plenty of room for it to slash prices while making a profit. As it has with other goods, Wal-Mart will slowly "collapse the price umbrella," squeezing check cashers and wire-transfer leader Western Union Financial Services, predicts Robert G. Markey Jr., consultant Bain & Co.'s director for financial services.

For the time being, though, the basic services it offers represent little more than a rounding error for the $287 billion goliath. Wal-Mart doesn't break out results for the unit, lumping them into the company's "other income," which totaled $2.1 billion in the first three quarters of the last fiscal year. That was up 31% but amounted to just 1% of total revenues. Still, there's huge potential for growth. Says banking consultant Bert Ely of Ely & Co. in Alexandria, Va.: "They're developing, in customers' minds, a link between Wal-Mart and going to the bank. That has powerful long-term implications."

PERFECT FIT FOR UNDERDOGS
Not all financial-service suppliers are willing to ride this tiger. Jane J. Thompson, president of Wal-Mart Financial Services, concedes that "some of the leaders in the industry don't want to hurt their margins and don't want to work with us." But Money-Gram, with a market share of around 1% in global money transfers, is a distant No. 2 to Western Union, which has 12%. For such players, Wal-Mart promises huge volumes of business through its 3,100 U.S. stores and more than 100 million customer visits a

Banking for the Masses?
Wal-Mart has a track record of careful experimentation, followed by domination. Will it be able to do the same in financial services? It won't be easy.

REGULATION	BRANDING	WILLING PARTNERS
Federal and state lawmakers shut down its efforts to buy an Oklahoma thrift and a California industrial loan company. And community bankers will put up a stiff fight to continue that separation of banking and commerce. They argue that Wal-Mart could drive small banks out of business nationwide.	Wal-Mart is famous for offering low-priced products of every sort. But as Sears learned in the 1980s, it isn't easy to sell mutual funds and insurance to the same folks who buy your socks and tires. That could make it hard for Wal-Mart to move beyond the basic money services it now offers.	Just as it does with manufacturers, Wal-Mart pushes for low prices and high efficiency from its financial-service partners. The huge potential volume it can offer is attracting suppliers now, even as Wal-Mart brings down prices. But will its demanding reputation scare off other providers?

(Cont.)

week. As the underdog, MoneyGram was already cost-conscious and focused on growth, not on protecting margins—a perfect partner for Wal-Mart, says MoneyGram Vice-President Daniel J. O'Malley. And it can't hurt to learn how Wal-Mart does business, notes SunTrust Executive Vice-President Christopher T. Holmes, especially if Wal-Mart achieves full-fledged banking status.

Could Wal-Mart really become a bank? First it would have to take on current prohibitions on combining banking and commerce. The laws were designed to prevent a big player such as Wal-Mart from denying credit to competitors or shifting losses from its retail business to an insured bank. But many expect Wal-Mart to overcome those rules. Ronald K. Ence, vice-president of Independent Community Bankers of America, says Wal-Mart lobbied last year to expand the banklike powers of the ILCs. A bill that passed the House, but not the Senate, in 2004 would have allowed unlimited interstate banking, but only for those with at least 85% of their business in financial services.

Wal-Mart denies any such lobbying. It tried to buy a savings bank in Oklahoma in 1999, only to be blocked by the Gramm-Leach-Bliley Act, which overhauled federal banking law. And the California legislature halted Wal-Mart's plan in 2002 to buy a small ILC.

Yet if Wal-Mart were to gain full banking status, it would be able to offer everything from checking and savings accounts to mortgages, car loans, and even small-business loans at prices that rivals could be hard put to match, let alone beat. "There's no question, they want to have a nationwide financial-services network. If they do, there's no doubt in my mind they'll be able to do to community banks the same thing they've done to the local grocery store and the local hardware store and the local clothing store," says the community banker group's Ence.

Wal-Mart insists its financial plans don't depend on owning a bank or a thrift. "Our strategy is what you see," says Wal-Mart's Thompson, who was once executive vice-president of Sears, Roebuck & Co.'s credit business. The services Wal-Mart offers are aimed squarely at its core, lower-income customers and employees. Many are among the estimated 200 million American adults who either don't have a bank account or use few bank services. "Helping the underserved customer gets right at what we like to be known for," says Thompson, who joined Wal-Mart in May, 2002. More important than the unit's profits, she says, is that these services bring customers into stores more often.

She seems to have learned from Sears' ill-fated effort in the 1980s to create a financial supermarket with its Allstate insurance, Dean Witter brokerage, and Coldwell Banker Real Estate units. Sears lost focus on its core business and found that many customers didn't want to buy mutual funds or insurance from the same place that sold them appliances. "My whole thing is about starting with the customer," says Thompson, who joined Sears in 1988 and took over its credit operation in 1993.

BEING SMART BY BEING WARY

Even though Wal-Mart may be following a gradual approach to avoid Sears' mistakes, it occasionally hints at bigger ambitions. On its Web site, Wal-Mart describes itself as "a trusted name in financial services." In stores, it's slapping its powerful brand on the money centers operating in them.

So far big rivals say Wal-Mart isn't hurting them. 7-Eleven, which offers check-cashing, money orders, and the like through 1,000 electronic store kiosks, says it's focused on convenience, not offering the lowest price. Likewise, Eric C. Norrington, a spokesman for Ace Cash Express Inc., the nation's biggest check-cashing chain, says Wal-Mart hasn't affected his company's pricing or growth. "Wal-Mart has validated the importance of this market segment. That's attention we welcome," he says.

But as toy retailers, grocers, and even jewelers have painfully discovered, complacency in the face of Wal-Mart can be suicidal. Given the giant's long interest in the financial arena, technological savvy, cheap capital, and instant national reach, small and midsize banks, in particular, are right to be paranoid. Even big ones should be wary. "The mistake would be to stick your head in the sand and try to convince yourself that Wal-Mart is not a factor," says Bain's Markey. For no matter what the obstacles, Wal-Mart seems determined to be a force in finance.

Wendy Zellner in Fayetteville, Ark.. Business Week.

58

China's New Entrepreneurs

McDonald's and KFC Race To Recruit More Franchisees As Rules Are Standardized

STEVEN GRAY AND GEOFFREY A. FOWLER.
WALL STREET JOURNAL.

WHILE WORKING on an M.B.A. at the University of Calgary in Canada, Meng Sun took a part-time job behind the counter at a McDonald's. "I thought it was a very good place to start as an aspiring entrepreneur," Ms. Sun says.

Then, last year, armed with about three million yuan ($360,000) in savings from previous work as a financial consultant, the Chinese national cashed in her degree and fry time to become the first McDonald's franchisee in China. Now she operates a bustling mall-based restaurant in Tianjin, a city of 10 million people about 70 miles southeast of Beijing.

Ms. Sun, 34 years old, is at the forefront of an emerging race between **McDonald's** Corp. and **Yum Brands** Inc., owner of KFC and other fast-food brands, to recruit and train the best of China's new entrepreneurial class. The goal is to tap their enthusiasm and capital to boost the number of McDonald's and KFC outlets in China, just as small-business owners propelled the U.S. fast-food restaurant boom decades ago.

Today, most McDonald's and KFCs in China are company-owned or operated in joint ventures with local companies. But the number of franchises is expected to grow now that China is set to impose newly standardized franchising regulations next month.

As part of its entry into the World Trade Organization, China will set a framework for everything from the recruitment and vetting of prospective entrepreneurs to the protection of brand and property rights. Previously, Western companies feared they could lose control of their trade secrets and brands by offering franchises in China, which offered them few legal protections. They also had to set up convoluted offshore entities to sell franchise rights. The new rules will change that and also make franchises more enticing

to Chinese businesspeople.

"Before, people in China couldn't imagine being an entrepreneur. They only tried to build large state-owned companies," Ms. Sun says. "But now, it's getting better, as people see that even Bill Gates is an entrepreneur."

For Yum, McDonald's and other Western fast-food operators, China is one of the few large economies with lots of room to grow. China's restaurant industry is projected to reach $91 billion in sales this year, nearly double 2001's $50.5 billion, says the consulting firm Bain & Co. (The U.S. industry is expected to take in about $476 billion this year.) While the U.S. chains face competition from Asia-based chains operating in China, including Shanghai YongHe King Co., controlled by **Jollibee Foods** Corp. of the Philippines, they see a bright future in the country, where the fast-food industry is widely viewed as being in its infancy.

KFC, formerly called Kentucky Fried Chicken, has been in the forefront of exporting U.S. fast food abroad, particularly in Asia. Capitalizing on China's culinary affinity for chicken, KFC arrived there in 1987 and has since amassed 1,200 restaurants. McDonald's, which opened its first Chinese stores in the early 1990s, has only half as many as Yum does today. Both expanded slowly.

Under the new franchise rules, industry analysts expect Yum to build at least 300 KFC stores a year in the coming decade, and McDonald's expects to have as many as 1,000 stores nationwide by 2008. To help meet these goals each needs to recruit armies of franchisees, who must be relatively wealthy to pass muster under the two companies' strict vetting rules.

The companies trust the franchise model. About 60% of the roughly 17,000 McDonald's restaurants outside the U.S. are franchised, as are about two-thirds of Yum's 12,000-plus non-U.S. outlets. In large markets, franchised restaurants tend to be better-managed and more profitable. (Under a franchise, a business person owns the restaurant and shares part of the proceeds with the parent company, among other requirements.) And American fast-food companies hope to tap the expertise of native franchisees steeped in vastly distinct Chinese markets. That should help the fast-food companies spread out well beyond the giant urban regions of Beijing, Shanghai and Guangzhou and into the 105 cities that have more than one million residents.

McDonald's is trolling for talent at business conventions and has fielded about 500 applications from Chinese businesspeople in China and abroad since September. McDonald's says it expects to have about nine new franchisees ready to own stores in China by the end of this year.

Yum executives are hunting for entrepreneurs in China, Australia and the U.S., some with advanced degrees from elite American

colleges, to own restaurants in China. Yum says it receives inquiries daily from would-be franchisees. The Louisville, Ky., company adds that it has sold about 55 franchised outlets so far in China, each for roughly eight million yuan, or more than double the franchise cost of a McDonald's outlet.

"Franchising today is a very small part of our total business. But we are planting the seeds for a bigger future," says Sam Su, president of Yum Restaurants China.

Yet in a country with an emerging economy and legions of poor people the American companies are proceeding cautiously. McDonald's says it plans to thoroughly investigate the finances of all franchisees, and prefers applicants with a history at a large, established company. Unlike in the U.S., McDonald's doesn't allow its Chinese franchisees to borrow money from banks. Similarly, KFC's Chinese franchisees must provide almost all of the start-up capital from personal savings.

Executives from both companies scout and compete for prime locations, build their restaurants from the ground up, and then hire and train the initial staff—all before turning over a store to a franchisee. Both companies require would-be owners to spend at least a year working at virtually every post in a restaurant.

For McDonald's, some of the skills are taught at a Hong Kong branch of its Hamburger University, which opened in 2001 and is modeled after the original program at the company's Oak Brook, Ill., headquarters. It resembles a business school, with case studies and breakout sessions. During a session with seven assistant store managers, instructor Grace Lau played the role of a testy boss. She scolded the managers for doing a poor job of presenting solutions to customer-service and management problems at an imaginary McDonald's.

Hamburger University instructors try to teach prospective franchisees and managers to think for themselves and make employees cheerful—skills not traditionally emphasized in Chinese universities and corporations. Instructors teach the importance of communicating and listening to employees so that workers can devise their own solutions.

Winning a franchise plugs entrepreneurs into an American business model that orchestrates everything from how to purchase food and manage workers to how to chop onions and mop floors. "Many restaurants in China don't have to offer such good service," says Li Kunyu, a KFC franchisee in the southern Chinese city of Dongguan. "The way that we greet customers, the hygiene levels that we ask for—these are pioneering in China."

Promotion

59

Why There's No Escaping the Blog

Freewheeling bloggers can boost your product—or destroy it. Either way, they've become a force business can't afford to ignore.
■ *by David Kirkpatrick and Daniel Roth*

Early in the evening of Dec. 1, Microsoft revealed that it planned to take over the world of blogs—the five-million-plus web journals that have exploded on the Internet in the past few years. The company's weapon would be a new service called MSN Spaces, online software that allows people to easily create and maintain blogs. It didn't take long for the blogging world to do what it does best: swarm around a new piece of information; push, prod, and poke at it; and leave it either stronger or a bloody mess. The next day, at the widely read Boing Boing blog, co-editor Xeni Jardin opted to do the latter.

She titled her critique of MSN Spaces "7 Dirty Blogs" and hilariously sent up the fickle censoring filters Microsoft appeared to have built in. MSN Spaces prohibited her from starting a blog called Pornography and the Law or another entitled Corporate Whore Chronicles; yet World of Poop passed, as did the educational Smoking Crack: A How-To Guide for Teens. Within the first hour of Jardin's post, five blogs had linked to it, including the site of widely read *San Jose Mercury News* columnist Dan Gillmor. By the end of the day there were dozens of blogs pointing readers to "7 Dirty Blogs," a proliferation of links that over the next few weeks topped 300. There were Italian blogs and Chinese blogs and blogs in Greek, German, and Portuguese. There were blogs with names like Tie-Dyed Brain Waves, Stubborn Like a Mule, and LibertyBlog. Each added its own tweak. "Ooooh, that's what I want: a blog that doesn't allow me to speak my mind," wrote a blogger called Kung Pow Pig. The conversation had clearly gotten out of Microsoft's hands.

Typically Microsoft would have taken the hits and kept powering forward. That is the Microsoft way. For years such behavior has done little but make people feel defenseless against the company. But this time Microsoft

deployed one of its most important voices to talk back: not Bill Gates or Steve Ballmer, but Robert Scoble.

Scoble has been at Microsoft only 19 months and has neither a high-ranking title (he's a "software evangelist" who works with outside programmers) nor such corporate perks as a window in his office. What Scoble does have is a blog of his own, Scobleizer, on which he weighs in daily with opinions about happenings in the tech world—especially the inner world of Microsoft. On a recent day he posted nine remarks, each averaging a paragraph, on topics ranging from how a company programmer had fixed a security bug to

the fact that his wife is becoming a U.S. citizen. Nothing too profound or insightful, yet Scobleizer has given the Microsoft monolith something it has long lacked: an approachable human face.

When it came to the criticism emanating from Boing Boing, Scoble simply . . . agreed. "MSN Spaces isn't the blogging service for me," he wrote. Nobody at Microsoft asked Scoble to comment; he just did it on his own, adding that he would make sure that the team working on Spaces was aware of the complaints. And he kept revisiting the issue on his blog. As the anti-Microsoft crowd cried censorship, the nearly 4,000 blogs linking to

KRYPTONITE'S BLOGSTORM
How ten days of Internet chatter crippled a company's reputation.

Complaint posted to bikeforums.net that a Bic pen can open a Kryptonite lock.

Videos showing how to pick a lock are posted.

Company assures public that its locks are effective.

New York Times and AP report the story.

Company announces free product exchange. **Estimated cost: $10 million.**

1,800,000
1,700,000
900,000
700,000
550,000   520,000
375,000
180,000
11,000
38,000

ESTIMATED DAILY BLOG READERS

Sept. 12 13 14 15 16 17 18 19 20 21 22

(Cont.)

THE IDIOT'S GUIDE TO BLOGGING

- **Step One** Go to Google's Blogger.com or Spaces.MSN.com and create an account. (If you're willing to pay for a more professional look, go to TypePad.com.)

- **Step Two** Come up with a name for your blog, peruse the templates, and click on one you like.

- **Step Three** Write something interesting.

- **Step Four** Want to find out if anyone's reading your blog? Register at a service like Feedburner to see how many readers you have and what posts they like best.

Scoble were able to see his running commentary on how Microsoft was reacting. "I get comments on my blog saying, 'I didn't like Microsoft before, but at least they're listening to us,'" says Scoble. "The blog is the best relationship generator you've ever seen." His famous boss agrees. "It's all about openness," says chairman Bill Gates of Microsoft's public blogs like Scobleizer. "People see them as a reflection of an open, communicative culture that isn't afraid to be self-critical."

The blog—short for weblog—can indeed be, as Scoble and Gates say, fabulous for relationships. But it can also be much more: a company's worst PR nightmare, its best chance to talk with new and old customers, an ideal way to send out information, and the hardest way to control it. Blogs are challenging the media and changing how people in advertising, marketing, and public relations do their jobs. A few companies like Microsoft are finding ways to work with the blogging world—even as they're getting hammered by it. So far, most others are simply ignoring it.

That will get harder: According to blog search-engine and measurement firm Technorati, 23,000 new weblogs are created every day—or about one every three seconds. Each blog adds to an inescapable trend fueled by the Internet: the democratization of power and opinion. Blogs are just the latest tool that makes it harder for corporations and other institutions to control and dictate their message. An amateur media is springing up, and the smart are adapting. Says Richard Edelman, CEO of Edelman Public Relations: "Now you've got to pitch the bloggers too. You can't just pitch to conventional media."

Of course, it's difficult to take the phenom-

enon seriously when most blogs involve kids talking about their dates, people posting pictures of their cats, or lefties raging about the right (and vice versa). But whatever the topic, the discussion of business isn't usually too far behind: from bad experiences with a product to good customer service somewhere else. Suddenly everyone's a publisher and everyone's a critic. Says Jeff Jarvis, author of the blog BuzzMachine, and president and creative director of newspaper publisher Advance Publications' Internet division: "There should be someone at every company whose job is to put into Google and blog search engines the name of the company or the brand, followed by the word 'sucks,' just to see what customers are saying."

It all used to be so easy; the adage went "never pick a fight with anyone who buys ink by the barrel." But now everyone can get ink for free, launch a diatribe, and—if what they have to say is interesting to enough people—expect web-enabled word of mouth to carry it around the world. Unlike earlier promises of self-publishing revolutions, the blog movement seems to be the real thing. A big reason for that is a tiny innovation called the permalink: a unique web address for each posting on every blog. Instead of linking to web pages, which can change, bloggers link to one another's posts, which typically remain accessible indefinitely. This style of linking also gives blogs a viral quality, so a pertinent post can gain broad attention amazingly fast—and reputations can get taken down just as quickly.

No one knows that better than Dan Rather. In a now infamous episode, the anchor fell like Goliath to the political bloggers during the presidential campaign. From the start, it was clear that these nobodies with laptops were going to have an impact. Conservative blogs, like the hugely popular InstaPundit, run by Glenn Reynolds, a University of Tennessee law professor, and Little Green Footballs, written by web designer Charles Johnson, or left-leaning sites like Markos Moulitsas's DailyKos, were rallying their hundreds of thousands of daily readers to whatever cause they alighted on.

Then, in mid-September, came what the blogosphere—the term used in the blogging world for the blogging world—calls Rathergate. On *60 Minutes,* Rather scooped rivals with memos that offered proof of George W. Bush's dereliction of duty while in the Texas National Guard—or that seemed to. Within a half hour of the broadcast, bloggers started questioning the authenticity of the memos. Others picked up on the suspicions and added their own thoughts and findings. After denying it at first, CBS later admitted it could "no longer vouch" for the memos. Soon after the election, Rather announced his retirement and the blogosphere declared victory—to the chagrin of the mainstream press. "We used to think that the news was finished when we printed it," says Jarvis. "But that's when the news now begins."

Just as Rathergate was breaking, corporate America got its clearest sign of blogger muscle—in this case, brought on not by memos but by a Bic pen. On Sept. 12 someone with the moniker "unaesthetic" posted in a group discussion site for bicycle enthusiasts a strange thing he or she had noticed: that the ubiquitous, U-shaped Kryptonite lock could be easily picked with a Bic ballpoint pen. Two days later a number of blogs, including the consumer electronics site Engadget, posted a video demonstrating the trick. "We're switching to something else ASAP," wrote Engadget editor Peter Rojas. On Sept. 16, Kryptonite issued a bland statement saying the locks remained a "deterrent to theft" and promising that a new line would be "tougher." That wasn't enough. ("Trivial empty answer," wrote someone in the Engadget comments section.) Every day new bloggers began writing about the issue and talking about their experiences, and hundreds of thousands were reading about it. Prompted

> ## "If you fudge or lie on a blog, you are biting the karmic weenie."
>
> —Steve Hayden, vice chairman, Ogilvy & Mather

by the blogs, the *New York Times* and the Associated Press on Sept. 17 published stories about the problem—articles that set off a new chain of blogging. On Sept. 19, estimates Technorati, about 1.8 million people saw postings about Kryptonite (see chart).

Finally, on Sept. 22, Kryptonite announced it would exchange any affected lock free. The company now expects to send out over 100,000 new locks. "It's been—I don't necessarily want to use the word 'devastating'—but it's been serious from a business perspective," says marketing director Karen Rizzo. Kryptonite's parent, Ingersoll-Rand, said it expects the fiasco to cost $10 million, a big chunk of Kryptonite's estimated $25 million in revenues. Ten days, $10 million. "Had they responded earlier, they might have stopped the anger before it hit the papers and became widespread," says Andrew Bernstein, CEO of Cymfony, a data-analysis company that watches the web for corporate customers and provides warning of such impending catastrophes.

Those who have tried to game the blogosphere haven't done much better. Mazda, hoping to reach its Gen Y buyers, crafted a blog supposedly run by someone named Kid Halloween, a 22-year-old hipster who posted things like: "Tonight I am going to see Ministry and My Life With the Thrill Kill Cult . . . This will be a retro industrial flashback." He also posted a link to three videos he said a friend recorded off public-access TV. One showed a Mazda3 attempting to break dance, and another had it driving off a ramp like a skateboard, leading in both cases to frightening crashes. Other bloggers sensed a phony in their midst—the expensively produced videos were tip-offs—and began talking about it. Suddenly Mazda wasn't being hailed; it was being reviled on widely read blogs. "Everything about that 'blog' is disgusting," wrote a poster on Autoblog. Mazda pulled the site after three days and now says it never intended it to have a long run. "It was a learning experience," says a spokesman. Tig Tillinghast, who runs the respected advertising industry blog Marketingvox.com, calls Mazda's blogging clumsiness "the moral equivalent of doing an English-language print ad that was written by a native French speaker."

"If you fudge or lie on a blog, you are biting the karmic weenie," says Steve Hayden, vice chairman of advertising giant Ogilvy & Mather, which creates blogs for clients. "The negative reaction will be so great that, whatever your intention was, it will be overwhelmed and crushed like a bug. You're fighting with very powerful forces because it's real people's opinions."

It all sounds like so much insanity: a worldwide cabal ready to pounce on and publicize any error a company makes. Yet it's not as if corporations are just sitting ducks. For one thing, not every negative voice is that influential. For every Rathergate or Kryptonite, there are thousands of other posts that disappear into the ether. Simply railing against Wal-Mart or repeating the latest conspiracy theory about Halliburton doesn't guarantee that the blogosphere will take notice.

More important, obsessive blogs can mean obsessive customers. The witty blogger behind Manolo's Shoe Blog may bash Birkenstocks and Uggs, but he drools over Coach, Prada, and, of course, Manolo Blahniks. Before blogs, finding someone like him—a person who probably helps others make buying decisions—would have been difficult and

> ## "Every company should have someone put into Google the name of the company or the brand, followed by the word 'sucks.'"
>
> —Jeff Jarvis, blogger and newspaper industry executive

costly. Now it's just a matter of Googling or searching on any of the blog-specific search engines like Technorati or Feedster. For those who want to go deeper, firms like Intelliseek and BuzzMetrics use sophisticated software to analyze the blog universe for corporate clients. They use this growing online database of constantly updated consumer opinion for marketing and product-development ideas.

But how to speak directly to this swarm? Wary of a Mazda-like fiasco, most companies that want to blog try to walk a fine line: telling employee bloggers to be honest but also encouraging evangelism. Corporate propaganda almost always drives readers away; real people with real opinions keep them coming back. At the GM Smallblock Engine Blog, employees and customers rhapsodize about Corvettes and other GM cars. Stoneyfield Farm has several blogs about yogurt. Not surprisingly, the earliest adopters have been tech firms. The biggest chunk of the 5,000 or so corporate bloggers comes from Microsoft, but others work at Monster.com, Intuit, and Sun Microsystems—where even the company's acerbic No. 2, Jonathan Schwartz, gets in on the action. (A recent Schwartz post openly criticizes competitor Hewlett-Packard: "Yet another series of disappointing announcements.")

At best, these blogs can act like tranquilizers in an elephant: slowing a maddened charge against a company but not stopping it. Macromedia three years ago set up a few employee blogs to give customers a onestop place for info and tech support. The blogs, and the employees running them, quickly became an important resource to customers—as well as to the company. When Macromedia in 2003 released software that was maddeningly slow, the company bloggers quickly acknowledged the need for fixes, helping ease some of the tension. "It was a great early-warning system and helped us frame the situation," says senior vice president Tom Hale. "It accrued a huge benefit to us."

"I need to be credible," says Microsoft's Scoble. "If I'm only saying, 'Use Microsoft products, rah rah rah,' it sounds like a press release, and I lose all ability to have a conversation with the world at large."

Unfiltered conversations aren't exactly the kind of things in-house counsel encourage, though. And employees have been fired at Starbucks, Harvard University, Delta, and social-networking software company Friendster for blogs the organizations apparently deemed offensive, though none will comment. Even blogging boosters Microsoft and Sun have hit bumps. Microsoft fired a temp who posted photos of Apple computers sitting on a company loading dock. Sun CEO Scott McNealy was urged not to blog after he showed trial posts to company lawyers and colleagues. "I've got too many constituents that I have to pretend to be nice to," he says.

As big companies try to maintain a delicate balance, it's often the smaller players who are nimbly working blogs to their advantage. Entrepreneurs like Shayne McQuade have learned that bloggers can be an easy—and free—marketing arm, if used right. McQuade, a onetime McKinsey consultant, in 2002 invented a backpack with built-in solar panels that enables hikers and Eurotrippers to keep their gadgets charged. He spent $15,000 getting the company up and running, outsourcing design and manufacturing to jobbers in Asia and warehousing and shipping to a company in New Jersey. The only thing left for him was getting the word out: He ended up outsourcing that to bloggers.

In late September, just after McQuade received an early sample of the Voltaic Backpack, he asked a friend, Graham Hill—who runs a "green design" weblog called Treehugger—if he'd mention the product. Start up the swarm! Within a few hours of Voltaic's hitting Treehugger, the popular CoolHunting blog mentioned McQuade's product, which got it seen by Joel Johnson, editor of Engadget competitor Gizmodo. Each step up in the blogging ecosystem brought Voltaic to a broader audience. (Yes, for all its democratic trappings, there are hierarchies of influence in the blogging world.)

In came a flurry of orders. Ironically, McQuade—who had helped research *Net Gain,* a seminal book on how the Internet would change business—was unprepared. "Overnight what was supposed to be laying a little groundwork became my launch," he says. "This is the

(Cont.)

ultimate word-of-mouth marketing channel."

These are still the early days of blogging, and the form is still morphing. Blogs that host music and video are popping up, people are starting to blog text and photos from their phones, and sites like NewsGator, using a technology called RSS, allow people to subscribe to blogs. Plus, an arms race is building behind the scenes. Venture capitalists last year invested a still tiny $33 million into blog-related companies, but that was up from $8 million the year before, according to research firm VentureOne. Blog ad companies, which place ads and pay per response, are enabling bloggers to earn money from their sites. And blogging publishers have emerged. Two of the most prominent, Jason Calacanis and Nick Denton, are going head-to-head with stables of popular blogs (Engadget and Autoblog vs. Gizmodo, Gawker, and Wonkette, among others). More important, some of the most competitive companies in tech are throwing their weight behind blogging.

The newest kid on the blog block, Microsoft, has already seen what the sites can do for it. Now it thinks it has a chance to grab the youth market. Blake Irving, the VP who oversees hotmail, the e-mail service, with 187 million users, and MSN Messenger, with 145 million IM accounts, views MSN Spaces as "the third leg of the communications stool," one that Microsoft hopes to turn into an advertising-fueled business. MSN is already selling ads on some Spaces for things like Lacoste shirts at Neiman Marcus online. E-mail is for old people, says Irving; kids prefer to communicate by phone and IM, and, now, by keeping blogs. So Spaces is tightly integrated with the latest version of MSN Messenger. Says Bill Gates, who claims he'd like to start a blog but doesn't have the time: "As blogging software gets easier to use, the boundaries between, say, writing e-mail and writing a blog will start to blur. This will fundamentally change how we document our lives."

Google, the company that Microsoft is playing catchup with (its Blogger.com division is the largest blogging service right now), also expects blogs to become as important as e-mail and IM. Right now, it's working on ways to better help people find content they want in blogs, says Jason Goldman, Blogger's product manager. But if Google's internal use of Blogger is any indication, it also sees it as an essential business tool. Since 2003, when it bought Pyra Labs, the company that launched Blogger.com, Google's employees have created several hundred internal blogs. They are used for collaborating on projects as well as selling extra concert tickets and finding Rollerblading partners. Google's public relations, quality control, and advertising departments all have blogs, some of them public. When Google redesigned its search home page, a staffer blogged notes from every brainstorm session. "With a company like Google that's growing this fast, the verbal history can't be passed along fast enough," says Marissa Mayer, who oversees the search site and all of Google's consumer web products. "Our legal department loves the blogs, because it basically is a writtendown, backed-up, permanent time-stamped version of the scientist's notebook. When you want to file a patent, you can now show in blogs where this idea happened."

But when you live by the blog, you die by the blog (or at least feel serious pain). Perhaps the best example comes from Mena and Ben Trott, the husband and wife team who founded Six Apart, creator of Movable Type, the blogging software that now runs some of the most prominent blogs on the web, includ-

> ## "If I'm only saying, 'Use Microsoft products, rah, rah, rah,' I lose all ability to have a conversation."
>
> —Robert Scoble, software evangelist, Microsoft

ing Insta-Pundit and Jarvis's BuzzMachine. The Trotts, both 27, started the company after the success of Mena's blog, Dollarshort.org. ("A day late and a dollar short," she says. "A lot of my stories were about people picking on me and being a dork.") Unhappy with the software she was using, Mena enlisted programmer Ben to design their own blog software. They announced the product in October 2001 with just a post on Mena's blog, and had 100 downloads the first hour. Companies paid a flat rate of $150 and individuals were invited to pay what they thought the product was worth. "If we got $50 or $60, that was nice," says Mena.

The Trotts soon started a hosting service for blogs, called TypePad, and lured $11.5 million in venture financing—along with some big customers, including Disney, the U.S. Air Force, Fujitsu, and Nokia. Yet until May, Six Apart was relying on its original pricing scheme. The Trotts decided to upgrade. Mena posted a long message describing the new fee structure on her company blog, Mena's Corner. Less than three hours later, the first comments started rolling in. "Looks like I'll be dumping Movable Type soon" was the first. Many others echoed that outrage in what became a total of 849 customer comments in about ten languages.

Six Apart didn't erase any of the comments, even the most negative ones. Mena read every comment in full, then kept posting notes explaining why the company had changed the pricing structure and that it was still working on revising it. Looking back now, she says, "We made people feel heard." And she knows that sooner or later, the process will start all over again. Says CEO Barak Berkowitz: "When everybody has a tool for talking to the rest of the world, you can't hide from your mistakes. You have to face them. Once you commit to an open dialogue, you can't stop. And it's painful." As the impact of blogs spreads through global business, that pain—and promise—will be something companies will have to deal with. And if they don't? You're bound to read about it in a blog.

60

Interactive: Pharma replacing reps with Web

Looking to cut costs, companies reach out to doctors through 'Net

Rich Thomaselli. Advertising Age.

PHARMACEUTICAL COMPANIES are looking for ways to replace the endangered species known as the sales representative, and they may have found it on the Internet.

The World Wide Web is becoming the place to be for big pharma to peddle its wares to healthcare professionals across the country. In an emerging trend, the drug companies are marketing their brands to doctors through e-mail and Web conferencing, capitalizing on the high efficiency and low cost of the Internet.

"I don't think it will ever replace a time-honored way of doing business, which is getting out there face-to-face," said a VP-marketing at one of the top 10 pharmaceutical companies. "But right now, I think the industry is dipping its toe in the pool and testing the waters. You need to keep all options open."

UNDER FIRE

Currently, pharmaceutical companies employ an estimated 87,000 sales reps to reach roughly 600,000 practicing physicians in the U.S. And more and more, those reps are coming under fire. The University of Pennsylvania Hospital System and Duke University hospitals, for instance, have severely curtailed visits by sales reps, who usually come armed with the latest details about drugs—and also come armed with gifts, some as small as pens and notepads but others as large as lavish lunches for entire medical staffs and trips for physicians.

A decrease in budgets as well as a decrease in numbers—Merck, for instance, recently cut 700 more jobs—are also factors in how pharmaceutical companies are restructuring their marketing.

"There's a larger audience of doctors out there using the Internet for drug information than are relying on reps," Mark Bard, president of Manhattan Research, said at a conference last year. Manhattan Research, a pharmaceutical marketing and services firm based in New York, estimated that last year more than 200,000 physicians participated in 'e-detailing'—the process of receiving drug marketing information via the Internet. The company estimated it was a 400% jump from 2001.

A similar firm, Jupiter Research, found that direct-to-physician online marketing budgets increased slightly in 2004 and will continue to rise this year. Although online spending accounted for only 9% of pharmaceutical companies' physician-directed marketing budgets in 2004—39%, the most, still went to sales representatives while 15% were for samples—Jupiter found that online detailing, product Web sites and e-mail marketing will receive increased spending in 2005.

Eric Bolesh, a senior analyst at Raleigh, North Carolina-based Cutting Edge Information, said he isn't surprised. "The

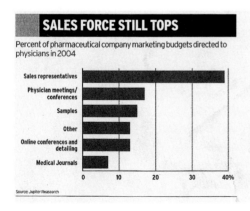

SALES FORCE STILL TOPS

Percent of pharmaceutical company marketing budgets directed to physicians in 2004

	0	10	20	30	40%
Sales representatives					
Physician meetings/conferences					
Samples					
Other					
Online conferences and detailing					
Medical Journals					

Source: Jupiter Reasearch

"There's a larger audience of doctors out there using the Internet for drug information"

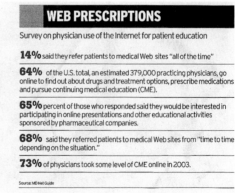

WEB PRESCRIPTIONS

Survey on physician use of the Internet for patient education

14% said they refer patients to medical Web sites "all of the time"

64% of the U.S. total, an estimated 379,000 practicing physicians, go online to find out about drugs and treatment options, prescribe medications and pursue continuing medical education (CME).

65% percent of those who responded said they would be interested in participating in online presentations and other educational activities sponsored by pharmaceutical companies.

68% said they referred patients to medical Web sites from "time to time depending on the situation."

73% of physicians took some level of CME online in 2003.

Source: MD Net Guide

(Cont.)

pharmaceutical industry's current competitive landscape makes choosing how to allocate sales force funds all the more difficult," Mr. Bolesh said.

That's where companies like The Maxwell Group come in. The Maxwell Group, based in Blue Bell, Pa., provides a service called MedConference, a direct-to-doctor Web conference that allows physicians using a standard PC with Internet access to see and hear live medical presentations. The doctors can also submit questions by voice or online chats. The three-year old company has already managed more than 5,000 presentations.

"Doctors need immense amounts of medical information, but their patient loads limit their ability to see pharma sales reps or attend outside conferences," said Bob Maiden, president of The Maxwell Group. "MedConference brings the experts directly to them whether in the office or at home using their own PCs."

And physicians aren't the only ones finding drug information on the Web.

Doctors are now writing "webscriptions" directing their patients to the Internet to research more information. Nearly 80% of the doctors who responded to a recent survey reported that they refer patients to credible online information at least some of the time. Fourteen percent said they refer patients to medical Web sites "all of the time" and 68% said they did it from "time to time, depending on the situation."

Approximately 800 specialists, ranging from pediatrics to cardiology, responded to the survey, which was conducted by the publishers of MD Net Guide, a series of medical journals designed to help physicians navigate the Internet.

"More and more patients rely on the Internet for medical information," said Todd Kunkler, MD Net Guide's associate editorial director, "and that makes it incumbent upon the responsible physician to check out what's available and recommend the most informative sites."

61

As Consumers Revolt, a Rush to Block Pop-Up Online Ads

BY SAUL HANSEL

The boom in Internet pop-up advertisement may be about to, well, pop.

The big ads that flash in separate windows above or below Web pages are among the most intrusive, and to many people, the most obnoxious features on the Internet. Not coincidentally, the pop-up format is also among the most effective for advertisers and the most profitable for Web site publishers.

But the potential reach of these ads is starting to be sharply curtailed as major companies, like **Time Warner's** AOL unit, **Yahoo** and **Google,** distribute software that blocks pop-up ads from opening. This summer, **Microsoft** will put a pop-up blocking feature in the next release of Internet Explorer, the dominant Web browser.

"There is a consumer revolt as forms of advertising get more intrusive," said Rob Kaiser, vice president for narrowband marketing at **EarthLink,** the first big Internet service provider to distribute pop-ups blocking software. The reaction to pop-ups, he said, is similar to the rush to join the government's do-not-call list to block telemarketing calls and the increase in the use of video recorders to block TV commercials.

Advertising executives, in television and the Internet market, note that consumers who block the ads are undercutting the economic model that provides them with free entertainment and information.

"I haven't spoken to any people who say I love pop-ups, send me more of them," said David J. Moore, the chief executive of 24/7 Real Media, an online advertising firm. "But they are part of a quid pro quo. If you want to enjoy the content of a Web site that is free, the pop-ups come with it."

But even companies like Yahoo and Microsoft, which receive significant revenue from advertising, have decided to bow to complaints from Web users.

"We are adding a pop-up blocker based on feedback from customers," said Matthew Pilla, a senior product manger for Windows at Microsoft.

Long a feature of AOL, pop-ups became widespread on the Internet about three years ago, as Web sites sought ways to replace the torrent of ad money that dried up after the dot-com boom. And a few advertisers, like X10, selling wireless cameras, and Orbitz, the online travel company, jumped onto the format early.

In December 2001, 1.4 percent of the Web ads measured by Nielsen/NetRatings were pop-ups or "pop-under" ads, which appear behind the main browser window. That rose to 8.7 percent in July 2003. But it has declined since, to 6.2 percent in December.

AdvertisementBanners.com, which places pop-under ads on Web sites, has found that 20 percent to 25 percent of Web users have pop-up blocking enabled on their computers, double the rate of a year ago, said Chris Vanderhook, the company's chief operating officer. Some advertising companies say that a smaller percentage of people are using blockers, but there is agreement that use of pop-up blocking is increasing.

In the year and half since EarthLink offered blocking software, one million of its five million customers have installed it. AOL added pop-up blocking to its software in 2002. Google added a blocker to its toolbar, a small program that adds some features to Internet Explorer. Yahoo, more recently, added a similar feature to its toolbar. And Microsoft's MSN just added a pop-up blocker to its most recent software.

The biggest potential impact will come this summer when Microsoft releases its Service Pack 2 for Windows XP, which will add a pop-up blocker and many other features to Internet Explorer. For now, Microsoft says Internet Explorer will not block pop-ups unless users enable the feature.

Still the prospect of nearly ubiquitous pop-up blocking unsettles some big advertisers.

"I don't want to see pop-ups blocked," said Matthew R. Coffin, the chief executive of LowerMyBills.com, a site that sells long distance and other services. Pop-up and pop-under ads, he said, attract more people than any other ad format. "People wouldn't click if they weren't interested."

The decline of pop-ups, he said, is all the more troublesome because it comes after the company had to slash use of e-mail advertising in response to the public backlash against spam. As a result, the company is moving to older forms of marketing.

"I'm very gung-ho on TV ads," he said.

Smaller Web publishers have fewer alternatives. Many independent Web sites are part of networks that pay them $3 to $5 for every thousand pop-ups they display.

"These pop-up blockers, as they become too widely used, will definitely cut into my income," said William Smith, who runs 40 Web sites from Winnipeg, Manitoba.

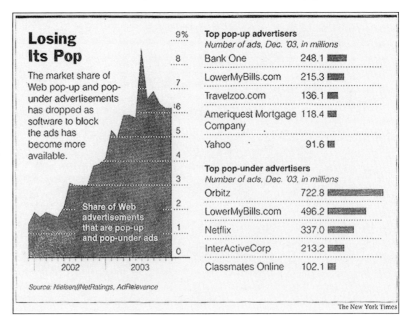

Losing Its Pop

The market share of Web pop-up and pop-under advertisements has dropped as software to block the ads has become more available.

Share of Web advertisements that are pop-up and pop-under ads

2002 2003

Source: Nielsen/NetRatings, AdRelevance

Top pop-up advertisers
Number of ads, Dec. '03, in millions

Bank One	248.1
LowerMyBills.com	215.3
Travelzoo.com	136.1
Ameriquest Mortgage Company	118.4
Yahoo	91.6

Top pop-under advertisers
Number of ads, Dec. '03, in millions

Orbitz	722.8
LowerMyBills.com	496.2
Netflix	337.0
InterActiveCorp	213.2
Classmates Online	102.1

The New York Times

(Cont.)

He says that 10 percent to 20 percent of his income comes from pop-up ads. Some of his sites, like thewinnipegpages.com focus on travel and others are pornographic.

Both types of sites take pop-up ads for products like Internet Eraser, software that eliminates records of what Web sites people visit. He said he tries not to have too many pop-ups interfere with users viewing his Web sites, but he does display pop-ups as they decide to leave.

"A guy has to make money," he said.

The larger Web publishers, by contrast, have reduced use of pop-up and pop-under ads. At Sportsline, pop-ups represented 5 to 10 percent of its ad revenue a few years ago, but now account for less than 1 percent. "We are totally ready for the day when you can't have any pop-ups," said Mark J. Mariani, Sportsline's president for advertising.

"Clients have started to shy away from pop-ups and pop-unders," he said. Sportsline now sets a quota of no more than one pop-up ad for each user in any 12-hour period. Instead, Sportsline, like many other publishers, is emphasizing larger advertisements woven into their main sites.

The Interactive Advertising Bureau, the major trade group representing both advertisers and Web publishers, has decided not to fight the pop-up blockers.

"If consumers tell us that pop-ups are a bad idea and they don't really like them, then it's time to stop doing them," said Greg Stuart, the group's chief executive.

Yet that is not a universal view even among major companies. DoubleClick, the big advertising software company, is developing technology that could let Web advertisers override the ad-blocking software in some cases. It is not planning to use that technology in instances where users have specifically chosen to activate the software.

"There are advertisers who want pop-up ads and publishers that want to serve them," said Douglas Knopper, general manager for online advertising at DoubleClick. "Our role is to help them do that."

House Training: Now, Employees Get Brand Boost

BRIAN STEINBERG. WALL STREET JOURNAL.

YOU'D THINK FEW people would know more about the virtues of Pedigree dog food than the workers at the company that makes it. But as part of a new marketing push, they're getting some fresh reminders.

Mars Inc.'s Masterfoods USA is launching a global advertising blitz for its Pedigree dog food valued around $200 million. While the effort is mainly intended to dazzle consumers, a chunk of the budget has been earmarked for an internal campaign to turn Masterfoods' 35,000 employees into better ambassadors for the brand, which the company says generates about $3 billion in annual global retail sales.

Rather than just sell more products, the inside job is meant to boost corporate morale by creating a seamless brand environment. Masterfoods, for example, had **Omnicom Group** Inc. ad firm TBWA\Chiat\Day design new business cards, as well as employee identification tags and office murals that feature employees' dogs. Masterfoods is also extending pet insurance to U.S. employees, and it has asked the ad firm to suggest ways to make some Masterfoods offices dog-friendly (the agency's 600-person Los Angeles office allows dogs at work). In another cute canine touch, TBWA created an employee handbook titled, simply enough, "Dogma." The company's traditional, consumer-focused TV ads, which play up the emotional bond between dog and owner, launch today.

Mars's internal effort represents the latest message from Madison Avenue to clients: If you want to sell more goods, increase market share or stand out to consumers, you must get your own employees to have a consistent, positive brand focus. Done well, agencies argue, the motivational process turns employees—even those who don't deal with the public in the course of their jobs—into

"evangelists" in the service of the corporation. In some ways, it's an extension of the current craze for viral or person-to-person marketing as traditional ad methods seem less effective.

But done poorly, the forced consumption of a company's culture can morph employee attitudes into something out of the dysfunctional-workplace farce "Office Space." These attempts at inspiration run the risk of being interpreted as getting workers to drink the proverbial Kool-Aid—an idea that carries with it darker implications. "As I understand cults, it's the first thing they try to do—they develop their own little language, a way of dressing, a corporate dress code," says Scott Adams, the creator of "Dilbert," the comic strip about the vicissitudes of cubicle life.

The Masterfoods program was developed with a team of volunteers from across the privately-held company, says Chris Jones, vice president of marketing for Masterfoods USA's pet-care operation. Employees would not accept an initiative that seemed forced or artificial, and "would see through that," he says. "This is true and it's genuine."

Still, Kathryn Yates, an organizational-communications specialist for human-resources consultancy Watson Wyatt Worldwide, says companies ramping up splashy internal communications efforts have to tread carefully. Employees "want to be entertained in some ways, but they do not want to be sold," she says.

Madison Avenue has dabbled in this sort of work before, but ad executives now see the business developing into something more fruitful—and with good reason. The giant companies that own ad agencies are sprawling concerns that offer dozens of services, and convincing marketers they can handle any communications need is paramount in the quest for dollars.

"You could argue that getting alignment inside companies is one of the critical issues," says Sir Martin Sorrell, **WPP Group** PLC's chief executive. He sees internal communications as an area of potential growth for his company. WPP's Ogilvy & Mather Worldwide has redesigned retail outlets for the former **AT&T Wireless Services** Inc.

and is helping **Delta Air Lines** Inc. and **Deutsche Post** AG's DHL with employee communications. The company's Landor brand-consulting firm designs workshops that have executives describe their visions of "brand heaven" and "brand hell."

It's hard for companies and agencies to resist the benefits of speaking to an audience that's not just captive, but beholden. At tony Champagne brand Moet & Chandon, for instance, when employees receive missives from management, "they have to go, 'Wow,'" says Stuart Foster, global brand director at the **LVMH Moet Hennessy Louis Vuitton** SA division. "Moet is all about panache and grandeur," he says. "Every document has to be fabulous." Moet has enlisted **MDC Partners Inc.'s** Kirshenbaum Bond & Partners to develop coffee-table-size employee guides that cover everything from brand colors to what letterhead should look like.

Smaller ad shops are also testing these waters. The Richards Group, an independent Dallas agency that works for marketers including **Chick-fil-A** Inc. and **Home Depot** Inc., formed Richards Inside last March. The operation has devised workshops and workbooks for clients and their employees, says David Cole, the unit's director.

Marketers see value in the idea. "You can't just have people working on something they don't feel passionate about," says Mr. Jones, the marketing official for Masterfoods USA's pet-care operation. As Masterfoods devised its program, the company enlisted the aid of its research-and-development, human-resources and marketing departments, as well as TBWA and other marketing firms.

"If the company doesn't walk the walk, somebody is going to point out the contradictions," notes Lee Clow, TBWA\Worldwide's chairman and chief creative officer. Mr. Clow himself is buying into the idea of personal involvement: His baby bulldog, Ms. Winston, appears in one of Pedigree's new ads.

Advertising: KFC 'Soul' Ad Poses *Global Issue*

U.K. TV Commercial Raises Racial-Stereotype Concern For World-Wide Marketers

ROBERT GUY MATTHEWS.
WALL STREET JOURNAL

London—**A CAMPY** new television commercial airing for KFC in Europe advertises fried chicken with the slogan: "Servin' Up Soul." The ad features two white Britons dressed in business suits who suddenly begin singing riffs of churchy-sounding soul music about their KFC chicken.

For a U.S. audience, the ad's musical style and the tagline could evoke a historical—and uncomfortable—stereotype of African-Americans eating fried chicken, notwithstanding the use of white actors. But while the U.S. long has had cultural associations with fried chicken, Britain has no such tradition.

Still, at a time when companies such as KFC operate in many countries and ads quickly can spread globally via the Internet, the commercial poses a delicate question for marketers: How much do ads in one country need to worry about images that might be considered off-limits in another?

Bartle Bogle Hegarty, the London agency partly owned by **Publicis Groupe** that created the ad, sees no problems with the commercial. It plans to use the "Servin' Up Soul" tagline in a series of KFC ads.

KFC, owned by **Yum Brands,** Louisville, Ky., says it doesn't think that it taps into any stereotypes, either U.S. or British, with the current ad. It says it hasn't received complaints. "We are delighted with the success of our campaign," says Claire Harrison Church, KFC marketing director in the United Kingdom.

"It is a funny ad," says Norman Sholkin, a branding consultant in London. "Frankly, I don't see how anyone could see it as anything offensive."

The ad isn't coming to the U.S., where KFC is running a separate marketing campaign called "Chicken Capital USA." Even so, many ads intended for one market are shared around the globe via the Internet, because watchers think they are funny, clever or even offensive.

Marketers have to be sensitive to even the most remote misinterpretations, and minority cultural traditions often aren't used in advertising, so ads that do use them receive particular attention, branding experts say.

"Blacks, Latinos, Asians often believe that they aren't portrayed effectively and believe that they are still stereotyped," says Pepper Miller, president of Hunter-Miller Group, a Chicago consulting firm that advises corporations on reaching various ethnic markets.

Learning of KFC's European ad, Ms. Miller said it raised some concerns to her. To be sure, KFC, along with **McDonald's,** for years has been lauded for its positive advertising using blacks in nonstereotypical settings, Ms. Miller says. The two companies in the U.S. continuously have used blacks in family and other congenial contexts that reflect more than stereotypes of the culture.

Stereotypes such as dumb jocks or sexy women are used all the time in advertising, but the key is not to use any that could be conceived as hurtful, says Howard Buford, chief executive officer of Prime Access, a U.S. ad agency that focuses on creative marketing to blacks, Hispanics and gays. He adds: "Something that is sweet and endearing in one location can be seen as crude and

New TV ads for KFC *show Brits singing to each other about their KFC fried chicken. The ad slogan: Servin' up soul.*

insensitive in other places."

The stereotype of fried chicken is an old one in the U.S., and the public is sensitive to it. In 2002, one Giant Food Stores supermarket in Pennsylvania advertised a special on fried chicken "in honor of Black History month." After customers complained, the store, a unit of grocery titan **Ahold** of the Netherlands, immediately removed the advertising and apologized, saying that the sale wasn't meant to offend.

Historians say the association of African-Americans with fried chicken dates back decades, when it was known in many black communities as the "gospel bird," because it often was served only on Sunday after church services. In later years, it gained wider popularity as a picnic food.

From *The Wall Street Journal,* January 27, 2005. Reprinted by permission of Dow Jones and Co., Inc. via The Copyright Clearance Center.

China Cracks Down on Commercials

Viewer Complaints Lead To Bans on Certain TV Ads; Prime Airtime Is Restricted

By GEOFFREY A. FOWLER

Beijing Resident Zhang Xiying recalls the awkward silence that fell over dinnertime conversation with her son and his friends when a TV commercial for a feminine-hygiene product appeared during the broadcast.

"What the ads bluntly said should only be talked about between women," says Ms. Zhang, 50 years old.

The Chinese government apparently agrees. In an attempt to bring decorum to China's often unruly broadcasting system, national regulators have banned ads for "offensive" products, such as feminine-hygiene pads, hemorrhoid medication and athlete's-foot ointment, during three daily meal times. Beer ads have been limited to two between 7 p.m. and 9 p.m. Regulators also sliced in half the amount of prime airtime available for ads on some stations—on some key channels, say media buyers, prime-time ads last year could run for up to 20 minutes straight.

The moves highlight the difficulties facing China, home to the world's biggest television audience, as it tries to apply cultural and broadcasting standards without driving away deep-pocketed advertisers.

Officials with the State Administration of Radio, Film and Television say they implemented the new rules Jan. 1 because viewers complained that commercials were too graphic—and too frequent—during dinner. They also instituted a special telephone hot-line for viewers to report infractions, which already has resulted in 600 orders from the government to change ads. China's fast development is creating cultural rifts between sophisticated urbanites and millions of rural farmers, who don't always appreciate or understand the commercials beamed in on CCTV from Beijing.

Political content on the airwaves in China always has been strictly regulated. But because China has become an increasingly competitive and important market for consumer goods over the past few years, advertisers are eager to push the limit of what is considered socially acceptable in order to get their message across. And even though Chinese ads already pass through government censor boards, the process can sometimes be finicky. Censors sent one **McDonald's** ad back almost a half dozen times because they

A Change in China

Average number of minutes used by advertising in 2003 prime-time TV programming

United States: 11 minutes, 16 seconds*
Singapore: 12 min.
Hong Kong: 10 min.
China: 11 min.

New in 2004:
China: 9 min.

* Includes only national commercial-minutes
Source: Universal McCann and CCTV Research

Don't worry, Whisper CD Ultra is here!

Ads by Leo Burnett China for **Procter & Gamble's** *Whisper brand of feminine-hygiene pads are among those now banned during meal times in China.*

objected to a scene showing a man licking drippings from his juicy chicken burger off a magazine page, says Ruth Lee, creative director of **Publicis Groupe's** Leo Burnett Shanghai.

Ren Qian, the radio-film-TV administration's vice director of the department of broadcasting affairs supervision, says the new laws are an attempt to bring consistency to censor enforcement. "We want to level the playing field by regulating the national standard."

But advertisers and media buyers complain that the new rules are too broad and are out of step with the country's quickly changing mores. "Banning sanitary products is definitely the wrong move," says Ravi Morthy, the general manager of Publicis Groupe media buyer Starcom, which will now have to place ads for **Procter & Gamble's** Whisper feminine-hygiene products during lower-profile time slots.

China's $14.5 billion ad market, already the world's fifth largest, grew 30% in 2003 and is widely expected to become the world's second largest in under a decade, according to Nielsen Media Research. Prime-time TV is the main tool many marketers use to build brand reputations in China.

But the new restrictions could potentially crimp the growth of the country's ad market because they limit the total number of ads shown at prime time to nine minutes an hour from a previous average of 11. The U.S. average is 11 minutes and 16 seconds during prime time.

Some channels were so ad-heavy that the cutback in ad time has resulted in a drop of nearly 50% of prime-time ad revenue. Last year, ads took up 30% to 40% of the prime-time programming of provincial broadcaster Hebei TV. "Now we're facing a pretty big challenge to fulfill the growth target of ads revenue," says Huang Wenxia, head of Hebei's broadcasting department.

They're Off to See the Wizards

Customers at Apple's Tech Bars Often Find an Elixir for What Ails Them

KATIE HAFNER. NEW YORK TIMES

IT was just past noon on a recent weekday at the Apple Store here, and the Genius Bar was buzzing.

At one end of the 40-foot maple counter, a cherub-faced Genius in a black T-shirt spoke soothingly to a middle-aged customer whose iPod kept erasing songs. After a few minutes of probing, the Genius announced his diagnosis: the firmware needed updating. Then he showed the man how to do it.

At the other end of the bar, another amiable Genius—Apple's term for its in-store technical support staff—greeted a couple who had arrived with an ailing PowerBook. "Hey, what's going on?" he said, and got down to work.

In an age when human help of any kind is hard to come by, the eight or nine Geniuses on duty at any given time here are a welcome anomaly.

In fact, go to any of the 102 Apple-owned retail stores in the world and—if you are willing to wait—you will be treated to what is an increasingly rare service: free face-to-face technical support.

The walk-up assistance has existed since the first Apple Store opened in 2001, in Washington. Over the years, as the concept gained momentum, the bars have become what Ron Johnson, Apple's senior vice president for retailing, calls the soul of the stores.

"It's the part of the store that people connect to emotionally more than any other," Mr. Johnson said.

For the first few years, there was general mayhem around the Genius Bars. Customers would stand four or five deep, broken gadgets in hand, waiting to speak to an expert. Now there is an online system for scheduling free, same-day appointments. And for $100 a year, customers can schedule appointments up to a week in advance with the expert of their choice.

But there can still be long waits. Just after Christmas, for instance, at the Apple Store in SoHo in New York, by 10 a.m. the earliest appointment that could be had was at 4 p.m. People left and came back, or sat for hours, reading, talking on their cellphones or milling about the store.

The San Francisco store, like all the others, has instituted a pager system for those who show up when all the experts are busy, like the man on this day who lugged his iMac to the bar, hoisted over his shoulder like a recalcitrant child. He took a pager and joined a dozen or so others waiting for help.

The concept of a bar came to Mr. Johnson one night when he was thinking about the kind of environment Apple wanted to create in its stores. He said he was inspired by Four Seasons, the Ritz-Carlton and other hotels where service is paramount.

"We believed you had to bring the people dimension back into retail," said Mr. Johnson, who joined Apple five years ago after 15 years at Target. "We thought, What about giving tech support that's as welcoming as the bar at the Ritz?"

Tim Bajarin, principal analyst at Creative Strategies, a high-tech consulting firm in Campbell, Calif., said Apple's strategy was sound. "It's all part of a sales process," he said. "They have these guys who are extremely articulate answering customers' questions, which is key not only to the sales process, but the support afterwards."

Other computer retail stores have technical support counters, too. A few, like CompUSA and Best Buy, even have traveling teams of tech support staff who make house calls. But those services are not free.

Further, Mr. Bajarin said, the wider spectrum of problems encountered at other stores dilutes the quality of service.

"A Best Buy could be handling not just H-P, but Gateway and Epson and whatever else they have in the store," he said. "These guys running the Genius Bars are extremely well trained around a single platform."

Hiring those Geniuses—the label was Mr. Johnson's idea, too—is not difficult. He said that when the company advertises for an opening, an average of 50 people apply within 24 hours. For the most part, the applicants already have extensive technical knowledge. Apple provides eight weeks of training, four weeks at the company's headquarters in Cupertino, Calif., and another four weeks at the store.

Mr. Johnson said an initial concern was that the people hired would be geeky, lacking the social skills for a job that calls for continuous interaction with strangers. But he soon found that more often than not, the employees were well-socialized young people who happened to know a lot about computers.

Each employee has an area of expertise—digital photography, say, or the Windows operating system. And they aren't too proud to call on colleagues for help.

"I borrow others' brain cells all the time," said Diana Souverbielle, an employee in the San Francisco store, who confessed to knowing "just enough about Windows to get in trouble."

David Marcantonio, 25, who diagnosed the firmware problem, is the resident iPod expert at the San Francisco store. Mr. Marcantonio, who studied criminology in college and has been fluent in most things Apple since age 14, stands out from his co-workers because his T-shirt reads iPod Genius.

"It's a bull's-eye," Mr. Marcantonio said of the shirt. Half of the customers at the Genius Bar these days have iPod-related problems.

Sometimes the public misunderstands the purpose of the Genius Bar, mistaking it for a think tank or an intellectual sounding board. David Isom, 29, who decided to defer a legal career in favor of a stint at the bar, said a man came in recently to discuss an idea he had for a solar-powered subway system. "He had technical questions, and he wanted to pitch it to us," Mr. Isom said. "I know nothing about solar power."

Indeed, they are humble experts. When confronted by a thorny problem on the fringe of their expertise, they might conduct a Google search to consult sources that are "not necessarily endorsed by Apple," Mr. Isom said.

And the experience of one customer whose keyboard had a sticky "e," which was cured by Ms. Souverbielle's mere touch, suggests that the experts might even have healing powers. Ms. Souverbielle declared that it was merely a coincidence.

Invariably in their 20's and 30's, and predominantly male, Apple's experts do keep lofty company. Behind each bar is a screen with a rotating display of quotations from half a dozen better-known intellectual luminaries, like Leonardo da Vinci ("The noblest pleasure is the joy of understanding") and Michelangelo ("If people knew how hard I had to work to gain my mastery, it wouldn't seem wonderful at all").

But could Michelangelo have executed a clean startup from an external drive on a PowerBook G4?

Could Leonardo have restored the video on Joe Montana's iBook?

That task was performed by Chris Tichenor, a 24-year-old Genius in San Francisco. No matter that the concierge mistakenly entered Mr. Montana, the famous quarterback, into the appointment queue as Steve Young, Mr. Montana's successor on the San Francisco 49ers. "He didn't seem to mind," Mr. Tichenor said.

By Mr. Johnson's estimate, each of the company's 500 experts handles some 200 customers a week, taking as long as is needed to solve each problem.

The stores in general and the Genius Bars in particular have been credited with creating a halo effect for Apple. The iPod owners who own PC's and go to the unrelentingly chic stores for an expert's help are often seduced by Apple's self-conscious hipness.

Paula Mauro, who lives in New York and recently spent several hours at the Genius Bar in the SoHo store, got that message when getting help with iPod-to-PC communication. As she sat at the bar with her 10-year-old son, William, who aspires to Macintosh ownership, it became evident to her that synching an iPod to a Macintosh computer is relatively seamless, while her three-year-old PC posed no end of technical challenges.

"The next computer I buy is going to be a Mac," she said.

The Geniuses are patient even when people show up with problems that only a technophobe could create. Mr. Isom said people have come to him with an iPod that they insisted was dead—until Mr. Isom showed them that they had pushed the Hold switch, which inactivates the iPod's buttons, mainly so that it cannot be turned on or off inadvertently.

If a problem can be solved on the spot, the Genius may disappear into the back and re-emerge with a piece of equipment restored to health. Broken iPods are often replaced at no cost, Mr. Marcantonio said, because if the warranty applies, the easiest thing to do is to hand the customer a new one.

In some ways, this has little to do with keen technical knowledge and a lot to do with astute customer service.

The experience of Cecilia Joyce, a marathon runner who claims to be unable to live without her iPod, is a recent case in point. Ms. Joyce's iPod is packed with music like Boy George's rendition of "The Girl From Ipanema," which inspires her to run longer, sometimes even faster.

When her iPod's battery stopped holding a charge, Ms. Joyce went straight to the Genius Bar in San Francisco. She apologized to Mr. Marcantonio for having bought the device at a different Apple Store. Unfazed by this mundane detail, and without further ado, he gave Ms. Joyce a new iPod.

Were it not for the Genius Bar, Ms. Joyce might have gone an untenable two weeks without a device, the amount of time it could have taken to send it to be repaired or replaced.

Soon after the elated Ms. Joyce left, Mr. Marcantonio glanced down at his computer to see what troubled device was coming next. "Oh, it's an iPod Shuffle—this is going to be interesting," he said, delighted by his first encounter with the tiny new flash-based iPod.

Mr. Marcantonio picked up the white plastic stick and gave its miniature controls a quick poke.

Unlike the clerk in the Monty Python dead parrot skit, who refuses to concede that the bird he sold to a customer was in fact deceased, Mr. Marcantonio knows a dead iPod Shuffle when he sees one. The solution: give the customer a new one.

Genius.

Giving Buyers Better Information

What's In Store: Hired-gun reps spread the word about new products.

. . . .

By Ken Spencer Brown
Investor's Business Daily

If you want something done right, the old saying goes, do it yourself.

That's why tech manufacturers, competing with a sea of rivals on retail shelves, often send their own representatives to stores to push their wares.

These on-site ambassadors answer customer questions, give demos and train the store staff on how to better sell the product. The aim is to persuade sales clerks to steer customers away from rival products and toward their own.

Fuji Photo Film USA Inc., better know as Fujifilm, wanted to do the same thing this winter to promote its new line of digital cameras for the holiday shopping season.

But Tony Sorice, who's in charge of the firm's hardware sales, knew he didn't have the budget to hire and train a brand new field sales team. So he put a new twist on the do-it-yourself approach: He outsourced it.

Sorice turned to sales and marketing company Campaigners Inc.

Campaigners saves clients money by quickly training a sales force to represent the manufacturer. Sometimes it trains retailers or pushes for better shelf placement. Other times, its workers stay in the stores during business hours, showing off the goods to customers directly.

"We were looking for an extension of our sales force as we became more involved in the digital imaging business," Sorice said. "There are tons of digital cameras out there, and it's important that we stay top of mind of the people on the (retail) sales force."

Such outsourced in-store marketing, long used by consumer products firms in grocery stores and at special events, is growing in popularity as a way of promoting tech products. Manufacturers can boost new product exposure in big chains such as Best Buy without having to hire a bigger sales staff year-round.

Hard To Explain

The effort doesn't replace the usual marketing work, which can include everything from ads to product reviews. But it does add a crucial step at that very point when customers make their final decision.

Redondo Beach, Calif.-based Campaigners isn't the only firm selling that type of marketing service. Its rivals include Acosta Sales and Marketing, Best Service Co. and Creative Channel Strategies Inc.

Samsung Electronics America uses Creative Channel for programs at Best Buy and other stores.

Erin Burns, Samsung's retail channel marketing manager, says it's not enough to just aim marketing at consumers. Keeping retailers abreast of current products is just as important.

For Fujifilm, the challenge was how to convey the benefits of its new digital camera. With just a product box sitting on a shelf, it wouldn't be easy to explain that the camera uses a new technology that doubles the resolution suggested by the 3.2 megapixel rating. With rivals offering higher megapixel models, Fuji knew it needed a way to stand out.

Campaigners tackled this by explaining the product better to retail clerks, who in turn did a better job explaining it to shoppers. That can be an improvement over a commercial or a Web site, since the message reaches the casual shopper at the very point of decision.

To do this, Campaigners needs to know the product nearly as well as the manufacturer. So the firm asks the clients lots of questions over a period of days to get familiar with the product and the company's style.

From there, the firm works with the client to craft a marketing message and approach.

One of the toughest parts is getting the right people. Campaigners culls a database of thousands of on-call workers to match skills, availability and other measures. Some work on a contract basis, and others are full-time employees.

Keeping up the pool of workers is key. To make sure Campaigners has enough workers ready for the next campaign, it often holds "casting calls" around the country to find people it can use.

The skills needed can vary from project to project.

"When you're on stage (representing) Microsoft, you need someone more technically competent than for Sierra Mist," said Campaigners CEO Melissa Orr.

Too Much Information?

Gathering attention on a college campus might be important in one setting. In others, it might be vital to keep loudmouth propeller heads in the crowd happy.

When auditioning, Campaigners puts wannabe reps through real-life scenarios to see how they react. After all, hecklers, product glitches and stolid crowds are routine in the field.

After selecting those who will work in the upcoming project, Campaigners brings them together for a two-to four-day training camp. Typically, the client directs the teaching, highlighting the intricacies of their goods.

"You would not believe how much there is to know about washing machines and dryers," Orr said, referring to client LG Electronics Co.

The final step of training is a day of rehearsed presentations. Campaigners puts workers through their paces, throwing all sorts of curves as they hone their performance.

Finally, the new reps are sent out into the field.

To retailers and shoppers, the Campaigners crew may as well be the manufacturer itself. Reps are decked out in outfits provided by the manufacturers and act as direct ambassadors.

One of their most valued functions is gathering field data: How familiar is the retail sales staff with the product? What do they think of rival products? For Fujifilm, the bottom line metric was sales. The company saw a noticeable spike in stores that got visits from the Campaigners staff. The work also keeps Fujifilm products on the minds of sales clerks.

If Sorice ever doubted that Campaigners was working closely enough with retailers, he got the proof he needed when one of his in-house sales staff visited a store with a Campaigners rep. The store's staff recognized the Campaigners rep and greeted her by name. Familiarity won't guarantee the clerk promotes the product, but it's a crucial first step.

"The retailers know these people," he said. "And they pass that on to the end customer."

Research: Study Says Some Should Take Pass on Super Bowl

Volvo, GoDaddy are ill-fit for game, though Bud scores high.

Kenneth Hein. Brandweek.

VOLVO, NOVARTIS, GODADDY.COM and others may be sorry they shelled out millions for their share of the Super Bowl spotlight, per a new study by Brand Keys, New York.

The survey, conducted earlier this month, asked consumers 18-59 who are likely to watch the game, to rate their top brands. Participants were then asked to rate them in the context of their appearance during the game for a "Return on Equity" (ROE) score.

"There are some companies whose brand values are better reinforced by the Super Bowl's values than others," said Brand Keys president Robert Passikoff. "If it doesn't reinforce your brand values, then you're throwing your $2.4 million away."

First-timers like GoDaddy.com, which had the lowest ROE score (-6), Consentino USA (-4) and Novartis Ciba Vision (-4) fared poorly because "there is some confusion as to what these brand values are and why they are mixing with the Super Bowl?" said Passikoff.

Volvo (-3), Ford/Lincoln Mercury (-2) and MBNA (-2) sank to the bottom because they don't align well with football. "Volvo is a car for soccer moms best-suited for a family program," said Al Ries, president of brand consultancy Ries & Ries, Atlanta. "A lot of advertisers miss the importance of matching the message to the medium. You wouldn't put a Bud ad in *Vogue*."

Not surprisingly, many of the brands that performed poorly in last year's survey—the American Legacy Foundation, Cialis, H&R Block, Levitra, Monster, Staples and the White House Office for National Drug Control Policy—won't be back.

As for the others that are staying on the sidelines, "It's not like P&G and IBM and others don't have the budget to buy these ads, they just think there are better ways to spend their media dollars," said Passikoff.

Brands that fit well in the context of Super Bowl parties, like Frito-Lay (+15), Pepsi (+13), Anheuser-Busch (+10) and Emerald of California (+7), got the best scores. Unilever's Degree scored a +10 because sweat is certainly a part of the game. Most of the movie ads fared well because they are a form of entertainment just like

MIXED BAG FOR THE BOWL	
ADVERTISER	ROE*
American Honda Motors	0
AmeriQuest Mortgage	+2
Anheuser-Busch	+10
Buena Vista Films (*The Pacifier*)	-3
Cadillac	0
CareerBuilder.com	-1
Consentino USA	-4
Emerald of California	+7
Ford/Lincoln Mercury	-2
FedEx	+3
Frito-Lay	+15
GoDaddy.com	-6
McDonald's	+8
MGM	+7
MBNA	-2
Tabasco	+3
Novartis Ciba Vision	-4
Olympus Imaging	+2
Paramount (*War of the Worlds*)	+1
Paramount (*The Longest Yard*)	+10
Pepsi	+13
Sony Pictures (*Hitch*)	+4
Unilever (Degree)	+11
Universal Pictures (tbd)	+3
Warner Bros. (tbd)	+4
Visa	+10
Volvo	-3
ADVERTISER	HALFTIME SHOW
AmeriQuest Mortgage	-2
ADVERTISER	POST-GAME
Cadillac	+6
Source: Brand Keys	**Return on Equity*

the NFL. Paramount Pictures' *The Longest Yard* got one of the highest scores at +10.

Cadillac's sponsorship of the postgame show scored well (+6) as it strongly intertwines the brand with a winner while AmeriQuest Mortgage's headlining the halftime show did not (-2). "Who wants to think about mortgages in the middle of the game?" asked Passikoff.

ENTERTAINMENT: YOUR FAVORITE TV SHOW IS CALLING

With quality video cell phones on the way, media companies are thinking small

FOX's thriller *24* is already a major TV hit in the U.S. and across much of Europe. And now a scaled-down version of the show is coming to an even smaller screen—the one on your cell phone. Later this month, Fox Broadcasting Co. will roll out one-minute "mobisodes"—mobile episodes, get it?—of *24* on Europe's Vodafone Group PLC network. And starting in February, Verizon Communications' U.S. subscribers may be able to get mobisodes of the show on their cell phones, too. If *24* is a wireless hit, the media giant may follow up with other programming, including reality shows.

Fox has plenty of company. With viewers increasingly abandoning TV for the Internet and video games, studios, and other media outfits are rushing to jump into the fledgling market for cellular video. In just the last month the likes of Fox, Warner Bros., and ESPN have all signed deals to bring everything from sports highlights to comic books to super-small screens.

With an estimated 170 million phone users out there, it's a potentially huge market. Industry analyst In-Stat/MDR figures the cell phone video market will generate just $32.7 million this year, but that could jump to $1.9 billion by 2008. The question is, will Americans want downsized video—and if so, can companies make money on it? "The business model is far from clear," says John Burris, Director of Wireless Data Services for Sprint Corp. "But this is a real business; a lot of content players want in."

Cellular providers and media giants are hoping to duplicate the success of video phone services overseas. Cell phone users in Japan and Korea already can watch TV on their handsets, and Vodafone offers sports highlights in Europe. Such services have been limited so far in the U.S. because the rollout of high-speed cellular networks has lagged behind other countries. Even now, the TV shows offered by 14-month-old California startup MobiTV are jerky at best.

All that could change this year. New third-generation phones running on beefed-up digital networks will hit the market during the first quarter. Cellular providers say they'll be capable of delivering near cable-quality video.

With the technological pieces finally falling into place, entertainment companies are scrambling to come up with programming. Warner Bros. aims to put *Looney Tunes* on some phones, as well as behind-the-scenes clips of its teen soap *The OC.* MTV Networks is negotiating with Microsoft Corp. to stream rock videos on AudioVox Corp. and other phones. And Verizon is expected to announce deals with several media companies, say industry insiders.

LOTS OF CLOSE-UPS

Success, of course, will require content that people actually want to watch on their

Coming Soon to A Phone Near You

FOX is creating one-minute "mobisodes" based on its hit drama *24* for Vodafone and Verizon

WARNER BROS. will offer cell phone users behind-the-scenes videos of teen drama *The OC*

ESPN aims to beam sports clips and news shows to a branded ESPN phone on Sprint's network

MARVEL COMICS has a deal with mobile game maker MFORMA to create comics and other content

cell phones. Analysts expect one- to three-minute video bursts to catch on initially—what Sprint's Burris calls "snack TV." The studios also have to tweak their content for those minuscule screens. In shooting its cellular version of *24,* for example, Fox featured more close-ups. At the outset, shows will be tailored to sports and news junkies and the younger viewers who live on their cell phones—and are the advertising sweet spot for TV execs.

How will companies make money? Subscriptions could be one way. MobiTV has signed up roughly 100,000 customers who pay $10 a month for more than 20 cable channels. Verizon and Fox won't reveal the per-mobisode price for *24.* But Warner expects to charge as much as $5.99 for each snippet of *The OC Insider;* it will also offer the show as part of a $24.99 yearly subscription to a fan club. Others plan to sell ads. Mobliss, a Seattle marketing firm that also makes original programs, is working with Nike Inc. and Coca-Cola Co. to cram product placements into its shows.

Another wrinkle: With TV rights to most shows still held by broadcasters rather than the media outfits that produce them, producers are being forced to come up with duplicate programs. The cell phone version of *24,* for example, will feature a new cast that doesn't include star Kiefer Sutherland.

With so much up in the air, some players are hanging back. "We're not sure it's a real business yet," says Sony Pictures Entertainment Chairman Michael Lynton, whose company is focusing instead on Internet downloads of its soaps. "But we're watching closely to see how Fox does with *24.*" With 170 million super-small screens out there, he'd be foolish not to.

Ronald Grover in Los Angeles. Business Week.

Web Search Sites See Clicks Add Up To Big Ad Dollars

JOHN MARKOFF AND NAT IVES, SAUL HANSELL CONTRIBUTED REPORTING FOR THIS ARTICLE.. NEW YORK TIMES.

When the year's largest television audience convenes for the Super Bowl on Sunday, advertisers will be spending an estimated $2.4 million for each 30-second cinema-quality commercial. But just as important to many of those same advertisers is the $1.50 or so a mouse click that they may spend on the Google Internet search site, at any hour on any day, for a few words of plain text that will link prospective customers to the advertisers' Web sites.

The fact that Eli Lilly, Napster, Novartis and Staples are among Super Bowl advertisers that are also regulars on Google is not the only evidence that Web advertising has come of age.

On Tuesday, Google, the most popular Internet search company, announced that it had passed a significant milestone by selling $1 billion of advertising during the last three months of 2004.

Each day on Google, hundreds of thousands of times an hour, Web surfers who type in search terms like "printer paper" end up clicking on paid links to sites like Staples.com—from advertisers that have bid to have their names appear in innocuous, no-frills text lists at the side of the search results page. The advertiser pays only when the prospective customer actually clicks on the ad link.

"In the past, advertising has been hard to track and hard to make accountable," said Tim Armstrong, Google's vice president for advertising sales. Now, he said, advertising has become a dialogue with the consumer.

Google did not invent the concept of keyword search ads, which predates the company's founding in 1998. And Google is not alone in capitalizing on the paid-click trend. Yahoo is also reaping rich, if somewhat lesser rewards, and Microsoft is expanding its considerable presence in the field. Small companies like Ask Jeeves are also in the hunt.

But so far Google has been the most successful in blending computer science, consumer behavior and merchant motivation into what, for now at least, is a considerable money machine.

With an overall market of about $3.8 billion last year, keyword search represented more than 40 percent of the total $8.7 billion in Internet ad spending last year in the United States, according to Merrill Lynch. And keyword search's share of the Internet ad market is growing.

No one expects Google-type ads to quickly render other forms of advertising obsolete in the United States, where marketers spent a total of $264 billion last year in all media.

"Avenues like the Super Bowl offer a tremendous outlet to reach consumers," said Richard Castellini, the vice president for consumer marketing at CareerBuilder.com, an online job listings company that has bought three 30-second spots on the Super Bowl broadcast.

A TV ad can put the company's name and brand before millions of viewers, Mr. Castellini said. But Google can direct prospective customers to his business by placing a CareerBuilder.com link on the screen of anyone using Google as part of a job hunt.

As for local advertising on radio and television and in newspapers, those media can still be effective ways to blanket large portions of the hometown audience with a uniform message. But individually focused Internet ads are already siphoning business away from locally oriented classified advertising and yellow pages directories—whether in their offline or online forms.

And as the Internet occupies an increasing part of the modern consumer's discretionary time, all the other forms of media advertising will probably have to adjust.

"You're seeing advertising move into advertising that people can seek out, and moving away from mass advertising," said Peter Sealey, a former Coca-Cola marketing executive who now teaches at the Haas School of Business at the University of California, Berkeley. "In the context of that shift, this little niche of Internet search will be a huge beneficiary."

Under the Google model, the Internet is also an equal-opportunity medium for advertisers. Sellers of all stripes have the opportunity to bid from 5 cents to $100 per mouse click to have their Web links appear alongside Google's pages of search results. Anyone who bids at least the minimum will appear on the list, but unless the bid is competitive, the bidder's name may appear so far down the list that the chances diminish that prospective shoppers will see it.

Unlike Yahoo, which ranks its lists of sponsored ads based on how much the advertiser has bid per click, Google continually adjusts the rankings on the basis of which ads are returning the most money. The merchant who bids $1 a click and gets 100 clicks per thousand people who see the ad, in other words, will receive a higher ranking than the seller who bids $10 but gets only five clicks per thousand. And to keep control of the cost, advertisers have the option of setting a spending cap—once reached, the ads stop running.

And so, keyword Internet ads—especially Google's version—are one of the few forms of advertising that potentially appeal to anyone, anywhere, of any size with something for sale.

Barnard Ltd., a small Chicago company that sells decorations and stage props like artificial food, has used Google keyword searches like "fake food" and "Styrofoam balls"—since 2002—to great effect.

The company finds itself consistently outbid for more common terms, like "decorations," by big retailers like Target and Amazon. Still, "in the first year it probably increased my sales by 70 percent," said June D. Barnard, the company's president. "It's enabled me to sell internationally and throughout the United States in a way that I could never do before."

The Internet ads have also allowed Barnard to halt its direct-mail catalog program, which attracted nearly no business, Ms. Barnard said.

Ms. Barnard's story is the kind that can set off fears—or hopes—that catalogs and all direct mail will disappear. But their demise has been predicted before, said Louis Mastria, vice president for communications at the Direct Marketing Association.

Instead, Mr. Mastria said, the Web and direct mail work best together. When a company mails a catalog, for example, it can count on a spike in traffic to its Web site within a day or two, he said. "A lot of these channels are coming together."

Google's wildly popular public stock offering last summer underscored the success of its approach. But the company itself expressed surprise at its robust fourth-quarter results; the earnings news sent the stock up 7 percent on Wednesday and it rose an additional 2.3 percent yesterday, to close at $210.86. That is up 148 percent since Google went public in August, raising worries by

(Cont.)

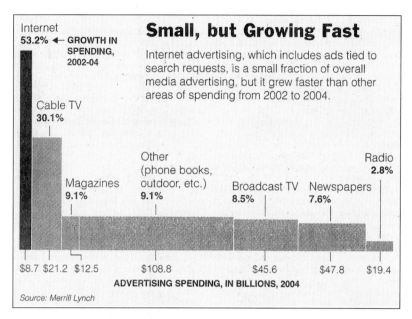

Small, but Growing Fast

Internet advertising, which includes ads tied to search requests, is a small fraction of overall media advertising, but it grew faster than other areas of spending from 2002 to 2004.

Internet
53.2% ← GROWTH IN SPENDING, 2002-04

Cable TV
30.1%

Magazines
9.1%

Other
(phone books,
outdoor, etc.)
9.1%

Broadcast TV
8.5%

Newspapers
7.6%

Radio
2.8%

$8.7 $21.2 $12.5 $108.8 $45.6 $47.8 $19.4

ADVERTISING SPENDING, IN BILLIONS, 2004

Source: Merrill Lynch

some that the stock may be overpriced even though its growth has been impressive.

The trend has also held some surprise for Bill Gross, the entrepreneur and software designer who was one of the pioneers of Internet advertising in the mid-1990's and is widely credited with inventing a way to make money from Web searches.

"I thought that the Internet was fantastic, and I was sure that it would become the ultimate direct marketing tool," he said yesterday. "But I had no idea that pay-per-click would ultimately be this big."

Mr. Gross recalls how resistant users were in the early days of the Web to pop-up ads that interfered with, rather than supplemented a person's search session. For him, the answer lay in making the advertising inconspicuous, but relevant to the Web user's search terms.

And yet he also remembers initial resistance to his approach. When he introduced his keyword search system, GoTo.com, at an industry conference in Monterey, Calif., in 1998, some people in the audience hissed. "They were upset that somebody would attempt to monetize search, which was widely believed to be a free good at the time," he said.

He later changed his company's name to Overture Services, which Yahoo purchased for $1.63 billion in 2003. Overture now sells ads for the search portion of Yahoo's Web site, and it also sells ads for other sites, most notably Microsoft's MSN Search service.

Google, by developing a reputation for returning the most relevant search results, became the most popular search site. In December, Google's site attracted 67.1 million different American users, who each spent an average total of 30 minutes on the site, according to Nielsen/NetRatings. By contrast, Yahoo's search service drew 47.9 million American visitors, who spent an average 12 minutes in December.

Google's reign at the top is not guaranteed, of course.

"Google has a very, very strong position in the marketplace, but they're competing against some of the most powerful, best-run companies in the world," said Ken Cassar, the director for strategic analysis at Nielsen/NetRatings, referring to Yahoo and Microsoft's MSN online service. And some Internet executives point out that keyword searches, representing less than half of all Internet advertising dollars, are not the only art form. A bit less than half of Google's fourth-quarter revenue, for example, came from ads it placed on other companies' Web sites, based on the context of the surrounding material.

Online ad spending is also increasing for video and so-called rich media advertising— interactive ads that use animation, audio and video. Jay Amato, the chief executive at Viewpoint in New York, a company that produces online video and interactive ads, said that while paid search may be getting its day in the sun, the time will come for rich media and video.

"It's very good for us, because people are seeing real results from online advertising," Mr. Amato said. "It says the years of the doldrums are over."

For now, though, the keyword search is king.

Ask Ray Allen, a former ad agency executive who is now the president of American Meadows, a wildflower seed supplier in Williston, Vt. "I used to spend millions of dollars of other people's money on TV, radio and newspapers," Mr. Allen said. He now spends about $300 a day to buy search terms like "wildflower seeds" and "hummingbird garden" from Google and Overture to advertise his own company, reaching a national audience of potential customers. "Never in the history of media," he said, "has a small business been able to have that much reach."

70

Advertising

Getting Buzz Marketers to Fess Up

Suzanne Vranica. Wall Street Journal

EVER WONDER if that guy striking up a conversation is really an actor hired to shill for a product? One trade group is hoping you'll never have to.

The Word of Mouth Marketing Association, a year-old Chicago trade group, is expected to announce today a new set of rules and guidelines for word-of-mouth advertising, one of the fastest-growing advertising practices.

The use of the marketing maneuver, also called buzz marketing or viral marketing, has soared in the past two years. Big advertisers such as **Procter & Gamble** and **Microsoft** have embraced the practice at a time when many traditional advertising venues are rising in cost while declining in impact.

While the practice includes a variety of techniques—from building Web communities so customers can chat about their product experiences to handing out product samples—a number of the methods that fall under the word-of-mouth umbrella, such as hiring actors to talk up a product in public places, have given the business a black eye.

"Some of these practices are deceptive because people think they are talking to a real person and they are talking to a shill," says Gary Ruskin, executive director of Commercial Alert, a Portland, Ore., watchdog group. "It's about the commercializing of human relationships."

In 2002, the U.S. arm of Sony Ericsson Mobile Communications faced wide criticism over a word-of-mouth effort for a camera phone.

The company, a venture of Japan's **Sony** and Sweden's **Telefon AB L.M. Ericsson,** hired 60 actors to haunt tourist attractions and act like tourists. Their task: ask unsuspecting passersby to take their pictures with the Sony Ericsson devices. The agency behind the effort, **Omnicom Group's** Fathom Communications, told the actors to identify themselves only when asked directly.

"That campaign is shilling, and it violates the 'honesty of identity' rule," says Andy Sernovitz, chief executive officer of the Word of Mouth Marketing Association, whose 40 members include marketing firms and advertisers.

Under the association's new rules, marketers must make sure that people talking up products or services disclose whom they are working for. They also must use real consumers, not actors, who discuss what they really believe about a product.

But getting every company to buy into self-regulation might not be easy. "I can't begin to image how one can regulate an industry that thrives on its covert nature," says Margaret Kessler, project coordinator at TMR Multimedia, a small marketing firm

in Hollywood, Fla. Ms. Kessler routinely hires "ad spies" to talk up local products. Recently, she hired several actors to stand in the long line at the local courthouse and strike up conversations about a sale going on at a nearby furniture store. Last year, a major snack-food company hired TMR to conduct a pilot project for a healthy snack, which included having ad spies hang around clinics while munching on the new product.

Larger concerns, too, are skeptical of the new guidelines. "The whole idea of marketing is to not make it look like marketing," says Jon Bond, co-founder of Kirshenbaum Bond & Partners. In the mid-1990s, the agency created an effort for Hennessy, a cognac brand now owned by **LVMH Moet Hennessy Louis Vuitton,** that involved hiring 150 actors to drink at trendy bars and chat with patrons about the pricey product.

Some buzz marketers already shun actors. **Edelman USA,** which opened a word-of-mouth division six months ago, recently did work for the launch of Halo 2, Microsoft's popular videogame. Instead of hiring actors, it gave some gamers—deemed to be influencers—tidbits about the alien-hunt game before its release so they could talk about the product with other avid gamers, who are inclined to be heavy users of chat rooms and videogame message boards.

Procter & Gamble says it never hires actors to promote products. Instead, the company has identified 250,000 teens whom it occasionally sends new products and information. Those teens are free to talk about the samples with friends and family. The Cincinnati company says it doesn't pay the teens. "They are free to form their own opinions," says Steve Knox, CEO of P&G's Tremor word-of-mouth marketing agency. "It's critical that marketers in the word-of-mouth space have ethics. The consumer must decide what he or she will say in the marketplace."

Up Close and Personal

With word-of-mouth marketing all the rage, a trade group wants to establish some guidelines for the practice. Among them:

■ **Honesty of Relationship** People talking up products or services must disclose who they are working for.

■ **Honesty of Opinion** Rather than hiring actors, companies must use real consumers to talk about what they really believe about a product.

■ **Honesty of Identity** Don't impersonate a consumer.

Source: The Word of Mouth Marketing Association

Price

71

Car-Rental Agencies Talk Of Realistic 'Total Pricing'

Obscure Fees and Surcharges Vex Drivers

BY CHRISTOPHER ELLIOTT

Nothing makes business travelers' blood boil quite like the unexpected fees and surcharges that car-rental companies tack onto their bills, from airport taxes to a $6-a-gallon charge for filling up the gas tank when the vehicle is returned.

A recent study by Travelocity, the online travel agency, found that the car-rental customer paid an average of 24.4 percent in taxes and surcharges over the base rate when renting at a major American airport. The list of these add-ons has been expanding steadily for the last decade, pushing many drivers to the point of revolt.

To blunt that anger, the car-rental industry and the online travel agencies recently began rolling out a program called total pricing, intended to quote a price that includes all taxes, fees and surcharges.

If this can actually produce a final bill that matches the advertised rate, it might just succeed in sidestepping a public relations disaster.

But that is a big if, industry insiders and business travelers say.

Travelocity.com, the first of the major online travel agencies to widely promote a complete price to its customers, guarantees that its estimate will be within 1 percent of the final bill.

A leading rival, **Orbitz,** promises that the price will be an exact match. And **Expedia** is expected to offer a similar warranty next month when it introduces a feature that will display an estimated rate at the end of each car-rental search.

Two other online travel sellers, Hotwire. com and **Priceline.com,** also guarantee all-inclusive rates in the form of prepaid vouchers.

But for business travelers, the road to a real, full price has been a bumpy one.

"I think rental customers are getting a more accurate idea of what a car rental will cost," said Neil Abrams, president of the Abrams Consulting Group. "But they aren't necessarily getting the whole picture. There are other optional charges, such as fuel-purchase options, loss-damage waivers, that aren't included. And the systems that generate a total price are costly, complex and not yet perfected."

For example, Travelocity, one of the earliest converts to total pricing, still does not offer a complete rate when corporate travelers use its Travelocity Business booking service. The reservations technology used by Travelocity Business is different from the one used on Travelocity, and is not yet capable of calculating a total price, according to the company. That is expected to be fixed with upgrades this spring.

In the meantime, "total pricing is always available on Travelocity," said Phil Kennewell, who is Travelocity's director of car and rail products.

But even when an online service promises a full price, it sometimes leaves out important details that can affect the rate paid. Chuck Reagan booked a car through Travelocity in January and was quoted a "total" price of $135. But when an agent at **Enterprise Rent-A-Car** found that he planned to drive from Portland, Ore., into Idaho, she increased the four-day rate more than 60 percent, to $218.

"Nothing in Travelocity's total price mentioned charging extra for driving into Idaho," Mr. Reagan, a salesman from Logan,

From discount Web site to airport counter, often a road map of consumer frustration.

Utah, said. "But Enterprise said that it is its policy to charge more for Idaho. It was a classic bait-and-switch scam as far as I'm concerned."

Travelocity said Mr. Reagan failed to read the fine print in his rental agreement, which outlined the geographical restrictions.

But Mr. Kennewell acknowledged that the booking display "could have been clearer." Enterprise refunded the difference between what Mr. Reagan was first quoted and what he was billed. Travelocity has pledged to redesign its booking page.

At times, travelers are not sure if they are being quoted a total price. Warren Bell, a South San Francisco, Calif., market researcher who rented a car through Orbitz in August, said that the rate offered by **National Car Rental** in Las Vegas for a midsize vehicle came up as $18.95 a day, including all taxes and fees. But Orbitz failed to mention that the daily rate jumped to $50.96 over the weekend, leaving him with a bill of $211.

"When I returned the car and saw my bill, I honestly thought they had charged me for the wrong reservation," Mr. Bell said.

Orbitz, which asserts that it has never had to reimburse a car-rental customer under its rate guarantee, said the quote Mr. Bell received did not represent a total price.

Sam Fulton, its director of car rental operations, said National had not upgraded its systems to send a complete price to Orbitz last summer. Since Mr. Bell's rental, Orbitz has begun offering total prices for its National cars, and it plans to extend that to all its rentals by year's end.

Mr. Fulton acknowledges that the concept of total pricing is not without its flaws. "If a municipality imposed new taxes that weren't in the system at the time of the rental, then there wouldn't be much we could do about it," he said.

Rental vouchers like the ones offered on "opaque" Web sites like Hotwire and Priceline have not been problem-free.

Bonnie Schollianos, a manager for a resort in St. Thomas, in the Virgin Islands, booked a car through Priceline two years ago. A rental agent at the **Hertz** counter in Oakland, Calif., charged her a $5 airport fee, which was supposed to have been included in her rate. Priceline said that the agent misunderstood the terms of the rental voucher and refunded the $5.

Priceline later revised its display to calculate all taxes and fees at the beginning of the booking process, and since then there have been no misunderstandings at the counter, a spokesman, Brian Ek, said.

"The price you see," he added, "is the price you pay."

Car-rental companies are offering total pricing both to placate customers and to meet rate disclosure requirements from states like California and North Carolina.

"It's important that a consumer knows exactly what they will pay," a Hertz spokesman, Richard Broome, said. "The last thing you want is a surprise at the end of the rental."

The improvements have not come cheap to car-rental companies. The cost for a small

(Cont.)

company to upgrade so a total price can be sent through its reservations system runs "in the tens of thousands of dollars," according to Mr. Abrams, the rental analyst.

For one of the major companies, it can be a six-figure technology investment. None of the online agencies would disclose its exact investment in total-pricing technology. Expedia's director of car programs, Noah Tratt, said it had a team of 10 developers working on the system, adding, "We are very committed to total pricing."

There are further complications. Total pricing is far from complete. Mr. Broome said current total-pricing systems, while sophisticated, still had to make certain assumptions. For example, when an Internet user

The car-rental rate quoted Chuck Reagan of Logan, Utah, rose more than 60 percent because he had to drive across the state line to Idaho.

asks for a quote on a Hertz car in Boston and does not provide flight-arrival information, the system guesses that it is being rented at a location other than the one at the airport.

But if a car is picked up at the airport, certain airport fees would apply. "If you were flying into Boston, your car would be more expensive," he said.

There is also the matter of when the total price is displayed—at the start of the reservations process when an Internet user is shopping for a cheap rate, or at the end

when a purchase decision is all but made.

Car-rental companies have resisted listing a total price at the start—in part because it forces the system to make assumptions about the rental that may be erroneous, but largely for competitive reasons.

No company wants to show the real price until it absolutely has to, according to Marie Benz, who manages the Web site Autorental-guide.com.

"Base rates are still artificially low," she said. "You have to pay attention to the fine print in your rental contract, even with total pricing."

72

Changing Course, Apple Offers Low-Priced Mac for the Home

JOHN MARKOFF AND SAUL HANSELL, JOHN MARKOFF REPORTED FROM SAN FRANCISCO FOR THIS ARTICLE AND SAUL HANSELL FROM NEW YORK.. NEW YORK TIMES.

Apple Computer introduced its first low-priced Macintosh on Tuesday, signaling its bet that most consumers now see computers as simply another appliance in the modern house.

While computers have long been sold as machines that can turn a home into an office, most Americans now use them in their bedrooms and kitchens as e-mail terminals; as hubs for playing music, storing and editing photos; and as stations for navigating the Web.

The new Mac Mini, priced as low as $499 without a keyboard, monitor or mouse, is aimed squarely at the needs of this new digital household.

The new Apple strategy, which moves the company deeply into the consumer electronics market, positions the new Macintosh as an entertainment and communication device. It also promises to intensify Apple's battle with Microsoft in the personal computer market dominated by machines using Windows software.

The move is in part propelled by Apple's success with its iPod digital music players; with 10 million sold in the last three years, the iPod has pulled Apple into the mass market. The popularity of iPod, analysts say, may persuade consumers who have not been Apple computer users to consider the Mac Mini.

"I wish I had a nickel for every time people have suggested that we do this," said Steven P. Jobs, Apple's chief executive, at a conference on Tuesday. "We want to price this Mac so that people who are thinking of switching will have no excuse."

But Apple's introduction of a low-priced machine is not likely to cut significantly into Microsoft's dominance in personal computing; more than 90 percent of PC's are Windows machines.

More important, Microsoft is also moving to turn PC's into entertainment centers with its Windows Media Center Edition software, which lets a computer double as a television and video recorder.

Gene Munster, an analyst at Piper Jaffray, said that Apple's consumers were probably not going to give up their Windows PC's but might buy a Macintosh as an additional computer for entertainment.

"It's not about switching but adding," he said. "People may still need a PC because of work activities, but this is for doing multimedia activities and searching the Internet."

For the last few years, Apple has deflected criticism of its roughly 3 percent share of the computer market by comparing itself to prestige brands like BMW. It tried to make sophisticated and attractive products that appealed to a small segment of consumers willing to pay a premium for superior design.

Mr. Jobs played down suggestions that Apple had any grand strategy to transform itself, saying instead that the new pricing strategy was one that came in response to things that Apple customers have been requesting.

In addition to the Mac Mini, which goes on sale Jan. 22, Mr. Jobs introduced a tiny digital music player, the iPod Shuffle, which is priced as low as $99. The less-expensive player has no screen and can hold about 120 songs, compared with 5,000 songs on a standard iPod.

"Today we saw the unveiling of a business strategy that people will be talking about for years to come," said John M. Gallaugher, a business professor at Boston College.

Even with the low price of the new iPod, Mr. Gallaugher said that Apple would probably make up the low profit margins from the music player by selling a series of accessories with higher margins.

Even loyal iPod users have resisted Apple computers because they are perceived to be expensive and not compatible with the so-called industry standard of personal computers based on Windows and Intel microprocessors.

But the advantages for consumers of using a Windows PC are less significant if they are performing common Internet and entertainment functions. Moreover, the computer viruses, worms and spyware that plague Windows machines have been far less of a problem for Macintosh machines.

The question still remains, however, whether PC users will try Macintosh machines in large numbers.

"This is not going to return Apple to a high level of profitability," said David Yoffie, a professor at Harvard Business School. "The margins on these new machines will be trivial. And I think they will add no more than one or two points of market share."

He said, however, that even a small growth in market share could be enough to attract software developers willing to write programs for the Macintosh.

Apple has struggled to break out of its

"Different by Design"

Since Steven P. Jobs, right, co-founder of Apple Computer, returned to help the company dig itself out of a deep slump in 1997, a series of eye-catching and space-saving reinterpretations of the PC as a stylish digital appliance have set Apple apart from other computer companies. The latest introductions, the Mac Mini and the iPod Shuffle are less-expensive versions of the Macintosh computer and the iPod music player.

iMac—Introduced in 1998
The iMac combined a monitor and central processor into one unit and stood out in the crowd of gray computers with its translucent, icy blue finish. Consumers lined up to buy iMacs even before Apple started delivering them. The current iMac is entirely housed within a flat-panel monitor that rests on a simple stand.

iPod—Introduced in 2002
The iPod married easy file management and a powerful digital music player. Then came the multi-colored iPod Mini, the U2 Special Edition iPod and the iPod Photo able to store and display digital photos. The unmatched popularity of iPods has led to a multitude of compatible products, including a BMW.

(Cont.)

niche position in the computer business since the Macintosh was introduced in 1984. Early on, Mr. Jobs defined the Macintosh as an all-in-one appliance, but he was forced to leave Apple just a year later after losing a management battle with the chief executive then, John Sculley.

During the 1990's, while Mr. Jobs was in exile from the company, Apple flirted with broadening its market by licensing the Macintosh operating system to companies that made systems that were Macintosh compatible.

The strategy backfired when those companies began stealing Apple's profits and Microsoft successfully imitated the Macintosh user interface with Windows version 3.1.

Mr. Jobs canceled the Macintosh operating systems licenses when he returned to Apple in 1997, focusing Apple instead on attractive industrial designs and a new operating system, Macintosh OS X, which he brought with him from Next, the company he founded in 1985.

Most of the decisions Mr. Jobs has made since returning to Apple have been well received, but the company's market share has continued to erode in the face of fierce price competition.

Some analysts said that the cheaper Mac Mini, which could cost several hundred dollars more than its $499 price with a monitor, keyboard and mouse, could help stop the erosion. The low-end Macintosh, called the eMac, sells for about $800.

"The product is sensational for the market it's designed for," said Charles Wolf, an analyst at Needham & Company. He said the new machine was designed to appeal to iPod users with Windows systems who have stayed away from the Macintosh in the past. "I think it's going to stem any further loss of market share, and I foresee the day late in the decade when they will double their market share because of a product like this."

Shares of Apple fell $4.40 Tuesday, to close at $64.56.

Mr. Munster said that investors had been guessing that Apple would sell more iPods in the fourth quarter than the 4.5 million the company reported. Apple will report its first-quarter results Wednesday afternoon.

Mr. Jobs made the announcements in front of an audience of more than 4,000 Macintosh enthusiasts. The announcements cap a year of both success and personal challenge for Mr. Jobs, who has seen Apple's stock more than triple.

Last summer Mr. Jobs was found to have a rare form of pancreatic cancer. After emergency surgery, he quickly returned to work at both Apple Computer and at Pixar Animation Studios, where he is also chairman and chief executive.

He has resisted speaking publicly about his personal crisis. Yet some at the conference thought the marketing slogan for the iPod Shuffle, "Life Is Random," was a reference to the fortunes of Mr. Jobs.

"It jumped out at me," said Roger Mc-Namee, a Silicon Valley venture capitalist. "It's existential marketing with maybe even a touch of nihilism."

Mr. Jobs said he had not created the slogan, which came from the company's advertising agency, TBWA/Chiat/Day, but he acknowledged that it had struck him as well. "I thought about it," he said.

73

Value Positioning Becomes a Priority

By: Jack Neff

For most of its history, premium-brand giant Procter & Gamble Co. treated the poor much like well-off persons treat panhandlers—avoiding direct eye contact but handing over some spare change in the spirit of philanthropy.

But something happened in 2001 when Chairman-CEO A.G. Lafley started making his top global managers spend time with consumers in homes or stores once a quarter. Take Rob Steele, for instance. P&G's president-North America was standing in the checkout line one day with his research subject, and she asked him to come up with the participation fee right then and there so she could pay her grocery bill.

Due to experiences like this, top P&G executives began realizing how many poor people there really are in the world, what a big potential market they made up, and how seldom they could afford or wanted to buy high-price P&G products.

Pampers: To take the focus off price the Premium line was renamed Baby Stages of Development.

At the same time, private labels and such rivals as Unilever's Suave and Alberto-Culver Co.'s VO5 were snatching money from P&G's wallet more figuratively as their value brands took share from P&G's stable of premium ones.

Close encounters with the cash-strapped have helped change the way P&G thinks about brands and marketing as it launches more value brands, value versions of premium brands and other marketing initiatives geared toward lower-income consumers both in the U.S. and overseas.

"It's important just that they've acknowledged as they try to become a global company that 80% of the world can't afford their stuff," said an executive for one P&G competitor. "It's just part of the gale force of competition with Unilever and Colgate, which are already value companies. At the same time, advertising prices are going through the roof. At some point, their business model has to evolve."

CLOSING THE GAP

Just in North America, P&G could add $3 billion in sales overnight if it could close the gap with rivals among low-income, African-American, Hispanic and French-Canadian consumers, Mr. Lafley said at a December investor conference.

Symbolically, P&G's most dramatic shift toward value may be with Ivory, its oldest surviving brand. Dubbed "The House that Ivory Built" in a 1987 *Advertising Age* commemorative issue on P&G's 150th anniversary, the company 15 years later sold the house that built Ivory—its century-old Cincinnati Ivorydale plant—to a Canadian contract manufacturer.

Following cost cuts derived in part from the outsourcing, P&G today markets Ivory as a "midtier" value brand, priced 10% to 15% lower-per-ounce than such rivals as Dial Corp.'s Dial or Unilever's Dove. Unlike most P&G brands, Ivory has no agency of record, but gets media support on a project basis from Benchmark Group, Cincinnati.

As P&G integrated its 2001 Clairol acquisition, it has similarly taken many of the lesser acquired brands, such as Daily Renewal 5x, Aussie and Infusium, down several price points. Most dramatically, Daily Defense, a failing premium brand Clairol had yanked in the U.S. as the deal was closing, came back last year priced at 99¢ or lower, positioned as what P&Gers called "a Suave killer."

The strategy hasn't immediately helped P&G's sales or share in U.S. hair care, both of which were down in 2003. But it did end several years of double-digit sales growth for Suave and helped ensure Unilever lost share in hair care despite its $100 million launch of Dove shampoo and conditioner.

DIFFERENT VENUES

Diana Shaheen, a hair-care marketing director whose portfolio spans Physique products priced north of $7 to Daily Defense, said having such a range "gives me more exposure to consumers in different venues. In shampoo, loyalty is not high, so learning their needs, having a lot of offerings and accelerating growth are really important."

Since the value strategy is global, P&G is sharing learning about appealing to low-income consumers among developing markets, lower-income European markets such as Poland and developed markets.

Mr. Lafley, in an interview with *Ad Age,* said he has been one of the chief drivers behind value brands, along with Kerry Clark, president-global market development, who oversees the units that handle local marketing and media buying efforts throughout the world.

Executives experienced in marketing to low-income consumers overseas are taking their knowledge to the U.S. and vice versa. Alex Tosolini, an Italian national who was marketing director for low-income consumers in P&G's U.S. fabric-care business, developing products for dollar stores, moved last year to become general manager for P&G's business in Poland. There, encroachment by German

(Cont.)

"hard discounters" like Aldi threaten to change the game in a market that had been one of the most favorable in Eastern Europe to premium brands, said Deutsche Bank analyst Andrew Shore.

DIFFERENT AUDIENCES

P&G's shift to value clearly won't mean heavy media advertising for these brands. Even if the thin-margin products could support the spending, it wouldn't necessarily be the right thing to do, said Dimitri Panayotopoulos, P&G's president-Central and Eastern Europe, Middle East, and Africa.

Value consumers "are very much different from the consumers who buy [premium] brands, which is good, because we don't cannibalize volume from the premium tier," he said. "Consumers who buy premium brands are more left-brained and pay for premium performance. [Value consumers] don't care so much about watching advertising and demonstrations and so on. They pride themselves on being savvy consumers who look for value."

After an initial ad push that included TV and print from Barefoot Advertising, Cincinnati, Daily Defense is now off the air, maybe for good, said an executive close to the company, though he added that the brand may remain on store shelves because it offers retailers a decent margin.

But the value focus isn't all about price, thin marketing budgets or even low-income consumers. Susan Arnold, president of P&G's global personal and feminine-care business, which markets some of the company's priciest products, last year had each of her top managers spend a month living on the median household budgets of their countries.

"The idea wasn't to think about price," she said. "It was to think about the value of our products compared with all the other things you could spend your money on with a limited budget."

Even well-off consumers often want value as they trade luxury in one area for thriftiness in another, said Paul Polman, P&G's president-Western Europe. "The Aldi consumer is not necessarily a low-income consumer," he noted. "You'll see plenty of Mercedes' in the parking lot."

74

EBay acknowledges changes that have alienated some users

Michael Bazeley. Knight Ridder Tribune Business News.

Feb. 8—EBay is moving to quell a wave of discontent among individuals and small merchants who sell on the leading online auction Web site.

In an unusual and contrite letter to members, a top eBay executive has acknowledged that recent fee increases, impersonal customer service and other changes to the site have alienated some users. President of eBay North America Bill Cobb vowed significant changes to customer service practices and announced a slight fee reduction that will affect many sellers of lower-priced items.

The letter, e-mailed Sunday to members, comes just weeks after eBay announced a series of unpopular listing fee increases, due to take effect later this month. But it also underscores the rising dissatisfaction among users about a series of changes at the world's largest online marketplace.

"The sense we've had is that sellers have felt increasingly disenfranchised," said Derek Brown, an equities analyst with Pacific Growth Equities in San Francisco. "They're disenchanted with the marketplace and the policies and the management and the fees. And the most recent proposed price hike was like pouring salt into the wound."

EBay users are especially passionate about the service and the San Jose company. That passion helped build the company into the dominant online marketplace with revenue last year of $3.27 billion. And it has allowed eBay to adopt several fee hikes over the years without significant dissent.

But the latest increases, aimed mostly at eBay users with online stores, came on the heels of a series of controversial changes and missteps over the past year. Those include billing problems last year that mangled invoices and double-billed some sellers, a redesign of portions of the Web site, and changes to the way some items are categorized.

Lori Teslow, a hobbyist eBay seller who uses the online moniker "virtualconsignmentstore," said she has moved much of her furniture sales to craigslist. Teslow, of Newport Beach, said a change to the eBay site made it harder for buyers to search geographically, and it "destroyed" her sales.

The fee increases announced in January were so steep—60 percent in one instance—that some sellers are questioning whether they can continue to make a living on the site. Many raced to the company's message boards to complain.

"Typically, we have a vocal crowd that gets stirred up," said Ina Steiner, editor of the online newsletter Auction Bytes. "This is not the usual crowd. These are people who usually buckle down and deal with it. These people who are complaining now are saying it's hurting their bottom line."

In his letter, Cobb said eBay would credit store owners $15.95—the monthly fee to operate a basic store—in May. The company is also lowering the listing fee—from 30 to 25 cents—on items that list for 99 cents or less. But that fee was not part of the January rate increases. The company is not rolling back any of those fees.

The reaction among eBay users has been mixed, with most feeling the changes do not go far enough, Steiner said.

"This is making people question whether they want to rely on eBay 100 percent," she said.

EBay spokesman Hani Durzy said the company is standing by the fee increases. But he said executives realize that many users are disgruntled.

"It would be disingenuous to say that everything about the community is happy," Durzy said. "We read the boards. We would lose a major source of our direction if we didn't hear the community. We're making changes that we think add value."

In his letter, Cobb said the company will overhaul its customer service practices, starting with a shutdown within 90 days of its automated e-mail response system.

"Our users will get a 'real' e-mail response to their questions—you'll hear from a human being who will try to help you with your problem or question right off the bat," he wrote. "We will only use auto responses to acknowledge receipt of spam or policy violation reports."

The company is also increasing the number of sellers who will qualify for telephone support, making it

(Cont.)

available to all store owners, not just the largest-volume "power sellers."

"This is a fantastic development," Steiner said. "I have to applaud eBay for recognizing that this is an issue."

Durzy would not disclose the specific staffing required to make the customer support changes, how much they would cost, and where any new jobs might be located. He called the financial impact "not material."

Nonetheless, analysts said they will be watching closely to gauge whether eBay finds a way to improve its customer service and keep sellers in its fold without eating too much into its bottom line.

The topic is sure to come up when eBay hosts a meeting with Wall Street analysts Thursday.

"Obviously it remains to be seen how eBay can balance the endpoints," Brown said. "It's interesting they chose to focus on customer service. Can it be solved easily? I don't think so."

Credit: San Jose Mercury News, Calif.

75

Europe Puts Consumers First

Market-Competition Rules at Odds With U.S. Approach

JAMES KANTER. WALL STREET JOURNAL.
Brussels—**THE CONCEPT SOUNDS** strange to American ears: Pulling a Pepsi can out of a Coke-branded cooler.

Under pressure from European Union regulators, though, mighty Coca-Cola Co. agreed last year to hand over one-fifth of the space in some of its familiar red-and-white coolers to archrivals such as PepsiCo Inc. The concession helped Atlanta-based Coca-Cola to avoid huge fines and punishments. It also underscores a profound difference between the way the U.S. and EU look at regulation and market power.

In several recent decisions—from soft drinks to software, beer and automobiles—Brussels has sought to use regulation to protect consumer choice much more aggressively than Washington does. Despite the European Commission's new emphasis on smoothing paths for business to encourage economic growth, this type of enforced competition is unlikely to change, antitrust lawyers say.

"Making a quick and concrete contribution to consumer welfare is rapidly becoming the paramount goal for EU antitrust," says Luc Gyselen, the former EU official who led most of the five-year investigation into Coca-Cola's business practices. He is now a Brussels-based partner at law firm Arnold & Porter.

For instance, a 2002 EU edict required car manufacturers to break off exclusive relationships with independent dealers, which theoretically would lead to consumers being able to shop among different brands of cars in one place. The rule hasn't yet had significant effects, either in the commission's own data on auto prices or in the view of consumer groups.

Yet they infuriated some car manufacturers, which traditionally have demanded that independently owned dealerships carry and service just a single brand. The EU's antitrust department is investigating complaints that some manufacturers are thwarting the rules.

The enforcement trend gained ground under former EU antitrust commissioner,

Making Room for Rivals

In recent rulings, the EU has sought to enforce consumer choice from store shelves in France, above, to pubs in Belgium, at left.

October 2004: Coca-Cola agrees to give space to rivals in its grocery coolers to help settle an EU case against it.

March 2004: EU tells Microsoft to share Windows with media competitors including RealNetworks.

April 2003: EU tells Interbrew to allow Belgian pubs to serve competing beer brands.

October 2002: EU requires car manufacturers to break off exclusive relationships with independent dealers.

Mario Monti, whose term ended in November, and is expected to remain a crucial part of new Commissioner Neelie Kroes's antitrust arsenal. "Mrs. Kroes is firmly convinced that it is crucial not only for Europe's competitiveness, but also for consumers who should be able to enjoy the benefits of a single market with access to a wide range of goods and services at reasonable prices," says her spokesman, Jonathan Todd.

Some U.S. officials are perturbed by the trend, which they fear adds up to a doctrine that allows rivals to piggyback on a dominant company's market power—punishing victors in business. They have warned that Europe risks eroding the value of big brands, trampling on intellectual-property rights and thereby chilling the already cool climate for innovation in Europe.

Going too far to help rivals of strong companies could "kill the goose that lays the golden egg," said Makan Delrahim, a senior Justice Department official, in a speech in London last year.

A common thread ties auto showrooms to soft-drink coolers—and to the EU's high-profile action last year against Microsoft Corp., which was ordered to unbundle a media player from its ubiquitous operating systems and to share code with rival server manufacturers. It is a legal concept known as dominance. Car makers rely on showrooms to brand and sell their cars in the same way that Coke relies on coolers or Microsoft on the base of Windows-installed computers. But European regulators have taken a skeptical view of such marketing tools if they allow dominant companies to hobble smaller competitors.

Europeans tend to find evidence of dominance more readily than Americans because European antitrust enforcement aims to maintain multiple competitors in any particular market segment. By contrast, U.S. regulators are more wary of intervention, preferring evidence of actual consumer harm, such as higher prices, before launching a crackdown.

The EU doesn't apply its toughest rules on sharing in every industry. In most cases, companies must have more than 40% of a particular market to trigger alarm bells.

(Cont.)

Some that have fallen prey to European investigators often have a far stronger presence in Europe than in the U.S. In Europe, Pepsi has about 10% of the market, compared with Coke's near 50%. In the U.S. the two cola giants are more evenly matched.

Leading European brands also are under pressure. Brussels enforcers settled an investigation into Belgian brewing giant Interbrew SA (now known as InBev SA) in April 2003, allowing lease holders of the company's own pubs, or those that accept loans or equipment from the company, to nevertheless offer competing beers.

Although the InBev order applied only inside Belgium, it set a standard that the commission intends to be followed by national competition authorities throughout Europe. To underscore that point, the commission last June held a conference in Brussels for national antitrust officials to learn how the InBev case's principles can be used to break up beer monopolies in their home countries.

Mary Jacoby contributed to this article.

Weak Dollar, Strong Sales

Declining Currency Allows Small U.S. Manufacturers To Reap Profits From Exports

TIMOTHY AEPPEL. WALL STREET JOURNAL.

Cleveland—**DONALD MOTTINGER** received an unexpected call last month from an Italian businessman, wondering if Mr. Mottinger's **Superior Products** Inc. factory here could make gas fittings for him.

Given the weak dollar compared to the euro, having the parts made in Cleveland is a bargain compared to what it costs in Europe. If the plan works out, it will be Superior's first Italian foray.

"Without currency shifts, our international business would have grown, but not like this," says Mr. Mottinger. The small company, with $8.7 million in sales last year, serves customers in a half-dozen countries, including Mexico, the United Kingdom, Australia, and Canada, and now is looking for business in Asia.

Superior isn't the only small manufacturing company benefiting in a number of ways from the falling dollar. The weaker dollar not only makes U.S. products cheaper for foreign customers, it also makes foreign products more expensive to sell in the U.S., leaving opportunities for American companies to do more business at home. The dollar's decline has made Mr. Mottinger's costs so competitive, for instance, that he's now poised to take business away from a former supplier from Germany.

Currency fluctuations also expand business for the larger companies that buy parts from smaller companies like Superior. Superior's customers, such as **Illinois Tool Works** Inc. and **Lincoln Electric** Co., are exporting more of their own products as a result of the weaker dollar.

A declining dollar has downsides. Some types of specialized machinery are only available in Europe or Japan, for instance, which means U.S. factories pay more for those items when the dollar is weak.

But generally the benefits for small U.S. manufacturers far outweigh the negatives. **Ohio Screw Products** in Elyria, Ohio, says when the dollar was strong it wasn't making any money on a line of quick-disconnect couplings it sold in Europe for plastic-injection-molding machines. Ohio Screw has long priced those parts in euros, so the profit margin eroded every time the dollar moved up. Now, the opposite is happening. "We aren't selling much more, but our margins have gone way up," says Dan Imbrogno, the company's president.

Big manufacturers, with factories around the world, can juggle production from one country to another to ease the impact of long-term currency swings. Smaller guys, typically limited to producing only inside the U.S., are affected more dramatically.

"They get hit first, but they also respond first when things turn around," says Frank Vargo, head of international economic affairs at the National Association of Manufacturers. Data aren't yet available to measure foreign trade expansion by smaller companies in the wake of the dollar's recent fall, says Mr. Vargo, but anecdotal evidence suggests they are moving quickly.

Between 1987 and 1997, exports by smaller U.S. producers grew by 169%, from $74 billion to $198 billion. That growth all but stalled as the dollar grew mightier relative to other major currencies in the late 1990s. That's now reversed. In the last year, the dollar has fallen about 5% against both the euro and the yen.

A few years ago, **Bison Gear & Engineering** Corp., a small manufacturer of power-transmission equipment in St. Charles, Ill., shut down an assembly and warehouse operation in the Netherlands largely as a result of the strong dollar. The machinery from Europe was packed in shipping containers and sent to St. Charles. The equipment is now being pulled out of the boxes and used in Bison's U.S. plant to supply growing demand, including a revival in Europe. The company is considering reopening a European operation.

Robert Lawrence, a professor of international trade and investment at Harvard University, estimates the strong dollar killed up to 750,000 U.S. factory jobs in recent years, including many in smaller companies that weren't able to adapt. Mr. Lawrence notes that—as in the 1980s, when the dollar fell sharply against other currencies—he expects U.S. producers to quickly take advantage of the shift.

That's certainly the case at Superior, an 80-employee company that sells 2,500 different types of gas fittings and assemblies used for everything from beer taps in barrooms to delivering oxygen to patients in hospital beds. Founded in 1946, Superior has long exported small amounts of its products, but only recently began pushing to expand that part of its business. Superior's exports have grown 65% since 2000, but still only amount to about $323,000 a year, or less than 4% of its sales.

The parts Superior formerly bought from Germany show how complex this dynamic can be, even for a small producer. Superior first started purchasing these valves used in welding equipment in 2000, when the company wanted to expand that line of business. Germany was the cheapest source, says Mr. Mottinger, largely because of the then-strong dollar. Superior imported the parts and sold them to its customers, mostly in the U.S., under its own brand name.

However, as the euro rose over the past year, "the Germans just kept raising their prices and raising their prices," says Gregory Gens, the company's vice president and grandson of the founder. Superior determined it would be cheaper to start making the parts itself. The German supplier has since offered a small reduction in its prices, recognizing that its former customer is now emerging as a major competitor in the crucial U.S. equipment market.

Leading the way out onto the factory floor, Mr. Mottinger points to the hulking machines that will be used to cut and shape the new parts. In another part of the plant, workers are installing a new automated testing machine needed to finish the product. This machine cost $40,000 and is made up of a mixture of used and new components. One of the ways Superior saves money is by purchasing equipment from **eBay** Inc. or some other source of used industrial equipment.

Mr. Mottinger says it's still too early to know how business with the Italians will develop. But if it takes off, he'll need to hire more workers, he says. During last month's visit, the Italian company—which he doesn't want to name—agreed that the two would share profits from any joint venture.

"Foreign business is important to our future," says Mr. Mottinger, but he adds that it isn't a quick sell. Superior worked on expanding its Mexican business for five years, but sold almost nothing in that country. It finally broke into the market in 2002 and last year had over $47,000 in sales in Mexico, making it Superior's third largest market after the U.S. and Canada.

While he says the lower dollar has opened doors to new markets—and he hopes it stays at favorable rates—he doesn't count on currency changes to carry his business into the future. "It's dangerous to bet on the dollar," he says. "You need to be low-cost and very efficient, no matter where the dollar is, and that's what we're doing."

"THE CHINA PRICE"

They are the three scariest words in U.S. industry. Cut your price at least 30% or lose your customers. Nearly every manufacturer is vulnerable— from furniture to networking gear. The result: A massive shift in economic power is under way.

From the rich walnut paneling and carved arches to the molded Italian Renaissance patterns on the ceiling, the circa 1925 council chamber room of Akron's municipal hall evokes a time when the America's manufacturing heartland was at the peak of its power. But when the U.S.-China Economic & Security Review Commission, a congressionally appointed panel, convened there on Sept. 23, it was not to discuss power but decline. One after another, economists, union officials, and small manufacturers took the microphone to describe the devastation Chinese competitors are inflicting on U.S. industries, from kitchenware and car tires to electronic circuit boards.

These aren't stories of mundane sunset industries equipped with antiquated technology. David W. Johnson, CEO of 92-year-old Summitville Tiles Inc. in Summitville, Ohio, described how imports forced him to shut a state-of-the-art, $120 million tilemaking plant four football fields long, sending Summitville into Chapter 11 bankruptcy protection. Now, a tenfold surge in high-quality Chinese imports at "below our manufacturing costs" threatens to polish Summitville off. Makers of precision machine tools and plastic molds—essential supports of America's industrial architecture—told how their business has shrunk as home-appliance makers have shifted manufacturing from Ohio to China. Despite buying the best computer-controlled gear, Douglas S. Bartlett reported that at his Cary (Ill.)-based Bartlett Manufacturing Co., a maker of high-end circuit boards for aerospace and automotive customers, sales are half the late-1990s level and the workforce is one-third smaller. He waved a board Bartlett makes for a U.S. Navy submarine-detection device. His buyer says he can get the same board overseas for 40% less. "From experience I can only assume this is the Chinese price," Bartlett said. "We have faced competition in the past. What is dramatically different about China is that they are about half the price."

WHERE THE JOBS WENT

"The China price." They are the three scariest words in U.S. industry. In general, it means 30% to 50% less than what you can possibly make something for in the U.S. In the worst cases, it means below your cost of materials. Makers of apparel, footwear, electric appliances, and plastics products, which have been shutting U.S. factories for decades, know well the futility of trying to match the China price. It has been a big factor in the loss of 2.7 million manufacturing jobs since 2000. Meanwhile, America's deficit with China keeps soaring to new records. It is likely to pass $150 billion this year.

Now, manufacturers and workers who never thought they had to worry about the China price are confronting the new math of the mainland. These companies had once held their own against imports mostly because their businesses required advanced skills, heavy investment, and proximity to customers. Many of these companies are in the small-to-midsize sector, which makes up 37% of U.S. manufacturing. The China price is even being felt in high tech. Chinese exports of advanced networking gear, still at a low level, are already affecting prices. And there's talk by some that China could eventually become a major car exporter.

Multinationals have accelerated the mainland's industrialization by shifting production there, and midsize companies that can are following suit. The alternative is to stay at home and fight—and probably lose. Ohio State University business professor Oded

---

CHINA PRICES

Machine Molds

PRICE GAP: Up To **50%**

XCel Mold of Ohio, bid $2.07 million to supply a set of plastic molds to a U.S. appliance maker. It lost the business when a Chinese supplier bid $1.44 million

Data: XCel Mold

Shenkar, author of the new book *The Chinese Century,* hears many war stories from local companies. He gives it to them straight: "If you still make anything labor intensive, get out now rather than bleed to death. Shaving 5% here and there won't work." Chinese producers can make the same adjustments. "You need an entirely new business model to compete."

America has survived import waves before, from Japan, South Korea, and Mexico. And it has lived with China for two decades. But something very different is happening. The assumption has long been that the U.S. and other industrialized nations will keep leading in knowledge-intensive industries while developing nations focus on lower-skill sectors. That's now open to debate.

"What is stunning about China is that for the first time we have a huge, poor country that can compete both with very low wages and in high tech," says Harvard University economist Richard B. Freeman. "Combine the two, and America has a problem."

How much of a problem? That's in fierce dispute. On one side, the benefits of the relationship with China are enormous. After years of struggling to crack the mainland market, U.S. multinationals from General Motors to Procter & Gamble and Motorola are finally reaping rich profits. They're making cell phones, shampoo, autos, and PCs in China and selling them to its middle class of some 100 million people, a group that should more than double in size by 2010. "Our commercial success in China is important to our

The China Challenge

Why should U.S. manufacturers worry when they have weathered decades of competition from Japan, Korea, and Europe? Because China is different. Here's why:

SPEED	BREADTH	COMPETITION	ALLIANCES	SIZE	ACCESS	U.S. POLICY
Earlier rivals usually took years to build up an American presence. Chinese competition often arrives en masse and seizes share rapidly with unbeatable prices, leaving little time for U.S. companies to adjust.	Other Asian nations shed labor-intensive work as they industrialized, but China is gaining share in low-end work such as garments and simple assembly at the same time it's advancing into higher-value areas such as digital electronics.	Japan and Korea are limited players in many industries. But in China, dozens of manufacturers battle for share in the domestic markets for appliances, cell phones, cars, and more, keeping everyone lean.	Unlike Japan or Korea, China welcomes foreign investment in key industries. Foreign ventures account for 60% of exports and a big share of local sales, so it's tough to complain that China is closed.	China is both an export power and is itself becoming the world's biggest market for cars, appliances, cell phones, and more. That gives China unparalleled economies of scale.	Retail giants such as Wal-Mart that import directly help Chinese electronics makers build U.S. market share without the need to spend as much on distribution and ads as Sony, Sharp, and Samsung did.	When imbalances got out of hand in the '80s and '90s the U.S. threatened sanctions to prod Japan and China to address trade grievances. China's entry into the WTO limits U.S. ability to act unilaterally.

competitiveness worldwide," says Motorola China Chairman Gene Delaney.

By outsourcing components and hardware from China, U.S. companies have sharply boosted their return on capital. China's trade barriers continue to come down, part of its agreement to enter the World Trade Organization in 2001. Big new opportunities will emerge for U.S. insurers, banks, and retailers. China's surging demand for raw materials and commodities has driven prices up worldwide, creating a windfall for U.S. steelmakers, miners, and lumber companies. The cheap cost of Chinese goods has kept inflation low in the U.S. and fueled a consumer boom that helped America weather a recession and kept global growth on track.

But there's a huge cost to the China relationship, too. Foremost is the question of America's huge trade deficit, of which China is the largest and fastest-growing part. While U.S. consumers binge on Chinese-made goods, the U.S. balance-of-payments deficit is nearing a record 6% of gross domestic product. The trade shortfall—coupled with the U.S. budget deficit—is driving the dollar ever downward, raising fears that cracks will appear in the global financial system. And by keeping its currency pegged to the greenback at a level analysts see as undervalued, China amplifies the problem.

AMERICA'S ERODING BASE

The deficit with China will keep widening under most projections. That raises the issue: Will America's industrial base erode to a dangerous level? So far the hardest-hit industries have been those that were destined to migrate to low-cost nations anyway. But China is ramping up rapidly in more advanced industries where America remains competitive, adding state-of-the-art capacity in cars, specialty steel, petrochemicals,

and microchips. These plants are aimed at meeting insatiable demand in China. But the danger is that if China's growth stalls, the resulting glut will turn into another export wave and disrupt whole new strata of American industry. "As producers in China end up with significant unused capacity, they will try to be much more creative in how they deploy it," says Jim Hemerling, a senior vice-president at Boston Consulting Group's Shanghai office.

That's why China is an even thornier trade issue for the U.S. than Japan was in the 1980s. It's clear some Chinese exporters cheat, from intellectual-property theft and dumping to securing unfair subsidies. Washington can get much more aggressive in fighting violations of trade law. But broader protectionism is a nonstarter. On a practical level the U.S. is now so dependent on Chinese suppliers that resurrecting trade barriers would just raise costs and diminish the real benefits that China trade confers. Also, unlike Japan 20 years ago, China is a much more open economy. It continues to lower tariffs and even runs a slight trade deficit with the whole world— which makes the U.S.'s deficit with China all the more glaring. Hiking the value of the yuan 30% might help. But that's unlikely. For one thing, Beijing fears what such a shift would do to jobs—and the value of its $515 billion

in foreign reserves. The real solution is for the U.S. to reduce its twin deficits on its own—but that's more America's issue than China's.

Meanwhile, U.S. companies are no longer investing in much new capacity at home, and the ranks of U.S. engineers are thinning. In contrast, China is emerging as the most competitive manufacturing platform ever. Chief among its formidable assets is its cheap labor, from $120-a-month production workers to $2,000-a-month chip designers. Even in sophisticated electronics industries, where direct labor is less than 10% of costs, China's low wages are reflected in the entire supply chain—components, office workers, cargo handling—you name it.

China is also propelled by an enormous domestic market that brings economies of scale, feverish local rivalry that keeps prices low, an army of engineers that is growing by 350,000 annually, young workers and managers willing to put in 12-hour days and work weekends, an unparalleled component and material base in electronics and light industry, and an entrepreneurial zeal to do whatever it takes to please big retailers such as Wal-Mart Stores, Target, Best Buy, and J.C. Penney. "The reason practically all home furnishings are now made in China factories is that they simply are better suppliers," says

CHINA PRICES

Networking Equipment

PRICE GAP: 25%

Datacom switch for corporations: Made in China for 3Com with a $183,000 list price. Cisco's comparable switch lists for $245,000.

Data: 3Com

AN UNBALANCED TRADE BALANCE

The U.S. has a growing deficit with China in most industrial categories—even in sectors where it is considered competitive. The U.S. mainly has trade surpluses in commodities such as iron and oil seeds. Some examples:

Where the U.S has big deficits...

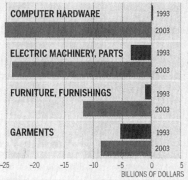

HANGZHOU The 3Com/Huawei joint venture

...and smaller surpluses

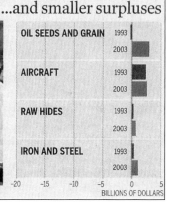

Janet E. Fox, vice-president for international procurement at J.C. Penny Co. "American manufacturers aren't even in the same game."

Fox's point is important. China's competitive advantages are built on much more than unfair trade practices. Some 70% of exports now come from private companies and foreign ventures mainly owned by Taiwanese, Hong Kong, Japanese, and U.S. companies that have brought access to foreign markets, advanced technology, and managerial knowhow. Aside from cheap land and tax breaks in some areas, private Chinese manufacturers get minimal government help. "The Chinese government cannot afford to offer financial support to the export economy," says business professor Gu Kejian of People's University in Beijing. And as capital floods in and modern plants are built in China, efficiencies improve dramatically. The productivity of private industry in China has grown an astounding 17% annually for five years, according to the U.S. Conference Board.

China needs U.S. imports, though not as much as imagined when Beijing agreed to join the WTO. U.S. exports to China have risen 25% to 35% annually in the past two years. But China's exports still outstrip its imports from the U.S. by 5 to 1. The U.S. sells about $2.4 billion worth of aircraft a year, and its semiconductor exports tripled in three years. Otherwise the U.S. looks like a developing nation. It runs surpluses in commodities such as oil seeds, grains, iron, wood pulp, and raw animal hides.

Meanwhile, the Chinese keep expanding their export base. Chinese competition arrives so fast that it's nearly impossible to adjust through the usual strategies, such as automating or squeezing suppliers. The Jap-

anese, South Koreans, and Europeans often took "four or five years to develop their place in the market," says Robert B. Cassidy, a former U.S. Trade Representative official who helped negotiate China's entry into the WTO and now works for Washington law firm Collier Shannon Scott, which wages dumping cases on behalf of U.S. clients. "China overwhelms a market so quickly you don't see it coming."

"SHOCK AND AWE"

Georgetown Steel Co. is a case in point. The Georgetown (S.C.) maker of wire rods used in everything from bridge cables to ball bearings had battled Asian and Mexican imports for years. But last year it shut its 600-worker plant, citing a tenfold leap in Chinese imports, to 252,000 tons, from 2001 to 2003. International Steel Group Inc. has since bought the facility after U.S. anti-dumping duties on imports and a rise in global demand helped hike domestic prices. The Gardiner (Mass.) plant of Seaman Paper Co., a maker of crepe and decorative paper, is highly automated. Yet Chinese imports have grabbed a third of the market. It sells 81-foot streamers to big retailers for as little as 9 cents each. That's below Seaman's cost of materials. "We thought we could offset Chinese labor cost by automating, but we just couldn't," says Seaman President George Jones III.

In bedroom furniture, 59 U.S. plants employing 15,500 workers have closed since January, 2001, as Chinese imports have rocketed 221%, to $1.4 billion—half of the U.S. market. Prices have plunged 30%. Dumping certainly seems to be one factor: At its Galax (Va.) factory, Vaughan-Bassett Furniture Co. displays a Chinese knockoff of one of its dressers that wholesales for

$105—below the world market cost for the wood. But the main competition comes from Chinese megaplants that sell directly to U.S. retailers and can get a new design into mass production in two months. The new Chinese factories of suppliers such as Lacquer Craft Furniture, Markor, and Shing Mark, some of them Taiwanese-owned, employ thousands and are so big they seem meant to build Boeing 747s, making most U.S. factories look like cottage industries. "The first wave is shock and awe," says John D. Bassett III, CEO of Vaughan-Bassett, whose sales and workforce have shrunk even though it has boosted productivity fivefold at its 600-worker Galax plant since 1995 by investing in computer-controlled wood drying, cutting, and carving gear. "American industry has never encountered [such] competition."

As component industries and design work follow assembly lines to China, key elements of the U.S. industrial base are beginning to erode. American plastic-molding and machine-tool industries have shrunk dramatically in the past five years. Take Incoe Corp. in Troy, Mich., a maker of steel components for plastic-injection machines. "When the economy turned soft, we anticipated the business would come back," says Incoe CFO Robert Hoff. "But it didn't. We saw our customer base either close or migrate to China." The U.S. printed-circuit-board industry has seen sales go from $11 billion to under $5 billion since 2001. In that time, PCB exports from China have more than doubled, to a projected $3.4 billion this year, says market researcher Global Sources Ltd. Most U.S. production of key electronics materials, such as copper-clad laminates, has fled, too. "The whole industry is hollowing out," says Joseph C. Fehsenfeld, CEO

(Cont.)

of Midwest Printed Circuit Services Inc. in Round Lake Beach, Ill.

The migration of electronics to China began when the Taiwanese shifted plants and suppliers across the Taiwan Strait in the late 1990s. As recently as four years ago, though, the U.S. exported $45 billion in computer hardware. Since the tech crash, that number has slid to $28 billion as the industry headed en masse for China, which is even more competitive than Taiwan. "All electronics hardware manufacturing is going to China," says Michael E. Marks, CEO of Flextronics Corp., a contract manufacturer that employs 41,000 in China. Flextronics and other companies are hiring Chinese engineers to design the products assembled there. "There is a myth that the U.S. would remain the knowledge economy and China the sweatshop," says BCG's Hemerling. "Increasingly, this is no longer the case."

A visit to Flextronics' campus in the Pearl River Delta town of Doumen vividly illustrates Marks's point. The site employs 18,000 workers making cell phones, X-box game consoles, PCs, and other hardware in 13 factories sprawled over 149 acres. The bamboo scaffolding is about to come down on an additional 720,000-square-foot factory nearing completion. Almost every chemical, component, plastic, machine tool, and packing material Flextronics needs is available from thousands of suppliers within a two-hour drive of the site. That alone makes most components 20% cheaper in China than in the U.S., says campus General Manager Tim Dinwiddie. Plus, China will soon eliminate remaining tariffs on imported chips. In the past five years, electronic manufacturing-services companies such as Flextronics have cut their U.S. production from $37 billion to $27 billion while doubling their China output, to $31 billion. That's likely to double again by 2007.

"GRAVITATIONAL PULL"

China is even making its presence felt in the U.S. market for networking gear, a bastion of American comparative advantage. On Nov. 15, struggling 3Com Corp.

in Marlborough, Mass., launched a data-communications switching system for corporate networks of 10,000 users or more. It claims twice the performance of Cisco Systems Inc.'s comparable switch. At $183,000, 3Com's list price is 25% less. Its secret? 3Com is settling for lower margins and taking advantage of a 1,200-engineer joint venture with China telecom giant Huawei Technologies Co. This is the first high-end piece of networking gear sold by a U.S. company that is designed and manufactured in China. For the price of one U.S. engineer, the joint venture can throw four engineers into the task of making customized products for a client. Even if 3Com does not succeed, similar tie-ups are expected, which could drive down prices of high-end gear sold in the U.S. Says 3Com President Bruce Claflin: "We want to change the pricing structure of this industry." 3Com hopes this is the start of a whole line of networking gear designed and made in China for the global market. Without referring to China, Cisco CEO John T. Chambers says "we are starting to see a stream of good, very price-competitive competitors, particular from Asia."

The next step for China is critical mass in core industries. Outside Beijing, Semiconductor Manufacturing International Corp. has just opened a chip plant fabricating 12-inch silicon wafers that experts say is just two generations behind Intel Corp. A foundry that makes chips on a contract basis, this plant won't compete directly with U.S. chipmakers. But with four more 12-inch wafer plants due by 2006 and many more fabs in the pipeline, the U.S. Semiconductor Industry Assn. warns that a "gravitational pull" could suck capital, people, and leading-edge research-and-development and design functions from the U.S.

Digital technologies aren't the only areas where the Chinese have huge ambitions. In the past decade, U.S. petrochemical makers have invested in little new capacity. But at a three-mile-long site in Nanjing, 12,000 workers are erecting a $2.7 billion network of pipes and towers for China's Sinopec and Germany's BASF that by next year will be among the world's biggest, most modern complexes for ethylene, the basic ingredient in plastics. An even bigger complex is going up in Shanghai. "The Chinese understand everything that scale means," says Fluor Corp. Group President Robert McNamara, who lives part-time in Shanghai and whose company has design

contracts at both complexes. "When they target an industry to dominate, they don't mitigate."

Can China dominate everything? Of course not. America remains the world's biggest manufacturer, producing 75% of what it consumes, though that's down from 90% in the mid-'90s. Industries requiring huge R&D budgets and capital investment, such as aerospace, pharmaceuticals, and cars, still have strong bases in the U.S. "I don't see China becoming a major car exporter in the foreseeable future," says GM China Chairman Philip F. Murtaugh. "There is no economic rationale." Murtaugh cites high production costs and quality issues at Chinese car plants, as well as just-in-time delivery needs in the West, as impediments.

BURNING RUBBER

Don't tell that to Miao Wei, president of Dongfeng Motor Corp. On Nov. 7, Dongfeng and Honda Motor Co. announced that their joint venture will invest $340 million to boost output of Honda CR-Vs and Civics fivefold, to 120,000, by early 2006. The plant aims to achieve world standards by employing Honda's flexible manufacturing system. "Honda will sell some of the Chinese-built cars in Europe," says Miao. Nissan Motor Co. is also talking about exporting with Dongfeng.

China's carmakers are developing the suppliers that one day could sustain exports. Auto-parts maker Wanxiang Group in Hangzhou started as a tiny township-owned farm-machinery shop in 1969. Now it's a $2.4 billion conglomerate that supplies the Chinese assembly plants of GM, Ford Motor, Volkswagen, and others and also exports 30% of its output. In two years, China will drop the rule that its auto plants buy at least 40% of parts locally. Wanxiang is getting ready: It is opening a $42 million plant loaded with U.S. and European testing gear. And since 1995, Wanxiang has bought 10 U.S. auto-parts makers. "Our goal is to acquire technology, management, and most important, to get access to overseas markets," says Chairman Lu Guanqiu.

Some U.S manufacturers hope China will run out of steam. This year, factories in Guangdong and Fujian faced serious labor shortages for the first time. Red-hot demand has meant skyrocketing costs for China's producers, most of which rely on imported goods such as steel, plastics, and components. Energy shortages have forced manufacturers

(Cont.)

to shut factories several times a week. In almost any industry one can think of, vicious price wars are biting into already razor-sharp margins. "There are so many small companies competing that they crowd out all profit," says Beijing University economist Zhang Weiying. Indeed, given the low emphasis on profits and the unsophisticated accounting of many Chinese companies, often their pricing isn't based on a full understanding of costs. Having gotten as far as they can on cheap production costs, Chinese manufacturers must develop their own technologies and innovative products to move ahead—areas in which they've made slow progress so far.

The juggernaut will slow, but only slightly. While salaries for top Chinese designers are rising fast, they are still a fifth to a tenth of those in Silicon Valley. If China's wages

CHINA PRICES

CREPE PAPER

PRICE GAP: **45%**

Chinese suppliers have sold crepe streamers to U.S. retailers for as little as 9 cents a roll—below the production costs of Seaman Paper.

Data: Seaman Paper

rise 8% annually for the next five years, says a Boston Consulting Group study, the average factory hand will still earn just $1.30 an hour by then. If China allowed the yuan to appreciate by around 10% in the next year, productivity gains would more than offset the higher costs, figures China expert Nicholas R. Lardy of the Institute for International Economics. "I don't think revaluation will have a significant impact," he says.

And Chinese producers are hardly standing still. In a recent survey of Chinese and U.S. manufacturers by *IndustryWeek* and Cleveland-based Manufacturing Performance Institute, 54% of Chinese companies cited innovation as one of their top objectives, while only 26% of U.S. respondents did. Chinese companies spend more on worker training and enterprise-management

software. And 91% of U.S. plants are more than a decade old, vs. 54% in China. Shanghai-based TV maker SVA Group, for example, has opened China's first plant to make flat panels, a venture with Japan's NEC Corp. That is enabling SVA to secure a U.S. beachhead by selling liquid-crystal display and plasma TV sets through channels such as the online sites of Costco Wholesale and Target. Starting price: $1,600—30% below similar models by Royal Philips Electronics and Panasonic.

More innovation. Better goods. Lower prices. Newer plants. America will surely continue to benefit from China's expansion. But unless it can deal with the industrial challenge, it will suffer a loss of economic power and influence. Can America afford the China price? It's the question U.S. workers, execs, and policymakers urgently need to ask.

Pete Engardio and Dexter RobertsWith Brian Bremner in Beijing and bureau reports. Business Week.

78

Spinning wheels got to go round for hip drivers

Status rims available at rent-to-own shops

Chris Woodyard.
USA TODAY.

INGLEWOOD, Calif.—For the young hip-hop crowd, a car without gleaming, oversize chrome wheels is like a birthday cake without candles.

But at $2,000 or more for rims and tires, a rolling dose of social acceptance can be out of reach for those in their first or second jobs.

That's where Rent-A-Wheel comes in.

Rent-A-Wheel is a sign of the times, a new wrinkle in the rent-to-own industry. The fast-growing chain and others like it are cropping up across the Sun Belt—tapping into the craze for giant bling-bling wheels that have become as essential to car enthusiasts as fuzzy dice were to their hot-rodding granddads.

"For our customer base, their cars are their status symbol. That's where they spend a lot of their disposable income," says Rent-A-Wheel's co-founder John Bowlin.

Most chains employ the same basic plan. Customers can take 90 days, or in some cases, up to 120 days, to buy a set of wheels and tires for the same price that they'd pay upfront.

If they don't make it in time—and many don't—they rent them, typically making weekly payments at a high premium for up to a year. If they make all the payments, their purchase is complete, and the wheels are theirs to keep.

If they can't keep up with the payments or don't want to own the wheels anymore, they can turn them in.

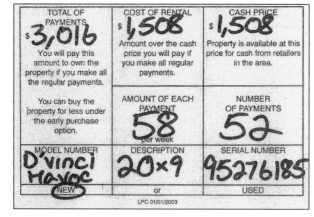

There are no credit checks. The chains usually rent to anyone who can show a steady paycheck.

The idea is borrowed from the rent-to-own furniture industry.

"While rims and tires are a minuscule part of the rent-to-own industry, it's the most exciting area because customers tend to be more upscale," says Bill Keese, executive director of the Association of Progressive Rental Organizations, a trade group.

Often, they are young drivers out for "the biggest, baddest-looking wheels they can find," he says.

To reach them, the rental wheel outfits typically advertise on hip-hop radio. The formula's success is showing up in how fast the businesses are growing:

► **Rent-A-Wheel.** From a single store in Los Angeles, Rent-A-Wheel now has 36 stores spread across California, Arizona and Texas, including the Rent-A-Tire chain it acquired in 1999. It plans to add about 15 stores a year.

► **Rent-n-Roll.** The Tampa-based chain has four company-owned stores and 23 franchises, and plans to have 100 stores under contract within five years.

► **Rent-A-Wheel of Florida.** Same name as the western chain, but not related, Rent-A-Wheel of Florida has five locations in the Tampa and Orlando areas and plans to soon add three, says Vice President Che Hatcher.

"What we cater to is young people who want to get wheels and tires and can't afford to pay $2,000 or $3,000. We do it on an easy installment plan," Hatcher says.

Despite their growth, the wheel businesses run into the same critics as the rent-to-own furniture business. Some fear young people will be strapped with wheel payments approaching what they pay monthly for the cars themselves.

"Rent-to-own has always been in the business of selling dreams with contracts that are very difficult to comply with," says Ed Mierzwinski, a consumer

(Cont.)

issues analyst for the Public Interest Research Group in Washington.

"The interest rates are so high that by the time you're done paying for the product, you've paid two or three times for it."

At the Rent-A-Wheel store in Inglewood, the cash price of a set of Zinik Adrian rims is $1,092, but at 52 weekly payments of $42, the total price balloons to $2,184. Tires, which can add $400 or more, are extra.

The cash price and the finance price are both posted prominently on the chrome rims throughout the shop.

Bowlin says the credit price has to be higher because of the inherit risk of defaults.

Some customers say they're happy buyers.

Actor Ray Smith, 29, of Inglewood pays $60 a week for his rims, which will amount to more than $3,000 over a year for a set that could be bought for $1,560 cash. "It's not that bad," he says. "It's affordable."

Smith, having had Zenetti rims mounted on a Mercedes-Benz C220, says he even looks forward to dropping his payment by the store every week.

"It gives me something to do on a Saturday," he says. Ephraim Garcia, 19, of Hawthorne, Calif., says a set of 18-inch Gitanos are a critical addition to the 2001 Honda Civic he recently bought for $16,000.

"It's really important," he says. "It gives you personality."

Marketing Strategies: Planning, Implementation, and Control

79

7-ELEVEN GETS SOPHISTICATED

With reams of research, a team of chefs, and technology that rivals Wal-Mart's, the legendary retailer is reinventing the concept of convenience.

Elizabeth Esfahani. Business 2.0.

There's something familiar about the place, with its muted orange-and-green color scheme. The aisles are wider, though, and the displays tonier. Chilling in the fridge is the house Chardonnay, not far from a glass case packed with baguettes and cream cheese croissants that come piping-hot out of the onsite oven. An aisle away is the snazzy cappuccino machine, which offers up bananas foster and pumpkin spice java. There's sushi and, of course, bouquets of fresh-cut flowers.

They're right next to the Slurpee machine.

Yes, this decidedly upscale little shoppe is a 7-Eleven—or it will be, when 7-Eleven CEO Jim Keyes and his team of ace technologists, trendspotters, and product developers wrap up one of the most ambitious makeovers in business history. The convenience king, most commonly known for low-brow if popular features such as the Big Gulp and around-the-clock access to Twinkies, is moving up the food chain in search of flusher customers and fatter margins. After all, the majority of convenience-store sales come from gasoline and cigarettes—two increasingly stagnant categories. So Keyes is banking on a new, inventive inventory mix that competes more with Starbucks than with Shell. In the process Keyes and his team are pumping new life into an icon that not long ago seemed in danger of financial oblivion—and providing an object lesson in how technology and merchandising savvy can amp up a fading business's metabolism.

The transformation is way more than skin-deep. Behind surface changes like the wines—which will roll out in April thanks to a partnership with California wine giant Mondavi—are some of the most sophisticated systems for gauging demand, predicting sales, and filling orders in business today. The company has spent more than $500 million on technology in the past decade, and it has imported processes that its licensee in Japan used to make stores there unlikely avatars of cool. Among the payoffs: Managers at 7-Eleven's 5,300 stores across the United States can order up, say, a single apple turnover, and it will arrive freshly baked by morning. Each humble pastry is backed by a fanatical devotion to research and development that features a team of in-house chefs and data crunchers who can determine the best weather for pastry sales. "Technology has allowed us to take back our destiny," Keyes says.

There have been plenty of obstacles along the way. Back in 1990, reeling from disastrous acquisitions and an ill-advised leveraged buyout, the company collapsed into bankruptcy. But Keyes, a veteran 7-Eleven executive of 19 years who became CEO in 2000, has helped the chain grind slowly, steadily back: In 2004, 7-Eleven rang up estimated revenue of $12.2 billion, up 12 percent from the prior year. It has had 32 consecutive quarters of revenue growth. Profits for 2004 came in at an estimated $106.4 million, held down by lingering debt the company is working off from its bankruptcy and its heavy tech investments—but still a 66 percent jump over 2003. Its stock price recently hit a post-bankruptcy high of $23.95 after diving to a low of $6.55 in 2003. And all of a sudden, some smart money is sensing that the formerly dowdy convenience chain is on the verge of a breakout. "They have some of the best technology in the business," says Adam Sindler, an analyst at Morgan Keegan. "Wal-Mart is the most powerful retailer, but now 7-Eleven is the most innovative merchandiser in the country."

As it happens, 7-Eleven has an underappreciated history of innovation dating back almost 80 years. In 1927 it invented the concept of convenience stores, when an employee at Southland Ice in Dallas started selling milk, eggs, and other sundries to customers dropping by to replenish their iceboxes. Recognizing that refrigerators would soon kill Southland's ice business, president Joe C. Thompson moved to capitalize on demand for convenience by opening a chain of stores that would stay open from 7 a.m to 11 p.m. The concept was an instant hit. By 1980, 7-Eleven had more than 6,000 outlets and had pioneered other ideas that are now commonplace, like 24-hour service and coffee to go.

But the firm faltered in the 1980s, beset by competition from oil companies that began turning their gas stations into mini convenience stores and by acquisitions

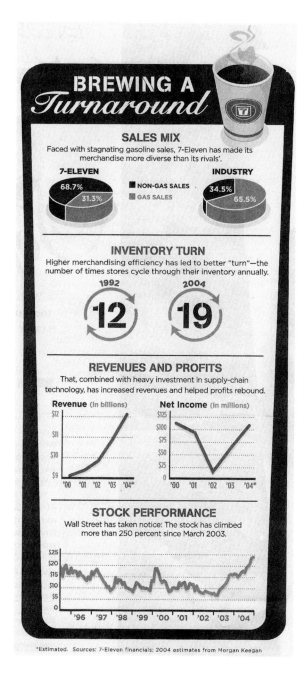

BREWING A *Turnaround*

SALES MIX
Faced with stagnating gasoline sales, 7-Eleven has made its merchandise more diverse than its rivals'.

7-ELEVEN
68.7%
31.3%

■ NON-GAS SALES
■ GAS SALES

INDUSTRY
34.5%
65.5%

INVENTORY TURN
Higher merchandising efficiency has led to better "turn"—the number of times stores cycle through their inventory annually.

1992 — 12
2004 — 19

REVENUES AND PROFITS
That, combined with heavy investment in supply-chain technology, has increased revenues and helped profits rebound.

Revenue (in billions)
$12 $11 $10 $9
'00 '01 '02 '03 '04*

Net Income (in millions)
$125 $100 $75 $50 $25 0
'00 '01 '02 '03 '04*

STOCK PERFORMANCE
Wall Street has taken notice: The stock has climbed more than 250 percent since March 2003.

$25 $20 $15 $10 $5 0
'96 '97 '98 '99 '00 '01 '02 '03 '04

*Estimated. Sources: 7-Eleven financials; 2004 estimates from Morgan Keegan

was a mess; stores might receive more than 80 deliveries a week, with everything from milk to magazines arriving separately and often during prime shopping hours.

At the same time, an odd thing was happening halfway around the world: In Japan, 7-Eleven had become the pinnacle of cool. There, licensee Ito-Yokado—Japan's second-largest retailer—had reinvented 7-Eleven's business model, centralizing distribution and cramming stores with fresh food. Ito-Yokado had also created an intricate information network, which let managers tailor inventory to the tastes of their customers. As a result, 7-Elevens had become hip hangouts—shoppers stopped by as often as five times a day—and sales were rising roughly 10 percent a year.

Among those most impressed by the Japanese success was Keyes, one of the managers sent from the company's Dallas headquarters to study the licensee's operations. After Ito-Yokado bought a 70 percent stake in 7-Eleven for $430 million as part of the reorganization that brought the chain out of bankruptcy, Keyes, then an up-and-comer in the finance department, was named to chair an eight-person committee charged with charting a new strategic course for the chain. Keyes had no trouble seeing the company's overarching problem. "We were a victim of our past success," he says.

That was reflected in the committee's fractious deliberations. Several members had spent their entire careers at 7-Eleven and were reluctant to shed the old ways. Moreover, there was antipathy between veterans and relative newcomers like Keyes. Keyes argued for a crash technology program that would give store managers more control over what went on their shelves—essentially, the Japanese model. Some of the old-timers pushed back, worried about the high cost of a massive technological overhaul. The old guard, Keyes recalls, saw the chain's customers as "blue-collar, truck-driving men" and harbored little hope that the company could appeal to a broader demographic. Keyes and his camp thought 7-Eleven was doomed unless it drew in more business-people, urbanites, and especially women.

Keyes bombarded the old guard with case studies depicting the benefits of more technology and empowerment of store-level employees. He hit them with countless demographic analyses of the customer base. After months of often-heated exchanges, Keyes won the day—and, many say, paved the way for his ascent to CEO. In the mid-'90s, 7-Eleven began pouring money into technology and upending the approach it had used for decades to run its stores and target new customers.

like its purchase of gasoline refiner Citgo (of which one of the only lasting benefits was to bring Keyes, a Citgo manager, into the 7-Eleven fold). Then came the ruinous leveraged buyout, which saddled the company with $4.1 billion in high-cost debt just after the market crash of October 1987. Meanwhile, the company's supply chain

"I'm a very stubborn and tenacious guy," says Keyes, now 49 years old. "And I had to be tenacious to internally transform the strategy and mind-set."

Ten years on, the results have been profound. Start with the tech transformation: Today, behind their unassuming glass doors, stores throughout the 7-Eleven empire have been turned into logistical marvels. In a matter of seconds, any store manager can tap into 7-Eleven's proprietary computer system and pull up real-time data on what products are selling best at that location or across the country. Instant weather reports, too, can dictate whether more umbrellas are needed for an impending storm or if a store should stock up on a muffin that sells particularly well when the temperature drops below 40 degrees. Employees are trained to stay current on upcoming sporting events or school functions to prepare for a surge in beer runs or notebook purchases. The constant tweaking means that slow-moving items are cleared away, so managers can make room for some of the 50 or so new ones 7-Eleven introduces every week. That leads to fewer overstocks and understocks, which begets happier customers. "There's no replenishment model in the world that can respond like the eyes and ears of a retailer," Keyes says.

But even the most informed manager would flounder without the strong tech backbone. 7-Eleven stores (about 60 percent of them franchises) are equipped with NEC handhelds designed exclusively for the chain. Meanwhile, engineers from NEC—just one of two dozen tech companies working in-house at 7-Eleven—are toiling on a second-generation version of the device, which will incorporate a touchscreen and wireless radio-frequency technology.

Using the handhelds, store operators place orders each morning for items that need replenishing the next day, and many of those requests are beamed to one of the 23 third-party distribution centers 7-Eleven has partnered with in the past decade. (The data also goes to HQ to be stored and analyzed.) At the centers, in warehouses akin to enormous refrigerators, local suppliers drop off their inventory for sorting. Every distribution center, too, is surrounded by a bakery and a commissary that churns out sandwiches, salads, and other fresh items. Each afternoon the orders are divvied up by store and route, and by 5 a.m. the next day, every doughnut and Slurpee cup has reached its destination. Consider that most of the 500 million items radiating annually from the warehouses are perishables, and the feat becomes even more impressive.

The system is a godsend for entrepreneurially mind-

7-ELEVEN'S HIT Parade

BRAIN-TWIST FLU & COLD DEFENSE Following the flu-shot shortage, a beverage startup sold 7-Eleven on a fortified juice to ward off illness.

COFFEE WIPES Inspired by the boom in cleaning wipes, 7-Eleven in December introduced a towelette to remove coffee stains.

TURKEY AND CAPPICOLA CLUB WRAPS A test offering in the Austin stores, the nouvelle sandwiches are meant to woo higher-end customers.

ANHEUSER-BUSCH ALUMINUM BEER BOTTLES CEO Keyes found the keep-cool casing in Japan and collaborated on a U.S. version in time for the Super Bowl.

PREPAID CELL PHONES Last April, 7-Eleven became the first national retailer to offer its own prepaid wireless service, aimed at young and low-income buyers.

ed store managers like Andrey Vinogradsky. At 8:30 on a recent morning, Vinogradsky prowls the aisles of his San Francisco store with the NEC handheld, scanning best-sellers like the King's Hawaiian Sweet Roll. The device instantly calculates how many have moved since last week and suggests an order, but Vinogradsky de-

(Cont.)

cides to up the number to 17, knowing that tomorrow is Thursday, his busiest day. As he works his way through the store, he passes several items that are there only because of his own initiative. Six months ago, for example, when Vinogradsky arrived at the outlet, he immediately noticed a flood of tourists who came in asking for maps, postcards, and other items that the store didn't carry; now it does, because Vinogradsky lined up a local vendor and began stocking them. He added snack foods from Mexico-based Bimbo for the Latino contingency. He even makes sure there's always a pot of macadamia-nut coffee for one special customer who comes in three times a day for a cup. "All of these tools allow me to provide what my customers really want," Vinogradsky says. "Without them, my job would be twice as hard."

The technological overhaul has done more than empower store managers. It has helped 7-Eleven regain control over distribution and product decisions that for decades had been dictated by its major suppliers. Traditionally, powerhouses like Anheuser-Busch and Coca-Cola have exerted enormous influence over which products a convenience store could carry, how much of them it got and when, and even how they were displayed.

Now 7-Eleven is getting suppliers to play by its rules, in part because the precise sales data it generates helps the suppliers predict demand for their products nationwide. "They'd been doing it the old way for a hundred years," Keyes says. Anheuser, for one, resisted giving up control. But, Keyes says, it eventually saw "the economic advantage" in ceding stocking and distribution decisions to 7-Eleven. Today store managers can communicate directly with Anheuser's delivery staff—face-to-face, by phone, and increasingly by handheld computer alone—to customize their mix of beverages. For the past four years, Keyes has seen a 6 to 10 percent annual increase in sales of Anheuser beer at 7-Eleven—a startling jump in an industry where 2 percent growth is considered healthy.

RECIPES FOR *Success*

A TEAM OF CHEFS AT 7-Eleven headquarters dreams up fresh-food concoctions—about 25 new concepts weekly. When a new item is approved—say, a holiday spice doughnut at Christmastime—individual store managers can include it in their morning orders. Requests are beamed to the nearest of 23 distribution centers stationed around the country, where nearby regional bakeries whip up the doughnuts. By 10 p.m., the pastries are en route to 200 or so stores within a 90-mile radius.

David Podeschi, 7-Eleven's senior vice president for merchandising, sits in a cavernous office lined with just some of the 2,000 products the retailer releases every year. It's his job to figure out new ways to mine the torrents of data that store managers and their machines are sending back to headquarters. Podeschi can see, for example, that cinnamon coffee does well in Southern California, while shoppers in the Northwest tend toward hazelnut. By combing through that kind of sales data, as well as monitoring outside stats and pop-culture trends, he and his team uncover clues about what their customers will clamor for next. "We've gone from having no idea what we were selling to predicting what customers want even before they know it," Podeschi says.

Now, when 7-Eleven spots a trend, it goes out and creates a product to match. Often that means partnering with small third-party manufacturers to create the perfect exclusive offering. In late 2003, for example, 7-Eleven noticed that supermarket sales of cleaning wipes were exploding. Bathroom and kitchen wipes didn't really fit 7-Eleven's convenience format, since those sorts of purchases could wait until the next grocery-store trip. Then, from one of the retailer's weekly brainstorming sessions, the perfect product emerged: a towelette specifically designed to remove coffee stains. At a chain where 10,000 pots of coffee are brewed each hour, it was a natural fit. The company chose a manufacturer to develop the wipes, and under 7-Eleven's guidance, it came up with a low-cost, sleekly packaged product that was small enough to fit in a glove compartment or desk drawer. Seven months later 7-Eleven Coffee Wipes landed in stores nationwide.

Called "team merchandising," that approach was also responsible for one of the quiet hits of the season: roadkill-shaped gummy candy, made for the chain by food giant Kraft. "We saw from sales data how popular Kraft's Trolli gummies were with kids," Podeschi says. "And we know that kids like things that are over-the-top

(Cont.)

gross. We literally handed Kraft this idea: 'Why don't you do Trollis that look like roadkill—squashed squirrels and snakes?'" Kraft's development team loved the idea, and by August, Trolli Road Kill candies were hanging on 7-Eleven racks.

The roadkill gummy set is an important demographic for 7-Eleven, but it's not the dream slice of the consumer universe on which the company has essentially staked its future. Keyes has already proven that he can make inroads with groups that 7-Eleven once thought were a lost cause—women, for instance. In the mid-1990s, Keyes championed a plan to put an early version of the credit card reader at 7-Eleven gas pumps. The notion was opposed by several high-ranking managers, who argued that the readers would just confuse many consumers and that, if they were deployed, they should be put inside the store rather than out at the pump. "Their logic was that you needed to drag people in for the impulse purchase," Keyes recalls. "But I said, 'We're in the convenience business, and I'm making it more convenient to buy gas.'"

The naysayers weren't convinced, and Keyes was forced to test the idea with a limited pilot project. It was a smash: Not only did sales of gas increase, but sales inside the store went up as well, as gas purchasers often popped in to pick up other items. More important for Keyes's long-range goal of broadening the customer base, the card-ready pumps brought in a surge of women customers. Why? It turned out that moms with kids loved being able to pay without having to leave the car—and the kids. Keyes was eventually cleared to put readers on all 7-Eleven pumps, making the chain one of the first convenience retailers to get them.

The hunt for new customers has since become dramatically more ambitious. Today, in an industrial kitchen at 7-Eleven headquarters, a staff headed by four culinary chefs is inventing the high-margin fresh-food offerings that will be key to making 7-Eleven a daily destination. One recent launch was a line of sandwiches on artisan breads aimed at attracting more upscale buyers, and executives stop by daily to sample everything from jalapeo and cream cheese taquitos (a big seller last fall) to turkey wraps, which will roll out nationwide this year. "At this job, you quickly learn to spit," jokes fresh-food director Alan Beach, who estimates he tries as many as 15 concoctions every day. Now fresh food is 7-Eleven's hottest growth area: Though only 8 percent of total sales, the category grew 15 percent in 2004 and is expected to beat that this year.

Keyes and 7-Eleven are clearly on a roll, but obstacles still loom. The company reduced its debt by 15 percent last year, but it still faces $1.5 billion left over from the leveraged buyout. (7-Eleven went public again in 1991, though Ito-Yokado and 7-Eleven Japan now own a 77 percent share.) 7-Eleven is the biggest U.S. convenience store chain not owned by an oil giant (Shell is No. 1), and it licenses its brand name to thousands of international outlets as well. But the industry is badly splintered, giving 7-Eleven only 4 percent of the estimated $317 billion U.S. market. Other convenience chains—2,300-store Circle K, 1,366-store Casey's General Store, 1,361-store the Pantry—are trying to bring technology to their operations too, although none is remotely in 7-Eleven's league. And Keyes says his company's biggest challenge now is making sure that store managers understand how to use the data at their fingertips: "You can supply all the technology in the world, and it won't matter if they don't think like entrepreneurs." Furthermore, he says his biggest rivals aren't other convenience chains but the likes of Starbucks and McDonald's. Taking them on is a tall order, but analysts think Keyes's initiatives have 7-Eleven on track for a record run of profits. According to Michael Coleman, an analyst with Southwest Securities, 7-Eleven's earnings are poised to grow at least 15 percent annually for the next five years.

Keyes has already begun to roll out smaller, classier stores in places the chain never ventured before: downtown business districts, airports, and universities. Several of the remodeled shops are in Austin, 7-Eleven's test market, where stores act as guinea pigs for the new merchandising concepts and food offerings that Keyes believes will really turbocharge growth.

In one Austin store on a recent afternoon, the aisles brim with fresh produce and salads, and the air is sweet with the scent of freshly baked cookies. A smartly dressed lawyer named Steven Hake stops in for a quick bite. Though he has worked nearby for 17 years, he never considered a 7-Eleven meal anything more than a last resort. But about a year ago, he stopped in to buy a drink and sampled a focaccia sandwich. He's been hooked on 7-Eleven's $3.49 lunches ever since. "When I eat out, this is hands-down my favorite place," Hake says. "If 7-Eleven is making these changes to attract customers like me, they're succeeding."

The Wegmans Way

THERE'S A NEW NO. 1 The 89-year-old Rochester-based chain is that rare breed: **a grocer beloved by its employees**—and one that is also trouncing its competitors in a very tough industry. Here's how the company does it.

■ *Matthew Boyle.*

SARA GOGGINS WORKS PART-TIME IN A GROCERY store. The blue-eyed 19-year-old attends college in upstate New York, aiming to teach high school history someday. Poor kid, slaving away at a thankless job for some faceless retail conglomerate. But her employer has a face—a ruddy, smiling one, topped with curly auburn hair—and it's right in front of Sara on this snowy mid-December day in the Rochester suburb of Penfield, N.Y., complimenting her on the display she has helped prepare in the store's French-inspired patisserie.

The face of Danny Wegman, president of Wegmans—the best company to work for in America—turns even redder when Sara whips out a picture she took of the two of them earlier this year, which she keeps behind the counter. "I love this place," she tells a visitor. "If teaching doesn't work out, I would so totally work at Wegmans."

Supermarkets aren't often thought of as desirable employers, what with low pay, grueling hours, annual turnover rates that can approach 100% for part-timers, and labor unrest such as last year's strike in California. Wegmans, however—along with the three other grocers on our Top 100 list—does things differently, including the way it deals with employees. The company has proved adept at battling the intractable problem facing grocery stores in this country—that there's no compelling reason to shop there anymore.

Privately held Wegmans—which had 2004 sales of $3.4 billion from 67 stores in New York, Pennsylvania, New Jersey, and Virginia—has long been a step ahead. Its former flagship store in Rochester, opened in 1930 by brothers John and Walter Wegman, featured café-style seating for 300. Walter's brilliant and pugnacious son Robert, who became president in 1950, added a slew of employee-friendly benefits such as profit-sharing and fully funded medical coverage. When asked recently why he did this, 86-year-old Robert leans forward and replies bluntly, "I was no different from them."

Robert is chairman now; his son Danny, a

sartorially challenged Harvard grad who came back to Rochester to cut meat for Wegmans, took the reins in 1976. Early on, Danny was keenly aware of the threat posed by nontraditional grocery outlets like club stores and discounters. (His 1969 senior thesis ended with these prophetic words: "The mass merchandiser is the most serious outside competitor to ever face the food industry.")

In 2003 those nontraditional grocers had 31.3% of the grocery market, and industry guru Bill Bishop projects that number will grow to 39.7% by 2008. That's because consumers think traditional grocers don't offer anything special; 84% believe all of them are alike, one survey has found. Most grocers responded to the competition by slashing

> **The company thinks nothing** of sending, say, cheese manager Terri Zodarecky on a ten-day sojourn to cheesemakers in London, Paris, and Italy.

prices, wreaking havoc on already razor-thin margins. From February 1999 through November 2004, the four largest U.S. grocery chains (Albertson's, Kroger, Safeway, and Ahold USA) posted shareholder returns ranging from -49% to -78%. Winn-Dixie Stores was booted out of the S&P 500 in December for its horrendous performance.

You don't see such problems at Wegmans. While it has no publicly traded stock, its operating margins are about 7.5% (the company will not disclose net margins), double what the big four grocers earn and higher even than hot natural-foods purveyor Whole Foods. Its sales per square foot are 50% higher than the $9.29 industry average, FORTUNE estimates, thanks to a massive prepared-foods department featuring dishes that rival those

of any top restaurant. (Wegmans asked famed Manhattan chef David Bouley for input.)

Each of the newer Wegmans stores is 130,000 square feet—three times the size of a typical supermarket. That means it can offer true one-stop-shopping for every taste. And unlike Whole Foods, which disdains products containing pesticides, preservatives, and other unhealthy stuff, Wegmans stocks both organic gourmet fare and Cocoa Puffs, at competitive prices. That vast selection helps explain why in places like Rochester, Syracuse, and Buffalo, the zeal for Wegmans often borders on kooky obsession. In 2004 the company received nearly 7,000 letters from around the country, about half of them from people pleading with Wegmans to come to their town. Ann Unruh, 52, an insurance manager in Sparks, Md., who has never set foot in a Wegmans, is so excited about a store opening in her area later this year that she plans to take the day off work to be there. She says there will be no need to visit Whole Foods anymore: "I will just shop at Wegmans."

Each Wegmans store boasts a prodigious, pulchritudinous produce section, bountiful baked goods fresh from the oven, and a deftly displayed collection of some 500 cheeses. You'll also find a bookstore, child play centers, a dry cleaner, video rentals, a photo lab, international newspapers, a florist, a wine shop, a pharmacy, even an $850 espresso maker. "Going there is not just shopping, it's an event," says consultant Christopher Hoyt. In an annual survey of manufacturers conducted by consultancy Cannondale Associates, Wegmans bests all other retailers—even Wal-Mart and Target—in merchandising savvy. "Nobody does a better job," says Jeff Metzger, publisher of *Food Trade News*.

But the biggest reason Wegmans is a shopping experience like no other is that it is an employer like no other. "You cannot separate their strategy as a retailer from their strategy as an employer," says Darrell Rigby, head of consultancy Bain & Co.'s global retail practice. Wegmans' hourly wages and annual salaries are at the high end of the market (the better to fend off unions). Consider the sous chef at Wegmans' store in the Rochester suburb of Pittsford, the chain's highest-grossing store at well over $2 million in sales per week. His name is Charles Saccardi, and his previous employer was Thomas Keller of the French Laundry, the famed Napa Valley restaurant. People like that don't come cheap.

But salaries aren't the whole story. The company has shelled out $54 million for college scholarships to more than 17,500 full- and part-time employees over the past 20 years. It thinks nothing of sending, say, cheese manager Terri Zodarecky on a ten-day sojourn to cheesemakers in London, Paris, and Italy. (It's no doubt easier to pamper employees like this when you don't have Wall Street breathing down your neck; a third of FORTUNE'S best companies to work for, like Wegmans, are private.) Even Wegmans is not immune to economic realities, however. Back in August 2003, the company—which previously covered 100% of employees' health insurance premiums—asked salaried employees earning more than $55,000 a year to contribute to the cost. This month Wegmans began asking all other employees to pony up too.

All that means Wegmans' labor costs run between 15% and 17% of sales, Bishop estimates, compared with 12% for most supermarkets (the company declines to comment). But its annual turnover rate for full-time employees is just 6%, a fraction of the 19% figure for grocery chains with a similar number of stores, according to the Food Marketing Institute. Almost 6,000 Wegmans employees—about 20%—have ten or more years of service, and 806 have a quarter-century under their belts. The supermarket industry's annual turnover costs can exceed its entire profits by more than 40%, according to a study conducted by the Coca-Cola Retailing Research Council. When you understand that, you begin to see the truth in Robert Wegman's words: "I have never given away more than I got back."

The proof is in the stores every day. The smiles you receive from Wegmans employees are not the vacuous, rehearsed grins you get at big-box retailers. They are educated smiles, with vast stores of knowledge behind them, cultivated perhaps through company-sponsored trips to Napa Valley's Trinchero winery. After all, what good is it to offer 500 types of specialty cheeses if you can't explain the origin of each, what type of cracker to serve them on, even what wines they should be paired with? "If we don't show our customers what to do with our products, they won't buy them," says Danny Wegman. "It's our knowledge that can help the customer. So the first pump we have to prime is our own people."

Priming the pump starts early. More than half of Wegmans store managers began work there as teens. "When you're a 16-year-old kid, the last thing you want to do is wear a geeky shirt and work for a supermarket," says Edward McLaughlin, director of Cornell's Food Industry Management Program. But at Wegmans, "it's a badge of honor. You are not a geeky cashier. You are part of the social fabric."

A cashier making $5.93 an hour part of the social fabric? But it's true. Wegmans employees don't work in any old supermarket. They work at Wegmans, and there's cachet attached to that. You're a culinary whiz, an ambassador of fine cuisine—even if you only stock shelves at night. "Just about everybody in the store

> **The Wegmans culture** "is bigger than Danny [Wegman] in the same way that Wal-Mart's became bigger than Sam [Walton]," says a consultant.

has some genuine interest in food," says Jeff Burris, who runs the wine shop at Wegmans' Dulles, Va., store. In fact, Wegmans has been known to reject perfectly capable job candidates who lack a passion for it.

Not all Wegmans cashiers are food connoisseurs, but a common denominator of passionate customer service sets Wegmans workers apart from those at other retailers. Simply put, no customer is allowed to leave unhappy. To ensure that, employees are encouraged to do just about anything, on the spot, without consulting a higher-up. One day it could mean sending a chef to a customer's home to clear up a botched food order. It could also mean cooking a family's Thanksgiving turkey, right in the store, because the one Mom bought was too big for her oven. Is that expensive? Sure. Is it worth it? You bet. A Gallup survey found that over a one-month period, shoppers who were emotionally connected to a supermarket spent 46% more than shoppers who were satisfied but lacked an emotional bond with the store.

Empowering employees goes beyond making house calls, though—it also means creating an environment where they can shine, unburdened by hierarchies. Kelly Schoeneck, a store manager, recalls the time a few years back when her supervisor asked her to analyze

a competitor's shopper-loyalty program. She assumed her boss would take credit for her work. But no: Schoeneck wound up presenting her findings directly to Robert Wegman.

That ethos exists at all rungs of the corporate ladder. For example, the Pittsford store sells "chocolate meatball cookies" made from a recipe passed down to Wegmans bakery employee Maria Benjamin from her Italian ancestors. About 15 years ago, Benjamin, who had been baking the cookies for other employees, persuaded Danny Wegman to sell them. How? She just asked him. "They let me do whatever comes into my head, which is kind of scary sometimes," says amiable part-time meat department worker Bill Gamer. Says operations chief Jack DePeters, only half-jokingly: "We're a $3 billion company run by 16-year-old cashiers."

Wegmans can save some serious coin by encouraging employees to step up to the plate. When the company opened a new, $100 million distribution center in Pennsylvania last June to serve its newer Mid-Atlantic stores, it needed truck drivers. Rather than hire experienced (and expensive) pros, Wegmans allowed current store employees to apply for the job. Twenty-one weeks later Wegmans had two dozen drivers with commercial licenses; they had previously been cashiers and produce clerks.

The Wegmans culture flows from the top: from Robert, Danny, and his two daughters, SVP of merchandising Colleen (33 and the likely heir) and 30-year-old group manager Nicole. But there is no shortage of folks to act as cultural conduits for new hires as the chain expands beyond its Rochester roots. (The company's expansion is slow and methodical: It generally opens only two new stores a year. In 2005, one is opening in Fairfax, Va., and one in Hunt Valley, Md.) The new stores may be tougher for the family to keep tabs on. But the Wegmans culture "is bigger than Danny in the same way that Wal-Mart's became bigger than Sam [Walton]," says Bain & Co.'s Rigby.

Wegmans guarantees that by populating new stores with the best and brightest from existing ones, a strategy that wouldn't work if the company were pursuing a more aggressive rollout plan. Take the Dulles store, which opened last February (it drew 15,500 shoppers on its first day, more than most supermarkets get in a week). All its managers came from different Wegmans locations—and that doesn't include the dozens of employees from other stores who jetted in temporarily to get the place up and running. Wegmans spent $5 million on training alone in Dulles. The company never opens a store until its employees are fully prepared. The Dulles store could easily have opened in November 2003 for the critical holiday-sales season, but Wegmans

(Cont.)

chose to wait until the following February. How many retailers would do that?

The emphasis on development over dollars attracts people who never thought they would work in retail, much less in a grocery store. Consider Heather Pawlowski, 38, an electrical engineering major at Cornell who began her career at National Semiconductor. "I was a techie," she recalls. But she had always enjoyed walking the aisles of retailers and wondering why people bought different brands. And in Rochester, what better aisles are there to walk than Wegmans'? So as a newly minted MBA, she entered Wegmans' store manager training program. While her classmates were off to Wall Street, she wore long underwear and got up to her elbows in fish guts. As she moved from packing fish to cutting meat to baking bread, learning all aspects of store operations, Pawlowski was amazed by how much time the store manager spent with her, talking about how things worked at Wegmans.

When asked what makes Wegmans tick, Pawlowski, now a vice president, replies, "We're taking customers to a place they have not been before." And once they arrive, shoppers often don't want to leave. Longtime customer Toni Gartner, 61, is spending the winter in Florida for the first time. But all things being equal, she'd rather be back in frigid Buffalo. "I am trying to get used to Publix," she says. "I understand that Publix is rated highly. Maybe—but it ain't Wegmans."

REPORTER ASSOCIATE *Ellen Florian Kratz*

81

Hotels 'Go to the Mattresses'

Marriott Is Latest to Make Huge Bet on Better Bedding

A Pledge to Wash the Covers

CHRISTINA BINKLEY. WALL STREET JOURNAL.

HOTELS ARE IN AN all-out battle over beds.

Marriott International Inc. today will launch a major initiative to replace nearly every bed in seven of its chains. At the Marriott chain, which is slated for the most extensive upgrade, each king-size bed will be getting 300-thread-count 60% cotton sheets, seven pillows instead of five, a pillowy mattress cover, a white duvet, and a "bed scarf" that will be draped along the bottom of the bed. The yearlong project will cost an estimated $190 million, and the company is saying that the cost, along with the planned marketing efforts, make it its biggest initiative ever.

It's the latest incursion in what has turned into a full-scale hotel bed war, launched by Westin's Heavenly Bed five years ago. Virtually every major chain is trying to outdo its rivals. Radisson, for instance, is buying 90,000 beds that allow each occupant to adjust the firmness of their side of the mattress with a remote control device that pumps air in and out. In recent years, Hilton, Sheraton, and nearly every other major chain has upgraded its beds, sometimes more than once. In October for instance, Sheraton Four Points added a new Sealy Posturepedic Plush Top Sleeping System bed, and tossed a few feather/down pillows on its beds.

PricewaterhouseCoopers estimates the industry this year will buy 1.4 million beds in the U.S. alone. In addition, some limited-service hotels, including Marriott's Residence Inn, plan to start "triple sheeting" their beds—a practice once reserved for five-star hotels, in which an extra sheet is laid over the blanket. One hotel consultant says that next up will be adjustable-height beds that can be raised or lowered electronically.

The bed wars raise some awkward issues, such as what to do with all the old beds. Some hotels are trying to give them to charity, but "homeless shelters don't really have a use for king-sized beds," says one Marriott executive. Housekeepers complain that stuffing

Comparing Hotel Beds

Chains are rapidly upgrading their beds and linens.

HOTEL	BED	COMMENT
Marriott	300-thread-count, 60%-cotton sheets; a "sheeted" white duvet (meaning an extra sheet is put on the bed); down comforter; plus either four or six pillows with bolster and a **decorative "scarf"** (a sort of table runner for a bed)	"Down-surround" pillows (an inner feather pillow is surrounded by down) are a luxury twist.
Courtyard by Marriott	200 thread count, 60% cotton sheets; nine-inch quilted-top mattress; three or five pillows plus bed "scarf."	Real comforters—no more fleece.
Radisson	250 thread count sheets; feather and down pillows; and a **firmness-adjustable** mattress called the Sleep Number Bed. Rolled out last summer.	Company claims researchers found people get more REM sleep on its new bed.
Westin	230 thread count sheets; down blankets; **"boudoir" pillows** (a small, tubular bolster-type pillow); pillow-top mattresses; feather and down pillows.	The 'Heavenly Bed' that revolutionized the U.S. hotel industry five years ago.
Four Points by Sheraton	11.5-inch Sealy Posturepedic Plush Top Sleep system; four pillows including two feather/down; cushioned duvet.	Introduced last **October**; dubbed the "Four Comfort Bed"

source: hotel companies

down comforters into all the new duvets is more time consuming than making a traditional bed with bedspread.

All the pressure to make hotel beds better is finally forcing the industry to reveal—and start to abandon—its dirtiest little secret: the fact that those colorful bedspreads on hotel-room beds sometimes get washed only a few times a year at most. Marriott hopes it will top rivals with a pledge to wash its white duvets between each guest visit, an initiative the company will call "Clean for You."

Hotels are doing all this because their research shows that people are willing to pay more for luxurious beds. Bill Marriott says he expects to be able to charge as much as $30 a night more in Marriott hotels once the new beds are installed.

And at Radisson, a unit of Minneapolis-based **Carlson Companies,** the decision to install new beds was easy after focus-group participants said they'd be willing to pay as much as $10 a night more for better beds. "The bed is paid for by a $1.89 increase in rate over five years," says Bjorn Gullaksen, Radisson's executive vice president.

Marriott plans to purchase 628,000 beds for hotels at seven chains. However, only the full-service Marriott and Renaissance chains

will get the new white duvets, which the company is planning to launder regularly as part of the Clean for You campaign. Less expensive Marriott chains like Courtyard and SpringHill Suites, along with Residence Inn, will triple sheet their beds by putting the extra sheet on top of the (less frequently laundered) outermost bedspread.

All this comes as the hotel industry is experiencing an economic boom, with room rates and occupancies rising faster than any time since the dot-com boom, leaving hotels extra cash to spend on improvements. Much of the increase in travel is coming from business travelers, who tend to be pickier and less price-sensitive than vacationers—meaning they want things like better beds and often don't mind paying for them since their expense accounts are picking up the tab.

At the same time, Americans are getting choosier about their beds at home and on the road. In fact, one hotel consultant says that more choice may also be in the offing for guests at some properties. For instance, one luxury chain currently in development, but not yet operating, is considering offering guests the choice of a duvet or bedspread at the same time they book their room, according to a person familiar with the plans.

The Westin innovation in the 1990s wasn't merely the bedding—a mix of pillow-top mattress, down comforters and pillows, and a crisp white duvet—but also the branding of it with the Heavenly Bed name. The effort helped turn around the Westin brand by lifting the loyalty of the chain's customers. The company says 30,000 guests have bought one of the beds from Westin.

It's not the first time Marriott undertook a bed-upgrade project recently. In its first attempt, three years ago, Marriott went as far as holding an in-house contest to find a catchy name for its thicker mattresses and a colorful polyester duvet. The naming contest was a flop, and the improvements failed to catch on with guests. This time, to promote Marriott's bed initiative around the office, Mr. Marriott says he plans to wear pair of brown-checked flannel pajamas to work today.

One reason the previous effort struggled: Risk-averse Marriott stuck with a more traditional colorful, patterned, polyester duvet. Colorful polyester materials can hide stains better and cut down on hotel cleaning bills, but the look Marriott chose didn't help set the new beds apart from its predecessor.

When it comes to bedspread sanitation, hotel chains are typically loath to reveal how often they wash the bedcovers. Regular laundering is costly, both in terms of housekeeping and laundering, as well as in wear-and-tear on expensive linens. So most hotels launder bedcovers only when absolutely necessary.

Westin's Heavenly Beds, with white duvets, are washed when a housekeeper identifies them as stained or wrinkled, says a spokeswoman. While that means the Westin duvets are laundered often, the spokeswoman adds: "I wish I could say we do it every time for every guest."

82

Reach Out and Upend an Industry

An Entrepreneur's Act II: Internet Calls

BY MATT RICHTEL

JEFFREY A. CITRON, the man who hopes to turn the telephone industry on its ear, works in a cubicle just down the hall from the "Tony Soprano" conference room. Nearby are the "Meadow" and "Uncle Jr." rooms, though if those are full, Mr. Citron's staff could gather in "Dr. Melfi."

The conference rooms at **Vonage,** an Internet telephone start-up in Edison, N.J., where Mr. Citron is chief executive, are named for characters from "The Sopranos." That hints at Mr. Citron's embrace of the un-conventional, a trait that has made him a dan-ger to some of America's most entrenched industries, but also at times to himself.

In the 1990's, he helped to pioneer com-puterized day-trading, putting a thumb in the eye of Wall Street's biggest companies. He amassed a fortune but wound up leaving the industry after he was charged with illegal trading by the Securities and Exchange Com-mission. Though admitting no wrongdoing, he agreed to pay a $22.5 million fine and was banned from the securities business.

Mr. Citron, the Sequel, is no less ambi-tious. Already one of the nation's wealthi-est 30-somethings, he aims to use Vonage's Internet technology to bring fundamental change to the telephone industry, one of the most entrenched and tradition-bound economic sectors. "I'm going to change the world," Mr. Citron, 33, said in an interview last month over lunch at the New York Palace Hotel. "I did it before. Why not again?"

There are plenty of reasons. Mr. Citron's own investors acknowledge that Vonage may be zapped out of existence if it somehow misfires, its customer care problems persist, major rivals provide better service or regu-lators take steps like insisting that Internet phone companies pay the same fees as the rest of the industry.

Yet even skeptics credit Mr. Citron with helping to create an inflection point in the telephone industry by turning Internet telephony—which had long been just a great-sounding theory—into a viable product line.

In a little more than a year, he has signed up 100,000 customers who use his black box to connect their traditional telephone to the Internet. Customers pay a flat fee of around $35 for unlimited local and long-distance phone service, though that figure does not include the more than $40 a month that sub-scribers must also spend for the high-speed Internet access used to transmit the calls.

Industry analysts say Mr. Citron's success has hastened development of the technology by major telephone and cable companies, which are clearly following his lead. **AT&T** and **Time Warner Cable,** for instance, have recently announced their own voice-over-Internet strategies; **Verizon, Qwest, Cox Cable** and others have said they intend to deploy the technology, too.

Their efforts come not only in response to Vonage, but in the larger context of the upheaval in telecommunications. Since the deregulation of Ma Bell, a simmer of com-petition has turned into a boil. Companies deploying many technologies, from cable to wireless, are vying to create voice infra-structure that they hope will enable them to generate and capture billions of dollars in fees from subscribers.

So Vonage faces competition not just from big telecommunications companies but also from start-ups even tinier than itself. One of them, **Skype,** makes free software that lets people talk directly over computers—like a voice version of instant messaging—thus bypassing the telephone altogether. Another start-up, **Net2Phone,** offers Internet phone service directly to consumers (as does Von-age) and works with cable operators to help sell phone service over their lines.

Facing off against them all is a man who, by many accounts, is a study in extreme capi-talism, not Harvard Business School nice-ties. Mr. Citron is not about polite cocktail conversation and low-carb diets; he leans more toward rolled-up sleeves, gut decisions and fast food. At the recent lunch at the Pal-ace hotel, he ordered the salade nicoise, but mispronounced it nih-KO-see.

In other words, he is not the kind of guy who asks for permission slips. Just as he barreled into Wall Street seven years ago, breaking china along the way, he is now barging into the telecom fray. In doing so, he has put himself in position for a great entrepreneurial comeback.

"He's out for redemption; he wants to prove he can do this, and do this properly," said Harry R. Weller, a partner at **New Enter-prise Associates,** a venture capital firm that invested $12 million last year in Vonage. After Mr. Weller's firm conducted extensive due diligence on Mr. Citron, it decided to forge ahead with the investment, despite what Mr. Weller described as the significant risk inher-ent in the technology and the man behind it.

That investment was followed last week by a $40 million round of financing from two other venture firms: **3i Group,** based in London, and **Meritech Capital Partners,** based in Palo Alto, Calif. As part of the deal, the investors have structured the board so that Mr. Citron does not have control over it—in part, Mr. Weller said, to make sure that Mr. Citron is kept within bounds.

Still, Mr. Weller said investors were convinced that it takes a personality like Mr. Citron's to shake the foundations of the telephone industry.

"You need somebody who knows how to disrupt an industry," he said. "You need to have a very, very aggressive entrepreneur. What we have to make sure to do is to take the best of Jeffrey Citron."

Mr. Citron grew up on Staten Island; his parents worked in the insurance business. As a boy, he says he did not know where his interests lay so much as where they did not: in school. He often skipped class, keeping mostly to himself, but he said he scored well enough on tests to offset his absences.

He made a quick transition from high school to Wall Street. In 1988, at the age of 17, he joined Datek Securities, where his father had close connections. By 20, he had made his first million as a trader.

Mr. Citron left Datek in 1991 to start his own firm, where, with a computer whiz named Josh Levine, he built the foundation of a computer-trading network called Island. It let individual traders swap shares inside the system—without help from the big Wall Street firms.

"Island was truly revolutionary," said Bill Burnham, who was an analyst at Piper Jaf-fray during the dot-com boom and is now a venture capitalist at Softbank Capital Part-ners. "It allowed individual investors to get direct access to the market to compete and get the same advantages that professional market makers do."

Mr. Citron returned to Datek Securities to create and become chief executive of Datek Online Holdings. Its technology al-lowed individuals to make their own trades automatically for $9.99, far less than the fees charged by full-service brokers. Datek Online became the nation's fourth-largest online trading firm.

But to regulators, Mr. Citron and his as-sociates were involved in something far less upstanding. The Securities and Exchange

(Cont.)

Commission contended that from 1993 to 1998, he and others were involved in a scheme to use automated trading systems to manipulate Nasdaq, exploit loopholes and make millions of dollars.

In October 1999, amid the scrutiny, Mr. Citron agreed to resign as chief executive of Datek Online. The investigations into Mr. Citron and his associates led to the agreement in January 2003 in which seven former executives and traders at Datek paid a total of $70 million in fines. Regulators said they had created fictitious customer accounts, used them to place their own trades and filed false reports.

The $22.5 million fine Mr. Citron paid—one of the largest in S.E.C. history—only dented his wealth. In 2000, he sold his stake in Datek to private investors for $225 million. Today he lives in a mansion in Brielle, N.J., with his wife and two children.

But wealth isn't everything. There is also reputation. And Mr. Citron says he wants his back. What happened at Datek "was 100 percent about being young," he said.

"We were young, we were naive, we were inexperienced, and, yes, there were backroom dealings," he added. "But that is part of a lot of industries. This time, we are doing it differently." "This time" began with a helicopter ride. Mr. Citron flew from New Jersey to Melville on Long Island in the summer of 2000 to meet with Jeffrey Pulver and the other principals of a company called Min-X.com. Min-X was trying to create a market where companies could trade excess phone network capacity in blocks of minutes, in much the same way commodities like oil are traded. The principals approached Mr. Citron for financing.

He invested what he calls a "significant portion" of the $12 million raised in that first round of financing. But it was far from an arm's-length transaction. He took an active role in the company, immediately replacing Mr. Pulver as chief executive and then changing the concept for the business. Mr. Citron said that it was while flying from California to New Jersey in December 2000 that he decided to focus the company on offering Internet-based telephone calls, transforming it into Vonage.

The quick decision jibes with his overall philosophy that a good business idea does not require endless analysis. "If you can't figure it out in four months, you shouldn't do it," he said. "If you can't figure it out in a week, you shouldn't do it."

The concept of Internet-based calling was not new. It generated much buzz during the dot-com boom and was being pushed heavily by technology companies like **Cisco Systems,** which wanted to sell equipment that would be used to route calls as data.

The basic idea is to transmit telephone with the same technology used to handle e-mail and other Internet traffic. Calls are digitized and delivered as packets of data, rather than as traditional voice signals.

That may sound simple, but the reality was much more complex, particularly because the existing telecommunications giants had spent a century investing in a different type of technology, called circuit switch.

Mr. Citron was hardly the first person to understand that Internet calls were potentially less expensive than those made using circuit switch—for a variety of reasons. With circuit switch technology, a telephone line is dedicated to a single conversation. But when the packets are sent as data, that line can send many signals at once, making far more efficient use of the telecommunications infrastructure. In addition, Internet equipment is less expensive and gives operators and consumers more control over voice traffic—for instance, allowing people to get an e-mail reminder each time they receive a voice mail message.

But for all the advantages, and the hype, no one had figured out the basics: how to affordably hook a traditional phone into the

"Speaking In Ones And Zeros"

Share of U.S. residential Internet phone subscribers (local and long-distance service using Internet protocol).

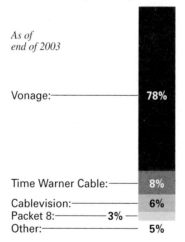

As of end of 2003

Vonage: **78%**

Time Warner Cable: **8%**

Cablevision: **6%**

Packet 8: **3%**

Other: **5%**

(Source by the Yankee Group)

Internet, then send a voice stream directly to another telephone. Mr. Citron and a small team spent the first half of 2001 working to solve the problem.

Louis Holder, a co-founder of Min-X who is now in charge of product development at Vonage, said it was a time of voracious fast-food consumption ("Everybody put on 10 pounds") and exhilaration. "Nobody had done this in the consumer space," he said.

The breakthrough came late on a Thursday night in June. Mr. Holder said he, Mr. Citron and two engineers figured out how to send a digitized call from one telephone to another through a firewall, a defense barrier between a computer or network and the wider Internet.

Initially, the company wanted to create partnerships with cable companies to help them in their assault on traditional telephone companies. But there was skepticism. Vonage was regarded by some executives as a leftover from the bubble. Besides, the cable companies were having their own problems, punctuated by the bankruptcy of @Home, which delivered Internet access over cable.

So in April 2002, Vonage started a consumer-based service. Secretly, the company hoped that if cable companies saw that Vonage was successful, they would consider signing partnerships, Mr. Holder said. But then Vonage took on a life of its own. Within 18 months, it has amassed 100,000 customers, and Mr. Holder said the company expects to have 250,000 by the end of this year, and 500,000 by the end of 2005. Vonage says it will be profitable this year.

Blair Levin, former chief of staff to Reed E. Hundt, chairman of the Federal Communications Commission during the Clinton administration, said that Vonage had proved that Internet calling could be done, and that it was forcing a giant industry to follow more quickly than it might have otherwise. "It's going to have a huge historical impact," Mr. Levin said. "Vonage was a match that was put on some pretty dry timber. But it was a match."

But Mr. Levin, like many others, said he wondered whether Vonage would be a historical footnote or a viable concern. "The question is: What is their defensible asset?" he said, noting that other companies can provide the same kind of service as Vonage, but with the added benefit of having well-known brand names and deep pockets. "They're playing in a world in which, traditionally, economies of scale and scope matter a huge amount."

An executive at a major telephone company, who requested anonymity, said Vonage was not seen as real competition. And the cable companies, which are vying to use their high-speed lines to deliver phone service, say they can do it far better than Vonage. Cox Communications, based in Atlanta, says that its version of Internet-based calling is more stable than Vonage's because it operates the data network, giving it more control. Even Mr. Citron conceded that this was a possibility. "Clearly, there might be some advantages," he said of the cable industry.

Indeed, Vonage acknowledges that it has two overriding challenges. One is the quality of calls made over its network. Customers often

(Cont.)

complain of having their calls dropped, or of hearing lags. Mr. Holder says that this happens because the high-speed Internet access in subscribers' homes can be spotty, and that when the lines falter, so does the call quality.

A related problem, Mr. Holder said, is insufficient customer service. The company is scrambling to hire and train qualified people to answer customer concerns. Vonage has 70 customer service employees and would like to have 110, he said.

Another major challenge is regulatory. So far, Vonage has been able to keep its costs low because it has been able to avoid the regulations that federal and state governments place on traditional telephone companies. But that may change: The F.C.C. said last Thursday that it intends to study the question of regulating Internet calling over the next year.

Mr. Citron said he hoped regulators would make the rules clear. He also said he did not intend to get into any gray areas, as he did in his first incarnation as a disruptive entrepreneur. But, in one way, he would like to see a similar outcome.

Internet calling, he said, "will be a large and transforming event."

83

Special Events Help Drive Customer Loyalty

For eBay, customers who attend special training events see increases in their online sales at the company's site

. . . .

By Marilyn Much
Investor's Business Daily

Last June, 10,000 eBay users gathered in New Orleans for the online retailer's third annual eBay Live users conference.

At the three-day show, eBay users networked, swapped stories, attended classes and heard talks from outside speakers and company executives, including CEO Meg Whitman.

They had informal chats with eBay executives and browsed the trade show floor, which featured products and services from exhibitors such as PayPal Buyer Credit (an eBay unit), Stamps.com and JJW Logistics. Plus, they got to play games, such as a treasure hunt, and if they came alone and gave their consent, they got matched up with people who shared common interests.

Other companies, including Whole Foods, use special events and educational programs to give consumers a chance to experience the brand. These efforts help build brand loyalty and affinity and in some cases drive added sales and draw new customers.

EBay also sponsors the eBay University program. It's a curriculum of education, tips, insights and best practices that enable individuals and businesses to fully leverage the Web site's capabilities. In 2004, eBay University visited 35 cities. Courses are also offered online.

Physical gatherings offer eBay a number of business benefits.

"They put a face on a virtual company and provide us with an opportunity to interface with customers, listen to them and understand their requirements to suc-cessfully build their businesses on eBay," said Mike Rudolph, director of education marketing.

EBay Live puts a face on the company, helps build the brand and gets users together, adds Abby Green, manager of eBay Live. The show also features eBay University classes, computer labs and round-table discussions that can help people grow their eBay businesses.

Learning to Boost Sales

Rudolph says the business goal of eBay University is to increase the knowledge and confidence of users. Users who start out on eBay and take an eBay University course are more successful after the course than users who haven't taken one. Once users attend the program, they can show increased sales and listings, he says.

The more successful the users, the better for eBay. It charges a "final value fee" if a seller's item is sold, ends with a winning bid or is purchased. For single items, the fee is based on the final sale price of your item. EBay also charges sellers a fee for listing each item.

Events such as eBay Live help companies drive sales, says Liz Bigham, director of U.S. brand marketing for Jack Morton Worldwide, a unit of the Interpublic Group. Jack Morton is an agency that focuses on experiential marketing events for clients.

Event marketing is a key platform for building relationships with customers and giving them an understanding of the brand, Bigham says.

Keeping that in mind, eBay has expanded its education efforts. At last year's eBay Live it launched an online program to train new teachers for the eBay University courses. Specialists, who charge from $39 to $69 a session, do the teaching face to face. This is a way eBay can offer courses in cities all the time. So far, 1,300 users have paid $149 to enroll.

Once a specialist passes the course, he or she gets listed in a directory that certifies credentials. This way, if someone needs eBay training in a particular city, he can access a specialist via the directory.

At Whole Foods, stores develop events geared to local communities. In-store events run the gamut from cooking classes and wine tastings to holiday bashes and yoga sessions. Events are offered in a separate classroom that typically holds about 25 people.

"Sponsoring get-togethers that let consumers experience its stores and products is a key component of Whole Foods' marketing strategy. It's a more intimate way than a print ad to connect with consumers," says Margaret Wittenberg, the chain's vice president of marketing and communications. She notes that Whole Foods doesn't do much mainstream advertising.

Events are geared to customers' lifestyles. For instance, last May, the natural and organic foods chain cosponsored a singles event with a group called ConnectStLouis. The St. Louis store had been known as a singles meeting place. So why not formalize it?

For $25, 25 singles got to socialize for two hours while munching on appetizers prepared by the store's chef. They also participated in activities and listened to ConnectStLouis talks on how to meet and attract other singles.

The bash was such a hit, people were turned away and urged to sign up for the next singles event.

The event gave exposure to Whole Foods and its products and forged an association between shopping there and having fun.

"(This type of event) is a great way to integrate Whole Foods with customers' lifestyles. And by reaching out and creating fun in a unique atmosphere within the store, Whole Foods becomes more than just a place to shop for groceries," said David Rosenberg, director of marketing for the Midwest region. "We make (Whole Foods) a place they look forward to coming back to."

Happy Birthday

These events not only help build the chain's brand image, they help drive sales. Whole Foods serves products from its stores at its gatherings, so customers get familiar with items they might not have tried otherwise. To entice attendees to come back, stores typically give away coupons at these events. For instance, at the St. Louis event, attendees got a coupon good for $5 off any $25 purchase.

Whole Foods also caters to parents. In Rosenberg's region, kids can have birthday parties in the in-store classrooms. Parents create the menu and format. It costs them from $5 to about $15 per attendee.

At the parties, educators talk to the kids about food and take them into the kitchen where they can play with the food.

Since parents transport the kids to and from the stores, these parties drive incremental traffic, says Rosenberg.

They also set a shopping pattern for kids and parents. If kids find it fun to go to Whole Foods, parents are likely to want to shop there.

84

Nature's Way— Behind a Food Giant's Success: An Unlikely Soy-Milk Alliance

At Dean Foods, CEO, Buddhist Team Up to Sell Silk Brand; And Gain Clout in Organics

Mr. Engles's Lesson on 'Sukha'

JANET ADAMY. WALL STREET JOURNAL.

Steve Demos started making tofu in a bathtub in the late 1970s. An earring-adorned Buddhist who once lived in a cave in India, he sold the tofu at a tai chi class he was taking in Boulder, Colo.

As his venture grew into an organic-food company called White Wave Inc., he sought to "prove that there is greater profitability in the green approach." He spent thousands of dollars in 2001 to relocate prairie dogs White Wave displaced when it built a soy-processing plant in Utah.

So when Gregg Engles sought control of the company that year, Mr. Demos was apprehensive. Mr. Engles, a Yale-educated lawyer, built Dean Foods Co. into a giant in the dairy business by rolling up little players and slashing costs. Now, Mr. Engles, Dean's chief executive, wanted to push into organics, one of the few hot areas in the slow-growth food industry.

Mr. Demos sued to block the takeover, alleging that Dean would damage his company's culture. "You've got to understand," he recounts saying at one meeting, "we're all about being green." Mr. Engles recalls retorting he also was committed to green: money.

Eventually Mr. Demos dropped his suit and the deal went through. Today Mr. Demos, 55 years old, and Mr. Engles, 47, are the unlikely partners behind one of the stars of the food industry. They make the most popular organic product in the supermarket, Silk soy milk—now a staple at Starbucks Corp. coffee shops. And they have helped transform Dean Foods from a low-margin milk producer into a Wall Street stand-out with a growing stable of high-margin brands. By the end of 2003, Dean's profit had tripled in four years, and its $9.2 billion in annual revenue made it bigger than Kellogg Co. and H.J. Heinz Co. Dean Foods' stock price has more than doubled since January 2000, far outstripping the food industry average.

While total food sales are growing by about 3% a year, organics are surging by about 20%. Dean's rivals, coveting that $10 billion U.S. market, have been snapping up organic brands. Organics now account for more than 5% of Dean's sales and are among the company's fastest-growing products. Along the way, Mr. Engles learned some Buddhist principles and Mr. Demos earned some new big-business management chops.

As the competition moves into Dean's market, the company faces some tough new challenges. Dean doesn't have a track record as a branded food company, and it is facing competitors who do. For example, General Mills Inc.'s 8th Continent soy milk is also posting double-digit sales growth and threatening to narrow the gap against market-leader Silk. The last Silk ad campaign didn't increase sales as much as Mr. Demos had hoped. Last year White Wave's sales grew 31%, shy of Mr. Demos's goal of 36%.

In the late 1980s, Mr. Engles made his first mark in business by assembling a collection of more than 30 packaged-ice companies. He grew skilled at boosting their margins by cutting costs. He thought the milk industry was ripe for a similar consolidation. In 1993, Mr. Engles bought Suiza dairy of Puerto Rico for $106 million. From Suiza's new Dallas headquarters, he acquired over the next several years more than 50 dairies accounting for about one-third of the nation's milk supply.

Mr. Engles's biggest deal came in 2001 with the $1.5 billion purchase of Dean Foods. At the time, Dean was buying other smaller dairies, too, but it wasn't as adept as Mr. Engles at making its purchases into winners. Mr. Engles felt he could do better. He moved Dean's headquarters to Dallas from suburban Chicago, but kept the family name of the founders.

As part of the deal, Mr. Engles got a toehold into White Wave, Mr. Demos's soy company. Dean had previously invested $15 million in White Wave, with an option to buy the rest.

It was an intriguing opportunity. The Food and Drug Administration had concluded soy protein could help people avoid heart attacks and allowed companies to advertise this claim. Mr. Engles's own effort to market soy milk hadn't gone well, in part because Mr. Demos got off to an earlier start. So he didn't hesitate when he got the chance to gain control of White Wave. "This was an underappreciated business," Mr. Engles says.

Mr. Demos took a roundabout route into business. He studied philosophy and political science in the late 1960s and spent four years traveling through Europe, the Middle East and India, learning about Eastern philosophy. In India, he says, he lived in a cave for several months to meditate and practice yoga.

After his Boulder tofu venture started to take off, he kept his hands in all aspects of the business. He came to the office one New Year's Eve and climbed into a waste-collecting pit to unclog it. He kept coveralls handy so he could fix food-making machines. He describes himself as a "benefic dictator" who told workers, "We're doing this, don't ask questions."

In 1996, Mr. Demos came out with Silk. At that point, most soy milk was sold in "brick pack" boxes that sat on store shelves because it wouldn't spoil in those packages. Mr. Demos put a fancy logo on a paper carton that required stores to stock it in the dairy case, where shoppers were more likely to be looking for milk products.

Mr. Demos tinkered with the taste and slapped on a heart-healthy label. But he needed more capital to expand from health-food stores to mainstream supermarkets, which charge suppliers hefty "slotting" fees to put their products on shelves. He approached Coca-Cola Co., Kraft Foods Inc. and others for money. Dean Foods bit, buying an initial 25% of White Wave in 1999 for $5 million.

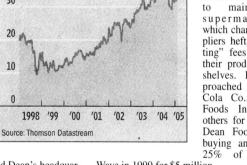

Cash Cow
Dean Foods' weekly closing share price
Source: Thomson Datastream

White Wave's sales continued soaring as grocery shoppers increasingly reached for foods grown without pesticides or genetically modified seeds. As a milk substitute, Silk also appealed to Asians and Hispanics, who for genetic reasons can have trouble digesting milk in adulthood.

In 2001, Mr. Engles flew to Boulder and told Mr. Demos that Dean wanted to exercise its option to buy the rest of White Wave for $154 million. Mr. Engles said Dean would give White Wave access to manufacturing capacity and stay out of Mr. Demos's way. Mr. Demos was polite but noncommittal.

Two months later in June 2001, Mr. Engles received a fax from Mr. Demos saying White Wave had sued to block the Dean purchase. Mr. Demos says he never thought the old Dean management believed in the potential of soy products, and he didn't trust Mr. Engles to treat him better.

Mr. Engles pressed ahead. He had seen that other big food companies also were buying organic food companies for their sales potential and wider profit margins. By the beginning of the decade, food giants such as Kraft and General Mills had bought all or part of more than a dozen natural and organic food companies.

After a judge ruled against his lawsuit, Mr. Demos prepared to leave White Wave. Former owners of food start-ups are rarely kept on in management after a takeover, but Mr. Engles wanted Mr. Demos to stay. He thought Mr. Demos, who owns a farm with 180 organic fruit trees, had keen insight into potential soy consumers. For instance, he was impressed by how Mr. Demos had engendered brand loyalty by touting the benefits of pesticide-free farming on Silk packages.

Mr. Engles flew back to Boulder. He boosted the price by about $40 million and offered Mr. Demos and his managers an additional $30 million in incentives to hit sales targets for Silk. He promised to keep White Wave's headquarters in Boulder. Mr. Demos became president and "head bean" of Dean's White Wave subsidiary.

Mr. Engles quickly approved a $22 million advertising campaign to keep Silk's sales growing and a $30 million plan to add soy extraction facilities to boost Silk production.

Last summer, Mr. Engles sat down with Mr. Demos and other White Wave folks to craft a mission statement for White Wave. Mr. Engles wanted it to spell out the company's focus on creating shareholder value and high-end brands. Mr. Demos wanted it to embrace "right livelihood," a Buddhist concept for work that is ethical and beneficial to a person's spiritual development. Someone in the meeting expressed concern that the term could be linked to an extremist group.

Having read up on Buddhism himself, Mr. Engles came to the rescue. He explained the principles of right livelihood to

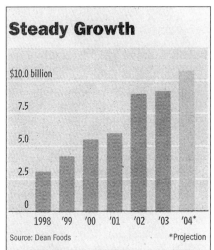

Steady Growth

Source: Dean Foods   *Projection

the group, using Hindi words like "dukkha" (suffering), and "sukha" (happiness) to show the concept wasn't radical. The statement eventually used "responsible livelihood." Mr. Engles says writing it "was one of the most rewarding things I've done in business."

Mr. Demos pushed to create a vitamin-enriched children's version of Silk. When Dean officials in Dallas asked for data showing demand for such a product, Mr. Demos said he had none, but, "there wouldn't be an opportunity if there was data trending," he recalls. Dean launched the product in June. Mr. Engles also agreed to spend $350,000 to convert White Wave's operations to run on wind power.

A big breakthrough came in 2003, after Mr. Demos asked Starbucks to make Silk its exclusive soy milk. Mr. Demos offered to create a blend that would complement espresso and chai drinks. The coffee chain accounts for a small fraction of White Wave's revenue, but the alliance has given the Silk brand valuable exposure.

Silk easily surpassed the sales targets Mr. Engles had set. Its sales are on track to reach $414 million this year. White Wave now controls about 65% of the dairy-case soy-milk market, which doesn't include restaurants and Wal-Mart stores, according to Information Resources Inc., a research firm in Chicago. Last year, Dean paid Mr. Demos an $11 million bonus.

In August, Mr. Engles named Mr. Demos to run Dean's new, $1.2 billion branded-products division, White Wave Foods Co. That more than doubled the amount of business Mr. Demos oversees. Along with Silk, he's now also responsible for Hershey's chocolate milk, Horizon Organic milk and International Delight flavored coffee creamers.

White Wave has been the most successful

organic food purchase in the industry, says Eric Katzman, a food industry analyst at Deutsche Bank. "They allowed this entrepreneur to thrive within a decentralized business model," Mr. Katzman says.

After several years of focusing on plain, vanilla and chocolate soy milk, White Wave is trying to extend the Silk brand with new products and sales venues. The company is pushing a variety with additional calcium for pregnant women and an unsweetened version.

White Wave is putting soy-milk vending machines in public schools to capture the children's milk market. The number of consumers who drink soy milk is "still quite small looking at the long-term potential," Mr. Katzman says. Industry experts have speculated that Dean Foods might try to sell or spin off Silk and other brands. Mr. Engles declined to comment. Last week, Dean said it will spin off its $700 million pickle and private-label foods business.

In 2003, Mr. Engles joined Mr. Demos at a natural-products trade show in Washington. There, Mr. Demos introduced Mr. Engles to Ziggy Marley, a musician and son of the reggae legend Bob Marley. Before Mr. Marley's performance at the show, the three toured the trade fair together, sampling natural foods. Mr. Engles attended the concert afterward.

"Steve has definitely caused me to think differently and more thoughtfully about certain aspects of the business," Mr. Engles says.

After watching Mr. Engles's management, Mr. Demos has started to delegate more. He lets others write White Wave's quarterly report to the Dean board, a task he'd largely handled himself. "He's certainly mellowed," says Pam Mettler, White Wave's information technology director.

Last summer, Mr. Engles and Mr. Demos hit a sticking point on who would research and develop new products. Mr. Engles wanted credentialed food scientists who were classically trained in flavor chemistry and other specific disciplines. Mr. Demos wanted at least one beanie-wearing chef who would propose unconventional new foods. "Wasn't that soy milk not too long ago?" he argued. The pair compromised by designating one position for a creative trend-spotter among the team of traditional food scientists.

In June the two men and their wives enjoyed a five-hour dinner in Paris on a business trip. After a few glasses of wine, Mr. Demos apologized for suing Mr. Engles when he first tried to buy his company.

From *The Wall Street Journal*, February 1, 2005. Reprinted by permission of Dow Jones and Co., Inc. via The Copyright Clearance Center.

85

LINUX MOVES IN ON THE DESKTOP

As more companies switch, Microsoft is hustling to protect its crown jewels

The doctors at Capital Cardiology Associates, with seven offices in New York and Massachusetts, pride themselves on latching on to the latest medical gizmos. But now they're pioneering in a different tech realm: computers. Employees at the 160-person company have traded in PCs running Microsoft Corp.'s Windows for machines using the up-and-coming Linux operating system. It spent more than $400,000 on a complete tech upgrade, but its president, Dr. Augustin DeLago, believes the investment will pay off handsomely over time in better security for patients' records and easier management of technology. "We're a small company, but I think we're out ahead on something," says Dr. DeLago.

Indeed, this could be the start of something big. After a long gestation period—and against all odds—Linux is finally gaining a toehold in Microsoft's backyard, office desktop computing. Market researcher IDC expects to announce within weeks that Linux' PC market share in 2003 hit 3.2%, overtaking Apple Computer Inc.'s Macintosh software. And the researcher expects Linux to capture 6% of this market by 2007. That's still tiny compared with Microsoft's 94% share. But it's clear now that Linux is becoming a viable alternative to Windows on desktop and laptop PCs for companies willing to put up with the trouble of switching.

Linux has made major strides in the past few months. In November, China declared it the operating system of choice. Starting on Jan. 1, the Israeli government plans gradually to replace desktop Windows with Linux. IBM CEO Samuel J. Palmisano late last year challenged his 319,000-employee company to move entirely to Linux PCs. And now, analysts say, dozens of major corporations in the U.S., Europe, and Japan are sizing up Linux. In a survey of corporate buyers by Merrill Lynch & Co., 43% said they would consider replacing Windows desktops with Linux. "I had expected governments to be interested, but now it's on the radar of corporate chief information officers," says analyst Steven Milunovich of Merrill Lynch.

FOREIGN FANS

Why the excitement now? Several factors are driving the growth. Linux, an open-source software package, has been steadily getting better and easier to use. It can be bought for moderate prices—or downloaded from the Net for free. Sun Microsystems Inc. in December introduced the Java Desktop System, which includes Linux, its StarOffice applications, a browser, and e-mail. The package sells for less than $100, while comparable Microsoft software for corporations costs more than $600. And corporations like to have alternatives to Microsoft software. What's more, unlike Windows, Linux has not been a big target of virus writers.

Even though Linux PCs are generating a lot of interest, don't expect them to bust Microsoft's monopoly anytime soon. That's because Windows is installed on 400 million PCs worldwide. Linux may have gained a 24% chunk of the market for server operating systems, but that's sold to techies. For Linux to chomp into Microsoft's PC lead, companies will have to make complicated transitions that might wipe out the initial cost advantages—switching not just operating systems but the applications that run on them. Tony Scott, chief technology officer for General Motors Corp.'s tech group, says GM will evaluate Linux, but "I'd be suspicious that it would be an easy swap in a large organization."

Clearly on edge, Microsoft is working overtime to protect its crown jewels. It has financed studies by market researchers that warn against switching to Linux, saying it could cost more over the long run. In high-profile cases, the software giant goes to great lengths to avoid losing out. When the city of Munich considered switching 14,000 PCs to Linux last year, Microsoft slashed its price by a third and dispatched CEO Steven A. Ballmer to woo the Bavarians. Munich went with Linux, but the city fathers may rue that day. *BusinessWeek* has learned that the project is behind schedule, bolstering Microsoft's message that Linux still isn't ready for prime time. "I haven't seen any of our customers use Linux in a mainstream way," says Martin Taylor, Microsoft's general manager for platform strategy.

Desktop Linux hasn't had any appreciable effect on Microsoft's finances yet, but it could do damage if Linux manages to grab a 10% share of the market, say analysts. IDC estimates that desktop Windows' share will shrink slightly, to 92% in 2007 as Linux' share doubles. Under that scenario, Microsoft would not only sell fewer copies of Windows than it might have otherwise, but it might feel pressure to lower prices, too, says IDC analyst Al Gillen.

If desktop Linux starts to hit Microsoft where it hurts, it will happen not so much among typical office employees but among specialized workers. These include stock traders, bank tellers, engineers, customer-

Linux Why Now?

Several factors are making the Linux operating system a stronger contender in the office

THE PRICE IS RIGHT Organizations can buy Linux and Sun Microsystems' StarSuite of word-processing, spreadsheet, and other programs for less than $100—or even download free versions. Comparable Microsoft software for corporations costs more than $600.

TECHNOLOGY IS IMPROVING While Linux and the desktop applications designed to run on it don't have as many features as Microsoft's products, they offer the capabilities most people need.

THE COMPUTER INDUSTRY IS BEHIND IT Computer makers, including Hewlett-Packard and IBM, have gotten behind Linux on the desktop. Sun and software maker Novell have made Linux the lynchpin of their desktop strategies.

(Cont.)

service reps, and warehouse employees. They rely on just a few applications and need PCs that are simple to use and rarely crash—which Linux can handle. Cole National Corp. uses Linux desktops in 1,700 Pearle Vision and other optical stores. And Delta Air Lines Inc. says it's considering using Linux on its airport desktop terminals.

This market is potentially huge. Microsoft has estimated that while the number of typical knowledge workers in the U.S. is about 40 million, the broader market for desktop computing is potentially 117 million. So it's no wonder this is where Linux suppliers such as IBM, Hewlett-Packard, Sun, and Novell are concentrating their efforts. While IBM previously focused on Linux server software, late last year its consulting unit started offering an array of Linux desktop services aimed at specialized workers.

Still, large corporations are reluctant to

Linux' spread could put pressure on Microsoft to lower its prices

discuss their Linux plans publicly. That's partly because SCO Group, Inc., a tiny company in Linden, Utah, claims Linux violates its copyrights and has threatened to sue users. They also don't want to commit to something that they aren't completely sure of yet. One major European bank that requested it not be named says it's considering switching tens of thousands of its desktop computers to Linux. "We want to be close to the front, but we don't want to be the pioneers with the arrows in our back," says one of the bank's CIOs.

In the short term, the best prospects for Linux on PCs are in governments and developing countries. Western governments are looking for ways to trim their budgets. At the same time, a number of governments, including Brazil and China, have adopted policies favoring the use of open-source technologies to help foster their own domestic software industries.

Think of this as the third lap of a 100-lap race. Desktop Linux could still spend a lot of time in the pits for repairs and tune-ups and continue to watch Microsoft zoom past. But if it gets up to speed, Microsoft better watch its behind.

By Steve Hamm in New York, with Spencer Ante in New York and David Fairlamb in Frankfurt

Puma Does Fancy Footwork to Stay Out of the Mainstream

BY SUSANNA RAY AND
MATTHEW KARNITSCHNIG

PUMA AG'S LOW-CUT sneakers and bowling-bag purses flew out the door for a couple years at "bruce," an upscale Vancouver fashion boutique. Then last summer, the shop's owner, Campbell McDougall, sensed that Puma and its retro athletic apparel was losing a little of its cachet. "I think it's cooling off. The brand has a reputation on the street as being mainstream," Mr. McDougall says. "One can only sit on re-issuing old styles for so long."

Stopping the slide from cutting edge to middle of the road is a challenge every trendy brand must face. It was only a couple of years ago that Puma's low-rise suede sneakers helped the company spring out of the shadow of athletic wear giants **Nike** Inc. and **Adidas-Salomon** AG, and its leaping-cat logo could be found on the feet of fashion plates like Madonna and Leonardo DiCaprio. Now, the popular brand is widely available and commonly spotted on folks far less glamorous.

And so Puma has had to grapple with keeping its cool while growing popular in the mass market. If the brand becomes too mainstream, it risks alienating the style-setters that fueled its comeback. Yet, if its sales don't grow, investors will flee.

It is up to Jochen Zeitz, Puma's 40-year-old chief executive, who guided the company back from the brink of collapse a decade ago, to manage the paradox. He wants Puma to stay hip by forging links with other hot icons.

Right now, Puma is rubbing elbows with the coolest name in cars—the BMW Mini. As part of a co-marketing agreement with **Bayerische Motoren Werke** AG, Puma has designed a black, two-piece driving shoe called the "Mini Motion 2 part shoe," which it is marketing as an accessory to the car. Puma says the shoe incorporates features of Formula 1 racing shoes. It consists of a flexible inner slipper, for comfort on long trips at the wheel or while puttering around the house, and a sturdier outer shoe, with ankle support and traction, to be worn outdoors and in city driving (to ease the strain of frequent gear-shifting).

Following a tried-and-true formula for maintaining an aura of exclusivity, Puma plans to limit production of the driving shoes to only about 2,000 pairs. They are expected

to sell for about $120 at Puma shops and Mini dealerships.

Puma also is limiting the availability of other shoes destined for stores. A new line created by Dutch designer Alexander van Slobbe (and there's nothing slobby about them) includes boots inspired by 1950s boxing shoes and black shoes stitched to look like old-time hockey skates. For the spring, Puma plans two apparel lines designed by the hipster label Vexed Generation Clothing of London, including a line of unisex garments inspired by martial-arts robes and a line with protective padding, for bike and scooter riders.

And later this year, Puma says, it will unveil a line of "modern, minimalist" shoes designed by French architect Philippe Starck. As it happens, Mr. Starck's credits straddle the divide between cool and mass market, encompassing avant-garde interiors for New York's Paramount and Royalton hotels and also a line of housewares for Target Corp. stores. "The fact that he's done so many different projects in different worlds is what made him interesting to us," says Puma spokeswoman Erin Cowhig.

Mr. Zeitz points to **Apple Computer** Inc. and **Porsche** AG as examples of brands that have maintained reputations for being cutting-edge while growing in mainstream popularity, Porsche with its Cayenne off-road vehicle and Apple with its iPod and iBook. "Puma is known for going its own way," Mr. Zeitz says. "It's a brand for individualists."

Puma's concentration on fashion contrasts with Nike and Adidas, which emphasize performance of their shoes and apparel and pay a stable of superstar athletes to wear them. Even when Puma does get into major sports, it still emphasizes style. For the national soccer team of Cameroon, which is known for its on-field flair, Puma recently created a striking one-piece uniform, with red shorts attached to a skin-tight green top. After the uniform's debut a month ago at the African Nations Cup tournament, soccer's ruling authority banned the suit because it violates the rule stating that uniforms must be in two pieces.

Puma says it was "shocked" by the ban, because it had received preliminary approval for the design from the soccer body. Of course,

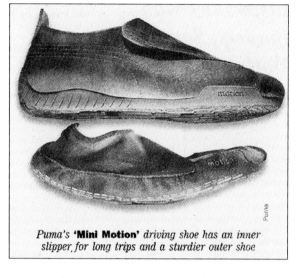

Puma's **'Mini Motion'** *driving shoe has an inner slipper for long trips and a sturdier outer shoe*

Puma also welcomes the free publicity: The uproar, after all, bolsters the brand's rebellious image, especially since the team defied the ban and wore the bodysuits for the duration of the tournament.

Mr. Zeitz's reliance on design is a bet against expectations in the athletic-shoe industry: The style pendulum is expected to swing from fashion back to function with the approach of soccer's World Cup and the 2004 Olympics in Athens. Mr. Zeitz, however, says 80% of the athletic shoes bought in the U.S. are for casual wear, not sports. "We will see more technical looks, but that doesn't mean it's shifting away from fashion," Mr. Zeitz says.

The focus on looks, at least for now, is still paying off. According to preliminary figures reported last month, Puma rang up a 40% leap in 2003 sales to 1.3 billion euros, or $1.65 billion. Net profit more than doubled to $226.7 million. The order backlog—an important indicator of demand—was a record $914.4 million. Final figures for the year will be released today.

Still, with management predicting sales could hit the $2.5 billion mark by 2006, it may just be a matter of time before Puma becomes so popular as to be passe. That would be bad news for Jana Cipa, a 15-year-old who bought a Puma belt and her fourth pair of Puma sneakers on a recent visit to the brand's spartan Frankfurt store. "Puma is definitely the most popular brand," she says and offers her own prediction: "They're going to stay trendy for another decade."

Electronics With Borders: Some Work Only in the U.S.

DAVID PRINGLE AND STEVE STECKLOW.
WALL STREET JOURNAL.

TO SAVE MONEY, Chris Caine, a resident of Fiji, always orders computers made by **Apple Computer** Inc. from the U.S., where they are significantly cheaper. Recently, he purchased Apple's newest desktop, the iMac G5.

Soon after the computer arrived from the U.S. he plugged it in. There was "a big bang, like an explosion, and white smoke out of the speaker grilles," he says. The machine then died.

Mr. Caine didn't have a defective unit. It turns out that, unlike the 17 other Apple computers that he had purchased in recent years for his DVD-rental business, the new iMac G5s sold in the U.S. are designed to work only with the electric power systems in the U.S. and Japan, which pump out a lower number of volts than in most other countries.

Mr. Caine fell foul of a little-noticed trend: Some consumer-electronics companies are designing products so they will work only in the U.S. For example, some of the latest printers from **Hewlett-Packard** Co. refuse to print if they aren't fed ink cartridges bought in the same region of the world as the printer. **Nintendo** Co.'s latest hand-held game machines are sold in the U.S. with power adaptors that don't work in Europe.

Such measures prevent thrifty foreign consumers and gray marketers—traders who sell goods through channels that haven't been authorized by the manufacturer—from taking advantage of the decline of the dollar against the world's major currencies to buy lower-price products in the U.S. In terms of euros, pounds or other strong currencies, U.S. retail goods are much cheaper today than they were two years ago.

U.S. multinational companies want Europeans to continue to buy their goods in Europe, however, rather than seeking out bargains in the U.S. The companies make more money if Europeans pay in euros for their goods at current exchange rates.

For example, H-P's European revenue in its fiscal fourth quarter, ended Oct. 31, rose 11.3% from the year-earlier period, while its U.S. revenue shrank 0.3%. The company said its total revenue, which is reported in dollars, was boosted by sales in euros and other strong currencies.

In the U.S., Apple sells the most basic version of the iMac G5 for $1,299. In the United Kingdom, the same machine costs GBP 765, or $1,430, before sales tax.

Of course, there have always been products, particularly electrical ones, that don't work universally; different countries have different voltages as well as incompatible television and radio broadcasting standards. But in the era of the global economy, with business people toting laptops, cellphones and digital music players around the world, the electronics industry had been moving toward making more products that work everywhere.

Now, there are signs that manufacturers feel that this kind of globalization has gone too far. H-P has quietly begun implementing "region coding" for its highly lucrative print cartridges for some of its newest printers sold in Europe. Try putting a printer cartridge bought in the U.S. into a new H-P printer configured to use cartridges purchased in Europe and it won't work. Software in the printer determines the origin of the ink cartridge and whether it will accept it.

The company introduced region-coding on several printers in the summer so it won't have to keep altering prices to keep pace with currency movements, says Kim Holm, vice president for H-P's supplies business in Europe, the Middle East and Africa. H-P eventually plans to introduce the concept across its entire line of inkjet printers, he adds.

This comes at a time when the sliding dollar has meant that H-P ink cartridges sold in Europe are becoming much more expensive than equivalent ones in the U.S. "We are not trying to make money on this," Mr. Holm says, adding that European customers will benefit from H-P's new approach if the dollar begins to rise in value against the euro—because H-P used to increase prices in Europe when the dollar rose in value to ensure consistent prices around the world. Under the new policy, H-P plans to leave prices in Europe the same even if the dollar rises.

But tech-savvy consumers already may be plotting to circumvent the system. A message recently appeared on an Internet bulletin board for people who specialize in refilling used printer ink cartridges to save money. "Does anyone have a solution to beat the regionalization that H-P has placed into the new 94 series cartridges?" it asked. (No answer has been posted yet.)

H-P is taking the same approach Hollywood has used with DVDs—and one that prompted a huge consumer backlash overseas. Movies sold in the U.S., which generally are cheaper, are designed not to play in European or Asian DVD players.

The European Commission in Brussels has been scrutinizing such practices including DVD pricing "for quite some time, and we are still investigating," says Jonathan Todd, the European Commission's spokesman for antitrust policy.

In the meantime, in response to consumer complaints, many manufacturers now sell DVD players in Europe that can be altered legally so they can play films bought in any country.

Consumer groups are also opposed to the latest region-coding measures. "Manufacturers don't like global commerce when it doesn't line their pockets," says Phil Evans, principal policy adviser at Which?, a British consumer watchdog. "In the long term, it's not a clever thing to do from a customer-relations standpoint."

Indeed, Apple shopper Mr. Caine says he felt ripped off. The iMac G5s Apple sells everywhere except the U.S. and Japan are dual voltage, meaning they can cope with the electrical systems in Fiji, Europe and most of Asia, as well as those in Japan and the U.S. Mr. Caine's new $1,500 computer is "a nice, pretty paperweight," he says.

Other Apple products including iPods, the new Mac Mini and its laptops are dual-voltage. Steve Dowling, a spokesman for Apple, which is based in Cupertino, Calif., declined to explain why the easily transportable iMac G5s Apple sells in the U.S. aren't dual voltage. He said only, "Apple does not discourage anyone, anywhere from buying an iMac G5."

Ironically, tweaking products for different regions can increase a manufacturer's costs. It is often easier and cheaper for a company to alter the power adaptors to work in the different voltage systems in Europe, Asia and the U.S. rather than make changes to the product itself.

Nintendo sells the same Game Boy Advance SP everywhere. But

Power Play

A comparison of the price difference for the same electronics in the U.S. and the U.K.

	U.S. PRICE	U.K. PRICE
Apple iMac G5	From $1,299	From £765 ($1,430)
HP printer cartridge 97*	$35	£22.97 ($42.94)
Nintendo Game Boy Advance SP	$80	£59.57 ($111.36)

Note: All prices before local sales tax
*Called the 344 cartridge in Europe.

Sources: Apple, Argos Amazon, HP, PC World

(Cont.)

the ones sold in the U.S., which cost nearly 30% less than in Europe, come with a single-voltage power adaptor that won't work in Europe. (So does the new Nintendo DS hand-held game machine, although it's not yet available in Europe.) Nintendo's older Game Boy Advance operated on batteries, which could be bought anywhere, but the newer machines must be recharged with a power adaptor.

That means the newer game consoles sold in the U.S. can't be recharged in Europe. The result: a cottage industry of substitute power adaptors. One dealer, Matthew Hudd, owner of U.K. online retailer Console Plus, says he sells 500 to 600 multivoltage adaptors a year, at about $10 each, that are specifically designed for U.S. or Japanese Game Boys used in Europe.

"Nintendo's power adaptors are designed to comply with the regulations found in the region in which they are sold," says Beth Llewe-lyn, a spokeswoman for Nintendo of America. "While the effect on gray-market trafficking is helpful, it is not Nintendo's primary design concern." She declined to elaborate.

James Kanter in Brussels contributed to this article.

From *The Wall Street Journal,* January 17, 2005. Reprinted by permission of Dow Jones and Co., Inc. via The Copyright Clearance Center.

88

New Destination

Airlines, Facing Cost Pressure, Outsource Crucial Safety Tasks

Heavy Maintenance on Planes Entrusted to Contractors; A Busy Hub in El Salvador

Ms. Biddle Is Laid Off Twice

SUSAN CAREY IN CHICAGO AND ALEX FRANGOS IN COMALAPA, EL SALVADOR.
WALL STREET JOURNAL.

JetBlue Airways doesn't offer passenger service to El Salvador. But this year, the discount airline will fly at least 17 of its 68 Airbus A320 jets to that country.

There, over six days, local mechanics working for an aircraft-overhaul shop under contract to JetBlue will inspect each plane nose to tail. They'll examine hydraulic and pneumatic systems, lubricate joints, service brakes and paint tray tables and toilet seats. Then the jets will fly back to the U.S.

America West Airlines also is sending some of its planes to El Salvador for check-ups required by the U.S. Federal Aviation Administration. Northwest Airlines flies wide-body jets to Singapore and Hong Kong for service by outside contractors.

As beleaguered U.S. airlines seek to cut costs, they are outsourcing a job that is crucial to passenger safety: long-term maintenance. While airlines continue to use their own mechanics for lighter maintenance between flights to ensure punctuality, half of U.S. carriers' heavy-overhaul work is now performed by outside vendors in the U.S. and overseas. That's up from less than a third in 1990, says consulting firm BACK Aviation Solutions in New Haven, Conn. The world-wide aircraft maintenance market is worth an estimated $37 billion annually.

Although U.S. airlines have had a good safety record recently, with 34 deaths from crashes on scheduled commercial flights between 2002 and 2004, some experts worry that the shift of work to third parties could

result in weaker regulatory scrutiny. Only supervisors at the outside repair stations—not individual mechanics—must be licensed by the FAA. At some shops, workers tend to be more transient and less well-trained than those employed by the airlines. Meanwhile the major U.S. airlines have been furloughing veteran mechanics.

Last year, the National Transportation Safety Board found that deficient maintenance by an outside vendor and lack of regulatory oversight contributed to a 2003 crash of a commuter flight in Charlotte, N.C., that killed 21 people.

In a 2003 report, the federal Department of Transportation's inspector-general faulted the FAA for inadequate oversight of outside contractors. Despite the rise in outsourcing, the FAA "has continued to concentrate its resources on oversight of air carriers' in-house maintenance operations," the report said. One airline outsourced 44% of its maintenance budget in 2002, the report said. The FAA did 400 inspections of that airline's own maintenance facilities but only seven at the outside shops.

The FAA concurred with the report's recommendations for tighter scrutiny of contractors. It is now phasing in rules requiring better record-keeping and training at contractors and raising the requirements for supervisors' experience.

Uniform Standards

All U.S. and foreign repair services that work on U.S. planes and parts must be authorized by the FAA and adhere to the same safety standards. James Ballough, the FAA's director of flight standards, says his branch inspects 4,500 domestic and 650 foreign repair stations. Nearly 700 inspectors are assigned to these outside servicers, while 220 inspectors look after U.S. airlines' in-house overhaul activities. Mr. Ballough concedes the FAA isn't present "for the turning of every wrench," but says "there certainly is no degradation of safety due to outsourcing."

Decades ago, airlines hired unionized employee mechanics to do most maintenance work. The jobs usually required each employee to have an FAA "airframe and power plant" license, and they paid well. Top airline technicians today can command as much as $37 an hour plus benefits. In the 1980s, U.S. airlines began sending engines for overhauls to the companies that built them, such as General Electric Co. and Rolls-Royce. Then they began seeking specialists to repair specific equipment such as landing gear and cockpit avionics.

The latest push involves outsourcing heavy inspections including those that take a few days and others, lasting as long as a month, in which planes are torn apart, inspected for cracks and wear, and then rebuilt.

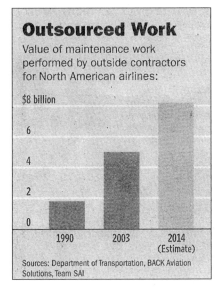

Outsourced Work

Value of maintenance work performed by outside contractors for North American airlines:

Sources: Department of Transportation, BACK Aviation Solutions, Team SAI

JetBlue's A320s go through checks every 15 months or 5,000 flight hours; the fourth check in this regimen, after 60 months, is a partial teardown and the eighth check is a big teardown. In these procedures, 65% to 80% of the total cost is labor, according to airlines and overhaul specialists.

Low-cost carriers such as Southwest Airlines and freight carriers such as FedEx Corp. have always outsourced most maintenance, but now older carriers are feeling pressure to follow suit. Even after extracting concessions from unions, the largest old-line U.S. carriers still have labor costs of $65 to $70 per employee-hour including supervisors and counting wages and benefits, according to Team SAI, a consulting firm in Lakewood, Colo. Outside shops in North America, Europe and Asia command only $40 to $50 an hour, while Latin American shops charge as little as $20 to $26.

One recent day in San Salvador, 29-year-old Oswaldo Colorado was underneath the wing of a JetBlue plane, lubricating parts for his employer, Aeroman. Aeroman is the maintenance subsidiary of Grupo Taca, a consortium of Central American carriers based in San Salvador. JetBlue started sending some of its planes to El Salvador last year. Mr. Colorado, a 10-year veteran of Aeroman, calls it "a beautiful place to work."

Aeroman was founded in 1983 and started performing third-party work in the mid-1990s. It has about 1,200 workers. Mechanics come from local technical colleges and the military, submit to lie-detector, drug and alcohol tests, and spend five to six months doing classroom work, then an equal amount of time as apprentices.

The individual mechanics have licenses from the Salvadoran aviation authority. They

(Cont.)

Cheaper Overhaul

Maintenance labor cost per hour:

Old-line North American carriers in 2001 $75–85

Old-line North American carriers today $65–70

North American outside contractors $40–50

Latin American outside contractors $20–26

Note: Figures are estimates and include cost of wages and benefits for supervisors, mechanics and other employees.

Source: Team SAI

aren't required to have an FAA license, but Aeroman pays for airfare and hotels for employees who choose to go to Miami to take the FAA exam, which is given only in English. They get a raise if they pass, and Aeroman says 30% to 40% of its technicians have these licenses.

Ranks of Inspectors

The Aeroman hangar was inspected 12 times last year by the FAA's Miami office, four times in 2003 and twice in 2002, the FAA says. Mr. Ballough says the facility also is scrutinized by other FAA inspectors assigned to JetBlue, the airline's own quality-assurance people, and the local aviation authority. Tom Anderson, JetBlue's senior vice president of technical operations and aircraft maintenance, says the facility also is examined by European regulators because it services European planes. "One could argue that the level of regulatory oversight they're getting is vastly superior to what they'd get on U.S. soil," he says.

Andres F. Garcia, Aeroman's commercial director, says the FAA checks are rigorous. "They say, 'What's that piece of paper doing there?'" he says, pointing to a candy wrapper on the shop floor that he jogs over to pick up.

Mechanics at Aeroman start at $300 a month and earn as much as $1,000 a month—a good salary in a country where per capita income is around $2,200 a year. Workers also receive pensions, private health insurance, and free airline tickets.

Aeroman recently won a contract from America West, which has overhauled its maintenance practices after being cited by the FAA for deficiencies in the late 1990s and 2000. The airline thinks outsourcing makes sense. "It's very difficult for a small airline to get the volume to do [all maintenance] in-house," says Hal Heule, America West's senior vice president for technical operations.

Outsourcing, he says, gives "a great deal of flexibility, particularly when you're growing. And it works when you're downsizing, too, because you don't have to have layoffs."

In the late 1980s, General Electric, which produces about 35% of the world's large commercial jet engines, had just three domestic shops that did engine-overhaul work for airlines. Today it has 17 facilities, half of them overseas in places like Brazil, Malaysia and Hungary. Revenues from spare engines, parts and maintenance, which stood at $3 billion a year in 1997, hit $5 billion in 2001 and, after an industry slump, are rising again, says Bill Fitzgerald, vice president of global operations for GE Aircraft Engine Services.

UAL Corp.'s United Airlines, parked in bankruptcy-court protection for more than two years, won union assent to close two heavy-maintenance bases and outsource as much work as it wants to outside vendors. Currently, planes needing heavy checkups go to Timco Aviation Services Inc., Greensboro, N.C., and ST Mobile Aerospace Engineering Inc., Mobile, Ala. In a new contract being voted on by its shrinking mechanics union, United is seeking permission to send some already-outsourced work overseas.

Greg Hall, senior vice president of the carrier's maintenance division, says United has found the outsiders' workmanship to be good. "We give them a lot of oversight," he says. "We give them training on our maintenance program and our tooling. We do frequent audits."

Northwest Airlines, also mired in losses, is bumping up against the maximum amount of work it can outsource under its contract with its mechanics. Northwest has been getting some DC-10s and 747s overhauled in Singapore, while farming out other 747 checkups to a Hong Kong servicer.

Some airlines admit to concern about turnover at contractors. Continental Airlines, which farms out about 60% of its maintenance work excluding line maintenance at airports, says it pulled out of some third-party sites in the 1990s because of high turnover. Southwest, which has an excellent safety record, has done the same on occasion. "We don't want transient labor on our aircraft," says Jim Sokel, Southwest's vice president of maintenance and engineering.

AMR Corp.'s American Airlines outsources only 20% of its maintenance. It keeps all of its heavy airframe checks in-house, says spokesman John Hotard, because it has "much more control over the whole repair process" and "a well-trained, seasoned work force." Still, to vie with competitors getting the work done for less, he says, American is working with its mechanics union to reduce costs.

Given that many vendors don't require FAA licenses and don't pay as much as the airlines, they are getting "warm bodies coming in off the street," says Brian Finnegan, president of the Professional Aviation Maintenance Association, a trade group that gets some support from mechanics' unions. "I don't take exception with the idea of outsourcing. I just want those people to be well-trained and supervised," says Mr. Finnegan.

Philip Anson Jr., president of STS Services, a Jensen Beach, Fla., company that places mechanics in maintenance jobs around the country, says outside vendors with which he is familiar generally pay up to $20 an hour.

Laid-off airline technicians are showing little appetite for the new jobs being created in their field. "We've lost a lot of guys to building maintenance and the police department," says Richard Turk, a United mechanic and union spokesman in San Francisco. "Most are smart enough to stay out of the airline business."

"The industry is losing its skills," says John Goglia, a former mechanic who recently stepped down after nine years as a member of the National Transportation Safety Board.

Jennifer Biddle, a mechanic at United's sprawling San Francisco maintenance base, was laid off in 2003 after eight years. She found a similar job in Oakland, Calif., for Alaska Airlines, only to lose that last September when Alaska shuttered its facility. Ms. Biddle, 39 years old, was a relatively junior mechanic although she held an FAA license gained after two years of schooling. She earned $63,000 a year at United before she was laid off.

She now works for a company that repairs laboratory equipment for the pharmaceutical and biotechnology industries, earning 30% less than she did at United. "I love airplanes," she says. "I wish I was still working on airplanes."

Melanie Trottman and Evan Perez contributed to this article.

From *The Wall Street Journal*, January 21, 2005. Reprinted by permission of Dow Jones and Co., Inc. via The Copyright Clearance Center.

Ethical Marketing in a Consumer-Oriented World: Appraisal and Challenges

89

BRANDING: FIVE NEW LESSONS

The P&G purchase of Gillette shows that innovation is key, and marketing is more diffuse and personal

The last time detergent and toothpaste giant Procter & Gamble Co. made a bid for razormaker Gillette Co., it was out of desperation. Back in 2000, when the Cincinnati giant made an unsolicited bid, Gillette was a bargain: Despite its hit Mach3 razor, a series of earnings disappointments had hammered the stock. P&G was struggling, too, and so were a lot of other once-invincible brands. With fracturing TV audiences moving to the Web and cable, the classic 30-second spot that had made household names of the likes of Mr. Clean and Tide was losing traction. Consumers were starting to identify more with niche markets than with the one-size-fits-all brands that had long been the backbone of the consumer-products industry. Retail shelves were stocked with private-label rivals. Most frightening of all: The information-packed Internet threatened to expose those brands as nothing special. The age of the giant, mass-market brand seemed to be dead—and so was a P&G-Gillette deal.

Oh, what a different story it was on Jan. 28 when it was announced that the wedding was on. Sales growth at both companies is on a tear, earnings and margins are up, and hit products are rolling out of their labs. P&G's sales growth is running at 8% a year, excluding acquisitions—double the rate of the late 1990s. And the once-struggling razormaker fetched a price of $57 billion, 19 times earnings before interest, taxes, and depreciation. Why did Gillette do the deal? "I have a simple formula," says CEO James Kilts. "Strength plus strength equals success."

Are brands back? Well, yes and no. Well, yes and no. It's not that the doomsayers were all wrong. Media are becoming infinitely more complex. Big retailers—especially Wal-Mart Stores Inc.—are more powerful than ever, pressuring the profits that big brands need to fuel marketing and innovation. And every year surveys show consumers becoming more cynical about advertising. No wonder so many brands have faltered: Coca-Cola, Levi Strauss, Kodak, Ford—the list goes on.

But the savviest brand managers have adapted, creating a new paradigm in which innovation is king, marketing is diffuse and personal, and size can be an advantage. Nothing shows this more than perennial No. 1 detergent Tide, where P&G's stepped-up consumer research, brand extensions, and ads have reawakened it within a moribund category.

Here are five lessons from classic companies and upstarts alike. All are thriving by managing brands differently than companies did in the heyday of the mass market.

1 INNOVATE. INNOVATE. INNOVATE.

Why would P&G tinker with Tide? Long the detergent leader, Tide would seem best left alone, a profitable annuity on years of mass-market flogging in the '60s, '70s, and '80s. But P&G has tinkered nonetheless, combining strong technology and consumer research to push sales up 2.6% over the last year in a category that is growing less than 1%. The secret: a widening family of detergents and cleaners that now includes everything from Tide Coldwater, for coldwater washing, to Tide Kick, a combination measuring cup and stain penetrator.

Innovation isn't always built from scratch. P&G is a master at transferring technologies from one brand to another. Tide StainBrush, a new electric brush for removing stains, uses the same basic mechanism as the Crest SpinBrush Pro toothbrush—also a P&G brand. Gillette, too, is adept at cross-pollination. Its latest winner is the battery-operated M3Power, the result of a collaboration between the company's razor, Duracell battery, and Braun small-appliance units. Despite a 50% price premium over what Gillette charged for its previous top-of-the-line razor, the M3Power has captured a 35% share of the U.S. razor market in seven months.

2 MOVE FAST—OR LOSE OUT

Not only are customers hooked on innovation, they're demanding it faster. Handbag designer Coach Inc. once introduced new products quarterly; now they come out monthly. On Coach's Web site, the new line currently features a bevy of options, from a $498 suede tote bag covered in an oversized pink and purple logo pattern to the "Coach Soho Nappa Small Tortilla," a white leather number with a tassel and a $328 price tag. "For brands to stay relevant, they have to stay on their toes. Complacency has no place in this market," says CEO Lew Frankfort. In any given month, Frankfort says, new products account for 30% of U.S. retail store sales.

3 MINIMIZE EXPOSURE TO WAL-MART

Wal-Mart is the key customer for any consumer product brand today. But balancing those sales with plenty of others is vital to a brand's health: For most suppliers, the more you sell to the world's biggest retailer, the less you make. In a recent study by consultant Bain & Co. of 38 companies doing 10% or more of their volume through Wal-Mart, only 24% sustained above-average profitability and shareholder returns. P&G, which sells 18% of its goods through Wal-Mart, was one. It has done so by shifting business away from basic products such as paper towels, which can easily be knocked off by a private label, to higher-margin products such as health and beauty care, including its line of Olay skin products.

It's not as if Wal-Mart is the only game in town—though sometimes it might seem that way. Besides low prices, Americans crave convenience. Increasingly, consumers are shunning supermarkets and buying food at convenience stores, fast-food outlets, club stores, and elsewhere. Recognizing that, Kellogg Co. began thinking outside the supermarket aisle in 2001 when it bought Keebler Co. and its links to vending machines. Now, Nutri-Grain bars, Pop-Tarts, and even single-serving cereal bowls are available at many more places, and the Battle Creek (Mich.) company has gone from providing breakfast cereals to round-the-clock snacks.

4 THE NEW MEDIA MESSAGE

The splintering media, it turns out, hasn't been all bad. P&G is a longtime master of what a former exec calls "surround-sound marketing"—everything from in-store demos to pitches on Wal-Mart TV, engulfing shoppers in the brand message. But it has also become a pioneer of new techniques, such as integrating its Crest Whitening Expressions

(Cont.)

Refreshing Vanilla Mint into a recent episode of the TV show *The Apprentice.* The goal is to both target specific customers and to fit the medium to the message. When research showed that girls wanted to know more about Tampax, P&G shifted a chunk of advertising from TV to print and created a Web site called Beinggirl.com. "It's hard to convey a lot of information and stuff that's kind of personal in a 30-second TV ad," says Ted Woehrle, vice-president for North American marketing. "Print and online were terrific."

5 THINK BROADLY

Rather than define itself by its products, P&G has expanded its mandate to become a solver of every problem in the home. While toothpaste rival Colgate-Palmolive Co. was focusing on the tube, P&G grabbed greater "share of the mouth" with innovations such as the inexpensive spin toothbrush and premium-priced Whitestrips teeth-whitening kits.

Apple Computer Inc., which was late to market with its digital music player, the iPod, took the lead nevertheless with a combination of great product design and marketing brains. But why were consumers willing to accept a computer maker as a consumer-electronics company? Because Apple made its brand stand not for desktop computing but for imagination and fun. "The iPod is about creative people doing creative things," says David Placek, president of Lexicon Branding in Sausalito, Calif.

Such thinking can fuel a rise to mega-brand status in a fraction of the time it once took. The proof: Starbucks Corp. The Seattle-based coffee chain does plenty of core innovation. Credit for part of its holiday profit surge of 31.2% belongs to its new pumpkin spice latte. But that's just the start. Anne Saunders, senior vice-president for marketing, sees the cafes not just as a place to slurp java but as somewhere "to connect with other people or as a getaway." That broader vision has led to offerings such as music and wireless Web connections.

Today, 30 million people visit a Starbucks each week. The average customer stops in 18 times a month. With no tagline and sparse traditional advertising, Starbucks has gone from an idea to being one of the most popular and valuable brands on the planet in under 20 years. "Starbucks, based on the old model, shouldn't be able to happen," says Kelly O'Keefe, CEO at brand strategy firm Emergence. But it has—and it's a whole new world.

Nanette Byrnes in New York and Robert Berner in Chicago, with Wendy Zellner in Dallas, William. Business Week.

90

Car Seats for 8-Year-Olds

States Toughen Laws Requiring Kids to Be Restrained in Vehicles; Finding One Your Child Will Use

MICHELLE HIGGINS. WALL STREET JOURNAL.

PARENTS WHO STOPPED wrestling their kids into car seats years ago may soon have to flex those muscles again.

A growing number of states are requiring children as old as 8—kids who have outgrown basic car seats, but who still are too small to use regular seat belts—to sit in booster seats. The seats, which cost as much as $70, are designed to raise a child up so that a regular seat belt can rest properly across his or her lap and shoulders. The concern is that, without such a seat, regular seat belts can pose a risk of abdominal or spinal-cord injuries to children.

Booster-seat laws, aimed at older children, have been on the books in some places since at least 2000. But efforts to toughen the rules, spurred by new research, are keeping more kids in seats for more years. Car-seat makers, seeing an expanded market—and aware that most kids resist the restraints long before they are 8 years old—are trying to design new models that will appeal to both parents and kids.

Six states passed or expanded their booster-seat laws in 2004, with most changes going into effect this year; those states include Indiana, North Carolina and New York. Several more states, including Connecticut and Minnesota, have legislation pending. These efforts follow those of 22 states and the District of Columbia, which have put such laws in place during the past four years.

In December, the National Highway Traffic Safety Administration issued a requirement that all new cars, SUVs and pickup trucks include lap-and-shoulder belts—which work with boosters—in the middle rear seat. Right now, an NHTSA spokeswoman said,

only 20% at most of kids who need to be in boosters actually use them.

While the state laws vary in their requirements, the upshot is that millions of parents are being told to keep their children in better, safer restraints until they are 5, 6, or even 8 years old, or reach a certain height or weight.

A 2003 study by Partners for Child Passenger Safety, funded by **State Farm** and conducted by the Children's Hospital of Philadelphia, found that use of a booster seat, instead of a seat belt alone, reduced injuries 59% for children ages 4 through 7 involved in crashes. Injuries ranged from facial lacerations to serious brain and spinal-cord injuries.

Car seats for infants and toddlers, first required by a state law in 1977, provide a complete seat-and-strap system, locked into place by the car's own seat belt. Booster seats, by contrast, are designed to position the child better to use the existing lap and shoulder belt. The seat raises the child and uses loops or guides to keep the belt resting properly across the child's lap and shoulders.

Eyeing this potential market, car-seat makers such as **Evenflo** Co. Inc. of Vandalia, Ohio, are bringing out boosters with an added cool quotient, such as built-in cup holders, armrests and reading lights, to help parents keep kids belted in longer—or woo back those who thought they long ago had graduated to grown-up seats.

This fall, Graco Children's Products of Exton, Pa., a division of **Newell Rubbermaid** Inc., launched a series of $70 booster seats with gender-specific patterns—Disney Princess cartoons for girls and Toy Story characters for boys.

And some companies are gearing up to meet demand for the booster seats in states

with new laws. "It's been a frenzy. There's none in stock anywhere" in North Carolina, where a law went into effect this month, says Joyce Kara, product manager for **Britax Child Safety** Inc., a Charlotte, N.C., unit of a U.K.-based company.

Several companies also make backless booster seats, which some kids prefer. From outside the vehicle, it looks like they are riding in a regular seat—a key feature for an 8-year-old arriving at soccer practice. These seats can be purchased for as low as $20, but should be used only in cars with high seat backs and headrests and only if the strap lies correctly across the shoulder.

Safe Traffic System Inc. in Lincolnwood, Ill., makes a $130 vest, styled like a robot or space costume, that uses a series of clips to position the seat belt appropriately. The RideSafer Travel Vest is designed to distribute crash force over a wider area of the body, decreasing potential injuries.

The first law on booster seats was enacted in 2000 in Washington state, according to Advocates for Highway and Auto Safety, a Washington, D.C.-based nonprofit. That law, which went into effect in 2002, was spurred by the death in 1996 of 4-year-old Anton Skeen, who was riding in an SUV and strapped in with just an adult seat belt. Also in 2002, Congress passed "Anton's Law," which required NHTSA to raise standards for booster seats and car restraint systems.

But only the laws in eight states and the District of Columbia cover children all the way to age 8, according to Advocates for Highway Safety. In 20 other states, the laws cover children only up to age 5, 6 or 7. NHTSA's recommendation, updated in 2002, specifies that children should be in booster seats "until they are at least 8 years old, unless they are 4' 9" tall." NHTSA emphasizes

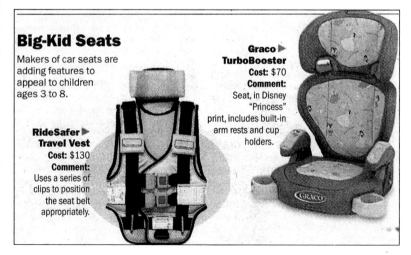

Big-Kid Seats

Makers of car seats are adding features to appeal to children ages 3 to 8.

RideSafer ▶ Travel Vest
Cost: $130
Comment: Uses a series of clips to position the seat belt appropriately.

Graco ▶ TurboBooster
Cost: $70
Comment: Seat, in Disney "Princess" print, includes built-in arm rests and cup holders.

(Cont.)

height rather than weight, the agency says, because it is a better guide to how children will fit in a seat belt.

Enforcement also varies. In some states, drivers can be stopped and ticketed if a child is riding without the proper restraint. In other states, drivers are ticketed only if stopped for another violation. (At about $10 to $25, penalties are usually modest.)

In North Carolina, the law that took effect this month requires children to ride in booster seats until they are 8 years old or 80 pounds. Sgt. Everett Clendenin, of the North Carolina highway patrol, says he can stop a driver if he sees a child who isn't properly restrained, or, for example, during a license check. But, he says, "What we do is take the parents' word" for it that a kid is big enough to be out of a booster seat. "Obviously we don't carry scales with us."

If a booster seat is used properly, the lap belt should rest below the child's hip bones, touch the thighs, and be snug. The shoulder belt should cross the center of the child's shoulder and not cut across the neck. To find NHTSA-certified technicians who can help install seats, parents can go to www.nhtsa. dot.gov/CPS/CPSFitting/Index.cfm. For a list of booster-seat laws by state go to saferoads. org/issues/BoosterSeatLawChart.pdf.

Parents do a pretty good job putting infants and toddlers in the right seats. In a study of crashes in 2003 involving children, Partners for Passenger Safety found that child restraints had been used for 100% of children younger than 1 and 96% of 3-year-olds, compared with 59% of 5-year-olds, 14% of 7-year-olds and 9% of 8-year-olds. Those figures showed increased use of child restraints over a study in 1999.

From *The Wall Street Journal,* January 27, 2005. Reprinted by permission of Dow Jones and Co., Inc. via The Copyright Clearance Center.

91

Drug Ills? Follow the Money

Do drug companies spend too much on marketing? Is marketing driving up drug prices? A close look at financial reports separates fact from fiction.

By Jim Edwards, Brandweek

Last year, Merck CEO Raymond Gilmartin gave two public policy speeches in which he displayed copies of *Time* magazine from 1952 and 2004. The older edition featured a photo of company founder George Merck and the quote, "Medicine is for people, not for profits." (Gilmartin keeps a copy in his office in a glass case.) The more recent issue carried the headline: "Why Your Drugs Cost So Much: Who's to Blame; What We Can Do About It."

"Today," said the CEO, "the pharmaceutical industry is far too often seen as a vehicle for greed, putting profits over patients."

Though he's been hit especially hard—the withdrawal of Merck's pain reliever Vioxx has already cost the company $1.3 billion in lost revenue and legal expenses—Gilmartin is not alone. Recently, several Big Pharma CEOs lamented that their companies are being bashed on the issues of drug pricing and marketing.

Last September, for instance, Novartis urged its employees to use generic prescription drugs to cut its healthcare costs, according to trade publication *Generic Line.* The magazine raised the question of whether drug prices have gotten so high that "one of the world's largest drugmakers no longer can pay for Rx medicines for employees."

The public's distrust of the pharmaceutical industry is "deeply troubling," AstraZeneca CEO Tom McKillop told the Pharmaceutical Leadership Forum on Nov. 16. His company has been sued over the marketing for its prescription heartburn medication Nexium; suits allege the drug is not significantly more effective than its less expensive OTC remedy Prilosec, even though the marketing claimed it was.

What is missing from this picture, however, is a detailed look at marketing expenditures and an analysis of the impact of such spending on the price of drugs.

A close inspection of financial reports reveals that the top 10 drug companies spend between two and three times on marketing what they spend on research. Marketing at those companies accounted for anywhere from 26% to 33% of sales. (In other industries, a more typical sales to marketing ratio would be 5-15%.) Put another way, for every dollar drug companies make in sales,

the first 26 cents, at least, goes to marketing. For some drug companies, such as Pfizer, the cost of marketing is the single biggest corporate expense, greater than either research or manufacturing.

It is statistics like that which have kept the public's attention on the rising cost of drugs and on the cost of the advertising that promotes them.

According to a study by the U.S. Government Accountability Office, drug prices jumped 21.8% between 2000 and 2004, or three to four times the rate of inflation. A similar study, published by the policy research group Families USA in June 2004, found a 22% price increase in the most commonly used remedies among the elderly since 2001. The price of asthma treatment Combivent, for example, increased 56% during the period, per the study.

At the same time, spending on direct-to-consumer advertising surpassed $3.8 billion in 2004, per Nielsen MonitorPlus. Industry critics claim that increasing expenditures on drug advertising and promotion are fueling rising prices, which are in turn passed down to patients in the form of higher bills.

"The industry average for research and development is about 15% [of sales]," said Jerry Flanagan, healthcare policy director at the Foundation for Taxpayer and Consumer Rights. "Profit is twice R&D and marketing is two to three times as much. Every dollar spend on marketing means the price of drugs will be more expensive."

In their defense, pharmaceutical firms often cite the exorbitant costs of research and development, which average more than $800 million per new remedy, according to the lobbying group Pharmaceutical Research and Manufacturers of America.

"R&D is risky, time-consuming and very costly. The drug approval process spans 12 to 15 years," said PhRMA spokesman Jeff Trewhitt. "On average four out of every five potential new medicines going into testing fail, generally for toxicity reasons . . . Companies lose millions of dollars on a single failed research project."

Who is right?

Consider the companies' own figures: The top 10 drug companies took in a total of $293 billion in global sales in 2003, the last year for which complete figures are available. (Comparable numbers, available in the next

(Cont.)

BIG PHARMA'S BIG SPENDING				
Top pharmaceutical companies, 2003 sales	Sales (billions)	Marketing and admin (billions)	Research & development (billions)	Advertising (millions)
1. PFIZER	$45.2	$15.2	$7.1	$644
2. JOHNSON & JOHNSON	41.9	14.1	4.6	232
3. GLAXOSMITHKLINE*	38.2	14. 2	5.2	487
4. BAYER**	35.9	10.6	2.4	44
5. ROCHE***	25.1	8.4	4.0	9
6. NOVARTIS	24.9	9.3	3.7	199
7. MERCK	22.5	6.3	3.1	342
8. BRISTOL MYERS-SQUIBB	20.9	4.6	2.3	142
9. ABBOTT	19.7	5.0	1.7	4
10. ASTRAZENECA	18.9	6.8	3.4	264
TOTALS:	293.2	96.4	37.9	2,367

Converted from: *pounds, **euros, ***Swiss francs

Sources: Hoover's Online, SEC filings/annual reports, SEC/annual reports, U.S. media spend/Nielsen Monitor-Plus

few weeks, are expected for 2004.) During the period, those companies spent $37.9 billion on research and development, or about 13% of sales. The companies' costs for marketing and administration far exceeded research at $96.4 billion, or about 33% of sales.

In typical annual reports, "marketing and administration" are recorded as one item, and most companies do not delineate between promotional activity and routine office bills. Only three of the top 10 firms—Bayer Group, Roche Group and Novartis—actually itemize the two expenses. In these cases, administration is a small minority of the total, between 13.8% and 20.6%.

It is not clear whether than range is a rough industry standard. Some corporations have large non-drug businesses, like Johnson & Johnson, and their cost ratios are likely to be different than Merck's, whose entire business is drugs. Even so, administration is expected to be a minority of the total, said David Moskowitz, managing director for healthcare at investment bank Friedman Billings Ramsey, Arlington, Va.

Taking the conservative end of the range, one can extrapolate that the top 10 companies spend $76.5 billion on marketing, or about 26% of sales. That's still twice what those companies spend on research.

The way drug companies delineate their expenditures can become slippery. In an October conference call to analysts, AstraZeneca "reclassified" $460 million out of "research" and into "marketing." The move did not go unnoticed.

"The size of the reclassification I think is quite substantial," said London's Redburn Partners analyst Paul Major, who followed with the question, "I was wondering if you could flesh out a little bit [why] you think what you have done is in line with industry practice."

AZ CFO Jon Symonds replied that it didn't make much difference. "There is a degree of discretion as to whether you do a local clinical Phase IV trial, or you do a different form of local product promotion," he said.

Symonds' implication—that certain clinical trials and local promotions are interchangeable—cuts to the heart of one of the main criticisms of the way the industry touts its commitment to research as a driver of prices. Drug companies have long paid hundreds of doctors to monitor their patients in massive tests of drugs that are already approved and on the market. In return, the company gets a little bit of post-market information about the drug's performance.

The main function of these trials is to get doctors into the habit of prescribing the drug being tested, critics contend, which is why Symonds was able to shift a sum larger than the entire ad budget of Verizon Wireless from "research" to "marketing."

"It's a major way to seed the market," explained Donald Light, a professor of comparative healthcare systems at Princeton University. "They plant the seeds for growing the market by paying physicians . . . a lot of money to recruit patients."

Such efforts also contradict the popular notion that

companies overspend on DTC advertising. As the financial statements confirm, DTC spending is a tiny fraction (about 2%) of average drug marketing activity. The real money—around $76.5 billion—is spent marketing drugs to doctors via ads in medical journals, free drug samples, office visits and entertainment at thousands of annual drug education seminars, dinners and lectures.

On paper, spiraling DTC spending is a red herring in the debate over drug pricing, a point on which even tight-lipped pharmaceutical firms are willing to speak out. "Our spending on direct-to-consumer advertising does not impact the price of drugs," said Michael Fishman, a Pfizer rep. "It's so minimal compared to the amount we spend on research and development. We spend more than 10 times on research and development what we do on [DTC] advertising."

While that is true, it is not the whole picture. The TV ads may draw the most scrutiny, but the real money gets spent on the sales reps, aka "detailers." Detailers visit doctors' offices carrying free samples of new pills they hope doctors will prescribe to their patients—the same way salesmen used to go door to door to sell vacuum cleaners.

From 1996 to 2001, industry-wide spending on detailing rose from $4.9 billion to $9 billion, according to the Blue Cross/Blue Shield Assn. In a similar period, the number of sales reps more than doubled, from about 42,000 to 90,000. Currently, there are between 80,000 and 100,000 detailers in the U.S., and about 500,000 doctors. Doctors can get five or six visits per day from sales reps. "Those ratios are pretty scary," said a pharma ad agency exec. "The average [salary] cost of a sales rep is about $100,000 a year . . . The fully loaded cost with benefits and cars goes far beyond that."

The retail value of the "free" samples is also enormous: $13.1 billion in the 12 months ending in September 2003, according to IMS Health, and another $15.4 billion in the same period for 2004.

Those are some pretty big numbers, and experts say they do, in fact, impact drug prices. Even John Calfee, a resident scholar at the conservative think tank American Enterprise Institute, admits that marketing "is certainly not irrelevant" to pricing. But most industry executives stick to the official line—that prices are driven by research.

"As much as people don't want to hear it, what drives the cost of drugs is how much it costs [in research] to get the damn drugs to market," said the pharma agency exec. "The number of years, the number of people, the number of clinical trials."

That argument may be wearing thin in Washington. Lawmakers are so concerned about the rising cost of drugs that several senators are urging bills that would allow U.S. citizens to buy prescriptions in Canada, where the government wields firm control over pricing. If such a reform were passed, drug marketers would find themselves in a price war with their own products, which are currently sold more cheaply across the border.

One bill is supported by John McCain (R-Ariz.), Trent Lott (R-Miss.) and Edward Kennedy (D-Mass.), a bipartisan coalition that may be enough to pass the legislation. "If [they] can get a clean floor vote they might have as many as 75 votes," predicted Bill Vaughan, director of government relations at Families USA. "That would send this issue back to the House, which has twice indicated over its leadership's opposition that they want to do something in this area."

The stakes in the debate go beyond what consumers will end up paying for their medications. "Policy makers are literally debating the future of the industry and how it's going to work in the next decade, and they're saying something has got to give," said Matt Giegerich, CEO of CommonHealth, a Parsippany, N.J., agency that counts several of the top drug companies as clients. "It could be the pricing model, it could be the role of the government, it could be the marketing."

However, is it fair to make a direct correlation between marketing costs and higher drug prices? At a basic level, the answer is yes. For most pharma companies, marketing is a major cost that companies need to cover in order to stay in business. But there are other schools of thought.

The industry's official line, as previously stated, is that the cost of research and development, not marketing, hikes the price of drugs.

"What driving up the price of drugs? At the end of the day it really is the cost of innovation," agreed Giegerich.

The other is a more complicated explanation, which argues that the fluctuations of the market dictate prices and companies simply tailor their expenses to stay competitive within that changing framework.

Research costs aren't a driving factor any more than marketing, said AEI's Calfee. "I know they sometimes say that but I think it's a mistake."

Calfee insists that drug prices are set by the market. Pharma companies work "backwards," he said, when considering whether to launch a new product. They try to estimate how many people might need the new drug, the prices of rival drugs and then they select the price.

(Cont.)

Only then do they factor in the cost of marketing and development.

The backwards calculation, experts say, is a nebulous one. Supply and demand are regulated by doctors and patients who don't know the real price of the drugs, and by pharmacies and benefit managers who can negotiate bulk prices downward but can't control what patients want or what doctors prescribe.

Thus, the drug companies are engaged in the equivalent of a series of boxing matches in which half the fighters are blindfolded and the rest have one hand tied behind their backs.

"The biggest challenge in the system is the transparency of prices," said one major drug company executive who asked not to be named. "What's wrong with it is nobody really knows what anything costs at the time they buy it . . . From the patient's perspective all medicines cost the same because they're paying the same co-pay."

In this school of thought, what consumers are actually complaining about is not the price of individual drugs but the total cost of their drug bills. Those bills have been rising because consumers are simply taking more drugs, not because each individual drug is getting more expensive. Blue Cross recorded that there were 7.8 prescriptions issued per capita in 1993. By 2001, it was 10.9.

The only flaw in this argument is the *reason* consumers are taking more drugs, which goes back to marketing. A study by Harvard University's schools of medicine and public health, published in 2003, found that for every 10% increase in DTC advertising, drug sales rose 1%.

That does not sound too impressive until it is translated into hard cash: Every additional dollar spent on DTC yielded an average of $4.20 in sales.

The bottom line? Americans' drug bills are going up because we're taking more drugs. And we're taking more drugs because the marketing works.

Drug companies seem to realize they have marketed themselves into the center of a storm, from which the escape route is not clear. Executives have retrenched even further in their public discussions of marketing and pricing ever since Congress started drafting the Canadian drug legislation. None of the top drug companies agreed to speak to *Brandweek* at any length regarding prices and the impact of marketing.

In the courts, Merck has been hit with hundreds of suits over Vioxx, a once heavily marketed pain reliever that may increase the risk of heart attacks. The Food and Drug Administration cited five of the top 10 drug companies for misleading advertising last year. Pfizer and Abbott Laboratories were warned twice. In recent weeks the FDA has highlighted misleading ads for pain relievers Celebrex, Crestor and Bextra.

Chastened, some industry insiders hope to see Big Pharma tone down their ads and lower their prices.

"Once a drug has been on the market for a number of years and it's a monstrous success, like Lipitor, for those drugs to take price increases, I don't know how the companies can justify that," said the ad agency exec, who asked not to be identified. "The price initially is reasonable, it's priced to recoup what's in development and marketing . . . But by year three, four or five, that's where you have to wonder about the sanity of some companies."

Still, there are also true believers, like Common-Health's Giegerich. "I don't think it's gone too far. Consumers need to know about their choices," he said. "It's going to be an interesting year."

At Merck's headquarters in Whitehouse Station, N.J., CEO Gilmartin still has both copies of *Time*. He might not like the more recent cover, with its cynical take on drug industry profits, but it gave him an idea of how consumers see his company.

"Not only is this [magazine] cover not hanging in my office," he said during one of his speeches, "the mail room wasn't even sure they should deliver it."

92

Lost in Translation

A European Electronics Giant Races to Undo Mistakes in U.S.

Philips Is Big Name at Home, But American Unit Muffed Chances to Build Identity

Now, Get Profitable or Close

By Dan Bilefsky

NEW YORK—For years, every time the Dutch bosses of Philips Electronics NV came here for a visit, Terry Fassburg would take them to Union Square, an area blanketed with electronics stores.

Then Mr. Fassburg, the communications chief for the company's U.S. operations, would bet them $100 that they couldn't find three products made by Philips, Europe's biggest consumer-electronics company. He never lost. "It was my way of showing European executives we needed help," Mr. Fassburg says.

Despite its role in inventing hundreds of products, including the compact disc and the audio-cassette recorder, Philips's consumer-electronics division has lost money in the U.S. for the past 15 years. Meanwhile, through a long string of self-inflicted fiascoes, it has watched many of its inventions become blockbusters in the U.S.—for its rivals.

Now Philips's troubled North American consumer-electronics division is facing its toughest challenge yet. About two years ago headquarters in Amsterdam ordered the operation to show a yearly profit for 2004—or be shut down. The division seemed to be making progress toward that goal under a new U.S. chief executive, Larry Blanford. He introduced a host of marketing and distribution efforts and helped dramatically shrink the division's losses. But Mr. Blanford has announced his resignation, and Gerard Kleisterlee, Philips's CEO, hasn't backed down from his threat to jettison the U.S. division.

"We are in the business to make profits, and we can't support operations that continue to destroy value for shareholders," Mr. Kleisterlee said in a recent interview.

Selling off the division, which accounts for roughly 9% of the company's total sales of $41 billion, would leave one of the world's leading electronics companies without a foothold in the world's largest electronics market. And it might make other European companies, which are closely watching Philips's moves, question the extent of their investments in the U.S.

In Europe, the Philips name resonates with both history and contemporary cool. The Eiffel Tower is strung with Philips light bulbs, the product that launched the company in 1891, and today Philips gadgets mesmerize European teenagers at hip electronics stores. But in the U.S., Philips's consumer-electronics division has distinguished itself largely by its disasters: a mix of marketing and distribution problems that undermined some groundbreaking products.

That was partly because Philips since the 1970s had primarily been known as the low-end brand Philips-Magnavox. Philips executives had calculated that they needed the large scale of low-end sales to be profitable, so they focused their marketing on less-expensive items instead of the upmarket products that were a hit overseas. The move hurt Philips's profit margin and deprived it of upmarket European cachet in the U.S.

A recent study by Philips showed that only about 35% of Americans recognize that Philips is a consumer-electronics company. Though brand image and loyalty are everything in the U.S. consumer-electronics business, Philips until recently treated marketing in the U.S. as an afterthought. Meanwhile, throughout the industry, competition from brand names and knockoffs alike has grown fiercer and profit margins have fallen to less than 1% on some products. Sony Corp. was forced to overhaul its consumer-electronics operation this autumn, shedding 20,000 jobs.

Reinier Jens, Philips's new U.S. CEO, acknowledges that a full turnaround—including a high U.S. profile for the Philips brand and big profits—is still a ways off. "You do not build a brand in one or two years," says Mr. Jens, a Dutchman who was until recently the London-based chief of Philips's Northern European consumer-electronics division. "It will take more time."

Cautionary Tale

Philips's history has been a cautionary tale. Though the company's engineers co-developed CD technology with Sony Corp., Philips lost out on U.S. profits because of its position as a low-end brand. Analysts estimate the company suffered $1 billion in losses between 1991 and 1996 with its CD-i machine, which let consumers play video games, listen to music CDs, watch movies and view digital photos. The product was chased from store shelves by Sony's PlayStation. Philips's version, which was pitched as a teaching device as much as a game machine, lacked its frenetic thrills. Even worse, the product was so complicated that it required a 30-minute demonstration.

In 1997, years before its competitors, Philips launched a $250 million U.S. advertising campaign for flat-screen TVs. But the company didn't get them into most stores until the market was overcrowded. "We ended up creating a buzz around the brand and then handed the flat television market to our rivals," says Mr. Blanford. One reason was the company's poor relations with upmarket retailers.

Matthew Foley, a manager at Provideo, an upmarket electronics retailer in Washington's

Oceans Apart

Troubles in America...
Losses at Philips's North American consumer-electronics division, in millions

Are a drain on the company
Philips's net income/loss, in billions of dollars

Note: Philips adopted U.S. generally accepted accounting principles (GAAP) on Jan. 1, 2002. All years have been restated accordingly. Figures are converted from euros at current rate.

Source: the company

Georgetown neighborhood, says retailers like him didn't take the flat-screen TV because of Philips's low brand recognition and because the company priced the sets too high. Indeed, when potential customers could find the sets, they were stunned to discover that they cost $15,000. Philips's rivals quickly produced their own models, many at cheaper prices.

Attempts to capture the U.S. markets for digital cable boxes and cellphones also faltered. Philips was among the first to come up with mobile-phone technology but was beat to the market by rivals while Philips divisions debated their model's design.

Such ventures weren't a total drain for Philips. In 2002, its global royalty revenue on inventions it helped create, such as the CD player, was $340 million.

When Mr. Blanford took over as U.S. CEO in 2001, he emphasized improving distribution, particularly at high-end stores. By wooing U.S. retailers and placing Philips on shelves where it had never been, he helped shrink the division's losses from $372 million in 2001 to $250 million in 2002 and $88 million through the first three quarters of 2003. Philips doesn't release revenue numbers for the division.

Mr. Blanford says he was stunned to discover that Philips's 12 U.S. salespeople never visited upmarket electronics stores. Tweeter, one of the biggest electronics chains in the U.S., with 175 stores in 21 states across the country, didn't carry a single Philips television.

Mr. Blanford increased the sales force to 50, and ordered salespeople into retail stores at least three times a week. He also left his Atlanta headquarters to visit the CEOs of Tweeter and Best Buy. "Larry was relentless," says Sandy Bloomberg, chairman of Tweeter, which went from carrying no Philips products to carrying more than 70.

Mr. Blanford split the Philips-Magnavox brand in two, for high-end and low-end products. And he made an aggressive grab for the youth market, organizing a "brand-management team" of twenty- and thirty-somethings who trawl retailers across the country to check out Sony's latest offerings, test Philips prototypes and attend extreme-sports events in search of ideas. The team joined forces with MTV, Nike and makers of surfboards and snowboards to help make the Philips name resonate among young buyers. The company has sponsored concerts and competitions, and introduced "youth" products such as a Nike-branded sweat-resistant portable CD player, which the company says is selling well with sports enthusiasts.

Just eight months after Mr. Blanford took the job, Mr. Kleisterlee surprised him with his threat to get rid of the U.S. division if it didn't become profitable. The threat was delivered in a December 2001 interview with the Dutch current affairs magazine Elsevier. Mr. Blanford wouldn't say whether the deadline was also handed down to him per-

sonally by his Dutch bosses. But when the Elsevier article appeared, Mr. Blanford was forced into fast action. He called the CEOs of Tweeter and Best Buy to ensure no sales contracts were canceled and sent a letter to Philips's 960 U.S. consumer-electronics employees, assuring them they still had jobs.

Some industry analysts say they suspect Mr. Blanford was asked to leave his post because headquarters was growing impatient with progress. The company denies this. Mr. Blanford says his parting with Philips is amicable; he never intended to stay beyond three years, and both he and the company wanted to make a change before the big International Consumer Electronics Show in Las Vegas, which starts tomorrow. Mr. Blanford, a 50-year-old former Maytag executive from Dayton, Ohio, says he wants to be chief executive of a company, not just a division, so he's leaving Philips by the end of this week. He doesn't have a new post lined up.

Mr. Bloomberg, the chairman of Tweeter, says Mr. Blanford brought Philips a new understanding of the U.S. market. Some industry analysts questioned the wisdom of appointing a European with little U.S. experience to the top job. "It's baffling that they replaced him with a European, given that most of their past gaffes resulted from Europeans not understanding the U.S.," says Bert Siebrand, technology analyst at Bank Oyens & van Eeghen in Amsterdam.

Mr. Kleisterlee, the Philips global CEO, himself has lamented in the past that Philips has too many "boring, white Dutch guys." Mr. Jens, the new U.S. CEO, says he has worked in the industry across the globe, and holding a Dutch passport is no impediment to running a U.S. business.

A major part of Philips' problem now is its lack of a breakout product. Aside from a range of gear targeted at teens in the U.S. and other markets—such as a digital camera the size of a house key and a pocket-size "audio jukebox" that can record from any source of music—the company's main offerings are hard to distinguish from many of its competitors'.

Long Shots

Philips does have some expensive long shots in the pipeline. It plans to market a television screen that becomes a mirror when it's turned off—first aimed at boutique hotels, but then within two years at home consumers, likely at $4,000 to $5,000. More ambitiously, it's offering a set of products it dubs "the connected home," in which computerized appliances such as televisions, computers and DVD players can "talk" among themselves and download digital photographs, music and video games from the Internet.

It's so determined to get these gadgets into American living rooms that it's hiring European architects to build prefabricated homes, fitted with this gear, that can be assembled in two weeks and shipped any-

where in the U.S. But industry analysts say the technology could take up to a decade to become popular with customers. Meanwhile, rivals such as Samsung and others have similar concepts in the works.

In an effort to avoid the snafus of the past, Philips last year hired its first-ever world-wide marketing chief. At the direction of the CEO, Mr. Kleisterlee, Philips's marketing division is now involved in product launches from the beginning. Philips has created a model home in Eindhoven, the Netherlands, where American teenagers are being recruited to test out new products under video and audio surveillance.

Philips now is outspending some of its rivals on U.S. marketing, putting nearly $31 million into advertising last year, according to TNS Media Intelligence/CMR, a New York-based research firm. The company sponsored the U.S. Open snowboarding competition in Vermont and organized a California surfing event where local grunge bands played on a Philips-branded stage. Philips products are among the prizes on MTV's "Real World Challenge" reality show.

In the past, says Diego Olego, managing director of Philips's U.S. research-and-development operation, "All our engineers cared about was winning patents and hanging plaques on their walls. Now they also want to be able to take their kids to a store in New York or San Francisco, show them the latest blockbuster and say, 'Look, daddy made that.'"

For Philips, maintaining relations with retailers and salespeople is a top priority now. In New York, Philips is now the exclusive video-equipment supplier for a new consumer-electronics boutique at Macy's flagship department store. Located near a gourmet sushi stand and the designer-underwear section, the boutique carries only the most expensive Philips products. Philips also is pushing for prominent display space at stores such as Jordan's Furniture in suburban Boston, which has a 262-seat IMAX theatre and a replica of New Orleans's "Bourbon street" running through its entrance.

Mr. Fassburg, the U.S. communications chief, no longer makes his Union Square wager with visiting Dutch executives, for fear of losing his $100.

But there is work to be done. Neill Salamack, the Philips regional representative for New York, Connecticut and New Jersey, recently stopped by J&R Music World, an electronics megastore in lower Manhattan, and confronted the store manager, John Jensen: The store's main Philips display was barely visible, its sign hidden under a staircase. The Panasonic sign nearby was nearly triple the size. "I'm not happy about this," he said.

Sri Lanka Is Grateful, But What to Do With the Ski Parkas?

Well-Meaning Donors Send Heaps of Useless Stuff; Pajama Tops, No Bottoms

PATRICK BARTA AND ERIC BELLMAN.
WALL STREET JOURNAL.

GALLE, Sri Lanka—The grateful people of Sri Lanka would like to make a humble request to all those who have offered succor to its devastated tsunami victims: Please, no more ski jackets, moisturizing gel or Viagra.

The recent outpouring of tsunami support has brought with it a mountain of unusable stuff from the Western world. That includes cozy winter hats, Arctic-weather tents, cologne and thong underwear. Dubbed "frustrated cargo" by aid workers—because it often has nowhere to go—these misfit items are gathering dust in warehouses and creating major headaches for relief workers in the field.

Mounds of donated clothes litter the coastal highway south of Colombo. Bottled water from European mountain streams is flowing freely, raising concern about empties littering the jungle. Medicines that are no longer needed, such as morphine, are feared to be loose in the country.

Some people are putting items of no apparent local value to creative use. Impakt Aid, a Sri Lankan group, cites two dozen goose-down jackets it recently received from a European relief agency. The group forwarded the coats to a refugee camp. There, they were used to wrap babies without diapers.

"People are just bringing anything and everything," says Melanie Kanaka, a World Bank administrator who is helping coordinate aid in the battered town of Galle. "We don't have the resources in this country to sort it all out."

Many vital needs still aren't being met, even as marginal donations pile up. Government figures record the arrival of 30,000 sheets, but only 100 mattresses. Colombo's main airport says it received 5,000 pajama tops from Qantas Airways, but no bottoms to go with them. The airline won't comment beyond saying that it sent a planeload of supplies to Sri Lanka, primarily medical supplies. Many of the country's more than 300 refugee camps face critical shortages of cough syrup and infection-fighting creams—even though there are plenty of skimpy undergarments.

Many aid workers don't know where all the useless handouts are coming from, or whom they're intended for. Although most aid that arrives is earmarked for specific relief agencies, such as the Red Cross, some shipments are addressed simply to "The People of Sri Lanka" and have no return address.

In other cases, the aid arrives unsolicited on the doorsteps of local charities, courtesy of foreign relief providers they have never heard of. Or, it wanders into the country in the suitcases of well-meaning tourists who then strike out on their own for the tsunami zone.

Western clothes are a particular nuisance. Although the nation's coastal regions have an average temperature of about 80 degrees and a preference for modest dress, aid groups are receiving sweaters and women's dress shoes. Much of the clothing arrives used and in bad condition. That is a major problem, aid workers say, because some Sri Lankans fear used clothing has been taken from dead bodies.

As a result, discard piles are popping up everywhere—including the second-floor hallway of Galle's government district office. One day recently, as officials processed aid requests, the moldy heap attracted just a handful of skeptical browsers.

One elderly woman pronounced the clothes "unsuitable" because they weren't appropriate for her age. The items included a heavy woven baby hat, a mustard-colored dress shirt and a leopard-print dress.

At the Kattugoda Jummah mosque near Galle, meanwhile, children spent their free time last week doing back flips and somersaults over a knee-deep bed of hand-me-downs. The children tied a shawl around a rafter so they could swing around in the air before dropping onto the soiled laundry below. "Clothes are really good to play in," said 10-year-old Mohamad Afral as he jumped around on the pile.

Kattugoda Jummah's adults are eager to unload all the stuff cluttering up the mosque. As laborers carted off some of the garments in a wheelbarrow, one of the mosque's leaders, Mohamad Nizam, fished a crusty pillowcase from the pile and frowned. "This is useless," said Mr. Nizam, who says he is more concerned about the mosque's dwindling supply of food.

Although essential in the early days of the relief effort, bottled water is now proving to be more trouble than it's worth because it is heavy and expensive to transport. Many villages have already restored their old water sources or are using purification systems.

At the White Pearl Hotel in Hikkaduwa just north of Galle, managing director Ananda Lal Waduge said he isn't sure what to make of the 600 bottles of Voslauer brand mineral water that recently showed up in his lobby. The bottles were parked there by an Austrian relief team staying at the hotel.

The water "has a different kind of taste" than locals are accustomed to, Mr. Waduge said. "Normal people can't drink it, only foreigners."

On the hotel's beachfront patio, the Austrian relief workers said locals loved the stuff. Dressed in matching red-and-white team jerseys emblazoned with the words "Austrian Water Support," the half-dozen volunteers were kicking back with some local Lankan lager and some cold Voslauer. After some discussion, they conceded that demand for bottled water is waning. "If we stay a month, maybe we will drink it," said Michael Gottwald, a 41-year-old volunteer with the group.

Unwanted medicines pose a more serious problem. Wary of potential epidemics, some doctors and private citizens appear to have unloaded their sample bins and medicine cabinets and shipped whatever they could find. The shipments have included useful antibiotics. But they also included drugs that aren't common in many villages and can easily be abused, such as Valium and antidepressants.

Complicating matters, much of the labeling is in languages most Sri Lankans don't understand. Jayantha Weerasinghe, a doctor at the Arachikanda Government Hospital in Hikkaduwa, says he had to turn away medicine because it was labeled in German. "I couldn't risk giving it to my patients because I wasn't sure what it was," he says.

Moahan Balendra, a volunteer for the Tamils Rehabilitation Organization in Colombo, says his group recently discovered five packs of Viagra in a shipment of medical goods from Australia. Now, he hopes the drug will somehow find its way to a needy home.

"We didn't know what to do with it," Mr. Balendra says. So "we gave it to the doctors and let them decide."

Nestlé Markets Baby Formula To Hispanic Mothers In U.S.

BY MIRIAM JORDAN

Anaheim, Calif.—By the dozens, mothers with strollers and protruding bellies approach the stand of the only infant-formula company exhibiting at an annual baby-products fair here. Like many others, Alicia Araujo leaves the booth clutching a free sample can. "They were very helpful," she says, pushing a carriage with her four-month-old, Danielle.

Nestlé SA is betting on Hispanic mothers like Mrs. Araujo to boost its share of the $3 billion U.S. infant-formula market—and some doctors and breast-feeding advocates are irate. The company has begun promoting Nan, a leading brand in Latin America, just as the U.S. government is poised to launch the first campaign in a century to persuade low-income, minority mothers to breast-feed.

At issue is whether companies should market baby formula to low-income immigrant mothers when health experts and government officials agree that breast-feeding is healthier, and saves in long-term health-care costs. Most health professionals say breast milk is superior to formula for infants, except in rare cases such as when a mother is HIV-positive. The American Academy of Pediatrics and the American College of Obstetricians and Gynecologists recommend that exclusive breast-feeding is ideal nutrition for the first six months after birth and that breast-feeding continue for at least 12 months, and thereafter for as long as mutually desired. An article on March 4 failed to state the entire recommendation, saying only that doctors recommend that all women breast-feed their babies for at least the first six months of life.

Nestlé came under fire in the 1970s for the way it marketed infant formula in the developing world to poor, illiterate women who often misused it. Health professionals at the time found bottle-fed babies sometimes became undernourished and suffered from chronic illnesses because their mothers were watering down the costly formula to make it go further or they were preparing it with contaminated water.

That prompted the World Health Organization, in 1981, to devise a voluntary code whereby countries and companies, particularly in the developing world, agreed to restrict the marketing of formula. And indeed, Nestlé doesn't advertise Nan in countries such as Mexico, which follows the WHO code.

The U.S. also signed the code, but never enacted laws to restrict marketing of formula here. The Swiss company takes care "to make sure that all advertising stays in the U.S.," says Kathy Mitsukawa, a marketing associate for Nestlé.

"We have launched Nestlé Nan in the U.S. with a fully bilingual label so that U.S. Hispanic moms, who choose not to or cannot breast-feed, can make an informed choice with regard to their child's nutrition," says Lisbeth Armentano, a spokeswoman for Nestlé's U.S. unit in Glendale, Calif. She adds that the company believes breast-feeding is better for babies and even says so in its advertising.

Nestlé entered the U.S. formula market in 1988 with Carnation's Good Start line. But the Swiss food titan has only a sliver of the market dominated by pharmaceutical companies. **Abbott Laboratories,** maker of Similac formula, and **Bristol-Myers Squibb** Co.'s Mead Johnson Nutritionals, which makes Enfamil, have long enjoyed an inside track in pushing their products because of their ties to the medical establishment. Many hospitals distribute free samples of Similac or Enfamil to mothers of newborns when they check out, a practice that breast-feeding activists and some doctors criticize. Research shows that many mothers end up using the formula they get for free at the hospital. While the two companies do some advertising, Nestlé alone markets with radio spots and promotions at baby fairs. However, the company also is trying to break into the maternity ward, Ms. Mitsukawa says.

The numbers help explain why Nestlé is focusing on the 38 million Hispanics in the U.S. They already make up 13% of the total population and that percentage is expected to grow to 20% of the U.S. population by 2020. "Hispanic households tend to be larger and have growing birth rates," Ms. Armentano says. In addition, Hispanic mothers in the U.S. tend to be less educated, and research suggests that women with less education are more likely to bottle-feed their babies. That makes them a desirable marketing target for formula companies.

Critics say that also means Hispanic mothers, who lack fluency in English, won't get enough medical advice to make an informed choice between formula and breast-feeding their infants. And, for many immigrant women from deprived backgrounds, bottle feeding has an aura of acculturation and prosperity. "Nestlé is using a vulnerable population for a grab at market share," says Marsha Walker, executive director of the National Alliance for Breastfeeding Advocacy, an organization that works to make breast-feeding a public-health priority.

Doctors also voice concern. "I am very much opposed to any marketing at all of infant formula. It should not be regarded as a growth area for companies," says Larry Gartner, neonatologist and head of the American Academy of Pediatrics' breast-feeding division.

Still, the reality is that many Hispanic mothers must work and can't be with their babies all day, or some find their babies aren't thriving with breast-feeding and are receptive to the formula makers' pitches.

Nestlé posters at the "Yeah, Baby" Expo proclaim in Spanish that "women in Latin America have trusted Nan for more than 40 years." To cater to Hispanic moms, Nan puts instructions in Spanish right on the can; other formula brands in the U.S. require customers to snip off the label for Spanish directions on the inside.

"Hispanic moms in the U.S. are familiar with Nan . . . and asked us to carry it," says Nestlé's Ms. Armentano.

Some Hispanic mothers dispute the claim that breast-feeding is better. At the Anaheim hospital where she gave birth, Eva Hernandez said the nurses encouraged her to breast-feed, but she didn't see any health benefits for Marcos, her firstborn son. He "got colds, ear infections and sore throats," she says. She breast-fed her second child only four months, then switched to formula and "he was much healthier," she says. She didn't breast-feed her third child at all: "I simply don't have time to breast-feed."

Nestlé officials decline to disclose details of the marketing strategy for Nan, including how much it will invest in ads. The company first advertised the brand last year on billboards in Hispanic enclaves of Los Angeles and Houston. But recently it kicked off a national campaign, placing ads in Spanish-language parenting magazines and radio.

"I filled out the form to get coupons," says Michelle Hernandez, 29, of Garden Grove, who was at the Anaheim fair. At as much as $13 per twelve ounce can, "formula can get expensive," she says.

The problem, critics say, is that a mother

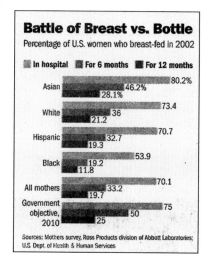

Battle of Breast vs. Bottle

Percentage of U.S. women who breast-fed in 2002

■ In hospital ■ For 6 months ■ For 12 months

Asian	80.2%	46.2%	28.1%
White	73.4	36	21.2
Hispanic	70.7	32.7	19.3
Black	53.9	19.2	11.8
All mothers	70.1	33.2	19.7
Government objective, 2010	75	50	25

Sources: Mothers survey, Ross Products division of Abbott Laboratories; U.S. Dept. of Health & Human Services

(Cont.)

who supplements with formula is likely to wean her baby from the breast early. At six months of an infant's life, 36% of white mothers breast-fed, 32.7% of Hispanic mothers and 19.2% of black mothers, according to a 2002 study by Ross Products, a unit of **Abbott Laboratories.**

Breast milk helps prevent allergies, infections and other illnesses in infants. Studies also show that raising breast-feeding rates would save families, insurers and the U.S. government millions of dollars each year on health care.

In the face of such evidence, the U.S. government is launching a major campaign to promote breast milk with public-service announcements. Created by the Ad Council, the spots will target minorities and low-income women because they show the lowest rates of breast-feeding, said people familiar with the campaign.

Back at the Anaheim baby fair, Rosie Sanchez, who works as a clerk, has formula-fed her two American-born children, and plans to do the same with the third on the way. "Women only breastfeed in Latin America because they can't afford to buy formula," she says.